Corpus-based Studies in Language Use, Language Learning, and Language Documentation

LANGUAGE AND COMPUTERS: STUDIES IN PRACTICAL LINGUISTICS

No 73

edited by
Christian Mair
Charles F. Meyer
Nelleke Oostdijk

Cover image: Morguefile.com

Cover design: HAVEKA BV | de grafische partner

The paper on which this book is printed meets the requirements of "ISO 9706:1994, Information and documentation - Paper for documents - Requirements for permanence".

ISBN: 978-90-420-3401-3
E-Book ISBN: 978-94-012-0688-4

Printed in The Netherlands

Corpus-based Studies in Language Use, Language Learning, and Language Documentation

Edited by John Newman,
Harald Baayen and Sally Rice

Rodopi

Amsterdam - New York, NY 2011

Contents

3. Language Documentation

Introduction

The present volume is a collection of selected papers presented at the American Association for Corpus Linguistics (AACL) Conference, held in Edmonton, Alberta, on October 8-11, 2009.[1] The call for papers for that conference was intended to elicit papers on a broad range of topics in and around the field of corpus linguistics. The organizers (John Newman, Sally Rice, and Harald Baayen) offered the following list as a guide to the range of topics which would be welcome at the conference: corpus linguistics and endangered languages, corpus creation, open source corpora (philosophy and practice), corpus annotation, linguistic analyses of corpora, visualization of large data sets, register/genre variation, lexicography, parallel corpora, tagging and parsing, software development, and the use of corpora in language learning and teaching. This openness to the full spectrum of research directions in corpus linguistics continued a tradition that had developed in previous AACL conferences. And indeed, just as the organizers had hoped for, all these topics found their way into the (more than 80) papers presented.

After the conference, the organizers, now wearing their co-editors' hats, invited abstracts from among the participants for a volume of papers based on the conference presentations. After a full review process of submissions for the volume, just eleven papers were finally selected for inclusion. The co-editors were also delighted to receive papers authored or co-authored by keynote speakers at the conference (Brian MacWhinney and Mark Davies). Altogether, therefore, thirteen papers have been included in the present volume. It seemed to the co-editors that the papers naturally fell into three main themes (despite some overlap of course), as reflected in the title of the volume: language use, language learning, and language documentation. The volume thus includes both linguistic and applied linguistic research, as well as new research relating to the construction of corpora which in some way serve as resources on languages.

1. Language use

General corpora, like the British National Corpus (BNC) and the Corpus of Contemporary American English (COCA), may be expected to include "standard" as well as "non-standard" usage. As such, they present opportunities for the study of non-standard usage, complementing rather than replacing other methods for investigating such usage (interviews targeting certain usages, interviews across socio-economic classes, attitudinal surveys, psycholinguistic experiments, etc.). **Kristina Geeraert** and **John Newman** turn to some commonly used general corpora (and the World Wide Web) to explore the use of a "standard" past tense of an English verb as a "non-standard" past participle in the perfect construction, as in *I would have took my two kids out of the house* (from the newspaper genre of COCA), where "standard" usage expects *would have taken* rather than *would have took*. The use of the quotation marks here is deliberate, acknowledging that notions of standard, prescriptive use of English can vary considerably. The authors document the varying degrees to which verbs are prone to this kind of "past tense spreading" on the basis of corpus evidence. Among other results, they find evidence for Bybee's Conserving Effect (Bybee 2006: 715): high frequency verbs like *GO* show far less past tense spreading than do low frequency verbs like *RING*, just as Bybee had found that high frequency verbs resist past tense regularization (*kept* -> *keeped*) more so than do low frequency verbs (*crept* -> *creeped*). The authors utilize the World Wide Web as a source of additional data in light of the relatively sparse occurrence of the phenomenon they are investigating. Even in a large corpus like COCA, for example, there are just eight instances of past tense spreading with *SWIM,* whereas more than 88,000 such cases were retrieved from the .com domain of the World Wide Web.

Corpus-linguistic methods are brought to bear on *–im* suffixation in Tok Pisin, an official language of Papua New Guinea and widely used throughout the country, in the chapter by **Conor Snoek**. In the most simplistic formulation of its usage, the presence of the suffix *–im* on verbs is associated with transitivity, and its absence is associated with intransitivity. It is clear, though, that the distribution of this suffix is more complex than this formulation implies. For the raw data, Snoek draws upon the online Slone Wantok Corpus, a collection of Tok Pisin stories based upon texts submitted to a column of the Tok Pisin newspaper *Wantok*, in the period 1971-1997. He focuses on a class of verbs which pose real challenges for the study of *-im* suffixation, since they have been analyzed as transitive and yet occur both with and without the *-im* suffix. Snoek illustrates the potential of various analytical methods which can be employed to explore aspects of the data retrieved from the corpus. These methods include the "behavioral profiling" technique (cf. Gries & Divjak 2009) in order to arrive at clusterings of the verbs used in the example sentences, with clusterings based on similarity of associated syntactic and semantic variables. This method can separate out fairly cleanly the cases where *–im* occurs and the cases where it does not occur (with an astute choice of variables), which lends credence to the method as a reliable clustering technique. Snoek also turns to another kind of multifactorial analysis to test the relative importance of particular variables on the distribution of the *–im* suffix, conditional inference trees. Snoek's chapter is a useful illustration of how various multifactorial methods can be applied to one and the same set of data obtained from a corpus.

"Complex extractions" are a class of syntactic rules which purportedly come into play in accounting for an invented sentence such as *What do you think it is likely people would have said?*, where *what* is supposedly moved from the object position after *said* across two clause boundaries to "land" in the initial position of the sentence. "Complex extraction" is also used for the purported movement of multiple constituents across a clause boundary to initial position in an invented sentence such as *In London tomorrow she has been told three bombs will explode*. **Gunnar Bergh** explores actual attested usage of such constructions in the history of English. To carry out his study, Bergh assembled a corpus of 1.4

million words, with an approximately equal number of words from each of the four traditional periods: Old English, Middle English, Early Modern English, and Late Modern English. Bergh follows, for the most part, the model of the Helsinki Corpus in choosing the 24 text types from which the data was taken. Complex extractions were found to be extremely rare compared with "simple extractions" (one constituent moved across one clause boundary) – just 2.8% of all extractions (680 in all) involved complex extraction. Bergh considers carefully the exact nature of the complex extractions attested in the corpus. Generally, the complex extractions do not show more than two clause boundaries being crossed or more than two constituents being fronted. Bergh considers the difficulty that this reality of historical usage (and perhaps in contemporary usage as well) poses for theories of syntax. Multiple fronting of constituents, in particular, presents difficulties, leading Bergh to earlier work by Cattell (1976) and Hudson (1990) as a way to accommodate the data.

Laura Teddiman's study of subject ellipsis in English presents an interesting challenge to a corpus-based approach: how to identify and count a missing part of a clause. Teddiman relied on the International Corpus of English Utility Program (ICECUP III) to retrieve from the International Corpus of English for Great Britain (ICE-GB) verb-initial sequences in declarative utterances/sentences and then manually filtered the results to obtain instances of subject ellipsis. She explores the attraction of particular elided subjects (which she takes to be pronouns, understood from the context of usage in the corpus) as well as verbs to the subject ellipsis construction. To measure the degrees of attraction, Teddiman adopts the Collexeme Analysis variant of Collostructional Analysis (Gries 2004), identifying the most strongly attracted subject pronouns and verbs across different genres of the corpus. By relying on the method of Collostructional Analysis, Teddiman takes into consideration the relatively high frequency of the items in the corpus as a whole and so arrives at statistically significant scores of attraction (or repulsion). One would expect certain spoken genres to show relatively high rates of subject ellipsis, compared with written genres, and this is borne out in the data to a large extent. Still, there are interesting findings which one could not so easily predict. The genre of written correspondence (social and business letters), for example, had the highest rate of subject ellipsis of any genre – a result influenced in large part by Teddiman's decision to follow the ICE-GB analysis of *thank* in *thank you* as a verb which in turn becomes an example of subject ellipsis for Teddiman. Verbs attracted to the subject ellipsis construction fall into a small number of categories, e.g., "mental state" verbs (*think, feel*), verbs describing impressions (*seem, look, sound*), and expressive verbs (*talk, tell*).

2. Language learning

Li-Shih Huang reports on a corpus-aided discovery learning (CADL) approach intended to enhance the acquisition of modern English grammar and usage in an undergraduate-level course taken by students across disciplines. The learners participating in this experiment were shown how to use three well-known online corpora: the Bank of English (COBUILD), the BNC, and the Michigan Corpus of Academic Spoken English (MICASE). Among other activities carried out over the fourteen weeks of the course, learners wrote biweekly language logs about a self-selected grammatical point that interested them, and also about what they discovered from using the corpora. Consider one such excerpt from a learner, quoted by Huang:

> "In BNC, I found that *different from* (3,281 hits) is used far more often than *different than*. From the examples, I noticed that in British English, *different than* tends to be followed by clauses. For example, *it's not very much different than what we had expected.* I also noticed that *different to* is more evident in British English than in American English. I also have another finding. The evidence from BNC suggested that *different to* is more commonly used in British English than *different than*."

Self-reports like this one, and others analyzed by Huang, point to the sense of discovery which all of us have undoubtedly felt as we work through concordance lines obtained from corpora. As part of her findings, Huang observes: "Time and time again, learners shared findings that contradicted what they had expected or predicted, or reported realizing that they were gaining a sharper awareness or becoming critical of the linguistic features in their own and others' spoken interactions or written texts". The heightened critical awareness which these learners arrived at, encouraged by their corpus-based learning, is surely laudable as far as intellectual growth is concerned, even if it might be judged "subversive" in some pedagogical contexts.

Laurence Anthony, **Kiyomi Chujo**, and **Kathryn Oghigian** concern themselves with the use of corpus-based learning of English by second and foreign language learners of English. Their data-driven learning (DDL) approach to language learning is guided by the same pedagogical considerations underlying Huang's chapter. In the particular course described by the authors, the learners were expected to identify patterns in a Japanese-English parallel newspaper corpus using a commercial parallel concordancer, followed by reporting of findings back to the class and further follow-up work by the teacher. Anthony, Chujo, and Oghigian's focus is on how to improve on the parallel concordancer software which could be used to support this kind of data-driven learning approach. They describe their own open-source software *AntWebConc-Bilingual* (still under development at the time of writing), a web-based parallel concordancer which was created in an attempt to remedy some of the shortcomings in other parallel concordancers. The authors report on the performance of their program in comparison with some other concordancers and find dramatic improvements in search times for individual words. In addition, the authors report on encouraging feedback on the program based on trialling a prototype version of it in 2010. Anthony, Chujo, and Oghigian emphasize the importance of developing user-friendly software tools designed specifically for learners of language, as opposed to tools intended primarily for analysis of language, and their own software is a move in this direction.

Christine Johansson and **Christer Geisler** turn to a new, specialized corpus, the Uppsala Learner English Corpus (ULEC), as the source of data for a study of stages in the syntactic development of Swedish high school students. ULEC derives from essays written by high school students using a web interface, consisting of about 136,000 words and includes metadata such as age and gender of each student. Their chapter analyzes data from a balanced sample of ULEC (10 boys and 10 girls from junior high, 10 boys and 10 girls from senior high). Their focus of interest is a variant of the "T-unit", i.e., a minimal terminable unit. For the purposes of the present study, Johansson and Geisler focus their attention on "syntactically error-free T-units". These are stretches of writing by a student consisting of either just a main clause or a main clause with one or more subordinate clauses attached to it. The authors proceed by analyzing the frequency and various properties of such units and arrive at a number of interesting conclusions supported by statistical analyses. The number of subordinate clauses per main clause (the "subordinate clause index"), as well as the relative frequencies of relative clauses and nominal/adverbial clauses prove to be reliable indicators of syntactic development from junior to senior high school. They find, on the other hand, that gender differences in syntactic development are not statistically significant.

Dispersion measures have attracted increasing interest in recent years (cf. the critical overview of such measures in Gries 2008). Various suggestions have been made to incorporate dispersion measures into the decision making about the headwords of dictionaries (cf. the discussion of dispersion in the Davies and Gardner chapter) or deciding on "core" vocabulary items for learners of a language. **Hanhong Li** and **Alex Fang**, in their highly original proposal concerning core vocabulary for EFL learners and learners' dictionaries, are also interested in a word's dispersion, but in their case it is dispersion of a word across different age groups (of native speakers) that is regarded as most critical. To achieve their goal, they construct an Age-Group Corpus, drawing upon a number of existing corpora (BNC XML, the Polytechnic of Wales Corpus, CHILDES, the Lancaster Corpus of Children's Project Writing, and the sub-corpus of Child Writing from the LUCY corpus), for which metadata on age of the speakers was available. They were able to assemble a well-balanced corpus with six age groups, each age-group containing about 1 million words (roughly half from the spoken domain and half from the written domain, except for the 0-14 age group where the data is mainly spoken). Li and Fang apply formulae for a "coefficient of usage" and a "dispersion index" based on Carroll (1970), in order to help them identify the words which are frequent and well-represented evenly throughout their corpus and these are the words that end up in the core vocabulary.

3. Language documentation

In the chapter by **Brian MacWhinney**, we are given a glimpse into a world of data and analysis encompassing much more than the traditional subject-matter of linguistics or, for that matter, the traditional contents of a corpus. MacWhinney sees the forms and functions of language as originating in the interplay of various adaptive processes, processes which operate at different levels and over different timeframes. So, for example, there is a "processing timeframe" in which the online processing of words and sentences takes place, a "turn-taking timeframe" of longer duration in which we take in data from our conversational partners and respond, an "activity timeframe" of even longer duration which encompasses goals beyond just the present conversation (e.g., our goal of buying a house will shape the form and content of a conversation we have with a real-estate agent), and so on. These timeframes, eight in all, may be in play at any moment of speaking. A full understanding of how these timeframes shape conversation will require far greater quantity and quality of data, based in the act of communication, than we are accustomed to in linguistics (an orientation which is in many ways reminiscent of the research carried out by Goodwin 1979, 1980, 1981 and other publications since). MacWhinney describes classes of analytical methods which have a role to play in this more encompassing view of linguistic analysis, including methods of both qualitative and quantitative data analysis, group and interlocutor comparisons, "change scores" which measure language development over time, and tracking of feedback from, say, a care-giver to a child. The data types and the associated analytical methods which MacWhinney advocates come together in the ComNet project as described more fully in the chapter. ComNet aims for full interoperability, universal access, "deep curation", sophisticated visualization, and wide coverage of data, all of which represent the emerging best practice in corpus linguistics.

Giancarla Unser-Schutz describes in some detail the design and contents of an innovative corpus based on Japanese *manga*, the popular Japanese comic genre. *Manga* occupy an important place in the lives of many younger Japanese (as well as gaining in popularity outside of Japan) and so a corpus based on their contents is potentially of great interest in tracking new styles of expression in Japanese. Unser-Schutz's approach to sampling *manga* for the purpose of corpus construction is in itself a valuable contribution of this chapter. She was guided by a list of the top-selling series reflecting sales of particular titles, but relied, too, on surveys she conducted among school students in Tokyo from which she was able to ascertain male and female reading preferences. By means of these combined methods, she carefully and methodically arrived at a corpus representing "a sample of male and female oriented series popular amongst high school students". The corpus itself is textual, incorporating various categories of language data found in the texts. Altogether, there are eight categories of text: "Lines" (text representing audible use of language as found in speech bubbles), Thoughts (text representing inner voices), Narration (details of plot, location etc.), Onomatopoeia, Background text (e.g., text appearing in names of buildings in a comic strip), Background "lines" (lines of text written by hand as part of the background), Comments, and Titles (metadata on the comic). The corpus, though consisting entirely of text, is thus complex and multi-layered, with additional challenges posed by various non-standard ways of representing some words. As Unser-Schutz reports, all the titles used in the corpus are available in English, thus clearing the way for future translation studies based on *manga*.

Christopher Cox reviews commonalities and differences between the practices and goals of corpus linguistics and language documentation, with particular attention given to ongoing work in Mennonite Plautdietsch communities in Saskatchewan, Canada. The notion of "language documentation", as used in this particular chapter, has its origins in Himmelmann (1998) and Woodbury (2003) where language documentation involving the development and utilization of multipurpose collections of linguistic data is construed as an independent sub-discipline of linguistics. Cox considers four specific areas in his comparison of corpus linguistics and language documentation: practices relating to the relationships between project stakeholders (with community stakeholders in language documentation projects typically exerting more influence than they do in corpus linguistic projects); sampling methods (the "balance" and "representativeness" aimed for in many corpora are not very realistic in practice in most language documentation); conventional technologies (the area showing the most commonalities between the two fields); and the treatment of data and metadata (considerably more automation of tasks can be expected in corpus linguistics than in language documentation). Cox is optimistic that there can be a productive interaction between the fields of corpus linguistics and language documentation, arguing for a view of linguistic corpora as "descriptive applications of language documentation, to be built directly upon the permanent documentary record".

Steven Weinberger and **Stephen Kunath**, in their chapter, introduce *The Speech Accent Archive*. Sometimes, archives and corpora can be quite similar (cf. the commonalities between the products of language documentation and corpus linguistics discussed in the chapter by Cox) and *The Speech Accent Archive* has some corpus-like aspects. The Archive, an online resource, is a collection of samples of speech (audio plus a narrow phonetic transcription arrived at by linguists manually carrying out the transcription), where each sample is based upon a non-native speaker of English reading the same short paragraph. The paragraph is designed in such a way that it contains a spread of consonants and vowels of English and numerous initial and final consonant clusters. Currently, the Archive includes non-native speakers of English from approximately 310 different language backgrounds. New types of data require new analytical tools, a point brought home convincingly by Roy (2009) in relation to the 230,000 hours of audio-video recordings (!) which constitute Roy's Human Speechome Corpus. The Archive, too, has its own accompanying speech transcription analysis tool which aligns one narrow phonetic transcription (e.g., a Vietnamese's pronunciation) with the transcription of another pronunciation, calculating a distance measure between the two pronunciations. The tool is quite flexible in what samples can be compared. It can compare, for example, pronunciations of a non-native speaker to a native speaker, or pronunciations of any two non-native speakers, or pronunciations of all speakers of one particular background. Weinberger and Kunath reflect on the *hybrid* nature of their project: "Humans create the phonetic transcription and the machine processes it".

Many readers will already be aware of Mark Davies' ground-breaking on-line Corpus of Contemporary American English (COCA). Now we have an equally ground-breaking dictionary based on that corpus (Davies & Gardner 2010), and in their chapter, **Mark Davies** and **Dee Gardner** introduce the dictionary and its unusual features. When it came to deciding on which words would be included as headwords in the dictionary, an unusual, though entirely appropriate, decision was made: the authors considered not just frequencies of words but also Juilland's dispersion (Juilland & Chang-Rodriguez 1964). The product of these numbers gives rise to a new score and the 5,000 lemmas with the highest such scores are the ones included in the dictionary. For collocates, a span of four words to the left and right of the node word (i.e., each headword in the dictionary) was searched in COCA with rating of the results by native speakers and filtering using variable thresholds for Mutual Information scores – again, a hybrid of human effort and machine power, as seen in Weinberger and Kunath's Speech Accent Archive. Each dictionary entry includes the top 20-30 collocates of the head word – the collocates appear in lieu of the definition one would find in a traditional dictionary. "Frequency" dominates the content and structure of the dictionary – the first head word in the dictionary, for example, is *the*; the collocates are ordered by part of speech and frequency; each head word has its rank order number shown next to it. An additional feature is the occasional (about 30) "thematic lists", e.g., kinship terms, a category of "words increasing most in frequency 1990s to 2000s", phrasal verbs, all listed by descending frequency of occurrence.

We are grateful for an Aid to Research Workshops and Conferences in Canada grant (#646-2009-0015) from the Social Sciences and Humanities Research Council of Canada (SSHRC) which provided funds to support administrative assistance in the preparation of this volume. We are particularly grateful to Diane McKen and Georgie Columbus for bringing the manuscripts submitted by authors to the final camera-ready stage.

John Newman, Sally Rice and Harald Baayen

University of Alberta
June 2011

Notes

1 The AACL 2009 website is available online at: http://www.ualberta.ca/~aacl2009/. The program schedule and abstracts booklet can be downloaded from the website.

References

Bybee, J. (2006), 'From usage to grammar: the mind's response to repetition', *Language,* 82: 711-733.

Carroll, J.B. (1970), 'An alternative to Juilland's usage coefficient for lexical frequencies and a proposal for a standard frequency index (SFI)', *Computer studies in the humanities and verbal behavior,* 3: 61-65.

Cattell, R. (1976), 'Constraints on movement rules', *Language,* 53: 18-50.

Davies, M. & D. Gardner (2010), *A frequency dictionary of contemporary American English: word sketches, collocates, and thematic lists*. London: Routledge.

Goodwin, C. (1979), 'The interactive construction of a sentence in natural conversation', in: G. Psathas (ed.) *Everyday language: studies in ethnomethodology*. New York: Irvington. 97-121.

Goodwin, C. (1980), 'Restarts, pauses, and the achievement of mutual gaze at turn-beginning', *Sociological inquiry,* 50: 272-302. (Special double issue on language and social interaction, edited by Don Zimmerman & Candace West.)

Goodwin, C. (1981), *Conversational organization: interaction between speakers and hearers.* New York: Academic Press.

Gries, S.Th. (2004), *Coll.analysis 3. A program for R for Windows 2.x.*

Gries, S.Th. (2008), 'Dispersions and adjusted frequencies', *International journal of corpus linguistics*, 13: 403-437.

Gries, S.Th. & D. Divjak (2009), 'Behavioral profiles: a corpus-based approach to cognitive semantic analysis', in V. Evans & S. Pourcel (eds.) *New directions in cognitive linguistics.* Amsterdam/Philadelphia: Benjamins. 57-75.

Himmelmann, N.P. (1998), 'Documentary and descriptive linguistics', *Linguistics*, 36: 161-195.

Hudson, R. (1990), *English word grammar*. Oxford: Blackwell.

Juilland, A. and E. Chang-Rodriguez (1964), *Frequency dictionary of Spanish words*. The Hague: Mouton de Gruyter.

Roy, D. (2009), 'New horizons in the study of child language acquisition', *Proceedings of Interspeech 2009*. Brighton, England. Available online at: http://web.media.mit.edu/~dkroy/papers/pdf/Roy_interspeech_keynote.pdf

Woodbury, A. (2003), 'Defining documentary linguistics', in: P. Austin (ed.) *Language documentation and description. Volume 1.* London: School of Oriental and African Studies. 35-51.

Language Use

I haven't drank in weeks: the use of past tense forms as past participles in English corpora

Kristina Geeraert and John Newman

University of Alberta

Abstract

We investigate a relatively understudied phenomenon, the use of the (standard) past tense verb form as a (non-standard) past participle in English, as in I haven't drank in weeks *and refer to this phenomenon as "past tense spreading". We explore this phenomenon in some familiar, large corpora of English, as well as utilizing the World Wide Web as a corpus through the Google search engine. The corpus-based approach allows us to examine details in the behaviors of many verbs across genres and to identify degrees of spreading among verbs. The web searches reveal differential behaviors for high-frequency and low-frequency verbs with respect to past tense spreading, an example, we claim, of Bybee's (2006) Conserving Effect. Past tense spreading also occurs more than expected with modal auxiliaries, a pattern which would not be predicted based solely on the non-standard character of the phenomenon.*

1. Introduction[1]

This paper is a corpus-based study of a phenomenon in non-standard usage of English which we call here "past tense spreading" (PTS).[2] PTS refers to the use of the past tense form of a verb in place of a distinct, prescribed past participial form in perfect tenses, as in *I haven't drank in weeks*, rather than *I haven't drunk in weeks*. PTS is by no means restricted to the verb *drink* and is found with a number of verbs in contemporary English.

We identify the verbs which show evidence of PTS and the frequency of the phenomenon in two readily available large corpora: the British National Corpus (BNC, see Aston and Burnard 1998: 28-41) and the Corpus of Contemporary American English (COCA, see Davies 2010a). Since the number of instances of PTS is relatively small in both of these corpora, we find it necessary to use the World Wide Web (WWW or web) as a "corpus", using the Google search engine. We also investigate the distribution of PTS across genres and its frequency with modal auxiliaries.

2. Background

PTS, though a relatively peripheral phenomenon in English, has existed for centuries. The phenomenon appears to have begun towards the end of the Middle English period with some increase in use in Early Modern English (Lass 1994:

89, Lass 2008: 170). The Oxford English Dictionary Online (2010) records, for example, *broke* as having been used as a past participle since the end of the 14th century, *took* since the 16th century, and *drank* since approximately the 18th century. In contemporary usage, PTS is documented in numerous non-standard varieties worldwide, leading Wolfram (2003: 146) to comment "past for perfect, as in *they had went there*, occurs in socially subordinate varieties of English wherever they are found throughout the world". PTS has been documented in the linguistics literature for a number of varieties of English, including the USA (Atwood 1953, Wolfram 2003), UK (Cheshire 1982: 46-49, Wright 1981: 118-120), and Australia (Eisikovits 1987). We believe it is very widespread, beyond just those cases described in the literature, though whether it is quite as widespread as Wolfram states remains an open question.

Research on PTS has received rather less attention than spreading in the opposite direction, namely the use of the past participle for the (prescriptive) past tense, as in *I drunk*, *I rung*, *I swum*, etc. (cf. Bybee and Slobin 1982; Bybee 1985, 1995). Research on these verbs and others like them has tended to focus on the phonetic structure of verbs which pattern in this way, in particular the presence of the vowel [ʌ], followed by a velar or a nasal consonant, in the past participial form. Anderwald (2007, 2009) further explores these verbs, which she fittingly calls "Bybee verbs", using some corpus-based methods (mining the Freiburg English Dialect Corpus and the Survey of English Dialects, containing dialectal data from across Great Britain – see Anderwald 2009 for details). As part of this study, Anderwald (2009: 8-11) calculated the approximate percentage of the number of verb types belonging to an inflectional type, using for this purpose Quirk et al.'s (1985: 115-120) list of strong verbs. The possible inflectional types she uses are based on identity (or not) of the infinitival, past tense, and past participial forms within the strong verb paradigm. Figure 1 is an adaptation of Anderwald's figure (Figure 1.1 in Anderwald 2009: 8) in which she summarizes her findings, with an example verb provided for each class. As can be seen in Figure 1, class (b) – precisely the group in which past tense and past participial forms are identical – contains the largest percentage of such verbs, where the percentage is calculated with respect to the number of verb types rather than the number of tokens in a corpus. Class (b), it will be noticed, is the class to which Bybee verbs are attracted (identical forms of *rung* in *I rung/I have rung*). It is also the class which many PTS verbs join (identical forms of *drank* in *I drank/I have drank*).[3] Class (b), therefore, is not only the largest one of the five, but it is also the class currently undergoing the largest increase in varieties of English where spreading between past tense and past participial forms occurs. Anderwald incorporates this observation in her account of the historical processes at work in the English verb paradigm, proposing that verbs from the other classes are in part motivated to undergo analogical leveling due to the comparatively large size of class (b), though other factors are also considered relevant. Another pertinent fact about the classes in Figure 1 is that the (e) class contains a greater complexity of forms (a three-way distinction, as in *drink*, *drank*, *drunk*) compared with the other classes. A change from class (e) to class (b), therefore, results in reduction of the complexity of the system in some sense (cf. the idea of "paradigm economy" as a factor motivating the evolution paradigms in Carstairs 1983). Simplification within the paradigm is also claimed to be indicative of non-standard usage (Cheshire 1994: 126).

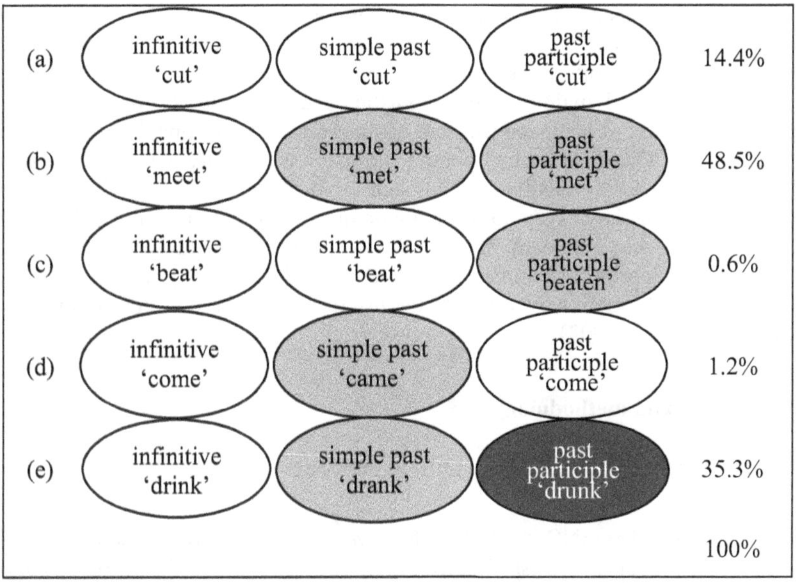

Figure 1: Identity of forms in the strong verb paradigm (adapted from Anderwald 2009)

It is clear that there are multiple forces which have shaped, and continue to shape, the variation in the form used as a past participle in the English perfect, in addition to any system-internal considerations such as economy within the paradigm. Miller (1987) illustrates the multi-layered complexity of the variation to be found with these verbs in his detailed account of the leveling at work in the English verb paradigm through three case studies of the verbs *bite*, *ride*, and *shrink*. Historical factors spanning England and the USA (all three verb paradigms have been leveling for centuries), geographical factors, social and ethnic factors, and education systems are all part of the larger story about each of these verb paradigms. A full account of PTS, in the spirit of Miller (1987), would necessarily involve many research methods (archival research, interviews targeting various populations, etc.).

The corpus-based approach which we have adopted in this paper can not possibly do justice to understanding PTS in its entirety or even do justice to all the distributional facts surrounding any one verb. We have demographic information for speakers in just one corpus (the speakers for the spoken part of the BNC). For the other corpora, we do not even have reliable information about exactly where the writers/speakers represented in the corpora are located, whether the writers/speakers are native-speakers, etc. It should be clear that we are working with a minimum of demographic information in the case of COCA and the web. However, a strength of the corpus-based approach lies in the fact that the corpora under consideration offer us a maximum amount of synchronic linguistic data from "ordinary" language use in the English-speaking world, with each corpus containing millions of words. Exploring PTS by means of these large corpora can reveal mainly "intra-linguistic" facts, i.e., facts from within the external products of language use, and can not reveal "extra-linguistic" facts (the "who, when, where, and why" behind the use). We readily acknowledge such limitations of the corpus-based approach to the study of PTS. We believe, nevertheless, that large corpora present a unique opportunity to explore PTS with reference to a large amount of naturally occurring data and for this reason a corpus-based approach should at least be tested in the way we proceed to do here (cf. also the informative overview of the use of corpora in the study of language variation in Bauer 2002).

3. Data and methodology

For the purposes of this study, we utilized three sources of data:

1. BNC. The BNC is a 100-million-word corpus of written and transcribed spoken British English. We accessed the BNC through Mark Davies' website (http://corpus.byu.edu/bnc/) and made use of the five major genre categories of the BNC, as provided for in the Mark Davies' interface at the time of carrying out this research in 2009-2010 (since changed): SPOKEN, FICTION, NEWSPAPER, ACADEMIC, MISCELLANEOUS.
2. COCA. The Corpus of Contemporary American (COCA) English contains over 400 million words (and growing). COCA was accessed in 2009-2010 through Mark Davies' website (http://www.americancorpus.org). COCA allows for easy searches across five major (and relatively equally represented) genres: SPOKEN, FICTION, MAGAZINE, NEWSPAPER, ACADEMIC.
3. World Wide Web. We utilized Google's search engine searching on the World Wide Web (WWW or web) in 2009-2010. Using the advanced search settings in Google, we restricted our searches to English websites.

Basically, we relied on one method of exploring PTS in these corpora which was by using individual search terms made up of fixed expressions, such as the sequences *have rode*, *has rode*, *had rode*, etc. for the non-standard forms and *have ridden*, *has ridden*, *had ridden*, etc. for the standard forms. This method had the advantage of directly targeting the patterns we were interested in, but it meant that we did not retrieve instances of the perfect where the auxiliary is separated by one or more intervening words, as in *Artists have in recent times dabbled in new media like acrylic.* We sacrificed the precision of our method in favor of the simplicity of searching for contiguous forms and reproducibility of results in all corpora.

Mark Davies' interfaces to the BNC and COCA allow for wildcard searches, as well as searches on parts of speech. For example, one can search for "vvd" (the part of speech tag for past tense of lexical verbs, i.e., verbs other than *be, have, do*, in both BNC and COCA), "vvn" for the past participle of the same verbs, as well as combinations of wildcard syntax with part of speech tags, e.g., "vv*" for all inflected forms of lexical verbs. We explored the possibility of utilizing such tags in the BNC and COCA, but we found the method too unreliable for our purposes. One needs to be aware, too, that the BNC and COCA have apparently been tagged using different algorithms and the difference in algorithms is directly relevant to the problem at hand. In the BNC, *took* in the sequence *we could have took over* (recorded as being spoken by an 80 year old retired miner) is tagged as a past tense. A comparable use of *took* in COCA *I would have took my two kids out of the house* (from the newspaper genre) is tagged as a past participle. Presumably, the tagging algorithm for the BNC relies primarily on the actual form of *took* to assign past tense status, whereas the algorithm for COCA relies rather on the occurrence in the frame *have X* to assign past participial status to a verbal *X*.

The Appendix lists all the verbs, their past tense and past participial forms considered as "standard" in this paper, selected from the same list used by Anderwald (2009), namely, Quirk et al. (1985: 115-120). Needless to say, we recognize that there is variation in usage (this is the starting point of our study, after all) and that some of these forms are local standards, so "standard" here simply means the reference forms assumed in this study. The (PTS) past tense forms *got*, *proved*, and *struck*, are well entrenched as past participles in the corpora used in this study, as opposed to *gotten*, *proven*, and *stricken*, respectively. In the BNC, for example, we found extraordinarily high percentages of use for the PTS forms: *got* (99%), *proved* (95%), and *struck* (99%). In other words, with these three verbs, the erstwhile past tense forms *got*, *proved*, and *struck*, represent the current dominant usage and we have not included these three verbs forms in the original list in Quirk et al. (1985) in our analysis.

There is currently much debate about using the web as a corpus (cf. Hundt, Nesselhauf, and Biewer 2007), with both pros and cons being highlighted. Some of the main criticisms leveled against relying on the web as a corpus are:

1. The web is "dirty" with numerous erroneous forms (Kilgarriff and Grefenstette 2003: 342).
2. Counts of the number of hits can be distorted due to the large amount of duplication on the web (Lüdeling, Evert & Baroni 2007: 14, Fletcher 2007: 31).

3. Search engines can be unreliable, returning substantially different counts for the same query on the same day (Kilgarriff 2007: 147-148), or returning hits that are not actually on the page itself, but rather contained in a link to the page (Keller & Lapata 2003: 469), or within titles or headings to these pages (Kilgarriff & Grefenstette 2003: 345).
4. Results are not returned in the format of easily readable concordance lines, a format much favored by corpus linguists.

Despite these issues, there is much to be said in favor of using the web as a corpus. Most obvious of all, the web provides data on a scale which is simply not matched by corpora such as BNC and COCA. Keller and Lapata (2003: 470) found evidence for claiming that counts obtained from the web were comparable to those obtained from standard corpora (a point we return to later). Importantly for our purposes, the magnitude of texts on the web makes the web particularly relevant when searching for relatively rare usage. Indeed, the web can be the only option to obtain data for a particularly rare phenomenon. Furthermore, some of the "dirty" forms referred to by Kilgarriff and Grefenstette (2003: 342) could be evidence of language change or evidence of a particular dialectal or regional use (Rosenbach 2007: 168-169), hence are potentially forms of some linguistic interest.

4. Results

4.1 Genre differences

Given the non-standard nature of the phenomenon under investigation, one would expect the more informal, spoken parts of the corpus to be where the phenomenon is most evident. We studied the occurrence of PTS forms in various genres in both the BNC and COCA. Figure 2 presents the results as mosaic plots, a simple but effective way to convey the relative proportions across categories. For these plots, the "expected" proportions are obtained by calculating the relative size of a genre compared to the whole corpus and applying that ratio to the total number of occurrences of PTS in the whole corpus. For example, in the BNC, the spoken part of the corpus consists of 10 million words = 1/10 of the total size of the BNC. The total number of PTS forms in the BNC is 323. Therefore, if PTS is proportionately distributed across all genres, we would expect 1/10 x 323 = 32.3 PTS forms in the spoken part of the corpus. In fact, 184 forms occur in the spoken part, so the "observed" size of PTS in the spoken part of the BNC (and COCA) is many times larger than the "expected" size, as shown in the darkest shaded portion in the top boxes of Figure 2.

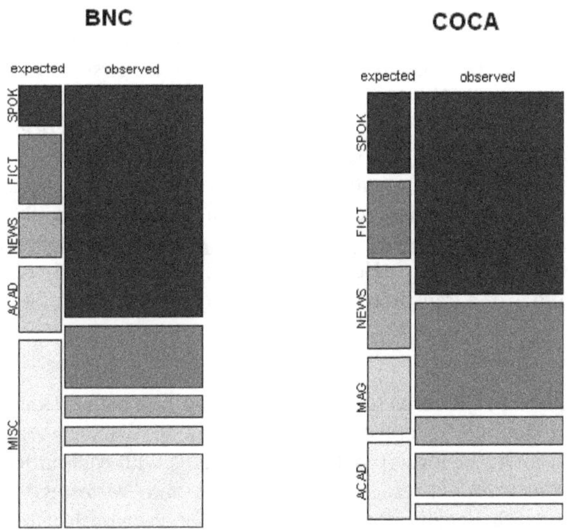

Figure 2: Observed and expected proportions of PTS use in BNC and COCA

What we see in Figure 2 is a snapshot of the corpus behavior of a particular non-standard usage: overrepresentation in the spoken part and variable degrees of representation in the other parts. In COCA, the fiction genre also has an overrepresentation of the non-standard, pointing perhaps to a greater tolerance and acceptance of non-standard forms in American usage, although one would need to follow up this observation with a closer study of genre preferences for individual instances of PTS. It may be surprising to see any occurrence of non-standard usage in the academic genre, but occurrences are found, in both BNC and COCA, and there can be various reasons for this. Sometimes, the non-standard form in the academic genre is reported speech, hence belongs more correctly to a conversational genre, as with *have wrote sic* in (1a), which occurs as part of a class drama where pupils are talking informally among themselves as part of the drama. The *sic* annotation here is part of the corpus itself. In (1b), *had wrote* also occurs as part of a direct quote, from the eighteenth century, a reminder as to how a corpus of contemporary Modern American English is not as clearly demarcated in time as one might expect. In (1c), *has showed* is part of serious academic writing in a journal.

(1) a. But a tribe member from the Onandage sic... said that we were taking their land and its sic realy sic ours and I have wrote sic down 3 suggestions for it. [COCA/ACADEMIC, *Social Studies*, Sep/Oct 1991, *82*(5), p. 179, reporting on a class drama]

b. He claimed Jekyll was "much incensed at the insolence of the Spanish protest which is to be considered in the Privy Council tomorrow August 18, 1737 by his Majesty. That Sir Jseph Jekyl sic had wrote a forcible letter to my Lord Chancellor Phillip Yorke, the first Earl Hardwicke on the occasion." [COCA/ ACADEMIC, Thomas H. Wilkins, "Sir Joseph Jekyll and his Impact on Oglethorpe's Georgia", *Georgia Historical Quarterly* 2007, 91(2), 119-134]

c. Although some observers have elaborated on the semi-democratic aspects of Palestinian rule, rather than a dictatorship, the Palestinian Authority has showed a certain degree of diversity in its rule. [COCA/ACADEMIC, Helena L. Schulz, "The 'al-aqsa intifada' as result of politics of a transition", *Arab Studies Quarterly* 2002, 24(4), p.21]

4.2 PTS verbs

In a larger study on PTS verbs (Geeraert 2010), the first author examined around 50 PTS forms not just in constructions with the auxiliary HAVE as a lemma (subsuming all inflected forms), but in constructions with each inflected form of the auxiliary (*have drank*, *has drank*, *had drank*, and *'ve drank*). In the larger study, patterns with negatives were examined for each inflected form of the auxiliary (*hasn't drank*, *hadn't drank*, etc.), as well as for morphologically complex forms (*have underwent*, *have misspoke*, etc.). For the purposes of the present paper, however, we content ourselves with discussing a selection of these results just for the simplex form of the verb (e.g., *went*, not *underwent*) from the three corpora mentioned, with frequency numbers aggregated for inflected forms of the auxiliary, ignoring negative constructions (e.g., *haven't went*).

In order to identify some main patterns in the fairly substantial amount of data obtained from the corpora, we begin by considering overall frequencies of the verbs and the extent to which they show evidence of PTS. In Figure 3, we plot the percentage use of PTS in the perfect construction against the frequency of the past participle, for all three corpora. The frequency count shown on the *X* axis is the ($\log_{10}$) frequency of the total number of past participial forms (standard + non-standard). The percentage use shown on the *Y* axis is based on the ratio of the frequency of the non-standard past participial forms relative to the total number of past participial forms (standard + non-standard). Each point represents one of the verbs, ordered from left to right in terms of increasing frequency on the *X* axis. This means that the verb represented by the nth point from left to right in one of these plots should not be equated with the verb represented by the nth point in either of the other plots, even though there can be quite a lot of overlap. Note that the scales for the *X* and *Y* axes in the three plots differ. This practice is usually avoided in presenting plots, but in this case, the main point to be made about these plots concerns the overall shape of the distribution of points and the axes have been adjusted to best reveal that shape. Extreme outliers have been removed from the BNC and COCA plots in order to reveal this distribution. These outliers include *bid*, *trod*, and *bade* in the BNC (with >6% PTS, see Table 1), and *bid*, *trod*, and *beat* in COCA (with >10% PTS, see Table 1).

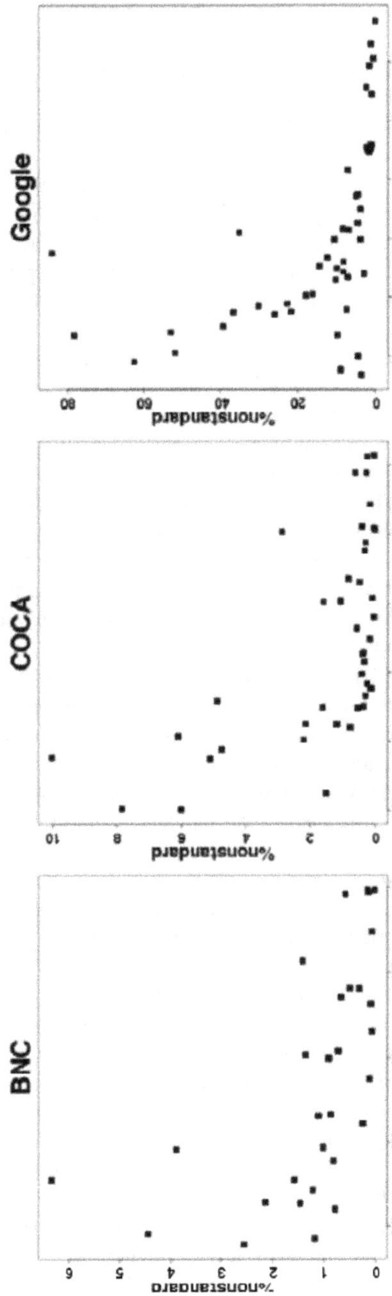

Figure 3: Scatterplots of % PTS x (log10) frequency of the perfect construction in the BNC, COCA and WWW (using the Google search engine). Note the different scales for the axes.

Figure 3 presents an intriguing series of plots. In the BNC, there is a hint of higher PTS use in the lower frequencies (<2.5 on the log scale, about 316 in absolute frequency). In COCA, this trend seems a little more pronounced in the lower frequencies (<3, or 1,000 in absolute frequency). Using the Google search engine on the web, the trend appears quite marked, with PTS use noticeably higher, on the whole, in the lower frequencies (<6, or 1 million in absolute frequency). Of course, as one proceeds from the smaller corpus size to the larger corpus size, the absolute frequencies increase, quite dramatically in the case of the web. And the range of percentages of PTS use also varies noticeably between the BNC and COCA on the one hand and the Google searches on the other. However, a similarity in the shape of the distribution in each plot nevertheless emerges, with the logarithmic curve showing more PTS with lower verb frequencies.

To appreciate better just what verbs occur where, we show the results from the web search in Figure 4. There are some verbs which appear as outliers, e.g., *bit*, *bid*, and *beat*. These three verbs have even higher PTS than verbs with similar frequencies and seem fairly well established as past participles. There is also a small group of verbs, *strode*, *wove*, *slew*, and *bade,* which appear as outliers in the lower left of the plot. These verbs have lower percentages compared with other verbs on the left side in this plot. Three of these verbs, *strode*, *wove*, and *slew*, would appear to be undergoing a different type of leveling to what we are exploring here, with *strided*, *weaved*, and *slayed* used more commonly as past participles. In the methodology we adopted for this study, only the past tense forms noted in the Appendix were searched and counted as possible past participles (*strode*, *wove*, and *slew* for these three verbs). So, in fact, a higher percentage of PTS use with these verbs would have been found if we had searched for *have strided*, *have weaved*, etc. *Bade*, however, appears to have a lower percentage of PTS because of the alternative verb form *bid*, which shows an 80% use with PTS. Putting aside these outliers, we see even more clearly the overall trend of higher PTS use in the lower frequencies and lower PTS use in the higher frequencies.

Even if each individual verb has its own unique history and set of sociolinguistic circumstances, the overall trend in Figure 3 calls for discussion. One might turn, most immediately, to Bybee's (2006: 715, 2007: 10-11) Conserving Effect as a motivating principle behind the trend: "high frequency sequences become more entrenched in their morphosyntactic structure and resist restructuring on the basis of productive patterns that might otherwise occur" (Bybee 2006: 715). One example of this principle from Bybee's work concerns regularization in the paradigm of the irregular verbs. For these verbs, Bybee observes how the regularization of the past tense suffixation of *-ed* to the stem of the base/present form, evident in the occurrence of *weeped*, *creeped*, *leaped*, etc., is resisted most in the case of high-frequency verbs where the past tense maintains a shortened vowel (*kept*, *slept*, etc.). Similarly, in our study, a high-frequency verb like *go* might be expected to "resist" a change to the structure of its perfect participial form more than a low-frequency verb like *ring* would.

Hence, the argument would go, *have gone* remains in a high percentage of cases, whereas *have rung* has "succumbed" to the new formation *have rang*.

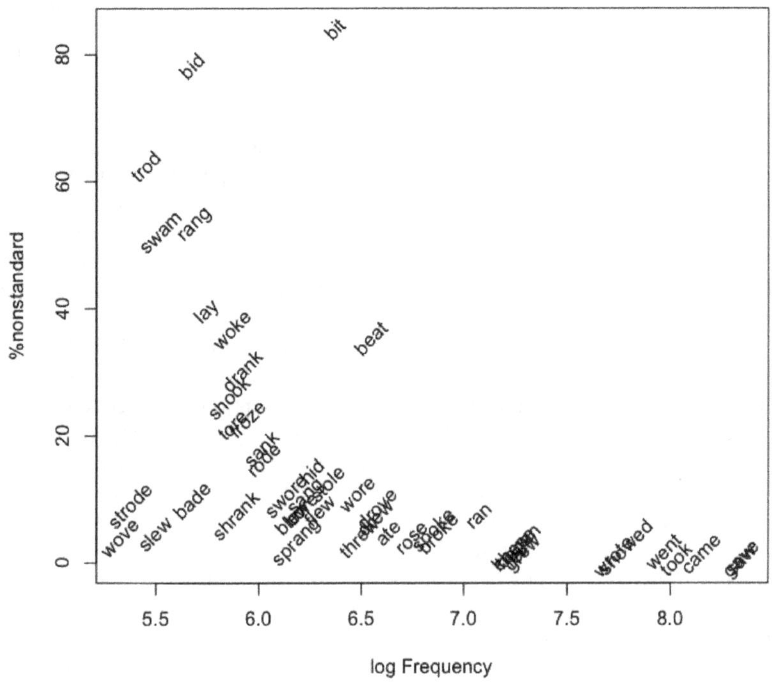

Figure 4: Detailed plot of PTS x Log_{10} Frequency of verbs, based on WWW hits using Google search engine.

While a Conserving Effect, or some principle like it, is undoubtedly real, it does not explain away exactly the distribution we see in Figure 3. By itself, the Conserving Effect says nothing about the stages which typify the historical course of a change like PTS, e.g., whether PTS spreads through the verb system in a linear way by, say, increments of 10% per century or whether PTS spreads in an S-curve manner with slower early and final stages and rapid middle stages (cf. Denison 2003 for a critical review of the S-curve hypothesis). The pattern in the plots in Figure 3 represent a snapshot in time and can hardly be used as a basis for arguing for any particular diachronic sequence of stages of implementation. Figure 3 would be consistent, for example, with a linear increase in PTS or an S-curve type of increase, both broadly consistent with the Conserving Effect. But the pattern in Figure 3 is also consistent with a "stable, low-frequency" phenomenon, as opposed to a change in progress. The phenomenon is then not a change making its way gradually through the lexicon. By this account, the change is contained within certain boundaries defined by genre, domain of "standard" usage, and the effects of stigmatized usage.

Let us turn to a more detailed presentation of some key results, beginning with Table 1, showing the verbs most prone to PTS in the BNC and COCA (with a PTS rate higher than 1%). A number of observations may be made about the two lists in Table 1. Notice, to begin with, that there is considerable overlap in the two lists – something which could not be inferred from Figure 3. All the verbs listed under BNC, except *swore*, *ate*, and *sank*, also occur under COCA. These three verbs do occur with PTS in COCA, just not with a percentage higher than 1%. The raw frequency of occurrence of the non-standard form can be small, e.g., 1 in the case of past participial *tore* in the BNC, but there are 85 occurrences altogether of the perfect construction with *tore/torn*, so there are a robust number of corpus occurrences of the construction. Clearly, though, the non-standard usage is very infrequent for most of these verbs. There are two verbs, however, that stand out as having significantly higher percentages of PTS than the rest, namely *bid* and *trod*, in both the BNC and COCA. These verbs were not considered "standard", like *got*, *proved*, and *struck* mentioned in Section 3, but appear close to achieving that "standard" status, especially within COCA.

Among the verbs showing PTS in the BNC and COCA, we have some basis here for identifying the lists in Table 1 as representing the verbs which are most advanced as far as PTS is concerned. It is precisely this kind of quantification of trends as seen in a broad spectrum of language use (even across continents!) where the corpus-based approach shows its strength. It is tempting to speculate on the phonetic and orthographic similarity of some past participles in Table 1. Two main phonetic patterns emerge. The first pattern is illustrated by *bid*, *beat*, *bit*, and *hid*. This pattern has a high front vowel followed by an alveolar stop. The second pattern is characterized by the verbs *drank*, *rang*, *sang*, *sank*, and *swam*, all of which have a low front vowel followed by a velar or a nasal (similar to the Bybee verbs mentioned earlier).[4] These phonetic patterns might be seen as phonetic templates functioning as prototypes within the PTS verbs (cf. Bybee & Thompson 2000: 384, Bybee 2010: 79), with the *bid–bit–beat–hid* group representing the most central exemplars.

Table 1: Non-standard past participial use of lexical verbs in BNC and COCA >1% of combined standard and non-standard use. Frequencies are based on co-occurrence with all inflected forms of the auxiliary HAVE.

BNC	*freq*	*% non-standard*	*COCA*	*freq*	*% non-standard*
bid	15	60.00	bid	89	89.00
trod	12	32.43	trod	36	76.60
bade	3	12.00	beat	150	14.07
rang	12	6.35	bit	26	10.04
bit	4	4.44	swam	8	7.84
beat	11	3.79	drank	21	6.10
rode	3	2.14	bade	6	6.00
froze	2	2.56	woke	12	5.11
drank	3	1.58	hid	30	4.88
swore	2	1.46	sang	13	4.73
showed	52	1.42	showed	301	2.87
broke	14	1.36	froze	7	2.18
sank	2	1.22	shook	9	2.13
tore	1	1.18	rode	9	1.61
ate	5	1.11	broke	51	1.58
			rang	2	1.52
			lay	5	1.20
			tore	5	1.18
			spoke	35	1.07

We decided to probe more deeply into the web behaviors of selected low-frequency and high-frequency verbs by examining the percentage of PTS use in three Internet domains (.com, .ca, .uk). We are aware that .com covers more than just American-based websites. Still, we relied on this web domain to represent American English usage in preference to domains such as .org, .edu, .gov, etc., since we felt that the latter are less likely to yield the non-standard usage being targeted in this paper. We chose five representative verbs from each of the low-frequency and high-frequency groups for this purpose, with results summarized in Tables 2 and 3, respectively. Percent PTS use in COCA is also included for the sake of comparison. As can be seen from these results, there is a surprisingly high degree of consistency across the three Internet domains in the behavior of these verbs, for both frequency groups.

Table 2: Five low-frequency verbs and the frequencies/percentages of their use as past participles using the WWW (searched by Google), compared with percentages in COCA. Frequencies are based on co-occurrence with all inflected forms of the auxiliary HAVE.

	.com		*.ca*		*.uk*		*COCA*
	freq	*% PTS*	*freq*	*% PTS*	*freq*	*% PTS*	*% PTS*
bid	330,600	**77.29**	5,388	**89.50**	37,235	**92.06**	**89.00**
bit	1,806,700	**83.99**	39,821	**89.35**	125,410	**81.62**	**10.04**
rang	217,400	**52.08**	1,399	**34.28**	43,280	**59.04**	**1.52**
swam	163,900	**54.07**	1,685	**43.46**	9,757	**31.06**	**7.84**
trod	164,900	**63.42**	2,269	**71.15**	9,970	**47.41**	**76.60**

Table 3: Five high-frequency verbs and the frequencies/percentages of their use as past participles using the WWW (searched by Google), compared with percentages in COCA. Frequencies are based on co-occurrence with all inflected forms of the auxiliary have.

	.com		*.ca*		*.uk*		*COCA*
	freq	*% PTS*	*freq*	*% PTS*	*freq*	*% PTS*	*% PTS*
came	1,513,000	**1.12**	26,866	**0.91**	46,640	**0.95**	**0.26**
saw	360,300	**0.17**	7,289	**0.23**	13,510	**0.21**	**0.04**
took	421,400	**0.43**	10,222	**0.37**	25,560	**0.49**	**0.27**
went	1,391,000	**1.61**	38,070	**1.97**	29,470	**0.67**	**0.62**
wrote	432,500	**0.88**	13,577	**1.06**	17,790	**0.77**	**0.31**

One difference between the BNC and COCA that is worth a special mention concerns the use of PTS for the verb *do*, omitted from Table 1, which reported only on full "lexical" verbs. In the BNC, the sequence HAVE *did* rarely occurs as a past participle. Instead, such sequences, to the extent they occur, usually are part of different constructions and must be categorized accordingly, as shown in (2).

(2) a. cleft constructions: *The job they had, didn't interest me.*
b. repetitions: *Did that have, did that have quite an impact.*
c. self-corrections: *So they had – did have a variety of different things.*
d. run-on sentences: *That was the first inkling we ever had – Did she have her cloth in hand?*
e. tag-questions: *Yeah we have, didn't you?*

f. interruptions: *At the moment Lincoln have [Did you know there's someone waiting for you at Radio].*

There are just three instances in the BNC that show *did* occurring in a past participle: *I've did er night shift once*; *...because the ones that we've did cost like I think it was eight hundred pounds*; and *you've did your undergraduate work at York*. The majority of instances of HAVE *did* in the BNC are not instances of PTS.

In COCA, however, the sequence HAVE *did* occurs quite frequently as a genuine past participle (89 occurrences in COCA), as in the examples in (3).

(3) a. he s got to protect his client, and he *should have did* it right then and then to start the clock ticking. (COCA: SPOKEN, 2008, CNN Nancy Grace)

b. if they wanted to express that way, they *should have did* it in another form (COCA: SPOKEN, 2008, NPR TalkNation)

c. There were a lot of things that night we *could have did* differently, and we should have (COCA: SPOKEN, 1998, ABC 20/20)

4.3 Modals and PTS verbs

One particularly intriguing usage context associated with a higher-than-expected incidence of PTS involves the presence of modal auxiliaries, as in *it must have took about three years, my father could have went to jail, it should not have came to this*, and *could one person have ran a massive scheme*. Eisikovits (1987: 23) had already noticed in her analysis of Inner-Sydney English that PTS occurred in this environment more often than one would expect. We found a similar pattern in our data. For example, out of the 81 instances of *have went* in COCA, 67 (82.7%) occur in constructions with a modal auxiliary. On the other hand, 3,623 (just 40.9%) out of the 8,860 instances of *have gone* occur with a modal. This amounts to a *percent difference* of 41.8% in favor of co-occurrence of PTS with a modal auxiliary. We rely on this simple statistical measurement of percent difference to report on the use of PTS and modal auxiliaries in COCA, though the same patterns were evident in all our corpora. This statistical measurement seemed most appropriate for this analysis as some verbs had extremely large frequencies which would lead too easily to statistical significance using, say, chi-square tests. We searched for all modal auxiliaries within five word positions to the left of *have*, (the "L1-L5" range), individually inspecting forms with lower frequency but relying on automatic retrieval of forms with larger frequencies. Only verbs which showed a minimum of three instances were used in these calculations of percent differences. The results are summarized in (4a-b):

(4) a. Preferred use of non-standard past participles in the context of a modal, with percent difference compared with standard past participial form in a modal context:

froze (64%), *shook* (61%), *saw* (61%), *drove* (60%), *fell* (60%), *swam* (59%), *ran* (50%), *hid* (47%), *gave* (46%), *came* (43%), *went* (42%), *wrote* (40%), *chose* (39%), *took* (39%), *showed* (33%), *broke* (31%), *sang* (31%), *beat* (31%), *began* (19%), *drank* (15%)

b. Preferred use of standard past participles in the context of a modal, with percent difference compared with non-standard past participial form in a modal context: *trodden* (40%), *bitten* (33%), *woken* (24%), *worn* (11%), *spoken* (7%)

The preference for non-standard past participial use in the modal auxiliary context, as seen in (4), is striking. It is not a matter of a subtle point or two in percent difference which is the basis for this conclusion – the percent differences are large, staggeringly so in some cases. Four modals appear most frequent with PTS: *would*, *could*, *should*, and *must* (which have variable overall frequencies in COCA, as reported in Davies 2010b).

We leave unanswered the question of *why* the non-standard form is so strongly associated with the modal auxiliary context. One fact that would seem relevant to answering this question in future research is the phonetic reduction that occurs, often but not always, in the infinitival *have* in these constructions, reflected in the orthographic representations *could've*, *would've*, etc., or the reanalyzed variants *could of*, *would of*, etc. Or perhaps the presence of the modal auxiliary introduces an extra degree of processing complexity which goes hand-in-hand with the selection of a more colloquial, more easily accessible variant of the verb. Whatever the explanation might be, it seems that we must acknowledge a recurring constructional schema in these cases with PTS firmly entrenched for some speakers.

5. Conclusions

The advent of corpora and the potential of using the web as a corpus have created the opportunity to use data from these corpora to explore non-standard English usage. Corpora such as the BNC and COCA and the web have, of course, not been constructed for the explicit purpose of studying non-standard usage – usually we would collect data in different ways if we were documenting and analyzing non-standard usage, e.g., interviews which target non-standard usage, specialized corpora based on local usage, etc. It is, therefore, of interest to learn what can be discovered about non-standard usage using these kinds of general, all-purpose resources.

As would be expected of non-standard usage, PTS is most common in the spoken genre of corpora which distinguish genres, such as BNC and COCA. But, interestingly, PTS occurs in all the genres of these corpora, reflecting in part the complexity and subtlety associated with some "genres" and their labels in corpus linguistics. The ACADEMIC genre of COCA, for example, can include quoted speech (including very colloquial speech) embedded in a piece of academic writing, giving rise to informal, colloquial variants which would not normally be found in highly self-conscious, planned, and edited written academic discourse. The presence of PTS in an academic sub-corpus of English, therefore, must be interpreted cautiously: some occurrences may reflect a new or emerging standard usage, but other occurrences may be "posing" as academic writing when they really belong to a conversational genre. It is a reminder of just how mixed the catch can be when we trawl in an ocean.

Relying on a corpus-based approach, we were able to identify the verbs in both BNC and COCA which are most prone to PTS. Despite some variation between the British and American varieties of English represented in these two corpora, there is a high degree of agreement in the results from the two corpora. We took a percentage of >1% PTS use as a basis for identifying verbs most prone to PTS (cf. Table 1) and found that there were 15 such verbs in the BNC and 19 in COCA. Two verbs had an exceptionally high percentage of PTS, *bid* and *trod*, while all other verbs in Table 1 had below 15%, suggesting that PTS remains a relatively peripheral phenomenon in these corpora. Of particular interest, though, was the comparison of PTS usage in these corpora with Google-based searches. On the web, we found a much greater range in percentage of PTS use and differential behaviors for high-frequency and low-frequency verbs. Specifically, we found that high-frequency verbs evidence PTS considerably less often than low-frequency verbs, a pattern which is discernible, though to a lesser degree, in the BNC and COCA results. For example, a high-frequency verb like *go* manifests relatively less usage of the non-standard perfect construction *have went* when compared with a low-frequency verb like *ring* and its non-standard perfect *have rang*. We believe this pattern is evidence of Bybee's Conserving Effect coupled, most likely, with the stable but marginal character of PTS. Additionally, one should explore potential correlations of PTS use with other frequency measures, such as frequencies of the past tense forms or the lemma. Recall that we used only the frequency of the combined standard plus non-standard past participial usage in the present study and this may not be the only relevant or optimal measure. In any case, other factors, beyond what we can measure using corpus-based methodologies, are most certainly relevant, as mentioned in Section 2. The intriguing strong association between a modal auxiliary context and PTS also invites further analysis, especially experimental analyses which investigate speakers' mental processing of modal vs. non-modal contexts of usage.

Notes

1 The authors would like to thank participants at the AACL 2009 conference and anonymous reviewers for helpful suggestions on earlier versions of this paper.

2 Past tense spreading is referred to as "preterite shift" in Lass (1994: 89).

3 Note that past tense spreading in some verbs results in one single form in infinitival, past tense, and past participial forms, such as *have beat*. In such cases, the forms migrate to class (a) in Figure 1.

4 There could potentially be a third pattern, all containing the vowel phoneme /ow/ (*rode*, *froze*, *showed*, *broke*, *spoke*). The preceding and following consonants around the vowel are quite varied in these cases, to the point that this pattern is less distinctive, phonetically, than the other two patterns.

References

Anderwald, L. (2007), ''He rung the bell' and 'she drunk ale' – non-standard past tense forms in traditional British dialects and on the internet', in: M. Hundt, N. Nesselhauf & C. Biewer (eds.) *Corpus linguistics and the web*. Amsterdam: Rodopi. 271-286.

Anderwald, L. (2009), *The morphology of English dialects: verb formation in non-standard English*. Cambridge: Cambridge University Press.

Aston, G. & L. Burnard (1998), *The BNC handbook: exploring the British National Corpus with SARA*. Edinburgh: Edinburgh University Press.

Atwood, E. B. (1953), *A survey of verb forms in the eastern United States*. Ann Arbor: University of Michigan Press.

Bauer, L. (2002), 'Inferring variation and change from public corpora', in: J. K. Chambers, P. Trudgill, & N. Schilling-Estes (eds.) *The handbook of language variation and change*. Malden and Oxford: Blackwell. 97-114.

Bybee, J. (1985), *Morphology: a study of the relation between meaning and form*. Amsterdam: Benjamins.

Bybee, J. (1995), 'Regular morphology and the lexicon', *Language and cognitive processes*, 10: 425-455.

Bybee, J. (2006), 'From usage to grammar: the mind's response to repetition', *Language*, 82(4): 711-733.

Bybee, J. (2007), *Frequency of use and the organization of language*. Oxford: Oxford University Press.

Bybee, J. (2010), *Language, usage and cognition*. Cambridge: Cambridge University Press.

Bybee, J. L. & D. I. Slobin (1982), 'Rules and schemas in the development and use of the English past tense', *Language*, 58(2): 265-289.

Bybee, J. & S. Thompson (2000), 'Three frequency effects in syntax', *Berkeley linguistics society*, 23: 65-85.

Carstairs, A. (1983), 'Paradigm economy', *Journal of linguistics*, 19(1): 115-128.

Cheshire, J. (1982), *Variation in an English dialect: a sociolinguistic study*. Cambridge: Cambridge University Press.

Cheshire, J. (1994), 'Standardization and the English irregular verbs', in: D. Stein & I. Tieken-Boon van Ostade (eds.) *Towards a standard English: 1600-1800*. Berlin: Mouton. 115-133.

Davies, M. (2010a), 'The Corpus of Contemporary American English as the first reliable monitor corpus of English', *Literary and linguistic computing*, 25(4): 447-464.

Davies, M. (2010b), *Word frequency lists and dictionary from the Corpus of Contemporary American English*. Available online at: http://www.wordfrequency.info.

Denison, D. (2003), 'Log(ist)ic and simplistic S-curves', in: R. Hickey (ed.) *Motives for language change*. Cambridge: Cambridge University Press. 54-70.

Eisikovits, E. (1987), 'Variations in the lexical verb in inner-Sydney English', *Australian journal of linguistics*, 7: 1-24.

Fletcher, W. (2007), 'Concordancing the web: promise and problems, tools and techniques', in: M. Hundt, N. Nesselhauf & C. Biewer (eds.) *Corpus linguistics and the web*. Amsterdam: Rodopi. 25-45.

Geeraert, K. (2010), I haven't drank in weeks: *preterite shift in English*, MSc thesis, University of Alberta.

Hundt, M., N. Nesselhauf & C. Biewer (eds.) (2007), *Corpus linguistics and the web*. Amsterdam: Rodopi.

Keller, F. & M. Lapata (2003), 'Using the web to obtain frequencies for unseen bigrams', *Computational linguistics*, 29(3): 459-484.

Kilgarriff, A. (2007), 'Googleology is bad science', *Computational linguistics*, 33(1): 147-151.

Kilgarriff, A. & G. Grefenstette (2003), 'Introduction to the special issue on the web as corpus', *Computational linguistics*, 29(3): 333-347.

Lass, R. (1994), 'Proliferation and option-cutting: the strong verb in the fifteenth to eighteenth centuries', in: D. Stein & I. Tieken-Boon van Ostade (eds.) *Towards a standard English: 1600-1800*. Berlin: Mouton. 81-113.

Lass, R. (2008), 'Phonology and morphology', in: R. Lass (ed.) *The Cambridge history of the English language volume 3: 1476-1776*. Cambridge: Cambridge University Press. 56-186.

Lüdeling, A., S. Evert & M. Baroni (2007), 'Using web data for linguistic purposes', in: M. Hundt, N. Nesselhauf and C. Biewer (eds.) *Corpus linguistics and the web*. Amsterdam: Rodopi. 7-24.

Miller, M. I. (1987), 'Three changing verbs: bite, ride, and shrink', *Journal of English linguistics*, 20(3): 3-12.

Oxford English Dictionary online, 2nd ed. (OED) (2010). Available online at: http://www.oed.com/.

Quirk, R., S. Greenbaum, G. Leech & J. Svartvik (1985). *A comprehensive grammar of the English language*. London: Longman.
Rosenbach, A. (2007), 'Exploring constructions on the web: a case study', in: M. Hundt, N. Nesselhauf & C. Biewer (eds.) *Corpus linguistics and the web*. Amsterdam: Rodopi. 167-190.
Wolfram, W. (2003), 'Enclave dialect communities in the south', in: S. Nagle & S. Sanders (eds.) *English in the southern United States*. Cambridge: Cambridge University Press. 141-158.
Wright, P. (1981), *Cockney dialect and slang*. London: B. T. Batsford.

Appendix

Verbs and their past tense and past participial forms, as assumed in this study

bear bore borne
beat beat beaten
begin began begun
bid bid/bade bidden
bite bit bitten
blow blew blown
break broke broken
choose chose chosen
come came come
draw drew drawn
drink drank drunk
drive drove driven
eat ate eaten
fall fell fallen
fly flew flown
freeze froze frozen
give gave given
go went gone
grow grew grown
hide hid hidden
know knew known
lie lay lain
ride rode ridden
ring rang rung
rise rose risen
run ran run
see saw seen
shake shook shaken
show showed shown
shrink shrank shrunk
sing sang sung
sink sank sunk
slay slew slain
speak spoke spoken
spring sprang sprung
steal stole stolen
stride strode stridden
swear swore sworn
swim swam swum
take took taken
tear tore torn
throw threw thrown
tread trod trodden
wake woke woken
wear wore worn
weave wove woven
write wrote written

Irregular *-im* suffixation in Tok Pisin: exploratory methods in multivariate analysis

Conor Snoek

University of Alberta

Abstract

In this paper, two methods appropriate for the visual and quantitative inspection of multivariate data are applied to a corpus of narrative texts in order to investigate the behavior of the Tok Pisin suffix -im. *The distribution of the suffix is subject to considerable variability. While this problem has been noted in the literature and various solutions have been proposed, there are a number of verbs whose behavior is not easily accounted for. The methods used are complementary explorative tools for the analyst. They are deployed in an effort to ascertain which factors govern the encountered patterns, and what weight these factors carry relative to each other.*

1. Introduction

Tok Pisin is spoken in Papua New Guinea. Much of its vocabulary is drawn from English, although other languages such as Kuanua and German have also had an influence. It is spoken primarily as a lingua franca, although communities of first language speakers also exist. This paper seeks to investigate the occurrence of the verbal suffix *-im* in a number of Tok Pisin verbs showing irregular patterns of behavior. The distribution is complex and influenced by many variables. Working from a corpus, I seek to exemplify how multivariate analysis can be fruitfully applied to such a problem. Data are not available for all the factors which have been suggested to play a role, especially regarding whether a particular author speaks Tok Pisin as a first or second language. While this is unfortunate, the methods deployed here allow in principle for such data to be added. Furthermore, they enable the estimation of relative importance of these variables. As more and better data become available, new variables can be introduced to the models presented here and more accurate results obtained. The variation in occurrence of the suffix in clauses sampled for a corpus of Tok Pisin stories will be investigated here using behavioral profiling and conditional inference trees. Both these methods are able to deal with large numbers of heterogeneous variable types. The former was recently developed for linguistic analysis by Gries (2006 *inter alia*) and provides a new means of assessing the similarity of linguistic objects characterized by sets of feature-variables. The latter method, belonging to a recursive partitioning framework, has been available for longer, but has not frequently been used in the analysis of corpus data. This paper seeks to show that both are important and profitable means of analyzing linguistic data and gaining insight into morphosyntactic problems.

2. The *-im* suffix in Tok Pisin

The *-im* suffix has been consistently linked to transitivity in the literature. In his grammar of Tok Pisin, Verhaar begins his discussion of the suffix by noting that "[in] Tok Pisin, transitive verbs are derived from other forms by attaching the suffix *-im*." (Verhaar 1995: 22). He then goes on to list examples for this pattern as well as a series of exceptions. His description includes cases where the *-im* suffix serves to derive transitive verbs from other transitive verbs (1995: 22), undermining his own analysis of the suffix, or at least acknowledging the suffix's variability. Verhaar mainly takes a traditional view of transitivity, in the sense of a formal approach to characterizing the phenomenon: the verb is considered to be transitive if it takes a direct object complement and intransitive if it does not (Rice 1987: 13). This is the approach also taken by Mihalic (1971) in his brief description of Tok Pisin grammar at the beginning of his definitive dictionary.[1] Mihalic admits that some transitive verbs do not occur with the suffix, and instead have a preposition (always *long* in Tok Pisin) interposed between the verb and the object. The presence of this type of construction therefore undermines the definition of transitivity used in identifying clause types, by running counter to the only explicit diagnostic. Verhaar, who classifies Tok Pisin verbs into ditransitive, intransitive, transitive and semi-transitive according to the same principle, never fully addresses this definitional problem. The distinction he uses is a syntactic one and is based on whether an object immediately follows the verb (direct object) or whether *long* occurs between the verb and the object. Verhaar notes a discrepancy between syntax and semantics with his class of semi-transitives which are "transitive semantically but intransitive syntactically" (Verhaar 1995: 305) because they occur with objects preceded by *long*. They are considered semi-transitives because they do seem to require an object, but this object is not syntactically a direct object. Verhaar thus introduces a semantic notion to his study of Tok Pisin verbs. Unfortunately, he neither elaborates nor clarifies these distinctions in any detail. Supporting evidence for the presence of obligatory objects occurring in *long*-marked phrases comes from ditransitive verbs. Here too, obligatory objects occur marked by *long*. The presence of verbs like the semi-transitives and the ditransitives leads to the conclusion that syntactic elements coding for obligatory arguments of the verb can occur either bare or accompanied by *long*. These arguments are considered obligatory because they are required by the semantic structure of the verb. The correlate of this requirement is that they are always present in the context of the verbs in the corpus. They may be missing only in those contexts where they are topical and retrievable from the context. In practice this means that they occur as overt syntactic elements either in the same sentence or the immediately preceding discourse, which was defined as the paragraph containing the sentence for the task at hand. The verbs in the study appear in the kinds of syntactic patterns listed in Table 1, where *Ø* marks the absence of the suffix, *complement* stands for cases where the verb is followed by an adjunct, subordinate clause, or verb phrase, and *zero* when nothing follows the verb.

Table 1: Construction types and frequencies of occurrence in the sample

pattern type	*number of tokens in the sample*
Verb-*im* + complement	5
Verb-Ø + *long* + complement	37
Verb+ Ø + complement	311
Verb Ø + *long* + Obj	6
Verb-*im* + Obj	503
Verb-Ø + *long* + Obj	197
Verb-Ø + Obj	289
Verb-*im* + *long* + zero	0
Verb-Ø + *long* + zero	2
Verb-*im* + zero	6
Verb-Ø + zero	205
total	1561

In addition to the monovalent verbs and the bivalent verbs in object-omission contexts, there appears to be an alternation between verbs with the *-im* suffix and direct objects and verbs followed by *long* and an object. What complicates the picture is that verb-suffix combinations, as in (1), can alternate with verb-Ø combinations in very similar environments, that is to say in syntactic situations which may well be categorized as transitive clauses, such as (2) for example:

(1) *...na goapim wanpela diwai.*
...and climb-im a tree
'...and [he] climbed a tree.' (Slone Wantok Corpus)

(2) *Em holimpas meri...*
3sg hold woman
'He held onto her…' (Slone Wantok Corpus)

It must be noted that there are further cases in which the absence or presence of the verb can be reliably predicted: when *-im* marks the causative it may not be omitted, and when *-im* marks a reciprocal or a reflexive meaning no object follows the verb. The sample studied here contained no examples of causative or reciprocal uses of *-im*, however. There was one sentence which was ambiguous between being a reflexive use of *-im* or an object omission context; in the event it was classed as a case of the latter.

To summarize, Tok Pisin verbs can be transitive or intransitive under the formal diagnostic of being followed by a direct object. In the transitive case, the verb may or may not carry the *-im* suffix. Formal clausal transitivity is no guarantor for the presence of the suffix. Therefore, it is justified to investigate whether there are semantic aspects to the clause that play a role in the occurrence of the suffix.

In a study based on a range of languages, Hopper & Thompson (1980) outline a number of features which they consider to correlate with transitivity. They describe the traditional notion of transitivity as "a global property of an entire clause such that an activity is 'carried over' or 'transferred' from an agent to a patient" (Hopper & Thompson 1980: 251). More precisely they see transitivity as a graded phenomenon -- clauses can exhibit features which correlate with high or low transitivity. This seems to imply that all clauses are transitive at some level or to some degree. The components they have identified as pertinent to transitivity "allow clauses to be characterized as more or less transitive" (Hopper & Thompson 1980: 253). They find the following variables to be decisive in differentiating high transitivity clauses from low transitivity clauses: (1) the number of participants, (2) kinesis (as a property of verb semantics), (3) punctuality, (4) volitionality, (5) affirmation, (6) mode, (7) agency, (8) affectedness of object, (9) individuation of object. These variables were operationalized in the following manner for the Tok Pisin data. The semantics of verbs were encoded in variables describing the lexical aspect covering features 2, 3 and 7 from the list above. Feature 4 was considered to the extent that the animacy of the subject was encoded. Feature 9 was encoded as the grammatical number of the objects. The other features proved difficult to instantiate for the corpus-based approach adopted here, in particular with regard to the affectedness of the object. While the animacy of the object was encoded, details to the extent of the affectedness of the objects as a function of the meaning of the verbs proved difficult to ascertain. With regard to affirmation, the data in sample were composed almost exclusively with affirmative sentences (only 7 of the sentences were negated cases) and all of these featured the *-im* suffix.[2]

In order to investigate the effects of these variables on the occurrence of the suffix and to examine their potential interaction, a clustering procedure known as *behavioral profiling* was used. This method and the results obtained with it are to be outlined in Section 7.3. The next Section continues with a description of the variables for which the corpus data were annotated.

3. The Slone Wantok Corpus

The data used in this paper are drawn from the *Slone Wantok Corpus*, a collection of stories written in Tok Pisin available freely from the internet at http:\\www.tokpisin.org. The corpus is searchable with regular expressions and these were used to match the desired strings. The entire contents of the corpus were made accessible this way, allowing for the complete contexts of each token sentence in the sample to be taken into account. The *Slone Wantok Corpus* (Slone 2003) is a collection of texts sent in to a column in the Tok Pisin language newspaper *Wantok* with the name "Stori Tumbuna" ('Ancestor Stories'). The corpus comprises about 800,000 words, and ranges over a time span from 1971-

1997. The stories were collected and translated by Thomas Slone. While Slone's editing appears highlighted in grey text over the webpage and can therefore be easily identified, no information is provided on the editing, if any, that was carried out by newspaper staff before publication.

The data for the *Slone Wantok Corpus* come entirely from stories. While this has advantages insofar as ensuring an equal status to all the data in terms of their genre, it does also have the limitation that no conversational or other type of Tok Pisin data is considered. It is then true to say that any results and insights gained from this analysis relate to narratological contexts only. This is not to say that the phenomenon under investigation necessarily behaves differently in other speech contexts, only that data from other genres have not been subjected to intense study in this paper.

4. Selection of verbs

The object of the investigation was to outline the factors involved in governing the distribution of the *-im* suffix. In the grammatical description provided by Mihalic (1971), Tok Pisin verbs are classified with regard to whether they occur with the *-im* suffix, and with regard to what effect suffixation has in each case. There is a large set of verbs, for example, for which the distribution of the *-im* suffix is predictable, so that the suffixed forms occur in constructions followed by a direct object, whereas the forms without a suffix do not. A second and somewhat more intriguing class of verbs are those described as having "two forms...[that] are transitive in both forms" (Mihalic 1971: 26). It is the verbs from this class that form the main group of the sample used in this study. These verbs are (English glosses in brackets): *abrus* (to pass by), *bilip* (to believe), *dring* (to drink), *goap* (to climb), *gris* (to flatter), *kalap* (to jump up), *lukaut* (to look out), *mangal* (to covet), *singaut* (to call), *spet* (to spit), *tekewe* (to take away), *tromoi* (to throw), *was* (to watch), *was2* (to wash),[3] *wet* (to wait). Another group exhibiting highly irregular behavior with regard to the suffix is verbs composed of a verb-stem carrying the *-im* suffix and an adverbial particle. Unfortunately, the corpus contained tokens of only one type from this group, *holimpas* (to hold); tokens of this verb were also taken into the sample. For the verbs in the sample many of the suggested possible sources for variation in suffix occurrence do not seem to hold. For example, they are not derived from nominals with the exception of *gris*. It has been claimed that *-im* does not delete in derived verbs of this kind, but *gris* does occur as a verb both with and without the suffix in the corpus. The verbs studied here do not show a meaning variation between versions of the verb followed by *long* or suffixed by *-im*, such as the differences between the verbs *glasim* 'to look thoroughly' and *glaslong* 'to signal with a mirror', both related morphologically to *glas*.

To the verbs listed above were added a number of verbs that were described as never occurring with the suffix: *gat* (to have), *luksave* (to recognize), *marimari* (to have pity on), *presen* (to give a gift), *tenkyu* (to thank) and *min* (to mean). The verb *aigris* (to desire) was added to this group. It is not described in the Mihalic dictionary but did occur in the corpus. This resulted in a total of 24 verb types in the sample.

5. Sampling method

Once the verbs were selected on the grounds outlined in the section above, all instances of token sentences with these verbs were retrieved from the corpus. 7,243 sentences were extracted from the corpus in this manner. If there were fewer than 100 token sentences featuring a given verb, then all sentences were taken into the sample to be coded. If there were more than 100 cases, then 100 random numbers from the sequence of unique identifier numbers corresponding to sentences featuring that verb were generated using a sampling function in the statistical programming environment R (R Development Core Team, 2011). The sample ultimately consisted of 1,561 sentences. Table 2 is an overview of the verbs in the sample along with the number of token sentences they feature in.

Table 2: The verbs in the sample and their token frequencies

verb	*token sentences*	*verb*	*token sentences*
abrus	91	marimari	4
aigris	29	min	40
bilip	90	presen	3
dring	98	ranawe	99
gat	67	singaut	96
goap	100	spet	62
gris	27	tekewe	31
holimpas	100	tenkyu	17
kalap	100	tromoi	99
lukaut	100	was	44
luksave	82	was2	50
mangal	33	wet	99
			total 1561

6. Coding

Each token sentence in the sample was annotated with information regarding its date of publication, the region of Papua New Guinea it originated in, syntactic aspects of the sentence, and semantic aspects of the sentence. The syntactic variables that were coded included the type of clause the verb in question occurred in (e.g., main clause, coordinate clause, subordinate clause), and the element directly to the right of the verb (e.g., the presence of the *long* preposition, the presence of a direct object, adjunct etc.). The semantic variables that were coded included the animacy of subjects and objects, the lexical aspect of the verb, the semantic values of modal verbs if they were present in the sentence, and the grammatical number of subjects and objects. Where available, information regarding the possible substrate language of the Tok Pisin author for each sentence was also provided.

7. Analysis

In this Section a number of hypotheses regarding the source of the variation of the *-im* suffix are explored and tested. The data are first considered from the perspective of regional and diachronic variation. However, these factors do not seem to explain the behavior of the *-im* suffix on their own. Therefore these investigations are followed up with methods capable of integrating large numbers of different variables. In this case, the methods are behavioral profiling and recursive partitioning in the form of conditional inference trees.

7.1 Regional and substrate based variation

The annotation of the data in the *Slone Wantok Corpus* make it possible to investigate whether the regional origins of the speakers or the languages that they speak besides Tok Pisin have an effect on the distribution of the *-im* suffix. The stories are annotated for the origins and first languages of their authors. An attempt was made to find these datapoints for each of the token sentences in the sample. This was not always possible, however, as data were not available for every token. Insofar as data were available, regional effects proved inconclusive. Therefore the hypothesis of a regional variation for the distribution of the suffix was dismissed. In order to show this, the number of occurrences of *im*-suffixed verbs as a subset of the token sentences from that region is compared across all the regions. Table 3 represents these data. Along with collecting the stories and translating them, Thomas Slone also attempted to provide data on the substrate language for each author. However, the data on substrates are not complete and only just over 50% of the token sentences could be assigned one of 143 substrate languages that were in the sample. For the available data no pattern in distribution could be found.

Table 3: Regional origins and *-im* suffix occurrence relative to all verbs in the sample from each region

region	*relative frequency of* -im
East Highlands	0.43
East Sepik	0.32
Enga	0.35
Madang	0.26
Morobe	0.23
Southern Highlands	0.37
Simbu	0.34
West Highlands	0.25
West Sepik	0.34
mean	0.32

It can be observed that three regions diverge from the general trend: the East Highlands region has a slightly higher frequency of *-im* usage, whereas the Morobe, Madang and West Highlands data exhibit lower than average frequencies. However, these differences are not stark enough to warrant dialectal difference as an explanation for suffix occurrence.

7.2 Diachronic variation

Another possible source for the variation in the occurrence of the suffix must be considered, namely the possible change in the frequency of the suffix over time. In this case only those token sentences with objects were considered. The corpus data spans three decades, from 1972-1997. The data were classified somewhat arbitrarily as belonging to one of these three decades so that there were 70s, 80s and 90s datasets. The occurrence of the suffix under the condition of the presence of an object was then cross-tabulated with the classes. In this case, the differences in the table are significant under a chi-square test (χ-squared = 20.7, df = 2, $p <$ 0.0001). The results are presented in Figure 1below.

However, the peak phase for *-im* suffix usage would be in the 1980s category, which seems to rule out the possibility that *-im* suffix usage has become more predictable over time. This overall pattern was thought sufficiently indicative of the general trend (or lack thereof), so that further classificatory possibilities with regard to the time partitions were not explored.

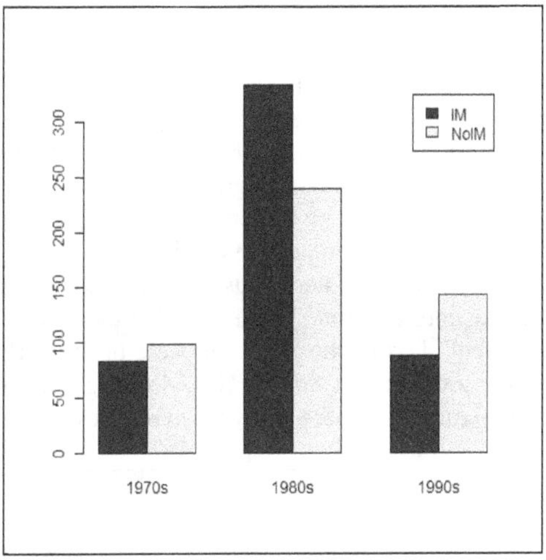

Figure 1: The change of occurrence of the *-im* suffix over time

7.3 Behavioral profiles

In a number of papers on the topic of corpus-based lexical semantics, Gries and others have outlined a method of analysis known as *behavioral profiling* (Gries 2006, Berez & Gries 2008, Gries & Otani 2010). The method involves annotating token clauses featuring the word under investigation with a set of variables that are considered to at least potentially influence the word's distribution. This set of annotations can then be compared and evaluated with the help of an implementation in the statistical programming environment R. The profiling method proved to be an important step in the exploration of the *-im* data as it allowed for easy manipulation of the variables and a visual representation of the effects of variable combinations on clustering patterns. The results in the form of clustered data gave insights into the relevance of certain variables. In each case, cluster diagrams were constructed through the use of the Canberra distance measure and Ward's amalgamation method.[4] The dendrograms representing the clusterings in the data carry information on the statistical reliability of each cluster. This information is rendered as numbers placed to the immediate left and right of each branch in the dendrogram. The number to the right is the Bootstrap Probability (BP) which represents the frequency with which that particular cluster reappears in the bootstrapped clusterings. The number to the left is the approximately unbiased probability value (AU). Heuristically, this value constitutes evidence for a particularly stable cluster if it reaches a size of 90 or more. This statistic is derived by applying a bootstrapping method and re-building the cluster from these bootstrapped samples (i.e., checking for the similarity of clusters if these are rebuilt multiple times by re-sampling from the same dataset). The details for this procedure are to be found in Suzuki & Shimodaira (2004). The behavioral profiles script is a useful exploratory tool run as it can be run a number of times with variations of the variables taken into the calculation.

A series of dendrograms of clusterings under different conditions can be produced allowing for a visual assessment of the effect of a range of variable combinations. The first clusterings produced by this method included all the variables that the data had been annotated for. This dendrogram provided a very mixed picture of the dataset, from which little could be discerned. The subsequent clusterings gave views of the data from different perspectives and paved the way for follow-up questions. The clearest, most consistent clusters were achieved taking only data from syntactic variables into account. These included the type of clause containing the verb, the functional class of the right collocate of the verb (direct object, adjunct etc.) and the presence of *long*. This dendrogram of syntactic variables is reproduced in Figure 2. There are two main clusters in

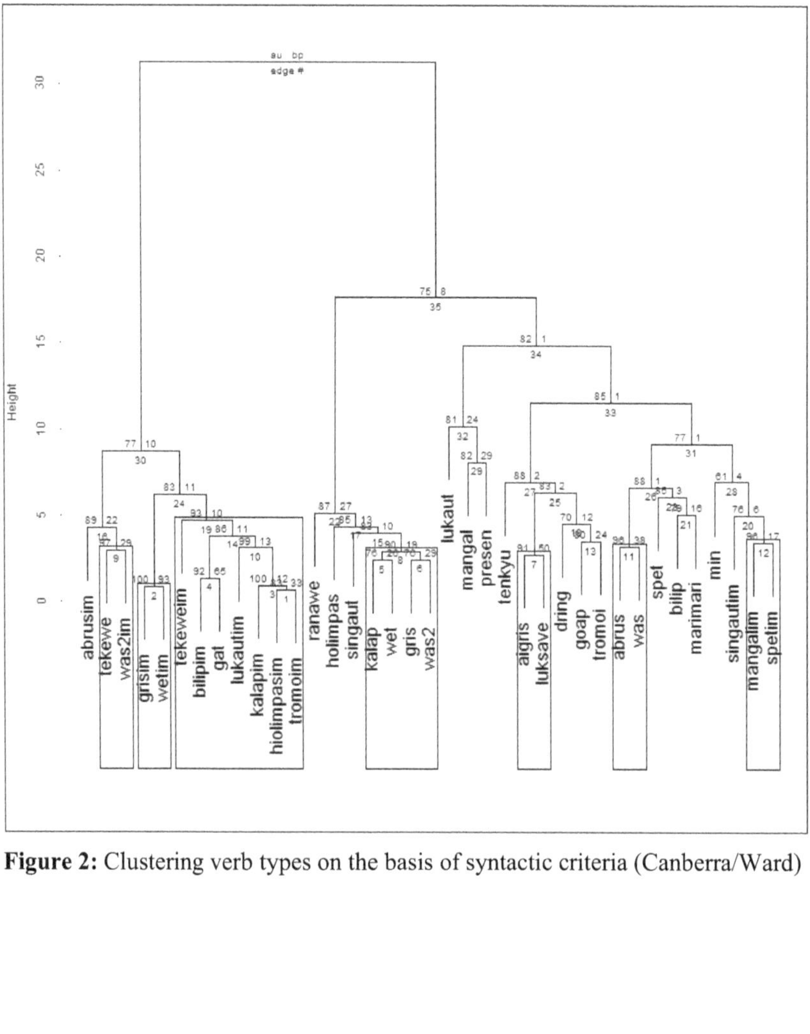

Figure 2: Clustering verb types on the basis of syntactic criteria (Canberra/Ward)

Figure 2. The verbs in the two groups are almost homogenously either *im*-suffixed verbs or bare verbs. The sole exceptions to this are the verbs *tekewe* 'take away' and *gat* 'have' on the left of the dendrogram, as well as *singautim*, *mangalim* and *spetim* on the right.

A second perspective on the data can be gained from looking at the divisions and stable clusterings from the perspective of the semantic variables only. This meant excluding the information regarding the element directly to the right of the verb, the syntactic construction the verb appeared in. Instead, only data relating to the number and animacy of subjects and objects, the lexical aspect of the verb, and the presence and type of auxiliary particles (perfective, completive, etc.) were taken into consideration. The picture of verb behaviors that emerges in Figure 3 is much more varied than that based on syntactic variables. It is interesting to note that here the verb pairs *kalap/kalapim* and *bilip/bilipim* form stable clusters with each other.

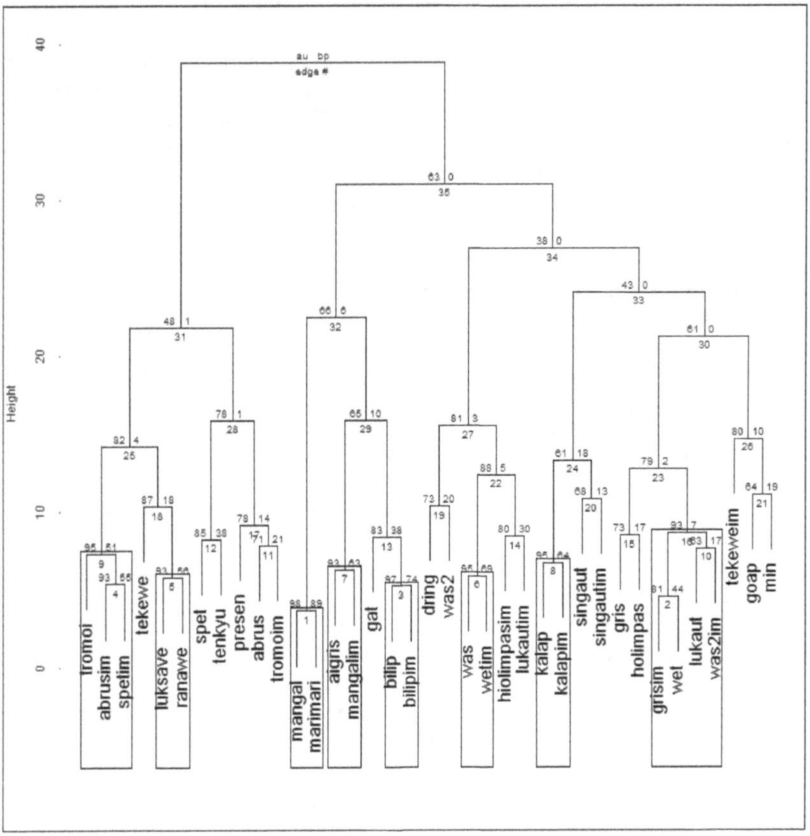

Figure 3: Clustering verb types on the basis of semantic criteria (Canberra/Ward)

Although these dendrograms allow some insight into the behavioral similarity of these verbs, it is clear that more information is required in order to trace their affinity for the *-im* suffix, and the conditions under which it is strong. The clear division of verb groups in the clustering based on syntactic criteria confirms the appropriateness of the standard analysis for the *-im* suffix in syntactic terms. However, what these dendrograms do not show is the effect individual variables have on the distribution of *-im*. These are important because they play a role in the distribution of the suffix in those cases that diverge from the standard syntactic pattern, such as *holimpas* in sentence (2) above.

7.4 Explorations of individual variables

The properties of subjects and objects are the first area of investigation. Contingency tables were used to gauge the effect of individual variables on the distribution of *-im*. In the first case, the animacy of the subject was investigated. However, results from this proved inconclusive as animate subjects dominate inanimate subjects overall. Investigations of the grammatical number of subjects proved similarly uninformative. The properties of the objects, however, showed greater differentiation. That is, the suffix is significantly more likely to occur with animate objects (χ-squared = 48.55, df = 1, p = 0.0001). The final semantic variable to be considered here is lexical aspect. The relationship between lexical aspect and the occurrence of *-im* is represented by means of a mosaic plot in Figure 4. In this plot it can be seen that accomplishment and activity verbs favor the *-im* suffix, while semelfactives, states, and achievements do not. This relationship is strongest for accomplishments. (located at the far left of Figure 4)

While these individual perspectives allow for interesting insights into certain aspects of the data, they are not easily related to each other. In order to gauge the relative influence of these factors on the distribution and investigate the interactions among these variables, a further computer-aided technique can be applied. This technique is known as recursive partitioning and its application and results are described in the next Section.

7.5 Modeling *-im* suffix occurrence with conditional inference trees

The variability in the data and the indications of interactions among several variables that ensued from the findings of the behavioral profiles methodology demand the application of a method capable of assessing the diverse influences on the distribution. From this perspective the conditions that govern the distribution of the suffix can be viewed as conspiracies among variables, particular combinations of which increase the likelihood for the occurrence (or non-occurrence) of *-im*. These conspiracies are here modeled as sequences of decisions, i.e., sets of cumulative conditions underlying the presence of the suffix in large numbers of instances. The conditional inference tree uses the variables to ask a series of binary questions and considers whether the answer justifies splitting the data into subsets in which one or the other response variable occurs

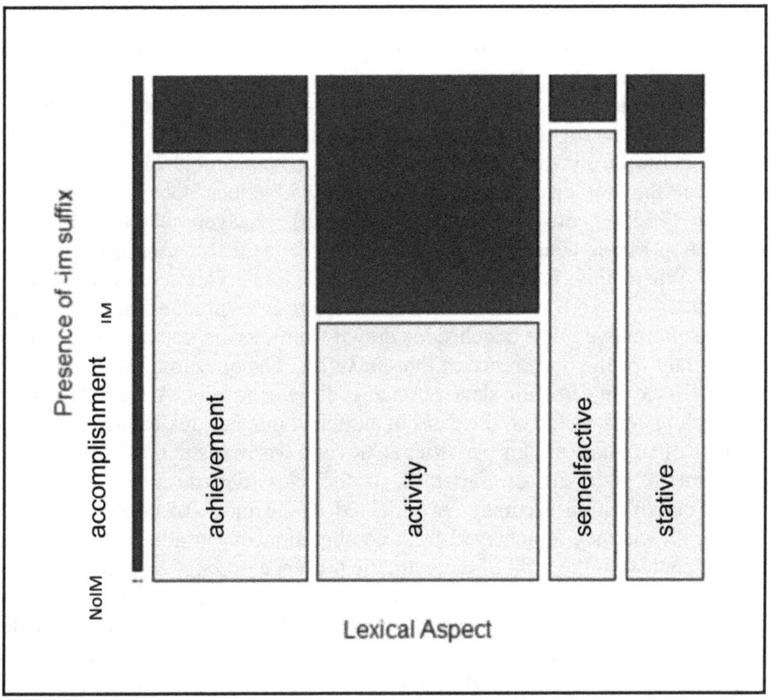

Figure 4: Mosaic plot showing the relationship between *-im* occurrence and lexical aspect (dark shading indicates presence of *-im*)

more frequently (Tagliamonte & Baayen 2011: 21). This results in a number of non-overlapping subsets, each described by a series of splits. The sequences of splits are visually represented by plotting the conditional inference tree. The final leaves of the tree constitute those instances which were classified according to the series of decisions undertaken in growing the tree. In the case at hand, instances were classified according to whether they would carry the suffix or not. This classification can then be examined to establish its accuracy and consequently, the usefulness of the variables involved in predicting the occurrence of the suffix. Accuracy in classification can be ascertained through the calculation of the Index of Concordance *C* (Baayen 2008: 281). Stemming from signal detection theory, *C* indicates the receiver operating characteristic curve area, which is frequently used in estimating classifier accuracy (Fawcett 2005: 861). It is a means of testing the predictive power of a model of the data against the actually observed data.

With this method it becomes possible to test the hypotheses that syntactic factors alone affect the distribution. This is of course testing a straw-man hypothesis to a certain extent, as Mihalic (1971), Wurm (1971), Mühlhäusler

(1979), Wurm & Mühlhäusler (1985) and Verhaar (1995) all admit that transitive clauses do not uniquely pattern with the *-im* suffix. Nonetheless, syntax has played a chief role in the description of the *-im* suffix to date and it is therefore justified to investigate whether syntactic features alone can account for distribution of *-im*. This hypothesis is tested by constructing a classifier that takes only syntactic variables into account: the nature of the syntactic construction to the right of the verb in question, and the syntactic status of the clause. The accuracy achieved by this classifier reaches a *C* value of 0.754. While this is better than the non-discriminating value of 0.5, values above 0.8 would be desirable (Tagliamonte & Baayen 2011: 18, Baayen 2008: 204). This classification rate is considerably improved if the presence of *long* is taken into account. When this is done, *C* jumps to 0.843. This confirms that the constructions of Verb + *im* and Verb + *long* are predominantly mutually exclusive alternatives. The conclusions drawn from this are that syntactic patterns are important for the occurrence of the *-im* suffix. The question now is whether a classifier based on semantic data can achieve better results. A second classifier was therefore constructed on the basis of animacy, number, lexical aspect, and the semantics of auxiliaries. This classifier achieves a worse result of $C = 0.723$.

Simple additions of variables to the classifier do not automatically improve classification accuracy, as reflected in the index of concordance. The best overall accuracy is achieved by a combination of variables coding for the syntactic context to the right of the verb, the presence of *long*- and the animacy of subjects, animacy of objects, and the year the utterance originated in. This last variable was added despite the conclusions reached in Section 7.2. While no clear trend could be discerned, there was nonetheless a significant difference in the occurrence of *im*-suffixed verbs among the decades. The addition of these variables helps to achieve an index of concordance value of 0.873. Figure 5 shows the variables and their respective importance. The branches are labelled with the variables affecting the decision showing both the splits and the p-values of the associated independence tests for each node. The first node, for example, represents the split between all constructions featuring a direct object to the left, and all other types of syntactic construction in the dataset to the right. The end nodes are annotated with the number of instances in the partition and the proportions of *-im*-suffixed and unsuffixed items in each subset. According to this model the 'best-case-scenario' for the occurrence of *-im* involves cases where the verb is followed by an object, there is no *long* before the object, and both object and subject are animate. However, it is also apparent from Figure 5 that the data still contains a lot of variability. From this perspective it can be said that this concatenation of variables describes a prototype for *im*-usage in Tok Pisin.

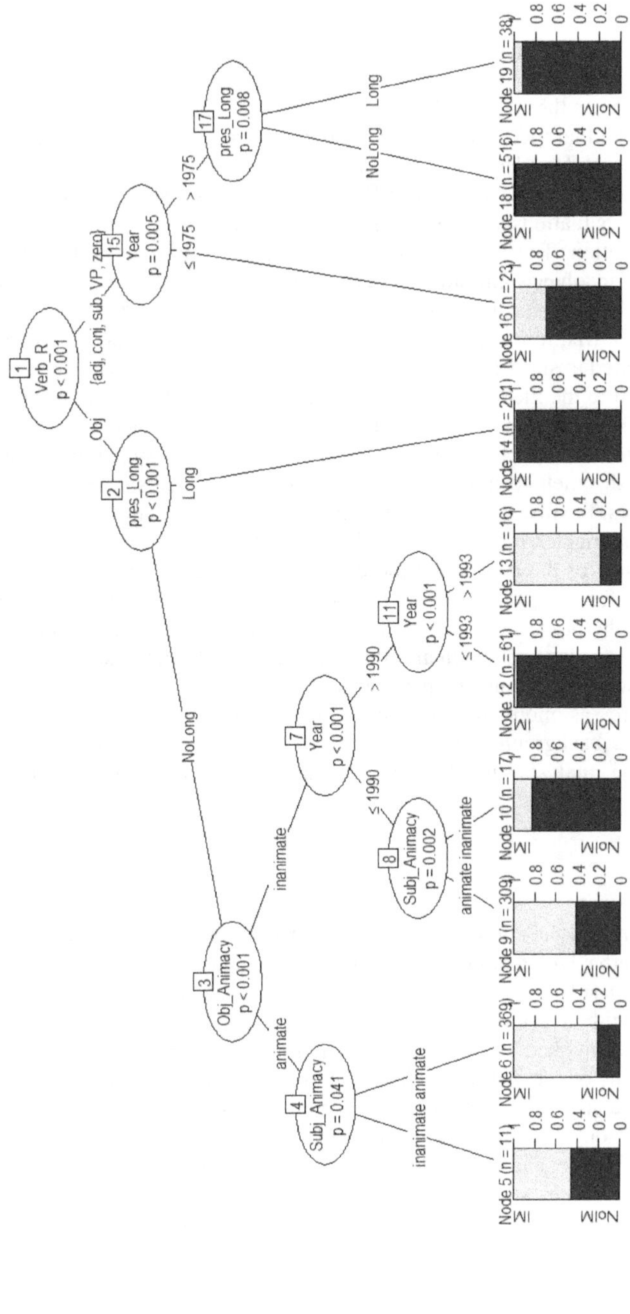

Figure 5: Conditional inference tree with highest prediction accuracy

8. Discussion

The above analyses show that there is no unitary phenomenon underlying the distribution of the *-im* suffix. It is a multi-functional element but these functions are not the same across the examined data. The classifier is most successful when it integrates a model that incorporates some important features of the Transitivity Hypothesis put forward by Hopper & Thompson (1980). However, not all uses can be accounted for in this way. The suffix is not thought necessary by some speakers, even for situations that otherwise would seem to fit a prototypically transitive interpretation. The tendency to pattern with transitivity as well as the use of the suffix in object-omission contexts may be related to its purported historical origins as an accusative/objective pronoun. The variability in the occurrence of the suffix, however, speaks against a stronger hypothesis by which the pronoun is related to substrate influences, such as Keesing (1988) proposed.

With regard to the methodologies employed it was found that a three-step approach can lead to important insights into the structure of the data. The initial clusterings provided by the behavioral profiles method, and the easy manipulation of variables that the method allows for, paved the way for closer scrutiny of individual variables. Finally, conditional inference trees provided an efficient way of combining the variables into a model with the possibility of ascertaining both the general accuracy of the model and the effects of individual variables. These methods allowed for the consideration of the full range of data types made available through the *Slone Wantok Corpus*, making them effective tools for the investigation of language phenomena that are not easily understood from semantic, syntactic or sociolinguistic perspectives on their own.

Furthermore, as more varied data become available (such as specific information on the backgrounds of the speakers), these variables can be easily integrated into the analysis and their effects gauged relative to the variables investigated here.

9. Summary

This paper investigated the conditions for the occurrence of the Tok Pisin suffix, in a group of verbs which appeared to behave irregularly with regard to a supposedly general suffixation pattern. By way of control, this group of verbs was augmented with a set of verbs that never pattern with the suffix. The properties that are invoked in order to account for the behavior of the suffix describe only a part of the Tok Pisin data encountered in the corpus. Instead, a number of factors conspire to account for the occurrence of the suffix. Beyond the syntactic construction, it is the animacy of subjects and objects that affect the distribution of the suffix. The role of these factors has been made discernible with the aid of multivariate analysis techniques like behavioral profiling and conditional inference trees, which hold the potential to integrate more diverse data as they become available.

Acknowledgements

I thank the anonymous reviewers and John Newman for helpful comments and suggestions.

Notes

1 Mihalic's (1971) *Jacaranda dictionary and grammar of Melanesian Pidgin* is still the most comprehensive dictionary of Tok Pisin. While no newer editions have been published, it is being revised and expanded as a web-based resource at www.mihalicdictionary.org.

2 Sentences were not considered when negated in toto. That is, with regard to the problem to be investigated here, cases of negation were counted only when the negating particle directly preceded the verb in question, i.e., between the predicate marker *i* and the verb. It was thought that the occurrence of sentence negating words such as nogat should not influence the use of the *-im* suffix or more generally the transitivity of the sentence. The reasoning being that nogat is more of a sentential marker, used in a manner perhaps similar to English but no or in contrast. These kinds of less direct negativity were not thought pertinent to the question at hand.

3 The verb *was* and *was2* are homonyms in Tok Pisin. The integer "2" was added to the orthographic form in this paper to distinguish them. *Was* has the meaning 'to watch' while *was2* means 'to wash'.

4 In the running of the bp script all other values, such as the significance value for the resample clusters, were left at default level, i.e., the significance level was left at 90, the graphic parameters left at 800 pixels and so forth.

References

Baayen, R.H. (2008), *Analyzing linguistic data: a practical introduction to statistics using R.* Cambridge: Cambridge University press.

Beck, D. (2000), 'Semantic agents, syntactic subjects, discourse topics: how to locate Lushotseed sentences in space and time', *Studies in language* 24(2): 277-317.

Berez, A.L. & S.Th. Gries (2008), 'In defense of corpus-based methods: a behavioral profile analysis of polysemous *get* in English', in: S. Moran, D.S. Tanner & M. Scanlon (eds.) *Proceedings of the 24th Northwest linguistics conference. University of Washington working papers in linguistics* Vol. 27. Seattle, WA: Department of Linguistics, University of

Washington. 157-166.
Burton, J. (2006), *Revising the Mihalic project.* Available online at www. mihalicdictionary.org.
Fawcett, T (2005), 'An Introduction to ROC Analysis', *Pattern recognition letters*, 27: 861-874.
Gries, S.Th. (2006), 'Corpus-based methods and cognitive semantics: the many senses of *run*', in: S.Th. Gries & A. Stefanowitsch (eds.) *Corpora in cognitive linguistics: corpus-based approaches to synatx and lexis*, Berlin/New York: Mouton de Gruyter. 57-99.
Gries, S.Th. & N. Otani (2010), 'Behavioral profiles: a corpus-based perspective on synonymy and antonymy.' *ICAME* 34: 121-150.
Hopper, P. & S. Thompson (1980), 'Transitivity in grammar and discourse', *Language* 56(2): 251-299.
Keesing, R.M. (1988), *Melanesian Pidgin and the Oceanic substrate.* Stanford (CA): Stanford University Press.
Mihalic, F. (1971), *The Jacaranda dictionary and grammar of Melanesian Pidgin.* Milton, Queensland: The Jacaranda Press.
Mühlhäusler, P. (1979), *Growth and structure of the lexicon of New Guinea Pidgin.* Pacific Linguistics, Series C, No. 52. Canberra: The Australian National University.
R Development Core Team (2011), *R: A language and environment for statistical computing.* R Foundation for Statistical Computing. Vienna, Austria.
Rice, S. (1987), *Towards a cognitive model of transitivity.* Doctoral dissertation, University of California San Diego.
Slone, T. (2003), *Slone Wantok Corpus.* Available online at: www.tokpisin.org.
Suzuki, R. & H. Shimodaira (2004), 'An application of multiscale bootstrap resampling to hierarchical clustering of microarray data: how accurate are these clusters?', in: *Proceedings by the Fifteenth International Conference on Genome Informatics* (GIW 2004) P034.
Tagliamonte, S. & R.H. Baayen (2011), 'Models, forests and trees of York English: *Was/were* variation as a case study for statistical practice.' Submitted MS.
Verhaar, J.W.M. (1995), *Toward a reference grammar of Tok Pisin: an experiment in corpus linguistics.* Honolulu: University of Hawai'i Press.
Wurm, S.A. (1971), *New Guinea Highlands Pidgin course materials.* Pacific Linguistics, Series D, No. 3. Canberra: The Australian National University.
Wurm, S.A. & P. Mühläusler (eds.) (1985), *Handbook of Tok Pisin (New Guinea Pidgin).* Pacific Linguistics, Series C, No. 70. Canberra: The Australian National University.

Complex extractions in a diachronic perspective

Gunnar Bergh

University of Gothenburg

Abstract

This paper deals with the structure and usage of extractions in historical English texts. Based on a corpus of 1.4 million words covering the language from Old English to the present day, it concentrates on how complex extractions are realized in terms of multiple embedding and multiple fronting. Apart from some purely descriptive work, including an account of common subtypes, the aim is to investigate the recursive power of these constructions in actual usage, and to determine how well their different variants fit into selected grammatical frameworks.

The results of the study show that complex extractions have been part of the English language throughout its history. Yet, these constructions, realized by means of either relativization or topicalization, turn out to be rather infrequent, and clearly more so than the work of many grammarians suggests. While theoretically unbounded in nature, they seem to be practically restricted to a complexity level of two or three, apparently due to the limiting effects of different perceptual, cognitive and stylistic factors. As regards their integration into syntactic theory, it is shown that whereas multiple embedding is a tractable structure in most contexts, multiple fronting presents problems for both generative and functional grammar, and seems best handled through the principles of dependency grammar.

1. Introduction

The present study is inspired by differences in perspective between rationalists and empiricists in discussions of grammatical structure. As such, it takes as its starting-point the treatment of so-called unbounded dependencies in grammatical theory, i.e., syntactic constructions where (at least) one constituent has moved across (at least) one clause boundary, and has the potential of moving across an infinite number of such boundaries. The central case of this class of constructions is represented by long movement (e.g., Haegeman 1991) or long-distance extraction (e.g., Hudson 1990) – or *Satzverschränkung*, as it is sometimes called by early historical grammarians (e.g., Behaghel 1928) – a construction which is recognized by the fact that the target constituent is extracted from a finite subordinate clause and moved across a higher (usually a matrix) clause to a position in front of it.

Long-distance extractions have been of particular importance within the field of generative grammar. As the descriptive efforts of this typically introspective approach have centered on the English language, it is only natural that much of the focus has been directed towards the properties of these constructions in present-day English. Specifically, we may note that extractions have been a central issue when grammarians have tried to formulate a descriptively adequate grammar for the language, not least because their postulated unboundedness poses as a constant challenge for any such formal system (e.g., Meillet 1934, Ross 1967, Chomsky 1965). This is so because the dependencies involved between the extraction site and the landing site span more than a local tree, i.e., the nodes covered by a mother and her daughters, which is taken to be the basic unit in the representation of mainstream generative grammar as well as many other theoretical frameworks. Accordingly, such structural interpretation seems to have created a general view that there are no restrictions whatsoever on the complexity of clausal embedding in any sentential position, despite the fact that there is little empirical data available to support it (e.g., Karlsson 2007: 110).

The properties sketched above have led to a situation where today we seem to know a great deal about extractions from a theoretical point of view and with regard to present-day English (e.g., Horrocks 1987, Haegeman 1997, Löwenadler 2007), but where we know much less about the practical side, the usage, of these constructions, and in particular their properties in earlier varieties of the language (but cf. Allen 1980, Bergh & Seppänen 1994). The aim of the present study, then, is to explore some structural possibilities of long-distance extractions, specifically the type we will be referring to as complex extractions, and investigate their patterns of usage in different periods of written historical English. Within this diachronic approach, particular attention will be paid to the relationship between rationalist claims of unlimited complexity, or unboundedness, and the results of the present empiricist investigation of actual occurrences of extractions featuring such complexity aspects.

2. Definition

Trying to stake out the field of complex extraction patterns, we may begin by looking at their logical counterparts, what may be referred to as simple extractions. Consider the following model examples:

(1) a. *He showed them a painting* ***which*** *he said [Strindberg had painted Δ].*
b. ***What*** *do you think [people would have said Δ]?*
c. *Was it Castro* ***whose brother*** *you said [you had met Δ in Cuba]?*
d. ***What an expensive car*** *it turned out [that they had Δ]!*
e. ***Those words*** *she confessed [Δ should never have come across her lips].*

Realizing the possible processes of extraction involved – relativization, as in (1a), question formation, as in (1b), clefting, as in (1c), exclamative formation, as in (1d), and topicalization, as in (1e) – these model sentences constitute exponents of long movement, where the fronted element is extracted from its logical position in the finite subclause and moved to the initial position of the matrix clause by means of, in traditional terminology, *wh*-movement (sentences (1a)-

(1d)) or topicalization (sentence (1e)). These relationships are coded in the formula below, where the fronted item is represented by a boldface XP at the front of the matrix clause (the host clause), while the gap it leaves behind in the subclause (the source clause) is marked by Δ:

(2) **XP** matrix clause [… Δ …]

It should be noted that the matrix structure in extractions can be very similar to parenthetical clauses functioning as general discourse markers. In particular, this is so in structures where there is no overt complementizer, and where the matrix elements consist of a first person singular pronoun and a simple present tense verb, e.g., *It was a painting which I think Strindberg had painted* and *Those words it is clear she should never have uttered* (cf. (1a) and (1e) above). However, there are certain tests indicating that the extracted element actually has a functional role in its matrix clause even in such sentences, thus establishing their status as extractions proper. For example, apart from using general substitution strategies for first person pronouns and present tense verbs, it is possible to insert a complementizer after the matrix verb, as in *It was a painting which I think that Strindberg had painted* (except in cases of subject extraction where the process is regularly blocked by the so-called *that*-trace effect, e.g., Löwenadler 2007). Similarly, interrogation can be used to show that the extracted element typically leads to (partial) inversion in the matrix clause, as in *What words is it clear she should never have uttered?*

What is interesting about simple extractions, furthermore, is the fact that these patterns can occur in more complex forms, giving rise to the notion of complex extractions. Founded on quantitative properties, this distinction involves primarily two syntactic parameters which may show different numerical values, viz. the clausal distance between the fronted element (XP) and the gap (Δ), often referred to as depth of embedding, and the number of fronted elements (XPs) occurring to the left of the matrix clause structure. Constituting the archetypal case of extraction in English, simple extractions thus illustrate the situation where the two target parameters exhibit the value ‘one’. Accordingly, in each of the constructions under (1) above, there is only one fronted element, forming the pattern of a one-element extraction. Similarly, in each of these cases the fronted element has crossed only one clause boundary, thus representing the pattern of a one-level extraction.

As implied by their recognized unboundedness, simple extractions also have the potential of multiplying their main elements, the fronted element as well as the matrix clause, all to serve the sophisticated communicative needs that may arise in actual usage in terms of signaling attitude, style, theme, focus, etc. Thus, each of the complex extractions under (3) and (4) is grammatically possible, with the two target parameters now showing the value ‘two’ instead:

(3) a. *He showed them a painting* ***which*** *he said [the experts believed [Strindberg had painted Δ]].*

b. ***What*** *do you think [it is likely [people would have said Δ]]?*

(4) a. ***In London tomorrow*** *she has been told [three bombs will explode ΔΔ].*
b. ***If I had left the ceremony, what*** *do you think [people would have said Δ Δ]?*

As we can see, the fronted elements in (3) have crossed two clause boundaries – the matrix clause and what will henceforth be called a link clause – exemplifying two-level extractions, whereas in (4) there are two elements moved out of one and the same source clause, representing two-element extractions. These examples, in turn, are represented by the following formulae:

(5) a. **XP** matrix clause [link clause [… Δ …]].
b. **XP** + **XP** matrix clause [… Δ … Δ …].

But, naturally enough, the complexity potential is not exhausted here either. It is equally possible to give the target parameters the value 'three', i.e., to add yet another link clause or XP, thus realizing three-level and three-element extractions respectively, as shown in (6):

(6) a. *He showed them a painting* ***which*** *he said [the experts believed [it was likely [Strindberg had painted Δ]]].*
b. ***Yesterday, if I had left the ceremony, what*** *do you think [people would have said Δ Δ Δ]?*

And, in principle, given the recursiveness of the grammatical rules involved, the same possibility applies to the values 'four', 'five' and so on. In (7) and (8), the model sentences illustrate some of these even more complex cases:

(7) a. *Was it Castro* ***whose brother*** *you said [that you thought [it was obvious [that everybody would more or less guess [that you had met Δ in Cuba]]]]?*
b. *This is the pub* ***which*** *Elizabeth remembered her husband admitting [that it had seemed to him [as if she had been led to believe [that Charles might think [it was not at all unlikely [that he used to visit Δ every night]]]]].*

(8) a. ***In Miami, on that wonderful evening in your house, if I had proposed to you as I had intended to, what*** *do you think [you would have said Δ Δ Δ Δ]?*
b. ***For reasons of sheer survival, in Siberia, when my parents were young, if the temperature went down to 50 below, how*** *do you think [they protected themselves against the cold Δ Δ Δ Δ Δ]?*

Evidently, the fronted element has crossed four clause boundaries in (7a) and five clause boundaries in (7b). Similarly, there are four fronted elements moved out of the source clause in (8a) and five such elements in (8b).

However, sentences like these are somewhat problematic, in particular when considering the distinction between grammaticality and acceptability. Hence, while the examples with low levels of complexity sound fully natural, it is clear that a point is soon reached where their naturalness decreases with every further addition to the number of link clauses and XPs involved. And, quite obviously, this is also the impression conveyed by the model sentences in (7) and (8). Yet, in generative studies, as well as in some other frameworks, it has been argued that it is not possible to fix any definite point as the upper limit of the degree of complexity allowed in a grammatical sentence (e.g., Chomsky 1965, Quirk et al. 1985, Pinker 1994). The acceptability of complexity has rather been described as a matter constrained by perceptual, cognitive, stylistic and other extragrammatical factors, a view supported also by psycholinguistic studies involving various processing tests of complex sentences (e.g., Lewis 1996, Gibson 1998).

These observations, then, bring us to the central aspects of the present study, what can be addressed in terms of the following questions:

(i) How often do complex extractions occur in written historical English?
(ii) What levels of complexity occur in actual usage?
(iii) Which fronting patterns are involved in producing these constructions?
(iv) How well can different descriptive frameworks handle their internal structure?

3. Corpus data

In order to try to provide answers to these questions, a project-specific historical corpus consisting of 1.4 million words of running text was compiled and analyzed systematically, using both automatic and manual search strategies. The corpus was modeled on the structure of the Helsinki Corpus (e.g., Rissanen et al. 1993) but differs from it on three counts, basically reflecting the specific scope and focus of the present study: first, it involves prose only; second, it contains fewer but longer text samples; and, third, it covers the history of written English in toto, i.e., from the 9th century to the present day. In accordance with this measure, the material was divided into the traditional four subperiods of English, i.e., Old English (-1150), Middle English (1150-1500), Early Modern English (1500-1710) and Late Modern English (1710-2000), with each period represented by a joint sample of 300,000-400,000 words of running text.

Among the 34 different text types recognized in the Helsinki Corpus, the present material contains 23, plus one additional type in the Late Modern English period, namely "drama, other". These 24 types were chosen so as to represent the widest possible range of subject matter and style, and are shown in Table 1.

Table 1: 24 text types in the corpus used for the present study

bible	law
biography, autobiography	letters, non-private
biography, lives	letters, private
documents	philosophy
drama, comedy	preface
drama, other	religious treatise
educational treatise	rules
fiction	science, astronomy
handbook, medicine	science, medicine
history	science, other
homily	sermon
journalism	travelogue

For further description of the structure and contents of the corpus, see Bergh & Seppänen (1994).

4. Results and discussion

Looking at the results of the analysis, we may begin by considering the overall frequency of extractions in the material, including their distribution in the different subperiods. These data are given in Table 2.

Table 2: Absolute and relative frequency of extractions in general across the four major subperiods of English

subperiods (word count)	*occurrences*	*occurrences/100,000 words*
OE (300,000)	122	41
ME (400,000)	144	36
EModE (300,000)	199	66
LModE (400,000)	215	54
total	680	49

As we can see, there were a total of 680 extractions in the material. Translated into relative terms, this means that there were almost 50 extractions per 100,000 words, or – using a smaller denominator – one extraction per 2,000 words. It may also be of interest to note that extractions are well represented in each of the four subperiods, although the Modern English periods tend to show a higher average frequency than Old and Middle English. This distributional imbalance is not surprising, however. Since the extraction pattern has previously been shown to correlate positively with informal text types (e.g., Bergh 1996), it seems reasonable to associate the relative infrequency of extractions in the early material to the shortage of informal text types in those periods. A main exponent of this shortage is, for example, the text type of private letters, which does not enter the corpus scene until just before 1500.

Furthermore, we can note that there were large differences in the distribution of fronting types. The relevant figures are given in Table 3.

Table 3: Absolute and relative frequency of extractions in general across the major types of fronting

fronting type	*occurrences*	*percentages*
relativization	390	57
topicalization	234	35
question formation	56	8
clefting	0	0
exclamative formation	0	0
total	680	100

With no extractions discovered involving clefting or exclamative constructions, the table shows that relativization is the most frequent fronting type, with 57% of the cases, followed by topicalization, with 35%, and question formation, with 8%.

Next, with regard to the question of the distribution of complex extractions, it turns out that the overall frequency of such constructions was rather low. Out of the 680 recorded extractions, only 19 satisfied the conditions for being labeled as complex extractions, i.e., only 2.8% of the total figure. Table 4 lists the distribution of such extractions over the main subperiods of English.

Table 4: Absolute and relative frequency of complex extractions across the four major subperiods of English

subperiods	*occurrences*	*occurrences/100,000 words*
OE	2	0.7
ME	1	0.2
EModE	8	2.7
LModE	8	2.0
total	19	1.4

As was the case with extractions in general, we can see that complex extractions are represented in each of the four subperiods of English. Two things are different now, however. On the one hand, the overall figures are very low, indicating that complex extractions seem to be rather infrequent in historical English texts, and on the other, the Modern English periods account for a clear majority of the cases, whereas the Old and Middle English periods make a marginal contribution only.

Let us elaborate the present figures further by looking at the data for the two target constructions separately. In the course of this discussion, we will then also have opportunity to consider the second and third of our target questions in detail, i.e., what levels of complexity occur in actual usage, and what patterns of fronting are involved. As a point of reference in this discussion, we may use Table 5, which shows the frequency for the two construction types as a function of the four subperiods involved.

Table 5: Absolute frequency of the two types of complex extractions across the four major subperiods of English

subperiods	*multiple embedding*	*multiple XPs*	*total*
OE	1	1	2
ME	0	1	1
EModE	4	4	8
LModE	3	5	8
total	8	11	19

4.1 Embedding

Starting with depth of embedding, Table 4 shows that there were eight complex embeddings in the material. Seven of them occurred in the Early and Late Modern English periods, as shown by the examples under (10) and (11), whereas the remaining case was found in one of the earliest Old English texts, as shown in (9).

(9) *he ... geliefđ đæt he suelc sie* ***suelce*** *he gehierđ [đæt his olicceras secgađ [đæt he sie Δ]* (Pastoral Care 111:11 – religious treatise)

(10) a. *my lord Archbishop hath sent a letter to my cousin William your son and a byll closed therin;* ***which byll and letter*** *I wold [ye gave good heed to Δ], and [understand [whether* ***it*** *be Kings comandement, or nay]].* (The Plumpton Correspondence 175:5 – letters, private)
b. *then he layd heinously to her charge, ye thing* ***yt*** *her self could not deny, [that al ye world wist [Δ was true*]] (More's King Richard 54:21 – history)
c. *Saynt Iames meaneth of the fruytfull workes that folowe after faythe the whiche gyve euydence of a lyfely faythe and these iustyfyeth a man. and* ***these*** *he saythe [[yf Abraham hadde not had Δ] he had not ben iustyfyed]* (Fisher's Sermons 328:28 – sermon)
d. ***The fast****, I make no question [but you heare [when* ***it*** *is appointed]]* (The Barrington Correspondence 53:29 – letters, private)

(11) a. ***If I can bring my Design to bear, and make the Maskers preserve their Characters in my Assemblies****, I hope [you will allow [there is a Foundation laid for more elegant and improving Gallantries than any [the Town at present affords] Δ]]* (The Spectator 63:14 – journalism)

b. *Your memory may fail; it is human; but the infernal conclusions you have drawn,* ***which*** *I see [you cannot, will not admit [Δ is too much]].* (Shelley's Correspondence 74:14 – letters, private)
c. *It is Aurora Leigh,* ***which*** *I think [you said [you had not read Δ]].* (Wilde's Correspondence 9:5 – letters, private)

Looking at the main properties of these constructions, we may note that all of them are extractions of the two-level type, i.e., the maximal distance of extraction was limited to movement across two higher clauses – a matrix clause and a link clause. Despite the frequent theoretical discussions by grammarians of multi-level embeddings involving movement across more than two clauses, there is thus no evidence of their existence in the present historical material. Interestingly enough, this outcome is well in accordance with previous findings for present-day English, both such derived from corpus-based studies and such elicited through psycholinguistic experimentation. Karlsson (2010), for example, shows that there is a general tendency for multiple embeddings collected from corpora to be restricted to two or three levels, although iteration in final-clause embeddings may occasionally increase this number to four or five levels. Lewis (1996) adds to this picture by concluding that there is a limit of two to three levels in short-term memory when processing complex sentences, among them multiple embeddings of the present type.

With regard to the fronting patterns involved, we can see that both obligatory movement (*wh*-movement) and optional movement (topicalization) are instanced, i.e., there were five cases of relativization and three cases of topicalization. Further, it turns out that the moved elements originate from different types of subordinate clauses: while the typical source clause is the *that*-clause, here represented by five instances, there are also two *wh*-clauses and one *if*-clause.

The occurrence of *wh*-clauses here is of particular interest. As commonly recognized in traditional generative grammar, such clauses are seen as linguistic islands from which no extraction is thought to be possible, thus introducing the notion of the *wh*-island constraint (e.g., Ross 1967, Chomsky 1986). However, there is one exception to this rule, and that is when the gap left by the extracted element is filled by a resumptive pronoun. This is a situation which in fact applies to both our examples, as shown in (10a) and (10d), and as such it gives credibility to the idea of the resumptive pronoun providing a form of amnesty for extractions out of *wh*-clauses (cf. Bergh & Seppänen 1994).

4.2 Fronting

Turning next to multiple fronting, we can see from the second column of Table 4 that there were 11 cases of this extraction type. Both obligatory and optional fronting are represented, with the movement processes involving four cases of relativization, one of question formation and 18 of topicalization. Concerning chronology, there is one case each in Old and Middle English, and four and five in Early and Late Modern English, respectively, examples which are found under

(12)-(15) below. As was the case with multiple embedding, then, most of the examples of multiple fronting derive from the Modern English periods, a fact which is likely again to be related to the combined effect of extractions posing as informal style markers and there being a higher proportion of informal texts in the later periods of the corpus (e.g., Bergh 1996).

(12) a. ***Toeacan đæm golde ealra glenga fyrmesđ on his hrægle*** *wæs beboden [đæt scolde bion se giem iacinctus Δ Δ, [se is lyfte onlicusđ on hiwe]].* (Pastoral Care 85:4 – religious treatise)

(13) ***On đan ilche daige đe đu tebrecst, ær đe sunne go te reste****, loce [đat tu bie sahtleđ Δ Δ]!* (Vices and Virtues 89:18 – religious treatise)

(14) a. *And here I brynge but one doctour.* ***whose testimony in the balance of any trewe christen mans herte****. me thynketh [Δ sholde weye downe Martyn Luther Δ].* (Fisher's Sermons 319:19 – sermon)
b. *And therefore they recken no pryuilege broken, though thei fetche him out.* ***Which if ye fynally refuse to deliuer him****, I verely thynke [they will Δ Δ].* (More's King Richard 37:17 – history)
c. *In Darby, who was the first Reprocher and scorner and giving the name to the people of god (quaker)* ***which sence in the nation*** *thou mayest see [what fruit* ***it*** *hath brought forth Δ Δ]* (The Journal of George Fox 7:16 – biography, autobiography)
d. ***if ye greatest necessity in ye world should happen, till some time in ye beginning of September next*** *I doe not see [that I shall have ye command of 500D of ye publick monys Δ Δ]:* (The Capel Correspondence 57:20 – letters, non-private)

(15) a. ***after I had crowded to the utmost, and began to despair****,* ***they*** *it seems [Δ saw me by the help of their Perspective-Glasses Δ]* (Robinson Crusoe 32:25 – fiction)
b. *But here I had like to have suffer'd a second Shipwreck,* ***which, if I had,*** *I think [Δ verily would have broke my Heart Δ]* (Robinson Crusoe 51:21 – fiction)
c. ***Often, even in His later days****, it is clear [that His words are Δ Δ the words of one who rejoiced in spirit]* (Farrar's Life of Christ 84:24 – religious treatise)
d. ***When the owner of the vineyard comes, how*** *do you think [he will deal with those tenants Δ Δ]?* (New English Bible 40:41 – bible)
e. ***In Rhodesia, during the war****, it was said [guerrillas had forced people at torture-point to co-operate with them Δ Δ].* (Gordimer's July's People 39:34 – fiction)

Let us look closer at the actual patterns behind the present figures. This is particularly relevant in this case because it has appeared from earlier discussions of the topic that the possibility of several fronted elements is restricted (e.g., Radford 1988), or at least dependent on the types of element in question (e.g., Hudson 1990). Examining our material from this point of view, we can immediately see that five cases – that is, nearly half of the recorded 11 instances – contain two topicalized adverbials, functioning as adjuncts rather than complements, as in (12), (13), (14d), (15c) and (15e).There are two further cases, both recorded from one and the same text, where the sentence is introduced by two topicalized elements, but functionally these elements are adjunct + subject and subject + adjunct, respectively, as in (15a) and (15b). Close to the above is the further case where similarly two adverbial adjuncts have been fronted but the second of them is a *wh*-interrogative, as in (15d). Finally, there are three cases where the topicalized adverbial – one or even two of them – is preceded by a relative element functioning as complement, as in (14a), (14b) and (14c). At the same time, we may note that the last of these examples, (14c), is the only case recorded where three elements have been fronted together – the complement *which* (subject) and the adjuncts *sence* (time adjunct) and *in the nation* (place adjunct).

What is the implication of these 11 examples of multiple-element extraction, then? Having already established the generally low frequency of the construction as such, we may note that its complexity seems to be limited to the level of two fronted elements, with the exception of the single case with three elements just referred to. Again, then, there is a contrast between the theoretical unboundedness of the construction and the actual occurrences of it in the present historical material. This is an outcome which is probably also related to "the magical number two (or three) in sentence processing" (Lewis 1996: 93), i.e., a complexity restriction based on the requirement for locality of syntactic dependencies, and the parsing limitation of constituents under the same syntactic relation (cf. also Gibson 1998).

Further, there is a certain pattern to be observed with regard to the different movement processes involved in the recorded 11 cases. Whenever two elements are moved together, one of them is always a topicalized adjunct – and if three elements are moved, two of them are topicalized adjuncts. From these data, then, we can formulate the following tentative rules:

(i) Multiple-element extraction must involve at least one fronted adjunct
(ii) Multiple-element extraction can only involve one fronted complement

How can we explain the differential behavior of fronted adjuncts and complements in this context? While most grammarians seem to have overlooked this question, there are a few scholars who have dealt with it and presented a theory which matches the present data rather well. Above all, this is the framework put forward by Cattell (1976), and later developed by Hudson (1990) in terms of his word grammar approach.

Addressing the question of why only one complement can be fronted in multiple extractions, Cattell suggests that the valency of the matrix verb has been saturated by the first extracted element, the result of which is that it cannot absorb a second one – and even less so a third one. In these cases the matrix verb is said to be overloaded, a situation which is exemplified by the sentences under (16).

(16) a. ****She him*** *I think [Δ met Δ].*
b. ****The teacher you the book*** *I'm sure [Δ showed Δ Δ].*

As we can see here, the subjects and objects of these sentences – i.e., two or even three complement-type elements – have been fronted simultaneously, and the matrix verbs *think* and *be sure* have therefore become overloaded, which leads to ungrammaticality. On the basis of such observations, Hudson (1990: 354ff.) postulates that each finite verb is allowed to have one or more "visitors", i.e., a type of fronted post-dependent preceding its head, where each such element generally falls into one of two types, depending on whether it is destined to be a complement or an adjunct. To illustrate his analysis in the case of multiple fronting, he cites the following examples (where the former sentence has been provided with a matrix predicate to qualify as a complex extraction):

(17) a. ***Last year in France because of the heat*** *I have to confess [we didn't go around very much Δ Δ Δ].*
b. ***On some days, sentences like this*** *I think [Δ are ungrammatical Δ].*

Thus, recognizing the grammaticality of having several topicalized visitors in this type of sentences, three adjuncts in (17a) and one adjunct and one complement in (17b), Hudson concludes that, in terms of dependency relations, there is no specific limit as to the number of adjuncts that a matrix verb can take, but that there seems to be a limit of just one on the number of complements.

Such observations bring us also to the question of how we can integrate the complement-adjunct distinction into the rule systems of major versions of grammar. Using the most complex of our recorded cases as our point of reference, here repeated as (18) and realized as a tree structure in Figure 1, we can show that this is a problematic issue for several grammatical frameworks, among them generative and functional grammar.

(18) *In Darby, who was the first Reprocher and scorner and giving the name to the people of god (quaker)* ***which sence in the nation*** *thou mayest see [what fruit* ***it*** *hath brought forth Δ Δ]* (The Journal of George Fox 7:16)

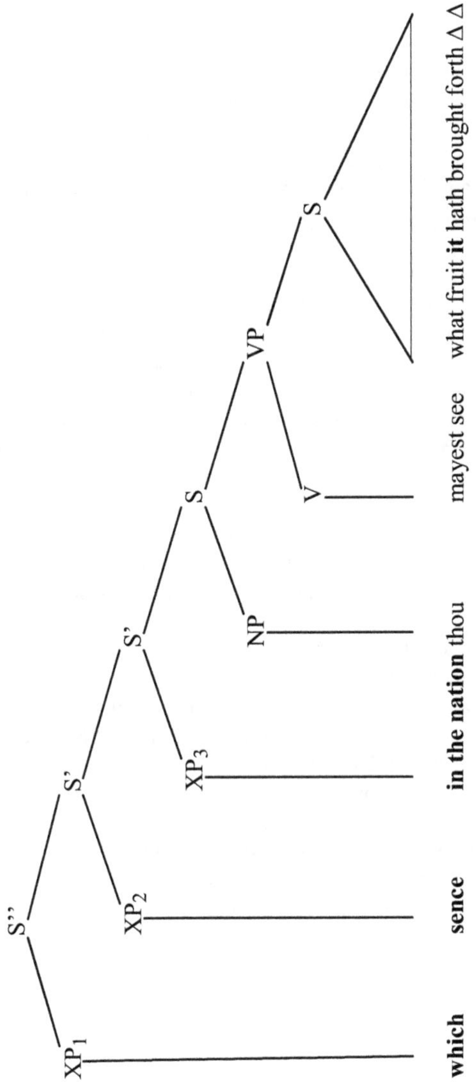

Figure 1: Tree diagram representing the structure of example (18)

Looking first at the different means of capturing fronted elements in generative grammar, it turns out that the mainstream framework is not properly equipped to handle the distinction in its entirety. Within traditional government and binding theory, the problem is that there is only one sentence-initial position available for moved elements, the C-specifier in the complementizer phrase (CP), which means that the rules automatically limit the number of extracted elements to just one (e.g., Radford 1988, Haegeman 1991). To solve this singularity problem, adjunction has later been brought in to allow projections to split, creating a split CP with several potentially recurrent positions for elements to occupy in the left periphery of sentences (e.g., Rizzi 1997, Radford 2009). While this reform has made it possible to reckon with multiple landing sites for moved elements, thus providing a descriptive framework also for multiple fronting, the theory seems as yet to fail to account for the basic deployment differences between complements and adjuncts, i.e., the behavior of *which* as a complement and *sence* and *in the nation* as adjuncts in our example.

If we look at functional grammar instead, it turns out that the idea of several fronted elements has received more attention here than in many other theories of grammar. Using Halliday's (1994) approach in terms of theme and rheme, we may draw on his suggestion of a maximally extended theme which is represented by the scheme in Table 6. As we can see here, the possibility of several front-positioned elements is well recognized within this type of grammar. In particular, there are no less than seven possible categories of elements that can be stacked together as multiple themes, and each of these categories is given a label which identifies the type of constituent involved. Yet, the system is problematic for our purposes in the sense that there is only one category which can accommodate fronted complements and adjuncts of the type that has been discussed here, namely the experiential (topical) category. This is necessarily so because all the other categories focus on textual and interpersonal elements, which are equivalent to peripheral elements such as disjuncts, conjuncts, vocatives, etc. In other words, given the example in (18), each of the elements *which*, *sence* and *in the nation* would fall under the experiential/topical category, a situation which is not allowed by the theory as indicated by Halliday's claim that "the theme always includes one, and only one, experiential element" (1994: 53). As it would be unsatisfactory to assign the topicalized elements to the rheme part of the sentence, i.e., to have the rheme as *sence in the nation thou mayset see what fruit it hath brought forth*, this indicates that Halliday's theory is not applicable in this case.

Table 6: Schematic representation of a maximally extended theme according to Halliday (1994:55)

theme							*rheme*
textual			*interpersonal*			*experiential*	
continuative	*structural*	*conjunctive*	*vocative*	*modal*	*finite*	*topical*	
well	but	then	Ann	surely	wouldn't	the best idea	be to join the group
	and	secondly		unfortunately		in spring	the house is far too cold

5. Conclusion

Trying now to summarize the present study, we may draw the following tentative conclusions with regard to the form and use of complex extractions in written historical English.

The present empirical data indicate that complex extractions are very infrequent constructions, and clearly much more infrequent than the work of many grammarians implicitly suggests. Rather, while theoretically unbounded in nature, they seem to be constrained by a combination of perceptual, cognitive, stylistic factors restricting their usage and complexity level. Furthermore, as measured by their overrepresentation in text types such as private letters and fiction, such extractions also seem to be style markers for informal text types, either speech-based varieties or such containing a fair share of dialogue.

With regard to recorded complexity levels, it tends to be the case that complex extractions show no higher value than two on this parameter, i.e., the typical outcome of our historical empirical analysis is the two-level embedding and the two-element fronting pattern. This usage limitation is well in agreement with previous work on complex sentences in present-day English, corpus-driven surveys as well as psycholinguistic experiments, where it has been shown that the complexity seldom exceeds levels two or three. Between the two extraction patterns, multiple fronting seems to be slightly more common than multiple embedding (11 versus 8 cases in the corpus) and perhaps also more natural, given the occurrence of even a three-element extraction in the material. Incidentally, this conclusion is also supported by the results of a pilot test of native English speakers: if extractions with three embeddings and extractions with triple fronting are juxtaposed, it is normally the case that the informants regard the instances of multiple fronting as more natural (or less unnatural) than those of multiple embedding.

While the main fronting pattern involved in extractions in general is relativization, followed by topicalization, multiple fronting in fact shows the opposite pattern, with topicalization as the most common type. This is however only natural given the positive correlation between, on the one hand, relativization and complements and, on the other, topicalization and adjuncts, and the fact that multiple fronting turns out to allow only one fronted complement but several fronted adjuncts. Also, it may be noted that when such elements are extracted from *wh*-clauses, the gaps they leave in the source clause seem to be regularly filled by a resumptive pronoun.

Finally, when it comes to the integration of complex extractions in a descriptive framework, there are several potentially adequate alternatives around. In particular, this is the case for multiple embeddings, where the different versions of grammar considered are well equipped to handle the unbounded dependencies involved, notwithstanding the pragmatic mechanisms constraining the levels of complexity. For multiple fronting, on the other hand, the situation is more difficult, since major theoretical frameworks, among them both generative and functional grammar, tend to fall short of crucial descriptive requirements.

Rather, the most profitable approach here seems to be the version of dependency grammar which is called word grammar, where, among other things, the particular fronting aspects of the adjunct-complement distinction are explicitly recognized and dealt with.

References

Allen, C. (1980), 'Movement and deletion in Old English', *Linguistic inquiry,* 11: 261-324.

Behaghel, O. (1928), *Deutsche Syntax. Band III.* Heidelberg: Carl Winter.

Bergh, G. (1996), 'Extractions in English: a stylostatistic account of the early and late modern English periods', in: G. Björhovde & G. Rogne (eds.) *Proceedings from the Sixth Nordic Conference for English Studies.* Department of English, University of Tromsö. 241-264.

Bergh, G. & A. Seppänen (1994), 'Subject extraction in English: the use of the *that*-complementizer', in: F. Fernández, M. Fuster & J.J. Calvo (eds.) *English historical linguistics 1992.* Amsterdam: Benjamins. 131-143.

Cattell, R. (1976), 'Constraints on movement rules', *Language,* 53: 18-50.

Chomsky, N. (1965), *Aspects of the theory of syntax.* Cambridge (MA): MIT Press.

Chomsky, N. (1986), *Barriers.* Cambridge (MA): MIT Press.

Gibson, E. (1998), 'Linguistic complexity: locality of syntactic dependencies', *Cognition,* 68: 1-76.

Haegeman, L. (1991), *Government and binding theory.* Oxford: Blackwell.

Haegeman, L. (1997), *Elements of grammar.* Dordrecht: Kluwer.

Halliday, M.A.K. (1994), *An introduction to functional grammar.* London: Edward Arnold.

Horrocks, G. (1987), *Generative grammar.* London: Longman.

Hudson, R. (1990), *English word grammar.* Oxford: Blackwell.

Karlsson, F. (2007), 'Constraints on multiple initial embedding of clauses', *International journal of corpus linguistics,* 12: 107-118.

Karlsson, F. (2010), 'Multiple final embedding of clauses', *International journal of corpus linguistics* 15: 88–105.

Lewis, R.I. (1996), 'Interference in short-term memory: the magical number two (or three)', *Journal of psycholinguistic research,* 25: 193-215.

Löwenadler, J. (2007), *A cross-theoretical approach to complementizer-gap phenomena,* Doctoral dissertation, University of Gothenburg.

Meillet, A. (1934), *Introduction à l'étude des langues Indo-européennes.* Paris: Librairie Hachette.

Pinker, S. (1994), *The language instinct.* Harmondsworth: Penguin.

Quirk, R., S. Greenbaum, G. Leech & J. Svartvik (1985), *A comprehensive grammar of the English language.* London: Longman.

Radford, A. (1988), *Transformational grammar: a first course.* Cambridge: Cambridge University Press.

Radford, A. (2009), *English sentence structure*. Cambridge: Cambridge University Press.
Rissanen, M., M. Kytö & M. Pallander-Collin (1993), *Introduction to the Helsinki Corpus of English texts*. Berlin: Mouton.
Rizzi, L. (1997), 'The fine structure of the left periphery', in: L. Haegeman (ed.) *Elements of grammar*. Dordrecht: Kluwer. 281-337.
Ross, J.R. (1967), *Constraints on variables in syntax*, Doctoral dissertation, MIT.

Subject ellipsis by text type: an investigation using ICE-GB

Laura Teddiman

University of Alberta

Abstract

This paper explores subject ellipsis in English across the text types represented in the International Corpus of English for Great Britain (ICE-GB), focusing on the identities of elided subjects, the verbs involved, and on differences between genres. All patterns are statistically significant, as revealed through the use of collostructional analysis (Stefanowitsch & Gries 2003). In the ICE-GB as a whole, I *and* it *are the pronouns most frequently elided, although this pattern is not observed within each sub-corpus. Subject ellipsis is most frequently observed in the private dialogue subcomponent of the ICE-GB, followed by unscripted monologues, correspondence, and public spoken dialogue.* I *and* it *remain the most frequently elided pronouns in the private and public spoken dialogues, as well as in correspondence. However, in unscripted monologues,* he *is the most frequently omitted pronoun. This reflects data from live sportscasts, where announcers describe the actions of a player who was identified earlier in the speech stream and update game information in real time. The verbs attracted to sentence initial position also differ by text type, with more active verbs such as* plays *and* turns *being present in unscripted monologues and mental state verbs such as* think *and* know *occurring in correspondence and private conversation. These results highlight the importance of examining linguistic structure across genres.*

1. Introduction

Subject ellipsis is not traditionally considered to be a feature of English grammar. This is in contrast to languages such as Spanish and Italian, where subjects in finite sentences are not obligatory, and where they may be omitted without sacrificing the grammaticality of an utterance. This permissibility is often linked to the verbal inflection available in these languages, where it is possible to determine the subject of a sentence by examining the inflection on a verb (Nariyama 2004). However, even though English has relatively poor inflectional morphology, the traditional assumption that English does not allow subject ellipsis is not reflected in corpus data. Outside of the second person imperative, subject ellipsis has been observed to be relatively common in conversation in the speech of both children and adults (Biber et al. 1999: 1048). While it is certainly much more common for English sentences to contain overt subjects, there are contexts where subject omission is understandable. For example, *don't know* is a comprehensible reply to a question, even though the subject *I* is omitted. Similarly, in closing a letter, the pronoun *I* can be reconstructed from *Will speak to you soon & definitely see you on 10th August* (ICE-GB: W1B-001 #211:5). In this example, only one subject is considered to be omitted in the co-ordinating structure. Subject ellipsis has also been attested in some written genres such as in diaries (e.g., Haegeman & Ihsane 1999) and in telegraphs (Barton 1998). This paper will examine the phenomenon of subject ellipsis across several different genres, focusing both on the elided subjects in main clauses and on sentence initial verbs.

The recoverability of the subject is critically important for the interpretability of subjectless sentences in English. The missing subject must be recoverable, whether from the surrounding context where the antecedent is directly available in a preceding sentence (e.g., Haegeman & Ihsane 1999) or a following linguistic structure (e.g., Kay's (2002) discussion of tag questions) or be available through knowledge of conventional expressions. Biber et al. (1999: 156) describe a number of different kinds of ellipsis observed in English, including textual ellipsis, where missing units can be recovered from context (e.g., coordinating structures) and situational ellipsis, where the interpretation of a missing element will depend on the surrounding (non-linguistic) context. In situational ellipsis, the choice to omit elements is also influenced by convention, and this is noted as being particularly common in conversation. Such cases of ellipsis should not be classed as errors because they are both fully interpretable and not uncommon in casual speech. Biber et al. (1999: 1104-5) also note that sentence initial pronouns may be subject to more general effects where less informative items are dropped at the beginning of a turn during speech.

Nariyama (2004) studied subject ellipsis in Australian English using a small corpus consisting of three casual letters, three recorded conversations, and dialogue from Australian television dramas. He observes that in this corpus, subjectless sentences in English carry less formal connotations than their ordinary declarative equivalents. Considering the size of the corpus and its composition, Nariyama (2004: 239) offers the corpus as "a sample of the qualitative problems encountered, rather than as a quantitative support for statistical evidence" in this area of research. In the television dramas, 53 cases of subject ellipsis were recorded, with *I* elided in 25 cases (47.2%) and *it* elided in 17 cases (32.1%). *You*, *s/he*, and *they* made up the rest, with *we* never being omitted. Data from the three conversations was similar in distribution: *I*-10 (20%), *we*-2 (4.1%), *you*-4 (8.2%), *he/she*-2 (4.1%), *it*-30 (61.2 %), *they*-1 (2%). The relatively higher percentage of *it* elision was interpreted as being related to the way in which conversations were elicited. Family members were provided with a topic of conversation, such as family holidays, and as they were talking about something specific, there was more call for the pronoun *it* to be used than what might be expected in free conversation. The utterances undergoing ellipsis are described as being less informative than their counterparts and less definite, and in some cases as being dismissive. There was also a tendency towards a casual attitude. Nariyama identifies four conditions supporting English subject ellipsis, which share similarities with Biber et al. (1999). These conditions are 1) when the subject occurred in the immediately preceding sentence, 2) when the elided subject referred to an entire preceding sentence/event or the topic of conversation, 3) when "dummy *it*" is removed and 4) when using conventional expressions (e.g., *dunno*).

Nariyama (2004) offers insight into more pragmatic uses of language, exploring aspects of usage by referencing a corpus of English texts. Even so, that corpus was quite small, and Nariyama does not address issues of statistical significance in his discussions of subject ellipsis. Larger corpora allow the researcher to more closely examine a given phenomenon in detail, and to determine whether an observed pattern is statistically reliable and not due to random variation. That is, we can use statistical tests to determine whether our intuitions about language are correct while also uncovering patterns that have been overlooked. In the case of subject ellipsis, we may observe that a specific pronoun is often omitted or that a particular verb often begins a subjectless sentence, but we will also want to know whether this occurs more often than would be expected by chance.

Among the most frequently used statistical tests for significance in corpus linguistics are the chi-square test and the log-likelihood test. Both of these tests compare the expected frequencies of words with their observed frequencies, with the latter not assuming a normal distribution (McEnery, Xiao & Tono 2006). However, traditional corpus linguistic analysis is often strictly linear, so that the association between words in a corpus depends on the number of times they occur within a set span (e.g.,within three words to the right and three words to the left of a search term, or node), without regard for syntactic structure (Stefanowitsch & Gries 2005). Stefanowitsch and Gries (2003) develop a method for determining the strength of the association between a lexeme and the grammatical structure (often formulated as a construction) in which it occurs, which they call collostructional analysis (cf. Gries & Stefanowitsch 2004a, 2004b, Stefanowitsch & Gries 2005 for extensions). Lexemes that are attracted to a particular 'slot' in the grammatical structure are called collexemes. By way of example, take the structure [N *waiting to happen*], presented by Stefanowitsch and Gries (2003). To determine the collostruction strength of any word, N, to the structure [*waiting to happen*], we need to know the frequency with which N occurs in the structure, the frequency with which N occurs outside of the structure, the frequency with which the structure occurs with words other than N, and the frequency of all other structures in the corpus. Association strengths are calculated using these values by the Fisher exact test. One of the most frequent lexemes in the N slot of this structure is *accident* (Table 1), which occurs 14 times with *waiting to happen* and 21 times outside of that structure in the British National Corpus (BNC) (The British National Corpus 2007). While the *waiting to happen* values were extracted directly from specific searches, the other values were obtained by subtracting those values from total values in the corpus. For example, to find the total number of other constructions (¬ [N *waiting to happen*]), the value for [N *waiting to happen*] was subtracted from the total number of verb tags in the corpus. These values can then be used as input to the Fisher exact test, finding that *accident* is strongly associated with the structure. This same procedure can be used to determine the association strengths of all the words (N) to [N *waiting to happen*], and gives them a relative ranking of association strength based on p-value.

Table 1: Cross-tabulation of accident and [N waiting to happen], with data from the British National Corpus (Stefanowitsch & Gries 2003)

	accident	¬ *accident*	*row totals*
[N *waiting to happen*]	14	21	35
¬ [N *waiting to happen*]	8606	10197659	10206265
column totals	8620	10197680	10206300

The same overall method can be applied to less specific grammatical structures. For example, Stefanowitsch and Gries (2003) also successfully apply collostructional analysis to a brief examination of the English imperative. Here they examined the verbs which begin imperative utterances and their relative attraction to the first slot in the imperative construction, and find that rather than giving the addressee direct orders, the most strongly associated verbs in this slot appear to be used to direct attention without imposing on the addressee. The successful application of collostructional analysis in this research is especially relevant to the work presented here, as the structure of elliptical sentences is similar in form to that of the imperative.

The purpose of the current paper is to explore the nature of subject ellipsis in English through the use of ICE-GB (the British component of the International Corpus of English, Aarts & Wallis 2006). Previous research has not focused on the verbs active in subjectless sentences, so in addition to examining the pronouns most involved in this phenomenon, the most frequent types of verbs involved in subjectless sentences, their identities, and other patterns in usage will be also outlined. After introducing the corpus and the methods used, we will provide an overview of results gathered from the whole of the ICE-GB, before moving on to look at the most active sub-corpora. The most important of these will be the sub-corpus of private conversation available in the ICE-GB. In addition to being a very active sub-corpus, the spontaneous speech recorded in private conversation is also of interest because it is arguably representative of a more basic type of interpersonal interaction than that observed in highly edited texts (cf. Newman 2008 for further discussion of this and other issues associated with spoken corpora).

2. The current study

The corpus used in this study, the ICE-GB, documents the speech of educated adult speakers in England, Scotland, and Wales through the period of 1990-1993. The corpus contains 1,061,264 words over 500 texts in a number of different genres, including casual conversation, scripted speech, and various types of writing.

2.1 Methodology

The corpus was searched using the International Corpus of English Corpus Utility Program, version 3 (ICECUP III, Wallis 1998). This tool allows the researcher to search not just for individual words or phrases, but also for syntactic structures that may be found in the data. The ICE-GB has been annotated using the TOSCA Tagger, which assigns word classes to individual lexical items and automatically parses sentences and outputs phrase and sentence structures. These phrase structure trees are searchable using "Fuzzy Tree Fragments," where parts of a grammatical structure can be specified. Searches using Fuzzy Tree Fragments (FTFs) return all examples in the corpus that match the specified structure. Using ICECUP III, the ICE-GB was searched for verb-initial sequences in individual declarative utterances using an FTF search (see Figure 1 for a screenshot of the FTF fragment search in ICECUP III). The identity of the first word (the verb) was left undefined, with the only requirement being that it occur first in the utterance. The following sentence elements were also left undefined, as was tense. This search was very broad, and was intended to capture as many instances of utterance-initial ellipsis as possible.

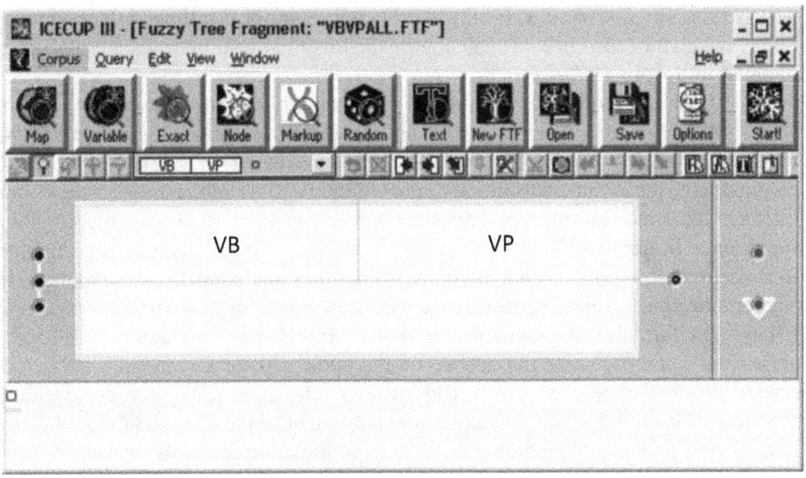

Figure 1: FTF fragment search in ICECUP III

The FTF search provided a starting point for manual analysis of verb-initial sentences for elided pronoun. Searches did not include verb-initial sequences in subordinate clauses. Following retrieval from the corpus, imperative utterances and other false positives were removed and the remaining results were manually coded for reconstructed subject. For the purposes of this study, the focus is on subject omission alone, and not on the omission of short phrases such as *I will*, as in [*I will*] *See you tomorrow*.

2.2 Overview of Results

Within the whole of ICE-GB, there were 694 instances of subject ellipsis found using the FTF search. The majority of these (516) were found in spoken texts, and of those, most (296) were from the private dialogue component of the spoken sub-corpus. Fewer instances were recorded in the public dialogue sub-corpus, which includes broadcast interviews, legal and political proceedings, and lectures, and the unscripted monologue sub-corpus, which includes unscripted speeches and commentaries in addition to demonstrations and legal presentations. In the written sub-corpora, subject ellipsis was attested primarily in correspondence, with smaller numbers reported in creative writing and non-academic writing. In most formal forms of writing, including scripted (spoken) newscasts, no examples of subject ellipsis were returned using our search. While the total size of the spoken sub-corpus in ICE-GB is greater than the written sub-corpus, (spoken: 637,562 words, written: 423,702), ellipsis remains more common in the spoken modality across the entire ICE-GB (occurrences per thousand: spoken: 0.46, written: 0.32). When the most active sub-corpora in both the written and spoken modalities are compared, the Correspondence (letter) sub-corpus stands out in the written component of ICE-GB as a very active area, primarily with the first person singular (see Table 2). Active sub-corpora are those which show a relatively high occurrence of subject ellipsis. Results by sub-corpus are discussed in detail in Sections 2.3–2.6.

The most frequently omitted subject, manually reconstructed from context, was *I*, followed by *it*, results that are in line with previous research. The breakdown of the ICE-GB by text type makes it possible to examine reconstructed pronoun distributions across genres. It is interesting to note how different the relative rates of omission are across genres, clearly marking the importance of genre and text type in corpus studies. Also of note is that although it is technically spoken, and therefore sometimes included as a component in spoken corpora, scripted speech (e.g., broadcast news) appears in many ways to behave like formal writing, suggesting that interpretation of spoken corpus results should take into account the source of the spoken data. Given the differences observed in text types, we will consider each of the most active genres, spending the most time on the private dialogue subcomponent of the ICE-GB before briefly considering public spoken dialogue, unscripted monologues, and correspondence.

2.3 Private dialogue

Private dialogue is the most active sub-corpus in this study. One hundred files are included in the private dialogue sub-corpus of the ICE-GB, all of which represent unrehearsed speech, with a total of 205,608 words. In this sub-corpus, there were 296 entries that fit the search criteria. Of these, about one third were negated (92). The understood subject in 141 utterances was unambiguously *I*, representing approximately 47% of the total omitted subjects, and in 126 cases was unambiguously *it*, representing approximately 42% of all omitted subjects. These

Table 2: Overview of elided pronouns by text-type represented in the sub-corpora of ICE-GB. The number of words in each sub-corpus is given in parentheses.

	spoken dialogue-private (205,608)	*spoken dialogue-public (171,059)*	*unscripted monologue (152,835)*	*letters (61,577)*	*creative writing (42,645)*	*non-academic writing (86,643)*
I	141	14	9	112	3	0
you	5	1	1	2	1	3
we	3	0	1	0	0	0
he	8	3	168	0	2	1
she	5	1	0	0	1	0
it	126	33	26	4	4	1
they	8	3	4	0	0	0
total	296	55	209	118	11	5
ellipsis per 1000 words	1.44	.32	1.37	1.91	.26	.06

numbers are similar to those reported by Nariyama (2004). Table 3 gives the ratio of rates of omission within the spoken sub-corpus compared to rates of occurrence.

The first person singular *I* is elided once for every 45 instances that it overtly appears in the texts. Compare this result to the first person plural form, *we*, which is elided once for every 463 times *we* occurs in the texts. Both *I* and *it* show much lower ratios of omitted frequency to corpus frequency than other pronouns. Although the answer in this case may appear to be obvious, the first question is whether these numbers are significant, or if they are an artifact caused by the overall relative frequencies of pronouns in the text. For example, is *I* elided more often than *he* because it is prone to omission in conversation, or are there more instances of omission for *I* simply because *I* occurs more often in speech and is therefore available to be omitted more often?

Table 3: Comparison of pronoun occurrence versus pronoun omission in the ICE-GB (private spoken sub-corpus)

pronoun	*elided frequency*	*corpus frequency*	*ratio (rounded)*
I	141	6313	1:45
you	5	1999	1:400
we	3	1390	1:463
he	8	1245	1:156
she	5	876	1:175
it	126	4788	1:38
they	8	1224	1:153

To examine overt pronominal subjects in comparison to elided subjects, this investigation turned to collostructional analysis, using Coll.Analysis 3 (Gries 2004) for the statistical package R (R Development Core Team 2008). This package presents three main options: Collexeme Analysis, which investigates the strength of an association between a word and a grammatical structure; Distinctive Collexeme Analysis, which compares the strength of the association between a single word and two similar grammatical structures; and Co-varying collexeme analysis, which investigates the strength of association between pairs of words in a grammatical structure with two open slots. The first question asked was whether the frequency of subject ellipsis by subject pronoun is significant in and of itself, and so the first statistical test was a collexeme analysis. This presented an interesting challenge, because collexeme analysis is designed to test the association between an existing word and a construction, but the subject pronouns being tested here are by definition not present in the grammatical structure. They can, however, be reconstructed based on context available in the corpus, and it is these reconstructed forms that make this test possible.

In these results, *I* and *it* are both significantly attracted to the elided subject construction (collocational strengths: *it*-58.45, *I*-42.03, where a collocational strength of >1.30103 is significant at the p <.05 level), while the other subject pronouns tested are significantly repulsed by it (collocational strengths with negative (neg) values: *you*-31.68(neg), *we*-23.28(neg), *he*-7.07(neg), *they*-6.72(neg), *she*-5.99(neg)). These results are similar to those found by Nariyama (2004), where *I* and *it* form the bulk of elided subjects. Note, too, that simple collexeme analysis is the best way to test the strength of association between pronouns and subject ellipsis in this corpus. A distinctive collexeme analysis comparing pronoun attraction to either the elided condition or the regular declarative condition found an overwhelming attraction to the latter, as might be expected in a language such as English.

Using the same test, association strengths between verbs and their position as the first element in an utterance can also be determined. A key virtue of ICE-GB and ICECUP III is that it is possible to determine the number of sentences in the sub-corpus that occur without an overt subject (296) and the identities of the verbs that fill that position, both of which are essential for collexeme analysis. Tables 4 and 5 present the main verbs and modal/auxiliary verbs most strongly attracted to sentence initial position, respectively (see Appendix 1 for a full list). Recall that collocational analysis takes into account the overall occurrence of an element, in this case, specific verbs, and compares their frequency inside of a construction against their frequency outside of it. Note that contracted negatives (e.g., *can't*) are considered here to be individual word-forms, separate from forms like *can not*. This is motivated by the existence of forms such as *dunno* (*don't* + *know*), where two word-forms have fused and appear to be analyzed as individual units by speakers, and also by recent findings that individual word-forms of a specific lemma can have strikingly different behavior. For example, Rice & Newman (2005) show that the verb THINK occurs most often in the first person singular form in casual conversation, and that this behavior is most marked in the present tense (93% of present tense *think* is with the first person singular in the BNC, compared to 65% in the progressive *I am/was thinking*).

Table 4: Main verbs significantly attracted to sentence initial position in the conversation sub-corpus of the ICE-GB. Values over 1.30103 are significant at p <0.05.

verb	*collocational strength*	*verb*	*collocational strength*
sounds	48.75	becomes	2.67
looks	21.78	thank	2.32
depends	19.97	sounded	2.25
watched	9.48	keeps	2.25
feels	6.48	talked	2.25
presumed	5.75	cost	2.08
picked	5.59	gives	2.08
tried	4.17	forgot	1.79
kept	3.86	seemed	1.67
seems	3.71		

Table 5: Modal and auxiliary verbs significantly attracted to sentence initial position in the conversation sub-corpus of the ICE-GB. Values over 1.30103 are significant at p <0.05.

verb	*collocational strength*	*verb*	*collocational strength*
can't	32.01	shouldn't	4.17
doesn't	20.46	haven't	3.87
must	15.59	should	2.61
don't	9.88	may	2.03
didn't	6.70	couldn't	1.90
could	4.81		

The verb most strongly associated with sentence initial position in the ICE-GB conversation sub-corpus is *sounds* (e.g., *sounds like a plan*), followed by *can't*, *looks*, *doesn't*, and *depends*. The past tense, *sounded*, is also significantly attracted to this position, although not to the same extent. There appears to be a preference in these data for verbs in the present tense, as the main and auxiliary collocates that show the strongest collocational strengths are in the present tense. This might be related to the nature of speech, where speakers may be speaking of the present time or in response to something someone else has said.

Results from the ICE-GB casual conversation sub-corpus are robust, revealing several patterns in subject ellipsis in English. There were 111 individual lexemes represented in the search results (72 lemmas). The nineteen lemmas most frequently encountered were: DO-66, CAN-44, HAVE-20, SOUND-18, MAY-15, WILL-13, LOOKS-9, BE-9, SHALL-7, THINK-7, COME-5, DEPENDS-5, MAKES-5, KEEP-4, SEEM-4, FEEL-3, and SAY-3. The phrase *thank you* also occurred 5 times, and could be interpreted in these utterances as a truncated form of *I thank you.* Subjects in phrases such as *thank you* are considered by Biber et al. (1999: 1104) to be defined by convention, similar to other elliptical phrases where larger clauses are omitted (e.g., *good luck* for *I wish you good luck*/*Have good luck*). *Thank you* represents a special case for the current study, as it is perhaps the most formulaic of the verb-initial utterances found in this study. The phrase is nevertheless included in analysis because it is considered to be a verb + object sequence in the ICE-GB.

These items can further be grouped broadly into auxiliary verbs (BE, HAVE, DO; 94 total instances), modal verbs (CAN, MAY, WILL, and SHALL; 75 total instances), verbs referring to internal states (THINK, FEEL; 10 instances in addition to words occurring only once, such as *remember*), and a related set of verbs describing impressions of external events (SEEM, *looks*, SOUND; 31 total instances) and reactions to them (*depends*; 5 instances). There is a strong preference for mental state verbs to follow *don't*, *doesn't* and *didn't*. This is likely related to the prevalence of mental state verbs observed as main verbs in the data, as here they are negated (i.e., one would not usually expect a form such as *I do think that* in casual speech when *I think that* would suffice). Expressions such as *doesn't matter*, *don't know*/*dunno*, and *don't think* (in *don't think so*, *don't think that...*, *don't think* [embedded sentence]) are prevalent.

There is a split between HAVE used as an auxiliary verb and as a main verb (e.g., indicating possession, *had* [something]). Of the inflected forms attested in ICE-GB, only *hasn't* fails to act as both main verb and auxiliary verb. Even so, the meaning of possession is maintained with use as an auxiliary, in examples like *hasn't got* [something]. Meanwhile, BE shows a preference in the negative past tense (*wasn't*) to occur in forms such as *wasn't*/*weren't as* [adj] *as*, although in these data there does not appear to be a preference in general for one tense over another.

Modal verbs also co-occur with mental state verbs. This is easily observed for the word *can't*, in *can't remember*. Otherwise, it appears that the modals are used to indicate the expression of opinion or to talk about possible activities. The negated verb-form *couldn't* was associated with actions, often physical (e.g., *couldn't bring*, *couldn't explain*), although this is not a pattern observed for the positive *could*. There was also a trend in the *won't* examples (e.g., *won't be costing us anything...*) to treat situations informally and to marginalize them. The phrase *must be* [something] occurred frequently, although there were no attested examples of *must be* occurring alone. This is in contrast to the examples *could*/*should do*, *could have*, and *could*/*should be*. These latter examples are reminiscent of Nariyama's (2004) conventional expressions.

As already noted, a number of verbs reflecting the internal or mental state of the speaker are expressed with modals and with DO (e.g., *shouldn't think [so]*). Many of these verbs also occur on their own, without negation, at the beginning of subjectless sentences. These include: *feel*-3, *forget*-2, *found* [emotion], e.g., *found* [something] *depressing*), *hope*, *knew*, *love*, *need*-2, *presume*, *suppose*-3, *think*-7, and *want*-1. The words *presume*, *suppose*, and *think* form a subgroup that can be termed 'thought verbs'. THINK itself occurs in both present and past tense, and appears to pattern either with *so* (*think/thought so*-3) or else is followed by an embedded sentence (e.g., *think I'll get that done first of all*-4). Some of these (e.g., *don't think so, don't like it*) may be going through a process of grammaticalization. This is especially true of the form *don't know*, which is also written in the corpus as *dunno*, exemplifying the way in which it is becoming a fused unit to some speakers.

Aside from mental state verbs, there are also examples of 'expressive' verbs, including items like *talk* or *tell*. These verbs often occur without auxiliaries, and include: *answered*, *explain*, *mention*, *say*-4, *suggest*-2, *speak*, *talk*, *tell*-2, and *thank*-5. *Thank* occurs exclusively in the phrase *thank you*. Another group of verbs can be defined as those having to do with sensory experience, or the senses, although *looks* is often used in lieu of *appears*. These words include: *heard*, *looks*-9, *see*-4, *smell*, *sound*-18, and *watch*-2. It is worth noting that *looks* is followed by either an adjectival phrase (e.g., *looks quite impressive*) or an embedded clause (e.g., *looks like it*-2). SOUND follows the same pattern, although there are relatively fewer SOUND + adjective combinations (e.g., *sounds lovely*). *Sounds like* represents 12 of the 18 total instances of SOUND. Within this category, the most frequently elided subject is *it* (e.g., [*It*] *sounds like a James Bond chase*, S1A-028: 103).

The final group of verbs attracted to sentence initial position in subjectless sentences consists of those making up common expressions. *Seems* occurs in sentences like *seems to me it will be a wonderful tool* (S1B-076: 098) or *seem*[*s*] *very reasonable* a total of 5 times in the ICE-GB casual conversation sub-corpus within a subjectless main clause. The verb *depends* forms the core of the next expression, sometimes standing on its own, but more often prefacing a prepositional phrase or verb particle phrase, as annotaed within ICE-CUP III (e.g., *depends on what you're talking about*, S1A-048:326). This expression is usually used in answer to a question that could have multiple answers or where the answers may rely on factors outside the speaker (e.g., *depends when my supervisor's busy*, S1A-039:028). It occurs 5 times within the given search criteria. In every case, the subject *it* is deleted. The final phrase described here is *doesn't matter*. This is another phrase that ordinarily would take the subject *it*. It occurs three times in the sub-corpus .

Results from the ICE-GB sub-corpus of spontaneous spoken speech have revealed a preference for *I* and *it* to undergo subject ellipsis in conversation. Several verbs and verb phrases have emerged as being attracted to sentence initial position in conversation, including *thank you*, which might be considered a fixed phrase, and phrases like *don't know*, which appears to be undergoing grammaticalization to *dunno*. Mental state verbs (e.g., *think*) and verbs referring to the speaker's internal state form a semantic class that is attracted to sentence initial position in this sub-corpus. Additionally, many verbs were in the present tense, which might be expected given the immediacy of conversation.

2.4 Public dialogue

The Public Dialogue subcomponent of the spoken sub-corpus consists of 171,059 words from publicly recorded conversations. With 55 total instances of subject ellipsis, the phenomenon is less frequent in public conversations than in private. This difference may be related to the different levels of formality represented: the private dialogue subcategory is composed of casual conversations, while the public dialogue subcategory includes legal proceedings, parliamentary debate, and classroom instruction, all of which, one might argue, lend themselves less to casual speech. A collexeme analysis for the pronouns in this sub-corpus reveals that *it* is more strongly associated with subject ellipsis than *I* for this text type, but that both are still strongly associated with ellipsis in declarative sentences (collocational strengths: *it*-198.46, *I*-0.54). Again, this is likely related to the relative formality of the genre and the nature of interpersonal communication in a public setting in comparison to private conversations. That is, speech participants are more likely to omit *it* when it refers to something being discussed than they are to omit *I* when referring to themselves.

The verbs most strongly attracted to sentence initial position in the public speech sub-corpus are main verbs, and not auxiliary or modal verbs, as in the private conversation sub-corpus. *Sounds* in *sounds like* remains significantly attracted to sentence initial position, as do *seems* and *looks*. In the public dialogue sub-corpus, the verbs that are significantly attracted to sentence initial position are *makes* with a collocational strength of 19.65 (where values over 1.30103 are significant), *describes*-17.15, *sounds*-16.61, *squashes*-10.46, *seems*-8.35, *works*-7.77, *gained*-7.70, *saves*-7.70, *strikes*-5.50, *couldn't*-5.30, *turns*-4.51, *thank*-4.40, *feels*-4.27, *sets*-4.27, *spoke*-4.06, *discussed*-3.40, *lost*-3.14, *looks*-2.82, *suggest*-2.25, *doesn't*-2.18, *can't*-1.70, *won't*-1.61, and *could*-1.35.

The most strongly associated verb, *makes*, acts both as part of the expression *[it] makes no difference* and as part of a larger discussion where the pronoun *it* is elided during a conversational turn during discussion, as in (1). The behaviour of other main verbs is similar.

(1) *Here's a private body, upon whose advice the*
minister acts to remove a statutory license
makes a definition of government difficult to say
the least when you see private bodies exercising public
regulatory power *(S1B-011: 027 – 028)*

2.5 Unscripted monologue

The unscripted monologue subcategory of the spoken sub-corpus contains 152,835 words, with 209 total instances of subject ellipsis. Results from this sub-corpus are dramatically different from both dialogue sections, in both preferential pronoun deletion and verb choice. The most frequently omitted pronoun in this sub-corpus is *he*. This is a result of the source texts: many of the texts come from live announcements of sporting events, such as soccer and boxing, a typical example of which is given in (2).

(2) *He'll sustain the England attack*
Plays it to Denis Wise on the right
Plays it back to Stevens again
He's got a little space
Plays it square infield to Parker who's pushed forward.
(S2A-001:133-137)

In these sporting contexts, announcers frequently omit subjects as they provide audiences with ongoing information about events as they unfold. *It* and *I* are still significantly attracted to the construction, but *he* is vastly preferred for omission (collocational strengths: *he*-1576.01, *it*-74.71, *I*-16.53). The relatively higher collocational strength of *it* over *I* relates to the type of speech present in this sub-corpus. *It* is often used to refer to things such as 'the ball' while a game is in play, and so is also likely to be omitted during fast reporting as old information. *It* is also more frequent than *I* in this sub-corpus in general. *They* was also significantly attracted to omission (5.27), where the elided subject refers to a few people or to a team as a whole.

Gone here are the verbs such as *think*, *remember*, *seems*, and *sounds*; most of the verbs in sentence initial position in this sub-corpus are words like *plays* (e.g., *plays the ball*), *comes*, *kicks*, and *tries*. The fifteen verbs most strongly associated with sentence-initial position are: *plays* with a collocational strength of 25.96, *gets*-10.23, *turns*-6.37, *played*-6.35, *tries*-6.29, *finds*-5.86, *headed*-5.18, *takes*-4.85, *comes*-4.15, *falls*-3.97, *bounces*-3.44, *bowls*-3.44, *sweeps*-3.44, *can't*-3.22, and *looks*-3.19 (see Appendix 2 for the complete list). These verbs tend to be strung along, one after another, describing the actions of a single player who is mentioned at an earlier point in the discourse. Where *it* is omitted, it can also be reconstructed by examining previous utterances, and usually refers to the ball in play, or some other aspect of a sporting event. *Looks* is still present, but here it refers to the physical action of looking (e.g., *Looks forward for support*). Similarly, where the modal *can't* appears, it does not precede a mental state verb, as observed in the private dialogue sub-corpus. Instead, *can't* precedes verb phrases describing actions that a player has failed to complete, as in *Can't retain the possession for England though and it's Turneskov who plays it forward* (S2A-001:224:1:A).The majority of these verbs are in the present tense, as might be expected given that they are produced to describe ongoing actions.

Sports casting has received attention in the past for its non-standard syntactic formulation (Ferguson 1983) and verbal routines (Kuiper 1996). Ferguson (1983) argued that sports announcer talk should be considered its own register, and included in his reasoning the simplification of sentences by the omission of the subject and copula. A key reason for subject omission is speed of reporting, but it also serves to make the announcer's play-by-play more accessible by avoiding excessive formality. This is a pattern observed elsewhere, for example in conversation, where subjectless sentences are often more informal than their regular counterparts (e.g., Narayama 2004). Ferguson (1983) also makes note that the lack of a subject (and copula) can mimic language used in headlines, and so may also be used to not only communicate but also to generate excitement. The lack of a subject during reporting may also be considered to be part of a syntactic routine, specific to the act of sports announcing (Kuiper 1996).

Formulaic language may also play a role in sports casting, where speed is a factor in reporting, and can require the use of what Kuiper (1996, 2006) calls formulae. A formula here is a phrasal lexical item that can only be used under certain conditions in specific contexts. For example, *catches the ball* can be used within the context of a baseball game as part of live sports coverage, and will be interpretable to speakers who are familiar with sports coverage. Out of context, or to uninitiated listeners, it can become more difficult to decipher the speaker's intended meaning.

2.6 Correspondence

The correspondence sub-corpus contains 30 texts (social and business) with a total of 61,577 words. Even at this size, subject ellipsis in declarative sentences is present in the recorded texts. In this sub-corpus, both *I* and *it* are significantly attracted to omission in declarative sentences (collocational strengths of *I*-795.2 and *it*-4.91), with *I* being omitted in most cases (112 of 118). These results are similar to Nariyama's (2004) results, where the majority of instances of subject ellipsis in three casual letters occurred with the pronoun *I*, and the rest with *it*. The letters in the ICE-GB do not represent solely casual communications, but are still the only major source of subject ellipsis across the written component of ICE-GB. Although correspondence has sometimes been likened to a form of monologue with an intended recipient (e.g., Nariyama 2004), there are few shared patterns across this grammatical structure with monologues as defined in the ICE-GB. Scripted monologues, represented by lectures, speeches, and broadcasts had no recorded instances of subject ellipsis according to our search criteria, while the active participants in subject ellipsis are quite different in the unscripted monologues of the ICE-GB. It might be more accurate to compare letters to diary writing, but with an assumed and specific audience, as the text tends to be self-referential.

Thank in the conventional expression *thank you* is the verb most strongly associated with sentence initial position, followed by [*I*] *thought*. Unlike in conversation, there are few instances of verbs describing external stimuli (*saw* is the only example). The verb *thought*, together with *can't remember* and *can't think* form a group of mental state verbs, which can be associated with *hope* and *wish*, verbs that are typically used to communicate affection to the reader (*wish you were here*, *hope to hear from you soon*). *Hope* and *wish* occur in the present tense, as they reflect communication with the reader rather than a retelling of events. The verbs significantly attracted to sentence initial position in the correspondence sub-corpus of the ICE-GB are *thank*-117.09, *thought*-2.78, *didn't*-2.67, *hope*-2.32, *traced*-1.86, *wish*-1.78, *saw*-1.75, *can't*-1.47, and *got*-1.39.

3. General discussion

This study has examined the phenomenon of subject ellipsis in English by studying its occurrence in a corpus of British English. ICE-GB is particularly well suited to the study of syntactic phenomena because the associated search program, ICECUP III, can be used to search for particular grammatical structures in the tagged corpus. It is the ability to search for grammatical structure that makes it possible to find instances of subject ellipsis in this corpus. Most English sentences contain overt subjects, but when subjects are omitted, they are most frequently left out during casual conversation. This is not surprising in and of itself, as similar observations have been made with regards to conversation in the past, but the active participants, pronouns and verbs, show some variation across text types.

I and *it* were the most frequently omitted pronouns in the entirety of ICE-GB, but this pattern was not present in the unscripted monologues, where *he* was most frequently omitted. Different verbs are also attracted to the sentence initial position in unscripted monologues, where there is more of a preference for physical action. This difference is related to the text sources and the composition of the sub-corpora. Likewise, the verbs most strongly associated with subject ellipsis change depending on the sub-corpus one is investigating. In private conversation, modal and auxiliary verbs appear to be among the most common verbs to take initial sentence position when a subject is omitted, particularly when these are negated. Other verbs that are strongly associated with this position include *depends*, *looks*, *sounds* and *thank* in the phrase *thank you*. In the unscripted monologues, active verbs describing motion and game play are most likely to be at the beginning of subjectless sentences.

In the majority of sentences analyzed in this paper, across several genres, the most frequently elided subject was *I*, which can easily be reconstructed by listeners in a spoken or written context. *It* was also frequently omitted from speech, often in phrases such as [*it*] *looks like*, where *it* is not referential. However, other third person pronouns (*he, she*) were rarely omitted, except in specific genres. Croft (1991: 112-113) describes the person hierarchy, a component of the larger animacy hierarchy, where the first and second person pronouns are less marked in comparison to third person pronouns. This is relevant in that, typologically, not all subject pronouns are equally likely to be omitted. Based on the person hierarchy, one would expect third person pronouns, which are traditionally considered to be more marked, to be preserved more often in speech. A further exploration of *it*-ellipsis in subject position could be explored to tease apart patterns of deletion within that pronoun to assess its status in the hierarchy.

The patterns in subject ellipsis and sentence initial verbs suggest that, although subject ellipsis is not as common in English as in many other languages, it is not an anomaly and occurs regularly in adult speech, particularly with specific verbs and in conventionalized expressions. The grammatical existence of subjectless sentences in English suggests that the distinction between those languages that typically feature subject ellipsis (e.g., Spanish) and those that do not (e.g., English) is gradient, not binary. The idea of gradience versus binary choice in syntax and elsewhere in linguistic theory has been explored with respect to hard and soft constraints on usage. Sorace & Keller (2005) explain the distinction between hard and soft constraints in terms of acceptability judgments, where hard constraints are those that "trigger categorical linguistic judgments" (Sorace & Keller 2005: 1502), while soft constraints result in gradient decisions along a scale. Consider, for instance, Bresnan, Dingare, & Manning's (2001) examination of the interaction of person and voice in English and Lummi. They argue that the hard constraints on passivization in Lummi are observed as soft constraints in English passives. In Lummi, the subject of a sentence must be higher in the hierarchy of person than any nonsubject argument that is also present. This hard constraint can force passivization when not met. In English, the subject may be lower on the hierarchy of person than a nonsubject argument, but a corpus analysis by Bresnan, Dingare & Manning (2001) reveals similar statistical patterns where English speakers prefer that the subject be higher on the hierarchy. This pattern is considered to reflect a soft constraint in English that is similar to the hard constraint of Lummi. The authors suggest that English and Lummi are part of a continuum, where Lummi is near an endpoint. The same may be said of subject ellipsis: there is a continuum along which languages may fall with respect to the permissibility of subject ellipsis, with English standing closer to an endpoint than languages in which subject ellipsis is more common. Given that English speakers do produce sentences without subjects, the need for a subject in English might then be considered a highly ranked soft constraint, rather than a hard constraint that forces the inclusion of a subject at all times.

It is possible to look at the ICE-GB corpus as a whole, but to do so might ultimately be misleading. The overall results from the ICE-GB do not match those from specific sub-corpora completely, and indeed, results like those found in the unscripted monologues sub-corpus may be obscured by patterning among other components of the corpus. Similarly, it would be incorrect to assume that the same results reported for the entire corpus apply to more formal sub-corpora (e.g., academic writing), where few or no instances of ellipsis were reported. Different patterns in subject ellipsis are associated with different genres and each presents possibilities for valuable research. The varied use of subject ellipsis in different situations and genres, as illustrated in ICE-GB, highlights the importance of examining linguistic pheonomena not only across, but also within different text types.

References

Aarts, B. & S. Wallis (eds.) (2006), British component of the International Corpus of English (ICE-GB), Release 2. London: Survey of English Usage, University College London.

Barton, E.L. (1998), 'The grammar of telegraphic structures: Sentential and nonsentential derivation', *Journal of English linguistics*, 26(1): 37-67.

Biber, D., S. Johansson, G. Leech, S. Conrad & E. Finegan (1999), *Longman grammar of spoken and written English.* Essex, UK: Pearson Education Limited.

Bresnan, J., S. Dingare & C.D. Manning (2001), 'Soft Constraints Mirror Hard Constraints: Voice and Person in English and Lummi', in M. Butt, T. H. King (eds.) *proceedings of the LFG '01 conference*. Stanford (CA): CSLI. 13-32. Available online at: http://cslipublications.stanford.edu/LFG/6/ lfg01bresnanetal.pdf

British National Corpus, version 3 (BNC XML Edition) (2007), Distributed by Oxford University Computing Services on behalf of the BNC Consortium.

Croft, W. (1991), *Typology and universals*. Cambridge/New York: Cambridge University Press.

Ferguson, C.A. (1983), 'Sports announcer talk: Syntactic aspects of register variation', *Language and society,* 12: 153 – 172.

Gries, S.Th. (2004), *Coll.analysis 3. A program for R for Windows 2.x.*

Gries, S.Th. & A. Stefanowitsch (2004a), 'Extending collostructional analysis: A corpus-based perspective on 'alternations'', *International journal of corpus linguistics*, 9(1): 97-129.

Gries, S.Th. & A. Stefanowitsch (2004b), 'Co-varying collexemes in the *into*-causative', in: M. Achard & S. Kemmer (eds.) *Language, culture, and mind.* Stanford (CA): CSLI. 225-236.

Haegeman, L. & T. Ihsane (1999), 'Subject ellipsis in embedded clauses in English', *English language and linguistics*, 3(1): 117-145.

Kay, P. (2002), 'English subjectless tagged sentences', *Language*, 78(3): 453-481.

Kuiper, K. (1996), *Smooth talkers: the linguistic performance of auctioneers and sportscasters.* Mahwah, NJ: Lawrence Erlbaum Associates.

Kuiper, K. (2006), 'Slipping on superlemmas', in: A. Hacki Buhofer & H. Burger (eds.) *Phraseology in motion 1*. Baltmannsweiler: Schneider Verlag. 371-379.

McEnery, T., R. Xiao & Y. Tono (2006), *Corpus-based language studies: an advanced resource book.* London/New York: Routledge.

Nariyama, S. (2004), 'Subject ellipsis in English', *Journal of pragmatics*, 36: 237-264.

Newman, J. (2008), 'Spoken corpora: rationale and application', *Taiwan journal of linguistics*, 6(2): 27-58.

R Development Core Team. (2008), *R: a language and environment for statistical computing.* R foundation for statistical computing, Vienna,

Austria, ISBN 3-900051-07-0. Available online at: http://www.R-project.org.

Rice, S. & J. Newman (19 July, 2005), 'Inflectional islands'. Paper presented at the 9th International cognitive linguistics conference. Seoul, Korea.

Sorace, A. & F. Keller (2005), 'Gradience in linguistic data', *Lingua*, 115: 1497-1524.

Stefanowitsch, A & S.Th. Gries (2003), 'Collostructions: Investigating the interaction between words and constructions', *International journal of corpus linguistics*, 8(2): 209-243.

Stefanowitsch, A & S.Th. Gries (2005), 'Co-varying collexemes', *Corpus linguistics and linguistic theory*, 1(1): 1-43.

Wallis, S. (1998), The Corpus Utility Program for the International Corpus of English (ICECUP), Version 3.0. London: Survey of English Usage, University College London.

Appendix 1

Verbs significantly attracted to verb initial position in the private conversation sub-corpus of ICE-GB (verbs listed in order of attraction, with the most strongly attracted verbs coming first).

sounds, can't, looks, doesn't, depends, must, don't, watched, didn't, feels, presumed, picked, could, shouldn't, tried, haven't, kept, seems, becomes, should, thank, sounded, keeps, talked, cost, gives, may, couldn't, forgot, seemed, sat, forget, needs

Appendix 2

Verbs significantly attracted to verb initial position in the unscripted monologue sub-corpus of ICE-GB (verbs listed in order of attraction, with the most strongly attracted verbs coming first).

plays, gets, turns, played, tries, finds, headed, takes, comes, falls, bounces, bowls, sweeps, can't, looks, cuts, hoists, doesn't, welcome, leaves, sends, goes, aimed, chips, feeds, frees, matured, punched, rebounds, recovers, scooped, spears, splits, strained, swings, threaded, thudded, twisted, weighs, wanted, clears, helps, lobs, pokes, right footed, shrugs, smiles, trickles, waits, thank, won't, boots, forgot, intercepts, lays, loses, scoops, switches, walks, makes, receives, slips, stood

Language Learning

Language learners as language researchers: the acquisition of English grammar through a corpus-aided discovery learning approach mediated by intra- and interpersonal dialogues

Li-Shih Huang

University of Victoria, British Columbia

Abstract

Despite advancements in technology and growing interest in a corpus-based learning approach in the field of second-language acquisition, there is a considerable gap between research and practice in the sense that learning to use and incorporate corpora in the teaching and learning process is still perceived as too time-consuming, complicated, daunting, or frustrating for instructors or learners. This paper reports on pedagogical applications and outcomes of incorporating a corpus-aided discovery learning (CADL) approach, mediated through peer-peer dialogues and individual written language logs, that enhances the acquisition of modern English grammar and usage in an undergraduate-level course taken by students across disciplines. The study involved 10 groups of students, with three participants in each group, over the course of 14 weeks. Findings from quantitative and qualitative analyses of the data offer a basis for using a CADL approach in this context and warrant further studies to obtain a fuller picture of the strategies and challenges involved in implementing the approach.

1. Introduction

Recent technological improvements have enhanced language learners' and instructors' access to corpora. Consequently, such pedagogical approaches as corpus-aided discovery learning (CADL), which actively engage learners in analyzing patterns and features, are increasingly workable options for instructors who teach English as an additional language (Gavioli 2001, Huang 2011). CADL is supported by theory (e.g., Johns 1991, 1994, Leech 1997), and, since Johns's (1994) seminal work on using corpora in language learning and teaching, attention and interest in corpus-based learning has increased (e.g., Bennett 2010, Flowerdew 2008, Foucou & Kübler 2000, Reppen 2010). As numerous researchers have pointed out, however, more empirical research about integrating corpora into the classroom is needed (e.g., Chambers 2005, Conrad 2005, Hunston 2005, Yoon 2008). Moreover, spreading corpus use to the classroom remains a great challenge (Conrad 2008). In addition to responding to researchers' calls for more empirical studies on the efficacy of corpus-based learning and corpus-related activities, this study is the first to explore the acquisition of grammar at the curricular level using a CADL approach mediated through peer-peer dialogues and individual written language logs.

2. Background

Corpus linguistics' contribution and potential usefulness in teaching and learning have been receiving growing attention and recognition (e.g., refer to Bennett 2010, Boulton 2010, Conrad 2005, Hunston 2005, Reppen 2010, Sinclair 2004). In recent years, corpus data have been acknowledged as resources for researchers that provide descriptive insights relevant to how people use language, and as tools that enable instructors and learners to analyze how people use language in the real world at various levels of formality and how language fulfills different speech functions across various contexts. These tools and endeavors promote the transferability of language skills and language-learning strategies (see Hunston 2005, Sinclair 2004). In the following sections, I define the key terms used in this study and then proceed with a brief overview of recent work that supports an investigation of the research questions.

2.1 Corpus-aided discovery learning approach

For this study, a "corpus" is defined as "a large collection of texts involving natural discourse in diverse contexts. Such discourses can be spoken, written, computer-mediated, spontaneous, or scripted and may represent a variety of genres, such as everyday conversation, lectures, seminars, meetings, radio and television programs, essays, and so on" (Huang 2011). Some examples of commonly known online corpora include the *British National Corpus* (BNC) (http://www.natcorp.ox.ac.uk/), the *Corpus of Contemporary American English* (COCA) (http://www.americancorpus.org/), and the *Michigan Corpus of Academic Spoken English* (MICASE) (http://micase.elicorpora.info/), to name a few. Central to the CADL approach used in the higher-education classroom is *enquiry-based learning* (Deignan 2009), which is learning that is driven by a process of enquiry and that works toward understanding or resolving a problem. In the field of corpora and language learning, CADL involves *data-driven learning* (Johns 1994), which encourages learners to take the role of language researchers engaged in discovery learning (Gavioli 2001) and to learn how to learn through activities that involve observations, analyses, and interpretations of language-use patterns through the use of corpora (Chen, Warren & Xu 2003). Both approaches have a similar philosophical orientation and intention: learners seek evidence to further their understanding and take responsibility for analyzing and presenting their findings, either as part of a group through peer-peer dialogues or as individuals through written language logs.

Over the past decade, a growing number of empirical studies have shown how learners can use data from corpora to further their language learning. As numerous corpus linguists have pointed out (e.g., Bernardini 2001, Gavioli & Aston 2001), activities that ask learners to analyze corpus data are consistent with current principles in language-learning theory. Such activities promote noticing (Schmidt 1990) and grammatical consciousness-raising, which enhance language learning and development. In their view, learner autonomy also increases when students are provided guidance on how to observe language and make generalizations. More recently, however, the amount of guidance or training required has been called into question. Some have suggested substantial training (e.g., Estling Vannestål & Lindquist 2007), while others have provided evidence for a minimal amount of required training (e.g., Boulton 2008a). Despite numerous publications emphasizing the benefits of using corpora in language learning (e.g., Bernardini 2002a, Kennedy & Miceli 2001), the empirical research that examines the effectiveness of the corpus-aided approach for language learning is insufficient (Chambers 2005). A growing number of empirical studies have focused on data-driven learning or corpus-aided approach, but scant studies have examined the link between corpus use and performance; the few quantitative studies that linked learners' performance to using corpora were based on pre- and post-test assessments (e.g., Boulton 2008b, 2009a, 2010, Chan & Liou 2005, Smith, Chen & Kilgarriff 2008).

2.2 Intra- and interpersonal dialogues

In the field of second-language acquisition (SLA), the term 'languaging' (Becker 1991, Swain 2006) has been used to refer to "the process of making meaning and shaping knowledge and experience through language" (Swain 2006: 98).[1] In the context of this study, participants were not exclusively second-language learners to whom the concept of 'languaging' may have been originally applied in the study of SLA. Still, the concept of 'languaging' applies in the sense that individual written language logs (intrapersonal dialogues) and peer-peer spoken dialogues (interpersonal dialogues) among English-as-a-first-language and English-as-an-additional-language learners mediated solutions to problems, whether the problems were related to how lexicogrammatical choices may vary depending on the contexts, to explanations of how one judges the grammaticality and appropriacy of a sentence, or to the determination of what grammatical voice should be used in information packaging.

In the field of cognitive and learning sciences, researchers have found that 'self-explaining,' a process comparable to languaging, facilitates the integration of new information into existing knowledge or one's cognitive system, and mediates problem-solving skills (e.g., Chi et al. 1989, Chi et al. 1994). In the field of SLA, in observations of learners' noticing or identification of learners' language development in their collaborative dialogue, previous work has used the language-related episode (LRE) as the unit of analysis to capture occurrences of attention to language (e.g., Swain & Lapkin 1998). Fortune and Thorp (2001), for example, identified grammatical, lexical, discourse, and orthographic LREs as main categories. LREs can vary in length and may consist of only two turns or multiple turns; they may entail learners talking, questioning, reflecting, or deliberating about language in order to understand, solve problems, self- or other-correct, and/or construct meanings (e.g., Leeser 2004, Swain & Lapkin 1998). The present paper focuses on identifying *negotiated* form-focused LREs (Basturkmen, Loewen & Ellis 2002, Ellis, Basturkmen & Loewen 2001) or, hereafter, *negotiated form-focused episodes* (NFFEs). Here, NFFEs include all interactions in which learners draw attention to form, whether it is grammatical features of English or discourse features (e.g., logical sequencing, stylistics, and structure) *through negotiations*.[2] Instances of minimal dialoguing, in which one learner suggested an answer or a solution and the other simply repeated or acknowledged the answer, or, instead, did not respond to the suggestion, were not included when calculating the number or outcomes of NFFEs. As previous research in instructional science has demonstrated, more interactive groups tend to generate more knowledge convergence, defined as "an increase in common knowledge following collaboration" (Jeong & Chi 2007: 289), than less interactive groups (e.g., Jeong & Chi 2007, Roschelle 1992). Moreover, as Jeong and Chi (2007) pointed out, for the contents of dialogues to be integrated into an individual's representation, learners must do more than pay attention to and acknowledge a contribution. The contents must be processed sufficiently. The NFFEs measured in this study provided an indication of the depth of processing (Craik & Lockhart 1972) or what Laufer and Hulstijn (2001) proposed in their work on vocabulary learning (adapted from Craik & Lockhart's depth-of-processing theory) as the extent of *involvement*. This involvement relates to learners' need to resolve a problem (i.e., the motivational component) and to generate and evaluate solutions (i.e., the cognitive component) (Hulstijn forthcoming).

The idea that learners operate with mediating tools (e.g., corpora, language logs) originated with Vygotsky's (1978, 1986, 1987) sociocultural theory of mind, which has received much attention over the past decade from those in education and those studying second-language teaching and learning (e.g., Lantolf 2000, 2001, Lantolf & Thorne 2006, Wells 2000). Researchers (e.g., Donato 1994, 2004, Ohta 2000) have advanced Vygotskian theory by arguing that for second-language acquisition to occur in a manner that will promote language learning, learners need to interact with their peers in small groups or pairs. Here, verbalization, whether spoken through interpersonal dialogues or written through intrapersonal dialogues, serves as a vehicle through which "thinking reaches a new level of articulation" (Smagorinsky 1998: 172) and "as a means of development by reshaping experience" (Swain 2006: 97). It is often through the effort of verbalizing, whether spoken or written, that an individual "has the feeling of reaching a fuller and clearer understanding for him or herself" (Wells 2000: 74). To use Williams's (2008: 18) words, for this study

> the role of talk [in this case both intra and interpersonal dialogues] is particularly important because, within the sociocultural perspective, knowledge construction is mediated by language; articulation makes the new knowledge available for inspection and discussion. This, it is argued, is a precursor to the internalization of knowledge.

3. Research questions

The goal of this study is to explore the efficacy of CADL in a peer-peer small group setting in terms of acquiring standard English grammar and usage in an introductory undergraduate-level course. This preliminary study addressed the following four questions:

1. How many negotiated form-focused episodes (NFFEs) did participants produce, and what is the distribution of outcomes of NFFEs (i.e., correctly resolved, incorrectly resolved, or unresolved)?
2. What is the relationship between the participants' overall course performance and the frequency of NFFEs produced?
3. What is the relationship between the participants' overall course performance and the outcomes of NFFEs produced?
4. How do participants perceive the relative usefulness of engaging in corpus-aided discovery learning through peer-peer dialogues and individual language logs?

4. Methods

4.1 Pilot study

A pilot study was conducted to field-test the data collection instruments and procedures. As a result, several changes were made in the design and implementation of the main study. First, recording equipment problems (human errors, improper equipment settings) were resolved so that the quality of recording could be maximized in the main study. Second, the organization of learner groups, which consisted of randomly assigned groups of five, was changed to triads in the main study for the following three key reasons: (a) Using a five-person group limited the number of turns that each participant could take in a 30-minute languaging session; (b) During the data transcription stage, it became very challenging to distinguish five speakers' voices and what each had said, especially when overlapping turns occurred; (c) A substantial body of recent research in interactional modifications, output, and collaboration has focused on dyadic interaction (e.g., Storch 2001a, 2001b, 2002, 2004, 2008, Swain & Lapkin 1998, 2002, Watanabe & Swain 2007), which may not reflect the everyday reality of classrooms.

4.2 Context

The main study occurred in an undergraduate-level course — "An Introduction to the Grammar of English Usage"[3] — in which corpora and peer-peer dialogue sessions have been recently incorporated. The course, which is a functional treatment of English grammar that emphasizes standard English usage from the descriptive perspective, focuses on the grammatical system that underlies how people actually speak and write the language. The course is offered three times per academic year and is taken by students across numerous disciplines who wish to improve their English grammar and usage in ways that will benefit their future academic and professional endeavors.

Table 1: Learner characteristics

age	Mean Range	20.5 18 ~ 23
length of residence	Mean Range	5.1 years 1 ~ 19 years
gender	Male Female	7 (23.3%) 23 (76.7%)
first-language background	Mandarin (12), Cantonese (6), Taiwanese (1), Korean(2), Japanese (2), Italian (1), French (1), English (5)	

As shown in Table 1, most students speak Chinese. Of the total, 25 participants speak English as an additional language, and 5 participants speak English as their first language. The mix of first languages could not be controlled because an intact class was used in this study. Participants who speak English as an additional language were all required to have met the university's English proficiency requirement for entry into their programs (i.e., 575 or higher on the paper TOEFL® test, 90 or higher on the TOEFL® iBT™ (internet-based test) test, 6.5 or higher on the International English Language Testing System (IELTS™), or a score of Level 6 on the Language Proficiency Index). Participants were students in a variety of disciplines, including psychology, biology, linguistics, applied linguistics, sociology, fine arts, chemistry, education, Pacific Asian studies, Spanish, Italian, and English literature, though the majority were students from economics.

4.3 Guidance on corpora use

Before learners stepped into the world of CADL, they were offered guidance by means of a familiarization process that first asked learners to explore the following three readily accessible, general corpora available online: COBUILD, the BNC, and MICASE.[4] Students were then shown how to use a corpus with its built-in search tools to obtain information about language use and data in various contexts. Both means of guidance aimed to meet the needs of those who were comfortable and/or competent in experimenting with corpora and their respective ways of performing searches as well as those who might have been wary about or resistant to using such tools. These means also provided opportunities for support during the learners' experimental stage when they might have been easily overwhelmed by the sheer amount of data generated by the corpus or might have had trepidations about how to make sense of the data.

4.4 Data collection

A total of 30 students across disciplines participated in the main study over the course of 14 weeks. Table 2 summarizes the types of information gathered and the data collection methods.

Table 2: Types of information and methods of data collection

information	*data collection*
students' backgrounds	background questionnaire
intra and interpersonal dialogues	weekly group audio-taped recordings bi-weekly individual written language logs
learning outcomes	quizzes and the final
perceptions about using the corpora	exit survey

The first week of the class was devoted to obtaining participants' consent, administering background questionnaires, and conducting an hour-long training session on the use of corpora. A questionnaire was distributed to all participants to collect information/histories about their backgrounds (e.g., gender, age, knowledge of other languages, educational experience, and length of stay in English-speaking countries) (refer Table 1). During weeks 2 through 11, participants used the corpora described above and engaged in weekly peer-peer dialogue sessions. Each group was given a tape recorder to record all dialogue sessions throughout the entire course. In addition, individuals wrote biweekly in their language logs about a self-selected grammatical point that interested or intrigued them, and also about what they discovered from using the corpus.

During the 10-week experimental period, three quizzes were also administered at intervals of approximately 3 weeks (see Appendix A for sample questions). In week 12, all students took a final exam, which included all content covered throughout the course, and, approximately 2 weeks after the exam, the participants were invited to complete an exit survey. The survey was conducted to elicit learners' perceptions of the corpora's usefulness and their opinions about interacting with their interlocutors. After students' final grades were submitted, I emailed all students and invited them to express their thoughts about using the corpus and engaging in the dialogue sessions. The survey focused on such questions as: *How have you utilized the corpus in your learning? In what ways has using the corpus helped (or not helped) your learning? What challenges have you encountered using the corpus?* The questions touched on students' experiences, which cannot be obtained only from test scores. The survey provided an additional source of information, which further informs the analysis so that it provides a fuller picture of students' learning and experiences.

4.5 Data analysis

The data generated from the dialogue sessions were transcribed verbatim. In the analysis of data from the weekly 30-minute dialogue sessions over the course of 10 weeks, the occurrences of NFFEs, as described earlier, were identified in the data first.[5] In addition to identifying NFFEs, the episodes were also categorized, following Leeser (2004), as correctly resolved (i.e., an NFFE in which the problem or question is solved correctly), unresolved (i.e., an NFFE in which the learner can neither solve the problem nor state the answer to the question), or incorrectly resolved (i.e., an NFFE in which a problem is solved incorrectly or an incorrect answer is provided to a question). When an NFFE was discussed multiple times during a single conversation, it was coded once, and the resolution was coded based on the outcome of the last discussion. When an NFFE involved discussion about different aspects of a grammatical feature, each aspect was coded separately. Two coders coded all the data for the NFFEs. The inter-coder reliability was 96%. Any disagreements were resolved by discussion.

As stated in the Data Collection section, three quizzes and a final exam were administered to assess students' learning outcomes throughout the course. The scores[6] were compared and correlated with occurrences and outcomes of NFFEs in the discourse data generated during the experimental period. Non-parametric correlational analyses, which were chosen on the basis of statistical tests for normality and the small sample size, were conducted to examine the relationship among the number of NFFEs, the outcomes of NFFEs, and test performance. All analyses were conducted using IBM® SPSS® Statistics 18.

The data gathered from the language logs and exit surveys were examined qualitatively (i.e., direct interpretation, patterns and themes, naturalistic generalizations and description). The goal for the two sources of data was to develop an emic view of learners' perceptions and use of corpora in the learning process.

5. Results and discussion

5.1 NFFE occurrences and distribution of NFFE outcomes

The number of NFFEs produced across the 10 groups ranged from 40 to 58, with a mean of 49. In terms of the distribution of NFFE outcomes, the percentage of correctly resolved episodes ranged from 57% to 90%, from 4% to 40% for incorrectly resolved episodes, and from 0% to 19% for unresolved episodes. Overall, 73% of the NFFEs were correctly resolved; 17% were incorrectly resolved, and 10% were unresolved. Table 3 summarizes the occurrences of NFFEs and the distribution of NFFE outcomes for each group.

For the three groups that had the highest percentages of unresolved outcomes (i.e., groups 1, 4, and 8), the total number of NFFEs produced also seemed to be higher. For the three groups that had the lowest percentages of unresolved outcomes (i.e., groups 3, 6, and 10), the total number of NFFEs produced was also lower. Previous research has shown that the higher the proficiency of a learner group, the greater the number of LREs the group produces and the more LREs the learners correctly resolve (e.g., Leeser 2004). Interestingly, in this case, a higher number of NFFEs did not necessarily lead to more correctly resolved NFFEs. Groups with a lower number of NFFEs (e.g., groups 2, 3, and 10), however, did have a higher percentage of incorrectly resolved outcomes. Insights from previous studies (e.g., Kuiken & Vedder 2002) indicated that groups with limited engagement, where the learners simply agree with the solution provided by another participant, without further discussion or deliberation, may have a lower number of unresolved episodes but a higher number of incorrectly resolved episodes, which may not contribute to learning.

Table 3: Total number and outcomes of NFFEs

	G1	*G2*	*G3*	*G4*	*G5*
total NFFEs	58	45	41	55	50
CS	37 (64%)	30 (67%)	23 (57%)	42 (77%)	45 (90%)
IS	10 (17%)	12 (26%)	16 (40%)	3 (5%)	2 (4%)
U	11 (19%)	3 (7%)	1 (3%)	10 (18%)	3 (6%)

Table 3 (continued)

	G6	*G7*	*G8*	*G9*	*G10*
total NFFEs	48	47	56	51	40
CS	41 (85%)	36 (77%)	24 (60%)	42 (82%)	27 (68%)
IS	5 (11%)	7 (15%)	10 (18%)	5 (10%)	13 (32%)
U	2 (4%)	4 (8%)	16 (28%)	4 (8%)	0 (0%)

G = Group; NFFEs = negotiated form-focused episodes; CS = correctly resolved; IS = incorrectly resolved; U = unresolved

5.2 Number and outcomes of NFFEs vis-à-vis test performance

To assess the associations among NFFE variables and test-score variables, tests were conducted to identify Spearman correlation coefficients, which measure the associations' direction and magnitude. A two-tailed test was used to determine whether the number and outcomes of NFFE variables correlated with the test-score variables.

Table 4: Correlations between the number of NFFEs and test performance

		Quiz 1	*Quiz 2*	*Quiz 3*	*final*
	mean	72.72	71.53	78.88	79.09
	SD	6.94	8.26	6.86	8.39
number of NFFEs	Spearman's *rho*	-.176	.855**	.742*	.879**
	sig.	.627	.002	.014	.001

NFFEs = negotiated form-focused episodes. * Correlation is significant at $p < .05$ (2-tailed). ** Correlation significant at $p < .01$ (2-tailed)

As presented in Table 4, the results indicate that there is a significant positive correlation between the number of NFFEs and test scores from quiz 2 ($r_s = .855, p < .01$), quiz 3 ($r_s = .742, p < .05$) and the final exam ($r_s = .879, p < .01$). In all cases, $r > .50$, which indicates a large effect size (Field 2005).[7]

In terms of the associations among the outcomes of NFFEs and participants' test performance, Table 5 shows that the results indicated a positive correlation between the quiz 1 score and NFFEs that were correctly resolved (r_s = .638, $p < .05$), with a large effect size. A significant negative correlation was found between the incorrectly resolved NFFEs variable and the final test score variable (r_s = -.661, $p < .05$), with a large effect size. This finding suggests that, the higher the number of incorrectly resolved NFFE outcomes, the lower the final test performance. Although the results did not show a significant relationship between the three quizzes and the incorrectly resolved NFFEs, all correlations were negative. For unresolved outcomes of NFFEs, the results indicate two positive correlations: for quiz 2 (r_s = .766, $p < .01$) and for the final test (r_s = .784, $p < .01$), with a large effect size for both.

Table 5: Correlations between outcomes of NFFEs and test performance

		Quiz 1	*Quiz 2*	*Quiz 3*	*final*
CS	Spearman's *rho*	.638*	.237	.354	.219
	sig.	.047	.510	.316	.544
IS	Spearman's *rho*	-.442	-.624	-.571	-.661*
	sig.	.200	.054	.084	.038
U	Spearman's *rho*	-.122	.766**	.561	.784**
	sig.	.738	.010	.092	.007

CS = correctly resolved; IS = incorrectly resolved; U = unresolved. * Correlation is significant at $p < .05$ (2-tailed). ** Correlation significant at $p < .01$ (2-tailed)

Overall, the results showed that groups with higher overall course performance tended to have higher percentages of NFFEs and higher percentages of correctly resolved outcomes, and those with lower test performance tended to have lower percentages of NFFEs and higher percentages of incorrectly resolved outcomes. It is interesting to note that a higher percentage of NFFEs with unresolved outcomes did not relate to lower test performance.

The following example (1) shows the interactions among learners on the topic of symmetric and asymmetric coordinations among members of one of the higher performance groups (group 5) that generated a higher number of NFFEs. (Refer to Appendix B for the transcription key used to transcribe the oral data.)

(1)

128. P2: *What does asymmetrical mean?*
129. P1: *Um... the two clauses are not the same?*
130. P3: *meaning they're not symmetrical? [laughs]*
131. P2: *Yeah, I know what it means in math. What does it mean in language?*
132. P3: *It means that they don't have the same weight? that because* =

133. P1: *=Because none of us are quite up to snuff with our studying.*
134. P3: *I haven't <had time to study>.*
135. P3: *Look at this example. Asymmetric is when you can't, change it. So it's, "we were left high and dry," we can't say "we were left dry and high."*
136. P1: *Yeah. That means something totally different…to be left dry and high.*
137. P2: *Okay. What about the example "He crashed into a tree and lost control of the car"?*
138. P3: *<I think>, that would be asymmetric, wouldn't it?*
139. P2: *Yeah, because you, you can't crash -*
140. P3: *//it has to do with time order. Does that mean anything to you?*
141. P1: *Yeah, yeah, 'cause for the car, to, to crash, you would have to loss control.*
142. P3: *//Yes, it's a sequence of events.*
143. P2: *He lost control of the* car –
144. P1: *Yep, and that was, that was exactly what she said in class, sequence of events.*
145. P2: *//and crashed into the tree. But, couldn't you say that crash into the tree and lost control of the car?*
146. P1: *Hmm….*
147. P2: *So it can be symmetric?*
148. P3: *No, it's NOT symmetric… You can't say crashed into the tree, and then lost control of the car.*
149. P1: *It can be both.*
150. P2: *I thought asymmetric was when it was grammatically incorrect.*
151. P1: *It just means that you can't change the clauses.*
152. P2: *So, if you look at this example, you can put this and that in any order right, so that makes it symmetrical.*
153. P1: *Yeah, you can't, if you can't take it, and reverse it and have it make grammatical sense, then it's asymmetric.*
154. P3: *Not only grammatical sense, meaning the same too… So the example "Talk to me like that again and you'll be fired. So –*
155. P2: *//So you can't be fired and then someone tell you not to talk like.*
156. P3: *Yeah you can't say you'll be fired and talk to me like that again.*

Here, none of the three participants had a clear idea of what symmetric and asymmetric coordinations are, but all came to an enhanced and expanded understanding of them, both individually and as a group. As a group, for example, the meaning of asymmetrical progressed from "two clauses not the same" to "not symmetrical," to "[not having] the same weight," "can't change [the clauses]," "grammatically incorrect," to "put [the clauses] in any order" and "make grammatical sense" and "meaning the same," as it was clarified by the contributions of different participants. Individually, in turn 136, for example, P1 commented that the meaning changed if the order of the two coordinates were changed, and later in turn 154, P3 followed up on P1's comments about the ordering and grammaticality of asymmetric coordination when considering the interpretation of the coordination.

Example (2), in contrast, shows interactions on the topic about adjectives used in attributive (e.g., *a diligent supervisor*), predicative (e.g., *he is diligent*), and/or postpositive (e.g., *someone diligent*) functions among members of another group (group 3) that generated a lower number of NFFEs.

(2)

11. P3: *Available... predicative, attributive, or postpositive?*
12. P2: *Did you search different combinations?*
13. P1: *Yes, and I would say it's, I would say it's a predicate, because you can say, -*
14. P3: *//Predicate. Okay...*
15. P1: *//something, someone is available.*
16. P3: *Yeah you can say... Ok uh available -*
17. P2: *//I think it works attributively. An available remedy, an available property, an available market, an available option, etc.*
18. P3: *OK. How about postpositive?*
19. P1: *I don't think that works, but I am not sure.*
20. P2: *How about the only person available?*
21. P1: *Oh yeah right.*
22. P3: *So all of them?*
23. P2: *Any other examples?*
24. P1: *No.*

Here, members of the group engaged in limited elaborative talk that would contribute to exploring a topic in that one learner offered a suggestion and another either attended to the suggestion by acknowledging it or responded with a phatic response.

As the results from the correlations demonstrated, a higher percentage of NFFEs with unresolved outcomes did not relate to lower test performance quantitatively. Qualitatively, using (1) as an example, the triadic dialogue contains an episode in which there was an unresolved outcome (turns 137-149), but the episode did not seem to hinder the dialoging process and outcome. Incidences like these point to the aspect of intersubjectivity (traditionally defined as "a state of overlapping individual 'subjectivities' or 'prolepses'" [Rommetveit 1979]) without agreement (Matusov 1996: 26). In cases of unresolved episodes, the disagreement may center on alternative ideas, rather than on always achieving an overlap of understanding or decision-making. It also points to the different layers of intersubjectivity (e.g., process, outcome, objective) and to the possibility that a lack of intersubjectivity in achieving an overlapping understanding or in group decision-making may not necessarily impede learning.

Researchers have pointed out that a knowledge convergence, the process by which two or more people share an understanding through social interaction, is one of the most fundamental aspects of the process of knowledge construction (e.g., Ickes & Gonzales 1996, Lave & Wenger 1991, Rogoff 1998, Vygotsky 1978). There are, however, different outcomes of collaborative interaction, as also revealed in the present study. The study's findings suggest that sharing a knowledge convergence, correctly or incorrectly, seems to have a more direct positive relation (with correctly solved NFFEs) or negative relation (with incorrectly solved NFFEs) with test performance. Most importantly, overall, the percentages of *unresolved* NFFEs did not seem to relate to test performance negatively, but, in fact, showed positive correlations with a large effect size for both quiz 2 and the final test, as shown in Table 5. One could postulate that negotiated dialogues may promote "deeper processing" (Lockhart & Craik 1990) or "involvement" (Laufer & Hulstijn 2001). The depth of processing of some piece of information or the degree of involvement in processing, as measured by the number of NFFEs, thus may be related to learning the information, as measured by test performance. Even though participants, such as those in example 2, provided evidence of grounding[8] by acknowledgement or with continued attention, the discussed information did not necessarily become a part of the participants' representation. As Jeong and Chi (2007) suggested, it is the depth of processing or what Hulstijn (forthcoming called the degree of involvement that facilitates the integration of new or newly learned materials with existing knowledge.

5.3 Written language logs and the exit survey

This section first reports findings from the written language logs and then the results from the exit survey. As mentioned in the Methods Section, learners wrote biweekly in their individual language logs about what they discovered while using a corpus to explore a question that was interesting or personally relevant to them. The survey focused on students' perceptions of their use of corpora in their learning.

The following examples demonstrate how learners engaged in research-like activities within just a few weeks (examples 3 and 4 were produced by English-as-an-additional-language students, and example 5 was written by an English-as-a-first-language student). In example 3, the learner, in her third language-log entry, chose to explore the usage of "stranded" (e.g., *This is the paper that the speaker was referring to)* vs. "fronted" prepositions (e.g., *This is the paper to which the speaker was referring.*).

(3)

When I was learning English in China, I was taught the standard British English. Therefore, I am always very careful with my prepositions and relating to my personal use, I always prefer the fronted version. This week, I used MICASE to search for stranded prepositions. Surprisingly, I found more than I anticipated. I found stranded preposition are used more common in "highly interactive" conversation. The ages of the speakers who use stranded preposition are distributed quite evenly. This shows that stranded prepositions are more common and in less formal situations. However, I also noticed that there are situations where stranded prepositions are obligatory. For example: "Who are you staring down?" In this case, you can't say "down whom are you staring?" because the phrase "stare down" is a verb idiom.

I found fronted preposition[s] used in many occasions also, for example: "...and to which religious order am I referring and to which famous Spanish Basque?" and "What sentence that person gets versus what sentence all the people to whom he distributed". I went through many examples and found most of the fronted prepositions were used by faculties and were happened [sic] in lectures, colloquiums, dissertation defenses and seminars. I think this is related to the "formal vs. informal" discussion we had in the class. I also observed examples to support the "syntactic feature" perspective. For example: "the angle at which things come out." If changed into stranded form, this sentence will be "the angle which things come out at." It is awkward to have two prepositions together. Therefore, fronted preposition may be preferred in this case.

I don't think I will restrict myself to the use of fronted prepositions only. There are clearly many things to consider when making a choice. (MG)

In example 4, the learner, in his eighth language log, chose to explore the usage of "*different from*" and "*different than.*"

(4)

I personally use different from *in almost all cases because I was taught that different should never follow than [sic.], and I don't really know the difference between* different from *and* different than. *In this log I would like to see how those constructions are used.*

When searching MICASE, I got multiple hits on "different than" (46 in 30 transcripts) and "different from" (88 in 53 transcript[s]). From the examples, I did not observe much difference in the manner in which the two phrases were used. Both uses seem to be followed by a full clause which shows the comparison of the antecedent to the final reference in the sentence or by an NP. While the use of different than is evenly distributed between the two genders, I did note different than *is used more often by female[s] than by male[s]. Of the 46 matches found, interestingly, 29 of them were used by female[s]. This may possibly suggest that besides cultural background and education I have previously discovered in my logs, gender could be another factor that contributes different language choices. I am still wondering whether there is any difference between* from *and* than. *I tried keying in* different from what *and* different than what. *The latter one is used slightly more often than the preceding one. This may suggest that when the following is a clause, the use of* different than *is preferred.*

In BNC, I found that different from *(3,281 hits) is used far more often than* different than. *From the examples, I noticed that in British English,* different than *tends to be followed by clauses. For example,* it's not very much different than what we had expected. *I also noticed that* different to *is more evident in British English than in American English. I also have another finding. The evidence from BNC suggested that* different to *is more commonly used in British English than* different than.

This initial exploration has drawn my attention to my own and others' preferences or choices in the use of different from, different than and different. For one, I did not know that all are acceptable constructions in a non-scalar comparison. (CS)

Excerpt 5 provides an example of what a learner who could not identify a subject or a verb when starting the course was able to do in her third language log: the usage of genitive and non-genitive subjects functioning as complements (e.g., *My supervisor is relying on my/me being there to implement the project.*) and of nominative and accusative forms functioning as adjuncts (e.g., *I first consulted with Professor Anderson, he/him being the project director.*)

(5)

I used three different corpora to explore the use of genitive and non-genitive subjects and observe any similarities, differences and trends between the two constructions. I started with the COBUILD and decided to try the gerund-participial as complement construction. I typed in "IN+me+being" and that produced approximately 41 results, while "IN+my+being" resulted only 26 hits. From this result, it seems that the informal accusative "me" is being used more frequently in English. I then entered the construction, "NN+he+being," and there was one match, and zero matches for "NN+him+being." I also tried different nominative and accusative pronouns. This resulted in only a few hits. So I decided to use BNC to see what I could find. There were 97 solutions for "_ my being" and 117 solutions for "_ me being." This seems to be similar to the results from COBUILD. Next I entered the gerund-participial as adjunct phrases. The query, "he being" returned 46 solutions while the query "him being" had 204 solutions. Based on this information, it seems that the accusative is being used in the gerund-participial as adjunct construction in British English…. (ML)

A common pattern observed among learners is that they identified a linguistic feature that interested them based on their own reflection on usage preferences or observations, a hypothesis concerning a chosen linguistic feature or construction, the collection of data from corpora through experimentation with different search combinations, observation of general and/or special usage based on the data gathered, analysis of the examples, or a generalization or verification drawn from observations and analyses. Through their self-exploration of the corpora, which promotes the noticing of specific grammatical features and languaging through a reflective language log as a mediational tool, students demonstrated a growing ability to perform searches, make observations, conduct analyses, and derive generalizations in their presentations of findings. Although learners expressed some frustration at the beginning stage about the "unintuitiveness," as one student put it, of the query syntax in performing searches, many students expressed how "interesting" or "fun" their explorations ended up being, regardless of whether their findings verified or contradicted their own hypotheses or beliefs.

For the exit survey, 28 out of 30 students responded. Among the 28 students, 27 reported that using corpora helped their learning. The following examples depict common themes (as underlined in the statements below) in students' responses regarding learner engagement and the clarification of personal understanding and assumptions.

(6) *"I used the corpora in every language log, and I <u>became very interested in exploring</u> how people speak English and how the language is used differently by people in different communication situations."* (MG)

(7) *"Often what I presumed would be spoken more frequently was not the case. Using the corpora help[ed] me to check my assumptions...."* (CS)

(8) *"I really enjoyed each exploration throughout the course. They gave me a chance to gain a better understanding of specific grammatical concepts covered in class that I may have otherwise just accepted. I also learned a lot from the explorations where I obtained [what was] contrary to what I had expected...."* (SD)

(9) *"Using the corpora has helped me to have a better, clearer understanding of my own questions. I was able to question previously [sic] ideas I had about particular usage. Subsequently, I was able to gather evidence and obtain new insights on areas that I was unclear about."* (LW)

(10) *"The conclusions I draw using the corpora are based on my limited skills from using the tool and content knowledge. Whether they are correct or not, it is still neat to see that there are definite discrepancies in opinion about the various usages in the English language, and that the corpus can be a useful tool in proving that there may be more than one acceptable answer to our questions...."* (JK)

The one negative response, presented below, should not be neglected, however, because such a response offers a pathway for instructors and researchers to ascertain the limitations of the tool or approach. The response also suggests the need to guard against an assumption that the approach works equally well across all learners, tasks, and contexts (Estling Vannestål & Lindquist 2007, Yoon & Hirvela 2004).

(11) *"I saw no need for using them, and I didn't really enjoy using them. I don't think that they contributed to my learning as much as the discussions and tangents within the class itself did. THAT is where I really got my knowledge. The classes and discussions themselves, rather than the corpora, were what I was really interested in -- people can't argue with a computer screen...."* (CL)

This input from the only participant who was majoring in linguistics also points to the need to be aware of individual differences in preferences for different modalities and mediational means for learning (Huang 2010). As another student put it: "I find that speaking an idea or concept clarifies it better than writing about it. In group discussion, I was able to talk about concepts and, hearing myself, confirm in my own mind that I interpreted and understood correctly or I was able to correct my own misunderstandings." This leads to the question: How would students' learning be enhanced (or not) if individual language logs could be integrated with group discussions, where the discussions follow students' corpus exploration, or the logs proceed before group members have an opportunity to discuss their personal exploration of a topic of interest?

The findings also unexpectedly indicated that all students affirmed, when asked, that the dialogue sessions helped their learning, even though, as indicated in the analysis of the outcomes of NFFEs, resolutions were not always achieved in peer-peer dialogue sessions. Common themes, as underlined below in the following examples from learners' responses, include problem-solving, having fun, gaining different perspectives, clarifying or deepening understanding, sharing responsibility, and enhancing memory/review.

(12) *"Personally speaking, the regular group discussions play a dramatically significant role in my learning.... Everyone felt a shared sense of responsibility for the learning because it affected other teammates. As such, it further stimulated all members' enthusiasm in studying. Finally, the study can be more efficiently [sic] because students can work together to solve problems, and study is no longer boring but is full of fun! I shared what I know and at the same time learned something new from others...."* (TL)

(13) *"For me, having people of different backgrounds in my discussion group allowed me to see different perspectives of the many usages of English from a lot of different angles. Although I had my opinions, it allowed me to see views of other people whose perspectives were just as valid as mine. It also allowed me to see how my perspectives blended and differed with those of people who are younger or older than I am. I think in many ways, as well, the group discussions allowed the three of us involved in the group to form more in-depth perspectives of the thoughts that we already had on a chosen topic, rather than having fragments put into a disorganized thought or a less-than-clear opinion on something that we may not really have a lot of clear ideas on...."* (CH)

(14) *"I like the group discussions very much. It is fun, interactive, and moreover helpful. The debates and arguments among group members encourage us to utilize the knowledge we have learned. In the discussion, we exchange our opinion and findings, learning from other people and come up with integrated solutions. I think most of my reviews for tests are done within group discussion, because when I debate, and accept or reject others' opinions, my memory of that knowledge is enhanced."* (LW)

In retrospect, I think it is important to point out that I have always encouraged learners to focus on exploring different explanations rather than on finding a "correct" answer to their questions. This prompts me to ask: how did that approach to learning, which was fostered early on, affect group members' interactional patterns, discussions, and learning outcomes? Social support (Clarke 2002) provided through the peer-peer dialogue sessions and the opportunity to use the corpus through written language logs may have contributed to the implementation of the CADL approach and warrant further investigation.

The findings demonstrate the efficacy of the CADL approach implemented in this study through the following aspects, some of which have also been supported by other researchers' work (e.g., Bernardini 2002b, Boulton 2009a, Gavioli 2001, Hadley 2002, Kennedy & Miceli 2001, 2002, Yoon 2008):[9]

Generativity

The data from the dialogue sessions, supported by data from the survey, show that students use language to develop, generate, and solidify knowledge within a community of learners. The research-like activities help learners engage in a recursive cycle of learning that consists of identifying topics, performing searches, making observations, conducting analyses, deriving generalization/conclusions, and sharing findings.

Relevance and engagement

The data from dialogue sessions, language logs, and surveys demonstrate that learners engaged in topics and discoveries that are of interest to them.

Independence and interdependence

Learners develop both independence and ownership of the discovery process while learning how to observe language and make generalizations, as demonstrated through learners' presentations of their findings. Learners also develop interdependence as members of a group that share responsibility for a behavioral synchrony that facilitates the mutually responsive interaction patterns that are evidenced in the learners' dialogue sessions and survey.

Noticing

Time and time again, learners shared findings that contradicted what they had expected or predicted, or reported realizing that they were gaining a sharper awareness or becoming critical of the linguistic features in their own and others' spoken interactions or written texts.

6. Limitations and future research

Although this preliminary study provides some very encouraging results, the findings should be considered in light of some potential limitations.

Using an intact class that contains a mixture of first and second languages may present a limitation.[10] When transferring the findings of this study to other English-as-an-additional-language teaching contexts, it is important to consider the particular mix of students' languages and how students were grouped. Having said that, the advantages of using an intact class also need to be taken into account. Using an intact class increases the study's pedagogical authenticity in the sense that courses like the one in the current study are prevalent across universities, and, at the institution where the study took place, such courses attract students from across disciplines, who sign up with the goal of improving their understanding and usage of English.

Some researchers have noted that group dynamics, interactional patterns (cf. pair dynamics in Storch 2001a, 2002), and levels of engagement (e.g., Storch 2008) may play important roles when group members have different proficiency levels (e.g., Kim & McDonough 2008). Others (e.g., Watanabe & Swain 2007: 121), however, have suggested that "proficiency differences do not necessarily affect the nature of peer assistance" in second-language writing; rather, patterns of interaction might matter more in language performance. Although I agree with Kim and McDonough's conclusion about the pedagogical importance of considering "proficiency and pair dynamics in order to create collaborative interactions" (2008: 230), I question whether such traits as "dominant" and "passive" can be considered global (i.e., relatively stable across contexts and tasks) and/or local (i.e., task- and context-dependent). It is also not clear how researchers who used those categories to code pair interactions dealt, for example, with learners who during one week might be identified as "dominant" because of their familiarity with the task or topic at hand, but during another week might be labeled as "passive" because of other situational factor(s) at play. This becomes an even more complex issue when interaction patterns that move beyond dyadic groupings occur, and a myriad of other factors, such as learning styles (e.g., Boulton 2009b), past and ongoing experiences with the tools or language-learning (e.g., Yoon 2008), corpus training (e.g., O'Sullivan & Chambers 2006), and so on come into play.

Patterns of peer-peer triadic interactions using a CADL approach warrant investigation. A substantial body of recent research in second-language acquisition, including studies on interactional modifications, output, and collaboration, has focused on dyadic interaction. The limited studies on *triadic dialogue* (Lemke 1990) in language classroom contexts (i.e., through a succession of three-move exchanges in which the teacher asks a question, a student responds, and the teacher makes some form of closing move) have dealt almost exclusively with *teacher-student* interactions (e.g., Gourlay 2005, Hanada

2005, Nassaji & Wells 2000, Radford, Ireson & Mahon 2006, Walsh, 2002). Research about the dynamics of triadic interactions and the role of triadic dialogue in peer-peer interaction in students' learning experiences is equally important, however, because, in the everyday reality of classrooms, learning does not occur only in dyadic or whole-class interactions. Theory and insights from social networks, which focus on explaining interpersonal mechanisms and social structures that exist among people within a social unit (e.g., Hatala & Fleming 2007), presents a viable framework to study and analyze how the mediational means facilitates CADL. Further examination is needed of peer-peer triadic interactions that take a micro-genetic analytical approach (i.e., tracking an individual learner's evolution in a process *moment by moment* during the development of an individual learner *over time*) (Vygotsky 1987); otherwise, it risks oversimplifying the diverse ways that human interpersonal processes influence individuals' behaviors or actions in pursuit of their goal(s).

Finally, I recognize that individuals' perceptions about the usefulness of a particular learning approach or tool may very well change over time. The survey in this study was conducted two weeks after the course ended and grades had been submitted to (a) obtain more truthful responses from participants (because they knew that whatever they chose to express would not affect their grades for the course), (b) recover information while their memories about using various mediational tools were not too distant, and (c) deal with the potential "power-over relationship" that raises ethical concerns. An understanding of whether, how, and why individual learners' perceptions vary over time may provide important pedagogical insights. Future studies that require learners to think aloud while interacting with corpora would provide important insights about the challenges associated with the learning approach.

Despite its limitations, this preliminary study has served as an important springboard that can lead to several lines of inquiry that have not yet been examined. Further research that includes a comparison group would provide empirical evidence about whether there is a difference between corpus-aided and non-corpus-aided groups in their patterns of interaction, the nature of their dialogues, and their learning outcomes across learners of different proficiency levels. Another question is whether there is a difference between a CADL approach mediated by group dialogue sessions and one mediated by individual written language logs. Such efforts will contribute to the development of a pedagogically sound method that is theoretically informed and empirically substantiated.

7. Conclusion

The potential for using corpora in language learning has attracted considerable attention and interest in recent years. Technological developments have also enhanced the accessibility of corpora to both language learners and instructors. In this study, the integration of dialogue sessions as a mediational means plays a critical role in this CADL approach. The results from this preliminary study point to the need for further investigation about this learning approach mediated by different means in different contexts with different learners. Such investigation may provide instructors and learners with a viable way to begin incorporating corpora that will not be perceived as prohibitive in terms of time, resources, or required knowledge and skills in corpus linguistics. This study used a learner-centered approach, because, after all, students should be at the center of any learning experience. Most importantly, the research and "learning how to learn" skills that learners develop and appropriate through this approach will probably have a greater learning impact than the mastery or understanding of any grammatical point. As one student put it: "Over the length of the course, my ability to use the corpora grew and my understanding also grew stronger. Sometimes I felt that I learned more about researching than I did about any specific topics." At the moment such a realization occurs, language learner and language researcher have become one and the same.

Notes

1 SLA studies that have explored languaging have focused exclusively on collaborative dialogue. One could argue, however, that an individual written language log is another tool of the mind that facilitates languaging, which may be "private" but quasi-social in nature (Vygotsky 1981).

2 This paper focused on NFFEs because the analysis of NFFEs provides clues about the quantity and quality of participants' peer-peer dialogues. Episodes related to corpus use were not included in this paper because they represent a very small percentage of the episodes identified. One may postulate that different sequences and forms of dialoguing activities (e.g., students dialoguing while exploring the corpora as a group or carrying out group dialogue sessions before/after written language logs) may produce different focuses, amounts, and types of LREs in group dialogue sessions.

3 Course description: The course is a functional treatment of English grammar that emphasizes standard English usage from the descriptive perspective. Students will be introduced to the difference between prescriptive and descriptive English, learn the parts of speech and their functional relations, and examine the grammatical system that underlies the way people actually speak and write the language by using data from a variety of texts that include natural discourse in diverse contexts.

4 The *Collins Wordbanks Online English Corpus* (COBUILD) (http://www.collins.co.uk/corpus/CorpusSearch.aspx) currently holds about 56 million words of both written and spoken text. The *British National Corpus* (BNC) (http://www.natcorp.ox.ac.uk/) contains 100 million words from both written and spoken language from a variety of contexts. The *Michigan Corpus of Academic Spoken English* (MICASE) (http://quod.lib.umich.edu/cgi/c/corpus/corpus?c=micase;page=simple) includes 1.8 million words of speech in various academic contexts. Throughout the course, learners were not limited to using the three corpora mentioned above, and they were encouraged to explore other corpora, although none did.

5 As stated earlier, instances of minimal dialoguing were not included. Such limited interaction does not provide sufficient information to understand and describe learners' noticing or to identify learners' development without further studies that involve asking learners to think aloud through stimulated recalls (Gass & Mackey 2000).

6 Overall course performance was not used to compute correlations between NFFE variables and test scores variables because it includes other components, such as marks for attendance, participation, and task completion.

7 Effect size (small effect: $r = .10$, medium effect: $r = .30$, and large effect: $r = .50$).

8 "Grounding" represents the interactive process by which learners present and accept ideas in building common knowledge through communication. Refer to Wilkes-Gibbs's (1997) collaborative theory.

9 For coverage of the pedagogical strategies related to this teaching approach, refer to Huang (2008).

10 In the random grouping of participants for the study, it happened that no group had more than one student who speaks English as his/her first language or who has near-native proficiency.

References

Basturkmen, H., S. Loewen & R. Ellis (2002), 'Metalanguage in focus on form in the communicative classroom', *Language awareness,* 11: 1-13.

Becker, A.L. (1991), 'Language and languaging', *Language and communication,* 11: 33-35.

Bennett, G. (2010), *Using corpora in the language learning classroom: corpus linguistics for teachers*. Ann Arbor: Michigan University Press.

Bernardini, S. (2001), '"Spoilt for choice": a learner explored general language corpora', in: G. Aston (ed.) *Learning with corpora*. Houston (TX): Athelstan. 220-249.

Bernardini, S. (2002a), 'Serendipity expanded: exploring new directions for discovery learning', in: L. Burnard & T. McEnery (eds.) *Rethinking language pedagogy from a corpus perspective*. Frankfurt am Main: Peter Lang. 225-234.

Bernardini, S. (2002b), 'Exploring new directions for discovery learning', in: B. Kettemann & G. Marko (eds.) *Teaching and learning by doing corpus analysis*. Amsterdam: Rodopi. 165-182.

Boulton, A. (2008a), 'Looking for empirical evidence for DDL at lower levels', in: B. Lewandowska-Tomaszczyk (ed.) *Corpus linguistics, computer tools, and applications: state of the art*. Frankfurt: Peter Lang. 581-598.

Boulton, A. (2008b), 'DDL: reaching the parts other teaching can't reach?', in A. Frankenberg-Garcia (ed.) *Proceedings of the 8th teaching and language corpora conference*. Lisbon: Associação de Estudos e de Investigação Cientifíca do ISLA-Lisboa. 38-44.

Boulton, A. (2009a), 'Testing the limits of data-driven learning: language proficiency and training', *ReCALL*, 21(1): 37-54.

Boulton, A. (2009b), 'Corpora for all? Learning styles and data-driven learning', in: M. Mahlberg, V. González-Díaz & C. Smith (eds.) *Proceedings of the 5th corpus linguistics conference*, July 20-23, 2009, University of Liverpool, UK. Available online at: (http://ucrel.lancs.ac.uk/publications /cl2009/)

Boulton, A. (2010), 'Data-driven learning: taking the computer out of the Equation', *Language learning*, 60(3): 534-572.

Chambers, A. (2005), 'Integrating corpus consultation in language studies', *Language learning and technology*, 9(2): 111-125.

Chan, T. & H.-C. Liou (2005), 'Effects of web-based concordancing instruction on EFL students' learning of verb-noun collocations', *Computer assisted language learning*, 18(3): 231-251.

Chen, W., M. Warren & X.-F. Xu (2003), 'The language learner as language researcher: putting corpus linguistics on the timetable', *System*, 31: 173-186.

Chi, M.T.H., M. Bassok, M.W. Lewis, P. Reimann & R. Glaser (1989), 'Self-explanations: how students study and use examples in learning to solve problems', *Cognitive science*, 13: 145-182.

Chi, M.T.H., N. de Leeuw, M. Chiu & C. LaVancher (1994), 'Eliciting self-explanations improves understanding', *Cognitive science*, 18: 439-477.

Clarke, N. (2002), 'Job/work environment factors influencing training transfer within a human service agency: some indicative support for Baldwin and

Ford's transfer climate construct', *International journal of training and development*, 6: 146-62.

Conrad, S. (2005), 'Corpus linguistics and L2 teaching', in: E. Hinkel (ed.) *Handbook of research in second language teaching and learning*. Mahwah (NJ): Lawrence Erlbaum Associates. 393-409.

Conrad, S. (2008), 'Corpus-based research is too complicated to be useful for writing teachers', in: J. Reid, K.S. Folse, C.M. Schuemann, P. Byrd, J. Bunting, K. Hyland, D. Ferris, S. Conrad, S. Cavusgil & P.K. Matsuda *Writing myths: applying second language research to classroom teaching*. Ann Arbor (MI): Michigan University Press. 115-139.

Craik, F.I.M., & R.S. Lockhart (1972), 'Levels of processing: a framework for memory research', *Journal of verbal learning and verbal behaviour*, 11: 671-684.

Deignan, T. (2009), 'Enquiry-based learning: perspectives on practice', *Teaching in higher education*, 14(1): 13-28.

Donato, R. (1994), 'Collective scaffolding in second language learning', in: J.P. Lantolf & G. Appel (eds.) *Vygotskian approaches to second language research*. Norwood (NJ): Ablex. 33-56.

Donato, R. (2004), 'Aspects of collaboration in pedagogical discourse', *Annual review of applied linguistics*, 24: 284-302.

Ellis, R., H. Basturkmen & S. Loewen (2001), 'Preemptive focus on form in the ESL classroom', *TESOL quarterly*, 35(3): 407-432

Estling Vannestål, M. & H. Lindquist (2007), 'Learning English grammar with a corpus: experimenting with concordancing in a university grammar course', *ReCALL*, 19(3): 329–350.

Field, A. (2005), *Discovering statistics using SPSS* (2nd ed.). Thousand Oaks (CA): Sage.

Flowerdew, L. (2008). 'Corpus linguistics for academic literacies mediated through discussion activities', in: D. Belcher & A. Hirvela (eds.) *The oral-literate connection: perspectives on L2 speaking, writing, and other media interactions*. Ann Arbor (MI): The University of Michigan Press. 268-287.

Fortune, A. & D. Thorp (2001), 'Knotted and entangled: new light on the identification, classification and value of language related episodes in collaborative output tasks', *Language awareness*, 10(2&3): 143-160.

Foucou, P.Y. & N. Kübler (2000), 'A web-based environment for teaching technical English', in: L. Burnard & T. McEnery (eds.) *Rethinking language pedagogy from a corpus perspective*. Frankfurt: Peter Lang. 65-74.

Gass, S.M. & A. Mackey (2000), *Stimulated recall methodology in second language research*. Mahwah (NJ): Lawrence Erlbaum.

Gavioli, L. (2001), 'The learner as researcher: introducing corpus concordancing in the classroom', in: G. Aston (ed.) *Learning with corpora*. Houston (TX): Athelstan. 108-137.

Gavioli, L. & G. Aston (2001), 'Enriching reality: language corpora language pedagogy', *ELT journal*, 55(3): 238-246.

Gourlay, L. (2005), 'OK, who's got number one? Permeable triadic dialogue, covert participation and the co-construction of checking episodes', *Language teaching research*, 9(4): 403-422.

Hadley, G. (2002), 'Sensing the winds of change: an introduction to data-driven learning', *RELC Journal*, 33(2): 99-124.

Hanada, M. (2005), 'Some functions of triadic dialogue in the classroom: examples from L2 research', *The Canadian modern language review*, 62(2): 313-333.

Hatala, J. & P. Fleming (2007), 'Making transfer climate visible: utilizing social network analysis to facilitate transfer of training', *Human resource development review*, 6(1): 33-63.

Huang, L.-S. (2008), 'Using guided, corpus-aided discovery learning to generate active learning', *English teaching forum*, 46(4): 20-27.

Huang, L.-S. (2010), 'Do different modalities of reflection matter? An exploration of adult second-language learners' reported strategy use and oral language production', *System*, 38(2): 245-261.

Huang, L.-S. (2011), 'Corpus-aided language learning', *ELT journal*, 65(4). First published on May 5, 2011, doi:10.1093/elt/ccr031.

Hulstijn, J.H. (forthcoming). 'Incidental learning in second language acquisition', in: C.A. Chapelle (ed.) *The encyclopedia of applied linguistics*. Oxford: Wiley-Blackwell.

Hunston, S. (2005), *Corpora in applied linguistics*. Cambridge: Cambridge University Press.

Ickes, W. & R. Gonzalez (1996), "Social' cognition and social cognition: from subjective to the intersubjective', in: J.L. Nye & A.M. Brower (eds.) *What's social about social cognition?* Thousand Oaks (CA): Sage. 285-309.

Jeong, H. & M.T.H. Chi (2007), 'Knowledge convergence and collaborative learning', *Instructional science*, 35: 287-315.

Johns, T. (1991), 'Should you be persuaded: two samples of data-driven learning materials', in: T. Johns & P. King (eds.) *Classroom concordancing (English language research journal 4)*. Birmingham: ELR. 1-16.

Johns, T. (1994), 'From printout to handout: grammar and vocabulary teaching in the context of data-driven learning', in: T. Odlin (ed.) *Perspectives on pedagogical grammar*. Cambridge: Cambridge University Press. 293-313.

Kennedy, C. & T. Miceli (2001), 'An evaluation of intermediate students' approaches to corpus investigation', *Language learning and technology*, 5(3): 77-90.

Kennedy, C. & T. Miceli (2002), 'The CWIC project: developing and using a corpus for intermediate Italian students', in: B. Kettemann & G. Marko (eds.) *Teaching and learning by doing corpus*. Amsterdam: Rodopi. 183-

192.
Kim, Y. & M. McDonough (2008), 'The effect of interlocutor proficiency on the collaborative dialogue between Korean as a second language learners', *Language teaching research*, 12(2): 211-234.
Kuiken, F. & I. Vedder (2002), 'The effect of interaction in acquiring the grammar of a second language', *International journal of educational research,* 37: 343–358.
Lantolf, J. (ed.) (2000), *Sociocultural theory and second language learning.* Oxford: Oxford University Press.
Lantolf, J. (2001), 'Sociocultural theory and second language acquisition', in R.B. Kaplan (ed.) *Handbook of applied linguistics.* Oxford: Oxford University Press. 109-119.
Lantolf, J. & S. Thorne (2006), *Sociocultural theory and the genesis of L2 development.* Oxford: Oxford University Press.
Laufer, B. & J. Hulstijn (2001), Incidental vocabulary acquisition in a second language: the construct of task-induced involvement', *Applied linguistics*, 22: 1-26.
Lave, J. & E. Wenger (1991), *Situated learning: legitimate peripheral participation*. Cambridge: Cambridge University Press.
Leech, G. (1997), 'Teaching and language corpora: a convergence', in: A. Wichmann, S. Fligelstone, A.M. McEnery & G. Knowles (eds.) *Teaching and language corpora*. London: Longman. 1-23.
Leeser, M.J. (2004), 'Learner proficiency and focus on form during collaborative dialogue', *Language teaching research*, 8: 55–81.
Lemke, J. (1990), *Talking science: language, learning and values*. Norwood (NJ): Ablex.
Lockhart, R.S. & F.I.M. Craik (1990), 'Levels of processing: a retrospective commentary on a framework for memory research', *Canadian journal of psychology*, 44: 87-112.
Matusov, E. (1996), 'Intersubjectivity without agreement', *Mind, culture, and activity*, 3(1): 25-45.
Nassaji, H. & G. Wells (2000). 'What's the use of 'triadic dialogue'? An investigation of teacher-student interaction', *Applied linguistics*, 21(3): 374-406.
Ohta, A.S. (2000), 'Rethinking interaction in SLA: developmentally appropriate assistance in the zone of proximal development and the acquisition of L2 grammar', in: J.P. Lantolf (ed.) *Sociocultural theory and second language learning*. Oxford: Oxford University Press. 51-78.
O'Sullivan, Í. & A. Chambers (2006), 'Learners' writing skills in French: corpus consultation and learner evaluation', *Journal of second language writing,* 15(1): 49-68.
Radford, J., J. Ireson & M. Mahon (2006), 'Triadic dialogue in oral communication tasks: what are the implications for language learning?',

Language and education, 20(3): 191-209.

Reppen, R. (2010), *Using corpora in the language classroom*. Cambridge: Cambridge University Press.

Rogoff, B. (1998), 'Cognition as a collaborative process', in: W. Damon (ed.) *Handbook of child psychology*. New York: Wiley. 679-744.

Rommetveit, R. (1979), 'On the architecture of intersubjectivity', in: R. Rommetveit & R.M. Blaker (eds.) *Studies of language, thought, and verbal communication*. New York: Academic Press. 93-108.

Roschelle, J. (1992), 'Learning by collaborating: convergent conceptual change', *Journal of the learning sciences*, 2(3): 235-276.

Schmidt, R. (1990), 'The role of consciousness in second language learning'. *Applied linguistics*, 11: 129–158.

Sinclair, J. (2004), *How to use corpora in language teaching*. Amsterdam: Benjamins

Smagorinsky, P. (1998), 'Thinking and speech and protocol analysis'. *Mind, culture, and activity*, 5: 157-177.

Smith, S., A. Chen & A. Kilgarriff. (2008), 'A corpus query tool for SLA: learning Mandarin with the help of SketchEngine', in: B. Lewandowska-Tomaszczyk (ed.) *Corpus linguistics, computer tools, and applications: state of the art*. Frankfurt: Peter Lang. 673-686.

Storch, N. (2001a), 'How collaborative is pair work? ESL tertiary students composing in pairs', *Language teaching research*, 5: 29-53.

Storch, N. (2001b), *An investigation into the nature of pair work in an ESL classroom and its effect on grammatical development*. Doctoral dissertation, University of Melbourne.

Storch, N. (2002), 'Patterns of interaction in ESL pair work', *Language learning*, 52: 119-158.

Storch, N. (2004), 'Using activity theory to explain differences in patterns of dyadic interactions in an ESL class', *The Canadian modern language review*, 60: 457-480.

Storch, N. (2008), 'Metatalk in a pair work activity: level of engagement and implications for language development', *Language awareness*, 17(2): 95-114.

Swain, M. (2006), 'Languaging, agency and collaboration in advanced second language learning', in: H. Byrnes (ed.) *Advanced language learning: thecontributions of Halliday and Vygotsky*. London: Continuum. 95-108.

Swain, M. & S. Lapkin (1998), 'Interaction and second language learning: two adolescent French immersion students working together', *The modern language journal*, 83: 320-338.

Swain, M. & S. Lapkin (2002), 'Talking it through: two French immersion learners' response to reformulation', *International journal of educational research*, 37: 285-304.

Vygotsky, L.S. (1978), *Mind and society: the development of higher mental processes.* Cambridge: Harvard University Press.

Vygotsky, L.S. (1981), 'The genesis of higher mental functions', in: J.V. Wertsch (ed.) *The concept of activity in Soviet psychology*. New York: Sharpe. 144-188.

Vygotsky, L.S. (1986), *Thought and language.* Cambridge (MA): MIT Press.

Vygotsky. L.S. (1987), *The collected works of L.S. Vygotsky. Volume 1. Thinking and speaking.* New York: Plenum Press.

Walsh, S. (2002), 'Construction or obstruction: teacher talk and learner involvement in the EFL classroom', *Language teaching research*, 6(1): 3-23.

Watanabe, Y. & M. Swain (2007), 'Effects of proficiency differences and patterns of pair interaction on second language learning: collaborative dialogue between adult ESL learners', *Language teaching research*, 11: 121–142.

Wells, G. (2000), 'Dialogic inquiry in education: building on the legacy of Vygotsky', in: C.D. Lee & P. Smagorinsky (eds.) *Vygotskian perspectives on literacy research.* New York: Cambridge University Press. 51-85.

Wilkes-Gibbs, D. (1997), 'Studying language use as collaboration', in: G. Kasper & E. Kellerman (eds.) *Communication strategies: psycholinguistic and sociolinguistic perspectives*. New York: Longman. 238-274.

Williams, J. (2008), 'The speaking-writing connection in second language and academic literacy development', in: D. Belcher & A. Hirvela (eds.) *The oral-literate connection: perspectives on L2 speaking, writing, and other media interactions.* Ann Arbor (MI): The University of Michigan Press. 10-25.

Yoon, H. (2008), 'More than a linguistic reference: the influence of corpus technology on L2 academic writing', *Language and technology*, 12(2): 31-48.

Yoon, H. & A. Hirvela (2004), 'ESL student attitudes toward corpus use in L2 Writing', *Journal of second language writing*, 13(4): 257-283.

Appendix A

Sample test questions

1. Reflect on our class discussions and your look into the corpora. Comment on the alternation between the use of singular and plural verb agreement for the following: (a) *neither/either* + NP... *nor/or* + NP; (b) *none of/no* + NP. Be sure to provide examples in your explanation.
2. Reflecting on our class discussions and your look into the corpora, explain and comment on the usage of the following constructions: (a) subjunctive mandative, (b) "should" mandative, and (c) covert mandative. Be sure to provide examples in your explanation.
3. Explain the syntactic differences between "integrated" and "supplementary" clauses in descriptive grammar. How do they differ from prescriptive grammar's "restrictive" and "non-restrictive" clauses? Be sure to provide examples in your explanation.
4. (a) Indicate the following examples as having stranded prepositions or fronted prepositions by circling S for stranded prepositions and F for fronted preposition. (b) Revise the stranded prepositions in the following sentences to corresponding fronted prepositions and fronted prepositions to stranded prepositions where possible. (c) Reflecting on our class discussions and your look into the corpora, comment on the use of stranded and fronted prepositions.

   a. S / F The place we are traveling to is so remote that we will need a local guide to take us there. →
   b. S / F This is the article to which the author was referring in his highly acclaimed book. →
   c. S / F He is the only person that everyone in the company can talk to. →
   d. S / F In what way did the career counselor help you? →
   e. S / F I'd like to share with you the invaluable documents which I came across. →

Appendix B

Symbols used in transcribing the oral data

Symbol	Meaning
.	Completion (with falling intonation)
,	A brief, natural pause
?	A question (with rising intonation)
?,	Uncertainty (with rising intonation, but is weaker than a '?')
!	Surprised intonation
<characters in chevrons>	Transcriber's guess; transcription doubt
(??? in parentheses)	Non-transcribable
[characters in square brackets]	Description of other non-verbal behavior or information
//	Overlapping talk
(……)	Long hesitation; pauses longer than five seconds
(…)	Short hesitation; pauses less than three to five seconds
-	Discontinued utterances
=	Continuous utterances

A novel, web-based, parallel concordancer for use in the ESL/EFL classroom

Laurence Anthony[1], *Kiyomi Chujo*[2] *and Kathryn Oghigian*[1]

[1]Waseda University
[2]Nihon University

Abstract

To date, the use of parallel concordancers in the classroom has been a largely unexplored area. As a result, there are few guidelines on the design of these tools or the functions they should offer. Also, the number of fully-developed parallel concordance tools is surprisingly few, and most of these are designed for use by corpus linguists and translators. In this paper, we describe a novel, web-based, parallel concordancer designed specifically for use by beginner-level second and foreign language learners of English. The software is built using standard web application tools, such as Linux, Apache, MySQL, and PHP, and thus can run in most university server environments. It is also designed on a similar architecture to the Google search engine, allowing it to work comfortably on very large corpora of hundreds of millions of words. To enable the smooth processing of both English and non-English texts, the concordancer is built to Unicode standards. Its internal token definition settings also employ Unicode character classes meaning that no cumbersome user-defined settings are necessary. Preliminary results show that the new software is considerably faster and easier to use than standard desktop parallel concordance programs. Also, because the tool is web-based, it can be accessed outside of class time, thus allowing students more time for hypothesis-verification and production activities.

1. Introduction

In recent years, an increasing number of studies have reported on the success of data driven learning (DDL) approaches in the teaching of foreign languages, mainly with advanced level students in a computer laboratory (Kennedy & Miceli 2001; Hunston 2002; Bernardini 2004; Granath 2009). In addition, success with lower level students has also been demonstrated. For example, Boulton (2008) shows that beginner-level learners can make substantial gains using paper-based DDL materials. Part of the success, he argues, is the removal of the computer software, which can be a major source of frustration, especially when the students are technophobic. One disadvantage of this approach, however, is the time it takes to develop the materials. Boulton reports that each item in his own study took half a day to prepare. This is slightly less time than the eight hours reported by Johns (1991) to create a DDL worksheet, but still impossibly long for most busy teachers.

Chujo and Oghigian (2008) have also reported on the success of DDL with beginner-level university students, but adopt quite a different approach. Here, students first form hypotheses about the target language through inductive corpus-based exercises using an English-Japanese newspaper corpus (Utiyama & Isahara 2003) together with a standalone parallel concordance tool (Barlow 2010a). Next, they receive explicit explanations from the teacher to confirm or correct their hypotheses, and then apply what they have learned in follow-up exercises inside and outside the classroom. In view of the work of Boulton (2008) described above, it might seem counter-intuitive to introduce a complex tool (i.e., a parallel concordancer) into the beginner-level language classroom. However, Chujo and Oghigian argue that the presentation of highly contextualized information from newspaper texts together with first language translations allows students to more easily focus on target items and manage the input. In fact, results from various trials over a five-year period confirm that this approach produces significant gains in students' understanding of grammar and vocabulary (Chujo 2008; Chujo et al. 2009). On the other hand, when students were asked about their views on this approach, many did suggest areas in which the current software could be improved, especially in regard to usability issues. This is not surprising considering that the tool used was developed primarily for corpus linguists and translators.

In this paper, we address the software issues raised by both students and teachers of Chujo and Oghigian's DDL course by proposing a novel, web-based, parallel concordancer. The software is unique in several ways. First, it is specifically designed for use by second and foreign language learners of English both inside and outside the classroom. As a result, it implements a simple, familiar, search engine-like interface, with minimum options and user settings. It is also built using standard web-application development tools (Linux, Apache, MySQL, PHP) and thus can be installed on almost all university server systems with little effort and limited cost. Second, the software is built on a similar architecture to most search engines, including Google, allowing it to work comfortably on very large corpora of hundreds of millions of words (Brin & Page 1998). Although the parallel newspaper corpus currently being used in the DDL classroom is only a fraction of this size at around 3.5 million words, the value of investigating an alternative architecture for large web-based corpus data is high. Finally, to enable the smooth processing of both English and Japanese texts, the software is built to Unicode standards, and its internal token definition settings also employ Unicode character classes, meaning that no cumbersome user-defined settings are necessary. No known mainstream standalone parallel concordancer has this ability.

In the following section, we will first outline the DDL course developed by Chujo and Oghigian (2008). Then, we will report on the students' performance gains and summarize their feedback on ways to improve the concordance software. In Section 3, we will detail the main features of the proposed web-based parallel concordancer, in terms of usability, accessibility, and scalability/speed. In Section 4, we will report on a preliminary survey given to students following initial tests of the software in the classroom. In Section 5, we will discuss our future aims for the software before making our conclusions.

2. DDL for beginner-level EFL/ESL learners

2.1 Course overview

Chujo and Oghigian's (2008) DDL course was developed for first year university engineering students at Nihon University, Japan. This course was initially implemented as a four-week case study in 2004, but has been expanded and modified in each subsequent year. The present study describes the course as it was implemented in 2009. In this year, the course was comprised of 20 classes that were held once a week for ninety minutes. Forty-two students took part in the course, with an English proficiency range from 290 to 520 on the *Test of English for International Communication* (TOEIC). This is equivalent to a *Test of English as a Foreign Language* (TOEFL) computer-based test score of below 137. In view of the beginner-level ability of the students, the course focused on developing receptive and productive knowledge of basic grammar and vocabulary items.

A four-step teaching procedure was adopted. In step 1, students identified basic grammar and vocabulary patterns in a Japanese-English parallel newspaper corpus (Utiyama & Isahara 2003) using the *ParaConc* parallel concordance program (Barlow 2010a). To overcome difficulties in the operation and understanding of the software output, students followed worksheets with carefully crafted exercises that guided them in the use of concordance program. An example worksheet is shown in Figure 1.

In step 2, students reported their findings to the class and the teacher provided further explanations of key patterns and rules. In this way, the students' own hypotheses could be confirmed or corrected. Then, in step 3, students were given follow-up homework exercises that involved hypothesis testing and production tasks. These were designed to internalize the key items. Finally, in step 4, the teacher gave feedback on the homework tasks in the following lesson.

2.2 Student performance

As reported in an earlier study (Chujo, Anthony & Oghigian 2009), students made significant gains in their knowledge of basic grammar items and vocabulary. Comparing pre- and post-test scores on vocabulary, word classes, derivations, countable and uncountable nouns, the structure of noun and verb phrases, and TOEIC-type questions, students showed gains from 3% to 33%. They were also shown to have higher gains than a comparable class that did not use the DDL approach.

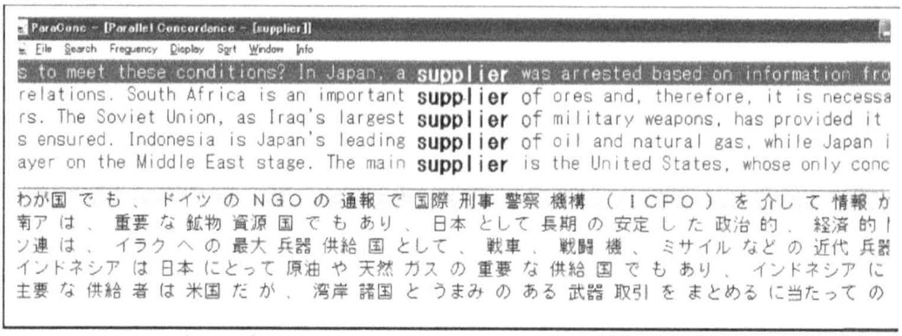

Choose five NPs containing ***supplier*** and write them below

	Determiner	Pre-modifier	Head Noun	Post-modifier	
1	( )	( )	supplier	( )	( )
2	( )	( )	supplier	( )	( )
3	( )	( )	supplier	( )	( )
4	( )	( )	supplier	( )	( )
5	( )	( )	supplier	( )	( )

Figure 1: Sample worksheet for identifying noun phrases in a Japanese-English parallel newspaper corpus

2.3 Student feedback

Students were asked to complete a survey regarding the course and, more specifically, the materials and corpus software used in the classroom. In general the responses about the course were positive, with over 70% of students stating that it was useful for grammar and vocabulary learning. The DDL worksheets, however, were deemed less useful with only 53% of students evaluating them in a positive way (Chujo, Anthony & Oghigian 2009). To further investigate this aspect of the course, both teachers and students were asked how the DDL experience could be improved. Here, three problem areas in software design were highlighted: usability, accessibility, and scalability/speed.

First, students expressed the need for an improved graphical user interface (GUI) to the software. Common problems included Japanese characters appearing garbled, font sizes being too small, and the long and complex procedure needed to initialize the software to process the corpus correctly. Students also mentioned that the search interface could be improved, with one student stating that "It required time to get used to the search operation". This is not surprising considering that the tool was originally designed for researchers and thus includes many high-level features that would rarely, if ever, be used by beginner-level students.The second problem was that of accessibility. One of the greatest limitations of the software was that it was a commercial standalone desktop tool that could only be installed in the university computer laboratory. As a result, students were unable to install it on their own computers and use it as part of follow-up homework exercises. As one student commented, "We can't use the software at home". Thus, both teachers and students felt a strong need for a more accessible web-based software tool that could be accessed freely anytime and anywhere.

A third issue related to the scalability and speed of the software. Because the Japanese-English parallel newspaper corpus used in the course was a moderate size of approximately 3.5 million words, the parallel concordancer could generate most results within just a few seconds. However, with new corpora of many millions of words becoming available each year, teachers of the course felt a need for software that could comfortably handle larger corpora and produce results almost instantaneously.

3. Design and development of *AntWebConc-Bilingual*

To address the issues raised by the teachers and students of the course described above, we started developing an alternative web-based parallel concordance tool, named *AntWebConc-Bilingual* in 2009. A screenshot of the latest version of the software is shown in Figure 2.

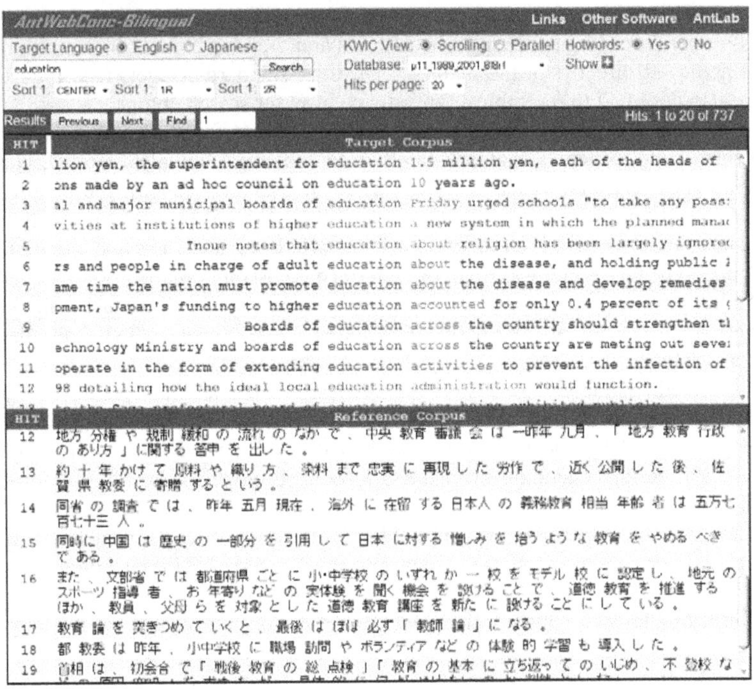

Figure 2: Screenshot of the web-based, parallel concordancer *AntWebConc-Bilingual*

The software is a freeware, open-source program written in the PHP 4 programming language using the ActiveState Komodo Integrated Development Environment (2010). The software is designed to run on a Linux operating system with an Apache web server and MySQL database. It is possible, however, to run the software on both Windows and Macintosh operating systems. To allow a fair comparison with comparable desktop tools, the performance tests described in section 3.3.2 were carried out on a Windows 7 operating system.

3.1 Software usability

To address the issues of usability mentioned by students, *AntWebConc-Bilingual* is designed specifically for use by novice learners rather than corpus linguists. Thus, almost all start-up settings are hardcoded, and users need only to select the target corpus and target language before performing a search.

Lonfils and Vanparys (2001) state that pull-down menus and pop-up windows can be confusing to both novice and expert users. They also recommend that software tools should have familiar buttons, lists, window adjusters and other interface widgets as this will improve their ease-of-use and intuitive operation. Following their advice, the interface to *AntWebConc-Bilingual* is designed so that common operations (e.g., entering search terms and viewing context information) can be achieved directly on the main screen using standard widgets (see Figure 3). It is also designed to resemble a typical web browser search engine.

Sommerville (2004) explains that good user interfaces should not only adopt terms and concepts that are familiar to the user, but also provide for different types of users. To cater for a variety of user preferences, the parallel KWIC concordance lines in *AntWebConc-Bilingual* can be viewed in two different ways: 1) in two fixed-height scrollable windows, and 2) in two variable-height non-scrolling windows. Also, the interface adjusts automatically for larger (or smaller) browser font sizes, and the entire theme of the interface can be swapped by selecting an alternative Cascading Style Sheet (CSS) from the browser menu bar.

Garbled characters in a software interface, such as those reported by students in the course, are usually the result of mismatches between the text encoding assumed by the software itself and that of the original corpus. For example, the default encoding of characters on an English Microsoft Windows operating system will be Latin 1 (cp 1252). However, the default on a Japanese Microsoft Windows operating system will be Shift-JIS (cp 932). To deal with this problem, all corpus data was re-encoded into the Unicode UTF8 encoding (The Unicode Consortium 2006), and the software is designed to process this encoding by default. In addition, Unicode character classes are used to define word tokens in the software, instead of ad hoc approaches such as hardcoded lists of characters that should *not* be included in the token definition. Adopting this design allowed us to simplify the interface and improve the user experience by providing noise-free KWIC concordance results.

3.2 Software accessibility

By developing the software as a freeware, web-based tool, it is immediately more accessible to students who require access in both the university computer laboratory and also in their homes. All teachers need to do is provide the students

Figure 3: Screenshot of *AntWebConc-Bilingual* showing more context for a KWIC concordance line and a choice of reference corpus keywords ("hotwords") to be highlighted.

with a login ID and password. In addition, the software is fully compliant with the HTML 4.01 standard and has been tested on all modern browsers, including the latest versions of Internet Explorer, Firefox, Chrome, Safari, and Opera. Finally, the software is developed in accordance with the Section 508 guidelines provided by the US government, which are designed to eliminate barriers to information technology for people with disabilities (W3C 2010).

3.3 Software scalability/speed

The English-Japanese parallel corpus used in the course is only approximately 3.5 million words in size. As a result, many alternative database architectures could have been used to implement the software.

One approach would be to design the software so that it could process raw text files. This is a common approach adopted by popular standalone desktop concordancers, such as *ParaConc*, *MonoConc Pro* (Barlow 2010b), *Wordsmith Tools* (Scott 2010), and *AntConc* (Anthony 2010). Although this design choice enables the tools to be highly flexible and operate immediately on a new corpus, it also means that they require a full-text scan of the corpus to find matches to the search criteria. This tends to limit the speed of the software and also puts a functional upper limit on the size of the corpus at around 100 million words.

A more common approach adopted by most web-based corpus tool designers is to use an indexed corpus. For example, this is the approach used by Heid (2010) for the IMS Corpus Workbench and by Davies (2010) for the Corpus of Contemporary American English. Indexes tend to allow very fast searching and sorting of results, even when the corpus is heavily annotated. The downside to using indexes is that they can take many hours to create and thus prevent immediate access to the target corpus. Of course, for a web-based system, this is usually not an issue because the index-building process can be performed before making the system available to users. Unfortunately, the details of different corpus indexing approaches are often only hinted at by their developers, making it difficult to apply similar strategies to new corpus databases.

Here, an indexed corpus was also adopted for the proposed parallel concordance tool. However, due to the problems involved in engineering one of the architectures used in current systems, an attempt was made to implement the architecture following principles that are well established in the field of Information Retrieval. Namely, the software was built on a standard Web search engine architecture, using a postings list and a merging algorithm, described below. This meant that the software would be scalable to handle corpora of many hundreds of millions of words and also process them at speeds in the order of fractions of seconds.

3.3.1 Database architecture

The first step in the processing of corpus data for the system was to create an SQL table ("corpora") that stored a unique ID number and the associated text in both English and Japanese, as shown in Table 1.

Table 1: SQL table storing corpus data

ID	*English text*	*Japanese text*
1	Europe is carrying out vigorously the Growth Initiative agreed in Edinburgh and strengthened in Copenhagen.	欧州 は 、 エディンバラ において 合意 され 、 コペンハーゲン において 強化 された 成長 イニシアチブ を 精力 的 に 実行 しつつ ある 。
2	We recognize the importance of improved market access for economic progress in Russia.	我々 は 、 ロシア の 経済 発展 にとって 、改善 された 市場 アクセス が 重要 である こと を 認識 する 。
...	...	...

The next step was to create two SQL tables ("eng_postings" and "jpn_postings") that stored inverted indexes of all words in both the English and Japanese texts together with an associated text ID, as well as the word position and character offset in the text (see Table 2). In Information Retrieval terminology, this is typically called a postings list (Manning, Raghavan & Schütze 2008).

Table 2: Postings list examples

English word	*record (text id, word position, character offset)*
Partnerships	3,0,12
market	2,6,46
the	1,5,38 2,2,16 4,6,47 5,8,54
Europe	1,0,7
unconstitutionality	4,9,79
...	...

Japanese word	*record (text id, word position, character offset)*
エディンバラ	1,5,14
で	2,30,49 3,4,8 3,24,47
発展	2,10,18
ね	5,20,32
ロシア	2,4,10
...	...

The final step in the processing was to create a script that found postings list entries that matched the search criteria. Once located, it would then be a trivial task to display the associated text matching the text ID by pulling the relevant data from the original "corpora" table.

One cautionary note regards matching search criteria in the postings list when multiple word units are specified, e.g., *the importance*. The postings list for individual words can be potentially very long, involving thousands (or millions) of entries. Thus, an efficient merge algorithm is necessary to prevent a huge number of redundant comparisons from being made. Take, for example, the postings lists for *the* and *importance*. A poor performance algorithm would compare each record for *the* against each record for *importance*, as shown in Figure 4.

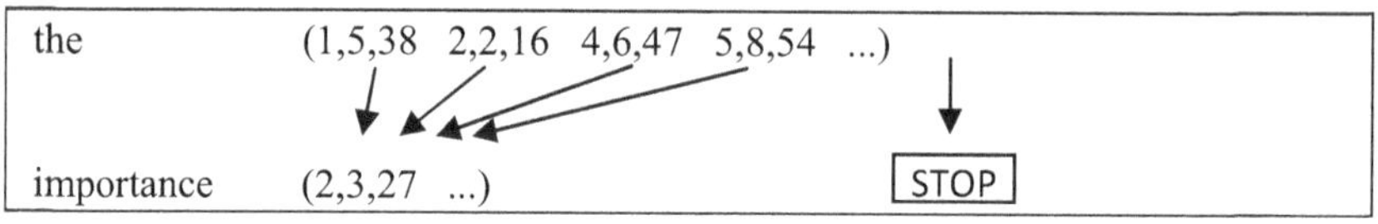

Figure 4: Inefficient merge algorithm for finding *the importance* (not used)

However, a much more efficient algorithm can step through each record in both lists, tracking which comparisons are necessary and terminating when no further comparisons are needed (see Figure 5). Such an algorithm is widely used in Information Retrieval, as reported by Manning, Raghavan & Schütze (2008) and illustrated in Figure 6.

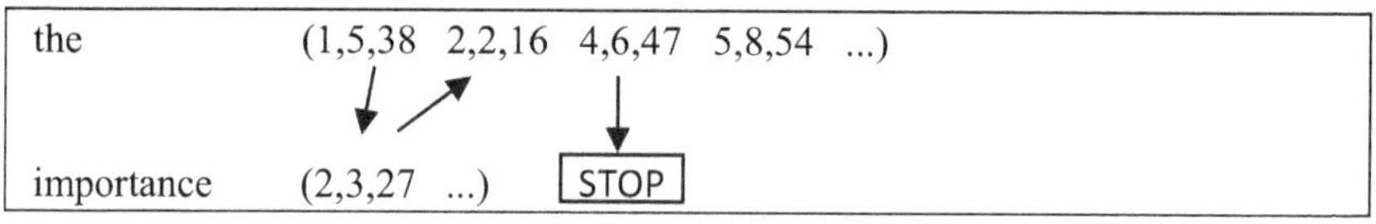

Figure 5: Efficient merge algorithm for finding *the importance*

```
INTERSECT(p1, p2)
    answer ← <>
    while p₁ ≠NIL and p₂ ≠ NIL
    do if docID(p₁) = docID(p₂)
    then ADD(answer, docID(p₁))
    p1 ← next(p₁)
     p2 ← next(p₂)
    else if docID(p₁) < docID(p₂)
    then p₁ ← next(p₁)
    else p₂ ← next(p₂)
    return answer
```

Figure 6: Pseudo code for the intersection of two postings lists *p*1 and *p*2 (adapted from Manning, Raghavan & Schütze 2008: 42)

3.3.2 System performance

The performance of *AntWebConc-Bilingual* was compared against that of *ParaConc*, as well as the monolingual *AntConc* concordancer (Anthony 2010). All tests were carried out on a desktop computer with an Intel Core 2 Duo 3.16 GHz processor running a 64-bit Windows 7 operating system with 8 GB of RAM memory. The English-Japanese corpus used for the tests was the same as that used in the DDL course. Details are given in Table 3 below.

Table 3: Corpus used for performance testing of *AntWebConc-Bilingual* [Indexing time: 426 sec.]

corpus	*total tokens*	*total types*
p11-1989-2001	English: 3,596,971 Japanese: 4,041,042	English: 47,362 Japanese: 52,327

The results in Table 4 show that *AntWebConc-Bilingual* clearly outperformed the other two concordancer tools, cutting processing times by nearly 50 times for single-word searches. *AntConc* and *ParaConc* were roughly equivalent in their processing times, which is not surprising as they both rely on a linear scan through the complete corpus texts before producing results.

Table 4: Performance measures for *AntWebConc-Bilingual, ParaConc, AntConc*

search term	*concordancer*	*time (sec.)*	*hit count*
the	AntConc	177	288,393
	ParaConc	209	287,461
	AntWebConc	4.47	288,393
education	AntConc	6	1,445
	ParaConc	3	1,433
	AntWebConc	0.02	1,445
apology	AntConc	6	100
	ParaConc	2	99
	AntWebConc	0.01	100
the best	AntConc	6	199
	ParaConc	2	194
	AntWebConc	5.14	199
Education Ministry	AntConc	6	176
	ParaConc	2	151
	AntWebConc	0.44	176
make an apology	AntConc	6	6
	ParaConc	2	6
	AntWebConc	1.07	6

The performance increase for *AntWebConc-Bilingual* was less dramatic in the case of multiple-word units, suggesting that further improvements to the merge algorithm are necessary. In particular, a search for *the best*, which involved merging postings lists for the most frequent word in the corpus, *the*, with that for a much less frequent word, *best*, resulted in a slow response of over five seconds.

Note that different hit counts recorded by the three software tools were the result of varying token definitions being implemented by the software. In *AntConc* and *AntWebConc*, the token definitions were based on a standard set of Unicode character classes determined by the Unicode Consortium (2006) for each language in the world. In the case of *ParaConc*, tokens were defined as characters that lie between a set of delimiting characters, such as commas, semicolons, and periods.

4. Preliminary in-class testing of *AntWebConc-Bilingual*

In January of 2010, a prototype version of the proposed software was tested by 42 students of the DDL course, who had previous experience using *ParaConc* for two semesters. The students were asked to rate both the speed and ease of use of the new software and also make suggestions for improving the software further. A summary of the results is shown in Table 5.

Table 5: Summary of survey responses on first impressions of using *AntWebConc-Bilingual* in the classroom

	YES ←				→No
	5	**4**	**3**	**2**	**1**
Was the software fast compared with *ParaConc*?	64%	24%	5%	5%	2%
Was the software easy to use compared with *ParaConc*?	21%	28%	31%	14%	5%
Selected positive comments					
The software response has improved.					
The speed is much faster and the interface is simple and easy to use.					
Selected negative comments					
It would be nice to have the colour highlighting as in ParaConc.					
It would be better if the search term was highlighted as in ParaConc.					
I would like the translation of the search term to be highlighted in Japanese.					
I think it would be easier to understand if the part-of-speech of words were highlighted.					
It is difficult to understand because the entire sentence of the English corpus does not appear.					
I would like the menu to appear in Japanese.					

The results suggested that students were generally happy with the speed of the software, rating it highly against *ParaConc*. However, some felt that it was not as easy to use as *ParaConc*. One reason for this could be that they had already been exposed to *ParaConc* for one year of study, and thus were more familiar with its operation. Indeed, the student giving *AntWebConc-Bilingual* the lowest rating for ease-of-use wrote "Although it is difficult to use now, once I get use to it (sic), it will probably be easier to use than ParaConc".

Most of the lower ratings given to *AntWebConc-Bilingual* for ease-of-use appeared to stem from its lack of colour highlighting of search terms in the KWIC display and its inability to show the sentence of target corpus hits. This was a known issue at the time of the trial and was subsequently addressed. Another issue was the inability to highlight the translation of the search term in the reference corpus. *ParaConc* includes a hotwords feature that achieves something similar to this by highlighting keywords in the reference corpus display (Barlow 2010a). Again, this was a known issue at the time of the trial and a similar hotwords feature was subsequently added (see Figures 2 and 3).

5. Discussion and future work

Boulton (2008) argues convincingly that concordance tools can be a major source of frustration for novice users of computers in EFL/ESL classrooms. This view is supported by Farr (2008), who found that technical difficulties associated with using concordance tools continued to trouble her students throughout a two-semester course. Also, in the DDL course described here, students reported on the technical difficulties associated with using a parallel concordance tool. These responses, however, are not unexpected. It should be remembered that the current monolingual and parallel concordance tools available to teachers and course developers have been designed primarily for corpus linguists and translators who are interested in *analyzing* languages, as opposed to *learning* them.

Clearly, much work needs to be done to develop more user-friendly monolingual and parallel concordance tools specifically for use by learners. In this study, a novel, web-based parallel concordance tool, *AntWebConc-Bilingual*, has been proposed. The database architecture for the tool is designed according to well-established principles from the field of Information Retrieval, and resembles that used by Web search engines such as Google. This results in very fast response times compared with commercial tools such as *ParaConc*. Also, the software has a greatly simplified interface, which was positively evaluated by students on the course in terms of ease of use. Some students suggested further improvements, such as highlighting of translations of search terms in the results window. Although the latest version of the software includes a hotwords feature, an automated detection tool to locate matching pairs in parallel corpora with high accuracy is now being developed. Also, further work on intuitive displays of KWIC concordance lines in a browser interface is now being carried out.

Acknowledgment

This research was funded by a Grant-in-aid for Scientific Research (21320107) from the Japan Society for the Promotion of Science and Ministry of Education, Science, Sports and Culture.

References

ActiveState (2010), *Komodo Integrated Development Environment* [computer software]. Vancouver, Canada.

Anthony, L. (2010), *AntConc* [computer software]. Tokyo: Waseda University.

Barlow, M. (2010a), *ParaConc* [computer software]. Houston (TX) Athelstan.

Barlow, M. (2010b), *Monoconc Pro* [computer software]. Houston Athelstan.

Bernardini, S. (2004), 'Corpora in the classroom: an overview and some reflections on future developments', in: J. Sinclair (ed.) *How to use corpora in language teaching*. Amsterdam: John Benjamins. 15-36.

Boulton, A. (2008), 'DDL: reaching the parts other teaching can't reach?', in A. Frankenberg-Garcia (ed.) *Proceedings of the 8th teaching and language corpora conference*. Lisbon: Associação de Estudos e de Investigação Científica do ISLA-Lisboa. 38-44.

Brin, S. and L. Page (1998), 'The anatomy of a large-scale hypertextual web search engine'. Available online at http://infolab.stanford.edu/~backrub/google.html (accessed 31 May 2010).

Chujo, K. (2008), 'Corpus ni motozuita syllabus design to sono jissen' (Corpus-based syllabus design and ELT), in: J. Nakamura and S. Hotta (eds.) *Corpus to eigo kyouiku no setten* (*A point where corpus and English education meet*). Tokyo: Shohakusha. 65-88.

Chujo, K., L. Anthony and K. Oghigian (2009), 'DDL for the EFL classroom: effective uses of a Japanese-English parallel corpus and the development of a learner-friendly, online parallel concordance', in: M. Mahlberg, V. González-Díaz and C. Smith (eds.) *Proceedings of the corpus linguistics conference, CL2009*. Liverpool University of Liverpool. Available online at: http://ucrel.lancs.ac.uk/publications/cl2009/.

Chujo, K. and K. Oghigian (2006), 'Discovering grammar in the beginning-level DDL EFL classroom', *Proceedings of the 7th international conference on teaching and language corpora (TaLC),* Paris, France: Department of Intercultural Studies and Applied Languages, University Paris 7 Denis Diderot. 168-170.

Chujo, K. and K. Oghigian (2008), 'A DDL approach to learning noun and verb phrases in the beginner level EFL classroom', in: A. Frankenberg-Garcia, T. Rkibi, M.R. Cruz, R. Carvalho, C. Direito & D. Santos-Rosa (eds.) *Proceedings of TaLC 8 - Lisbon, 8th Teaching and Language Corpora Conference, 3-6 July 2008*. Lisbon: Associação de Estudos e de Investigação do ISLA-Lisboa. 65-71.

Chujo, K., A. Uchibori, C. Nishigaki and K. Miyazaki (2009), 'Corpus wo riyoushita kiso bunpou shidou to sono hyouka (Corpus-based basic grammar teaching and its evaluation)', *Journal of the college of industrial technology, Nihon University,* 42: 53-65.

Davies, M. (2010), 'The corpus of contemporary American English'. Available online at: http://www.americancorpus.org/.

Farr, F. (2008), 'Evaluating the use of corpus-based instruction in a language teacher education context: perspectives from the users', *Language awareness*, 17: 25-43.

Granath, S. (2009), 'Who benefits from learning how to use corpora?', in: K. Aijmer (ed.) *Corpora and language teaching*. Amsterdam: John Benjamins. 47-65.

Heid, U. (2010), 'IMS Corpus Workbench (CWB)', Available online at: http://www.ims.uni-stuttgart.de/projekte/CorpusWorkbench/.

Hunston, S. (2002), *Corpora in applied linguistics*. Cambridge: Cambridge University Press.

Johns (1991), 'Should you be persuaded: two examples of data-driven learning', in: T. Johns and P. King (eds.) *Classroom concordancing. English language research journal*, 4: 1-16.

Kennedy, C. and T. Miceli (2001), 'An evaluation of intermediate students' approaches to corpus investigation', *Language learning & technology*, 5(3): 77-90.

Lonfils, C. and J. Vanparys (2001), 'How to design user-friendly CALL interfaces', *Computer assisted language learning*, 14(5): 405-417.

Manning, C.D., P. Raghavan and H. Schütze (2008), *Introduction to information retrieval.* Cambridge: Cambridge University Press.

Scott, M. (2010), WordSmith Tools [computer software]. Liverpool: Lexical Analysis Software.

Sommerville, I. (2004), *Software engineering*. Boston: Addison Wesley.

The Unicode Consortium (2006), *Unicode standard, Version 5.0.* Boston: Addison-Wesley.

Utiyama, M. and H. Isahara (2003), 'Reliable measures for aligning Japanese-English news articles and sentences', in: E. W. Hinrichs and D. Roth (eds.) *Proceedings of the 41st annual meeting of the association for computational linguistics. Volume 1.* Stroudsburg (PA): Association of Computational Linguistics. 72-79.

W3C (2010), Web Accessibility Initiative (WAI). Available online at: http://www.w3.org/WAI/.

Syntactic aspects of the writing of Swedish L2 learners of English

Christine Johansson and Christer Geisler

Uppsala University

Abstract

The present study focuses on syntactic development in Swedish high school students' writing. The data is drawn from the Uppsala Learner English Corpus *(ULEC), consisting of essays written by Swedish junior and senior high school students. In measuring syntactic development in the students' writing, we make use of various indices, including number of T-units, proportion of syntactically error-free T-units, and the subordinate clause index. In the statistical analysis of the data, syntactic development is analyzed across age, school level, and gender. Senior high school students write longer and more complex T-units, in that they have a more frequent and varied use of subordinate clauses. Contrary to previous research on gender differences in second language acquisition, our results show that, controlling for age and school level, there are no statistically significant differences between boys and girls when they write essays in English.*

1. Introduction

The present paper studies some aspects of syntactic development among Swedish junior and senior high school students. The data is drawn from a new corpus of learner English, the *Uppsala Learner English Corpus* (ULEC), which is a collection of essays by Swedish junior and senior high school students. The study investigates how writing differs between junior and senior high school and between the first and the third year of senior high school. Given that previous research has suggested that girls outperform boys when studying languages, we address the question of gender differences in ULEC. First, we describe the data and discuss various indicators of syntactic development in learner English, such as the number of T-units, the proportion of syntactically error-free T-units, and the subordinate clause index. We show that students' increased use of subordination in the form of relative clauses and nominal and adverbial clauses is a better tool for measuring syntactic development. In addition, two sets of pragmatic features are studied to detect possible gender differences.

The acquisition of second language syntax has been discussed in, for example, Braidi (1998), Hawkins (2001), Hawkins (2004) and Saville-Troike (2006: 31-65). In the present study, the focus is not on how Swedish high school students acquire grammatical structure. We limit ourselves to analyzing the development of students' syntax as exhibited when they write essays in English.

2. Corpus data

The *Uppsala Learner English Corpus* (ULEC) currently contains approximately 136,000 words. The corpus consists of 86 essays (19,000 words) written by junior high school students and 510 essays (117,000 words) written by senior high school students. The junior and senior high school students write their essays using a simple web interface. The ULEC data is collected by student teachers who use the essays when writing their degree projects (see Johansson 2006, Johansson & Geisler 2009). Each essay in the corpus is coded for extra-linguistic categories such as date of composition, essay genre (argumentative, narrative or descriptive), number of years in school, level of English course (English A, B, or C; only in senior high school) type of educational program (academic or vocational), gender and age of the writer, as in (1).

(1) <D 20081104><G ARG><Y 3><K C><P S><S M><A 18>
I think that people is fascinated by the unknown because they are scared of it. Like sharks or crocs, you can't see them, that's what scaring about them, but you are also fascinated by them. For example, who doesn't like the Jaws movies?
(male student, aged 18, senior high, year 3, English C, academic program)

The data forms a subsample of ULEC consisting of twenty essays from junior high school and twenty essays from senior high school. The students were instructed to write an essay of approximately 200-300 words. The total sample size equals 9,127 words of running text. The essay topic given to the junior high school students was "A dream journey" and the topic for the senior high school students' essays was "Do you believe in ghosts?". Ten boys and ten girls from junior high (school years 7 and 9, ages 14-16) and ten boys and ten girls from senior high (year 1 in the English A course, and year 3 in English C, ages 16-19) are represented, as shown in Table 1.

Table 1: Distribution of the data across Level, School year and Gender

		boys		*girls*	
level	*school year*	*mean essay length*	*number of essays*	*mean essay length*	*number of essays*
Junior high	Year 7	228.0	5	217.0	5
	Year 9	221.8	5	234.0	5
Senior high	Year 1	220.8	5	190.0	5
	Year 3	277.8	5	245.0	5
total		237.1	20	221.5	20

Junior high school students are typically between 14 and 16 years old and have studied English for approximately 4-7 years. Junior high school education is compulsory. The senior high school students, who are between 16 and 19 years old, have studied English for 8-10 years. In the third year of senior high school, one course, the English C course, is special in that it is an elective course that can only be taken by students in the academic programs. This course, which is designed to prepare students for university studies, is the only English course whose curriculum stresses correct writing among the grading criteria.

The rest of this paper is organized as follows. First, in Sections 3-4, we outline various tools for measuring syntactic development in learner English, such as the T-unit, error-free T-units, and the subordinate clause index. Section 5 details the statistical analysis of the data in the form of linear regression and ANOVA tests. The findings in ULEC are presented and analyzed in Sections 6-9 and, finally, in Section 10, we summarize our results.

3. T-units

The concept of the T-unit was first defined by Hunt (1965, 1966). T-units are "minimal terminable units", each of which consists of one main clause and any subordinate clauses attached to it or embedded in it (see Hunt 1966: 737 and 1968: 12-14). The T-units in (2) are illustrated in (3a-e). As is obvious from (3), a T-unit can be quite long and complex, as in (3b-c), which include adverbial *when*- and *if*-clauses, and in (3d), which includes nominal clauses.

(2) *i want to go to the space. and be a astronaout. when i'm in the space i want go on the moone and meet extraterrestials, but only if them is nice, if them not are nice i don't want meet them, but i want to see them anyway, if them existens. why i'm wanna travel too the space are becouse i have never be there befor and not so many other people have was there too.* (female student, aged 15, junior high school, year 9)

(3) (a) *i want to go to the space. and be a astronaout.*
(b) *when i'm in the space i want go on the moone and meet extraterrestials, but only if them is nice,*
(c) *if them not are nice i don't want meet them, but i want to see them anyway, if them existens.*
(d) *why i'm wanna travel too the space are becouse i have never be there befor*
(e) *and not so many other people have was there too*

According to Hunt (1965: 45-47), a short T-unit includes a maximum of eight words, and a high frequency of short T-units is characteristic of immature writing, as is the co-ordination of short T-units with *and* or *but*. A long T-unit is defined as one containing more than 20 words. In both the junior and senior high school data, there are many short T-units or several T-units strung together with a comma or coordinated with *and* or *but*, as in (4).

(4) *When I went to Stromstad. I went there whit my cousins. We had a lot of fun! I and my brother fished and catched crabs, that was really fun. Me and my youngest cousin played in the sand, we build sandcastles nearly every day...*
(male student, aged 14, junior high school, year 7)

It is characteristic of the junior, and to some extent also of the senior, high school students' writing that subordinate clauses are treated as main clauses, as if they were independent T-units, as in (5). In (5'), the student's writing is divided into proper T-units.

(5) *My dream journey would be to go to Spanien. Becaus its a big contry and i can buy a lot of stuff there cheap like cloths and other stuff.*
(male student, aged 16, junior high school, year 9)

(5') *[$_1$My dream journey would be to go to Spanien. Becaus its a big contry.]*
[$_2$and i can buy a lot of stuff there cheap like cloths and other stuff.]

The notion of the T-unit as such has been questioned as an indicator of syntactic development, particularly in second language acquisition (see, e.g., Gaies 1980, Foster, Tonkyn & Wigglesworth 2000, Ellis & Barkhuizen 2005: 147-155; for alternative methods of measuring syntactic development, see e.g., Casanave-Pearson 1994 and Szmrecsányi 2004).

4. Error-free T-units and the subordinate clause index

The concept of *error-free T-units* has been proposed as a more suitable measure of the developmental errors that occur in second language acquisition (see Larsen-Freeman & Strom 1977, Larsen-Freeman 1978, Scott & Tucker 1974, Gaies 1980, Homburg 1984 and more recently, Larsen-Freeman 2006). However, there are different definitions of an error-free T-unit. The strictest definition is provided by Larsen-Freeman & Strom (1977), who state that an error-free T-unit must be correct in all respects including spelling and punctuation. In the ULEC data, T-units that are error-free according to this definition are infrequent. Spelling is the area in which the most errors are made, particularly in the junior high school students' writing. Example (6) below, however, is one of the few instances of an error-free T-unit according to the Larsen-Freeman & Strom (1977) definition.

(6) *I believe in supernatural phenomena because I and people I know have experienced things that can't be explained by science.*
(male student, aged 18, senior high, year 3, English C)

In this study, we opt instead to measure *syntactically error-free T-units*. These are defined as consisting of either just a main clause or a main clause with one or more subordinate clauses. The concept of syntactically error-free T-units refers to the students' ability to use subordination correctly. Example (7) is syntactically error-free, whereas example (8) is not, since the subordinate clause introduced by *because* is treated as a main clause. See also example (5) above.

(7) *I believe that most things have a scientific explanation but I don't judge people who believes in ghosts or any other type of supernatural phenomena.*
(male student, aged 18, senior high, year 3, English C)

(8) *I don't believe in ghosts and supernatural strength or something like that. Because it's not for real, Halloween is just a funny week when al the people has a great time.*
(male student, aged 18, senior high, year 3, English C)

In example (7) a grammatical error occurs (subject-verb agreement in the verb *believes*), but we regard the T-unit as syntactically error-free. One problem with using the concept of syntactically error-free T-units in the junior high school data in ULEC is that many students write predominantly main clauses, and thus, by default, produce many syntactically error-free T-units (see example (4)).

We chose to analyze not only the frequency of error-free T-units, but also the proportion of error-free T-units across the total number of T-units in students' writing. In the ULEC data, we analyze this proportion across school year, level, and gender.

T-units can be lengthened by adding subordinate clauses to the main clause. The number of subordinate clauses per main clause is termed the *subordinate clause index* (SCI), where an SCI score of 1 represents a sentence with just one main clause (see Hunt 1966: 733). The subordinate clause index can be expected to be higher the more advanced the students are. Relative clauses used as postmodifiers constitute the type of subordinate clause that is the most reliable indicator when syntactic development is measured. Hunt (1966) suggests that the occurrence of relative clauses increases with student age. In the next section, both syntactic indicators based on the T-unit and the use of subordinate clauses are analyzed.

5. Statistical analysis of the data

The investigation of the ULEC data includes the analysis of the following indicators of syntactic development: average T-unit length per essay, number of T-units per 100 words, number of error-free T-units, proportion of error-free T-units, SCI, number of relative clauses per 100 words and number of nominal/adverbial clauses per 100 words. These seven variables are analyzed across three categorical variables, namely level (junior vs. senior high school), school year (junior high school years 7 and 9, and high school years 1 and 3), which serves as a proxy for age, and gender (male vs. female).

The statistical analysis of the data includes linear regression and ANOVA tests. Tables 2a-2b show the results of the linear regression analysis in the form of R-square values (R^2), F-values, and their associated probabilities. The various indices of syntactic complexity, such as number of T-units and SCI in the left-most columns, are so-called response (or outcome) variables. The variables Level, School year, and Gender are predictor (or explanatory) variables.

Table 2a: Summary of statistical analyses of syntactic features across Level and Gender

response variable	*level*	*gender*	*level* gender*	R^2	*F-value*	*prob.*
number of T-units	+	–	–	*0.11*	*4.82*	*0.03*
T-unit length	+	–	–	*0.09*	*3.94*	*0.05*
number of error-free T-units	–	–	–	<0.01	0.02	0.88
proportion of error-free T-units	+	–	–	*0.09*	*3.92*	*0.055*
subordinate clause index	+	–	–	*0.37*	*22.04*	*<0.001*
number of nominal/ adverbial clauses	+	–	–	*0.33*	*18.32*	*<0.001*
number of relative clauses	+	–	–	*0.53*	*43.12*	*<0.001*

Table 2b: Summary of statistical analyses of syntactic features across School year and Gender

response variable	*school year*	*gender*	*school year* gender*	R^2	*F-value*	*prob.*
number of T-units	+	–	–	*0.25*	*4.10*	*0.01*
T-unit length	+	–	–	*0.25*	*4.09*	*0.01*
number of error-free T-units	–	–	–	0.08	1.00	0.40
proportion of error-free T-units	–	–	–	0.14	2.03	0.13
subordinate clause index	+	–	–	*0.46*	*10.06*	*<0.001*
number of nominal/ adverbial clauses	+	–	–	*0.40*	*8.15*	*<0.001*
number of relative clauses	+	–	–	*0.56*	*15.40*	*<0.001*

In these tables, statistically significant tests are italicized, with the standard cut-off point of p.≈0.05. R^2-values (R-square) provide estimates of the amount of variation explained by the predictor variables: for example, relative clauses in Table 2b have an R^2-value equaling 0.56, which means that 56% of the variation is due to the predictor School year. In Table 2a, the predictor variable Level represents a contrast between junior and senior high school, whereas School year, in Table 2b, has four levels (coded 1, 3, 4 and 6 in the regression analyses). The predictor variables Level and School year were tested together with Gender (boys vs. girls), including a possible interaction effect with Gender (a star, *, between two predictor variables marks the interaction effect, as in the column labeled Level*Gender in Table 2a). A plus sign (+) indicates a statistically significant predictor, and a minus sign (–) indicates a non-significant predictor.

There are some general tendencies in the statistical tests in Tables 2a-2b: (a) The variable Gender and interaction effects involving Gender never reach statistical significance for any of the response variables, (b) School year can be interpreted as a stronger predictor than Level, since R^2-values for School year are consistently higher than those of Level. In addition, based on the size of the R^2-values, we see that relative clauses form the strongest predictor, followed by SCI and nominal/adverbial clauses. Three response variables are statistically significant but of less importance, with lower R^2-values,—namely, number of T-units, T-unit length, and proportion of error-free T-units. The response variable proportion of error-free T-units is only statistically significant across Level, with a probability of 0.05 (see Table 2a).

6. How important is gender?

It is generally assumed that the study of languages is something which is better suited to girls' learning strategies. English is regarded as a girls' subject (probably also in L2 acquisition), since it requires concentration and long hours in the classroom (see Swann 2005: 634). Certain components of an English class are also supposedly better suited to girls, for example, learning vocabulary and writing. A task such as that given to the students in ULEC, writing a 200-word essay, might therefore be an activity in which girls could be expected to do better than boys.

Previous research has identified important differences in the writing styles of male and female learners. Boys have a more sparse and concise style of writing, whereas girls often show a preference for cautious, discursive, and synthetic approaches (Murphy & Elwood 1998: 179). Examples (9) and (10) from ULEC serve to illustrate the differences in male and female writing styles referred to by Murphy & Elwood (1998) (see, however, the discussion of pragmatic features below).

(9) *My reason tells me that I do not believe in ghosts or the supernatural phenomena. Everything has a logical explanation. At least through my experience so far.*
(male student, aged 18, senior high, year 3, English C)

(10) *I do belive that there is something overnatural in our strange world, but I'm not really sure what it is. I don't think that you will be a ghost when you die, but I think that the spirit of your soul is still in the air after death, and to be honest, I think that sometimes, this spirit can show, and maybe that's what people who says they have experienced strange things can feel.*
(female student, aged 18, senior high, year 3, English C)

Several studies report on gender differences in second language acquisition (see Ekstrand 1980, Ellis 1994: 202-205, Murphy & Ellwood 1998, Swann 2005, and Eckert 2005). Most of these studies try to explain why girls outperform boys, mentioning differences in attitudes, learning strategies, and verbal activity. However, in our study there are no statistically significant differences between boys' and girls' performance either in junior high school or in senior high school. In more directed written assignments, such as writing an essay of about 200-300 words, gender differences would appear to be leveled out, at least when different aspects of the T-unit and the subordinate clause index are considered (see Tables 2a and 2b).

In order to detect possible gender differences between boys' and girls' writing, we investigate pragmatic features, namely *stance* expressions (see Biber 2006: 87-88). Example (10) above shows a girl's use of stance expressions, such as *I think*, *really* and *maybe*. We identify two sets of stance expressions that denote certainty, likelihood or attitude: stance adverbs (such as *really* and *maybe*), and stance verbs (such as *know*, *believe*, *think*, *expect*, *feel* and *wish*) (see Biber 2006: 92). Stance expressions occur mainly in the senior high school students' writing. This could be because the argumentative essay topic ("Do you believe in ghosts?") favors the use of various hedging devices. *I think* and *I know* are the stance verbs that occur most frequently. The analyses of stance adverbs and stance verbs are presented in Tables 3a and 3b.

Table 3a: Statistical analysis of stance expressions across Level and Gender

response variable	*level*	*gender*	*R^2*	*F-value*	*prob.*
stance adverbs	+	–	*0.129*	*3.889*	*0.029*
stance verbs	+	–	*0.391*	*13.52*	*<0.001*

Table 3b: Statistical analysis of stance expressions across School year and Gender

response variable	*school year*	*gender*	R^2	*F-value*	*prob.*
stance adverbs	+	–	*0.162*	*2.883*	*0.037*
stance verbs	+	–	*0.508*	*11.06*	*<0.001*

The results of the regression analysis and ANOVA tests of the two pragmatic features show that, in line with the findings in Tables 2a and 2b, there are no statistically significant differences across gender, as indicated by the minus sign (-) in both Tables 3a and 3b. However, Level (junior and senior high school) and School year are both statistically significant.

7. Measuring syntactic development in the writing of junior and senior high school students

As shown in Table 2a, the following variables are statistically significant across the variable Level (junior vs. senior high school): average number of T-units, T-unit length, proportion of error-free T-units, SCI, average number of nominal/adverbial clauses, and average number of relative clauses. Looking first at the number of T-units and T-unit length, it is evident from Table 4 and Figure 1 that the number of T-units decreases from junior high school (8.34 per 100 words) to senior high school (7.17), whereas the length of the T-units increases from 12.39 to 14.45 words per T-unit. This is because the junior high school students write many short T-units in the form of main clauses, while the senior high school students write comparatively fewer but longer T-units.

Table 4: Distribution of indicators of syntactic development across Level (normalized frequencies per 100 words)

	Junior high	*Senior high*
number of T-units	8.34	7.17
T-unit length	12.39	14.45
proportion of error-free T-units	0.51	0.62
subordinate clause index (SCI)	1.33	1.84
nominal/adverbial clauses	2.39	4.93
relative clauses	0.40	1.53

T-units in junior high school students' writings are exemplified in (11) and (12). In example (11) there are short T-units (mainly main clauses), whereas example (12) is one long sentence made up of three T-units coordinated with *and*. Example (11) is from the first year of junior high school (year 7) and example (12) is from the last year (year 9).

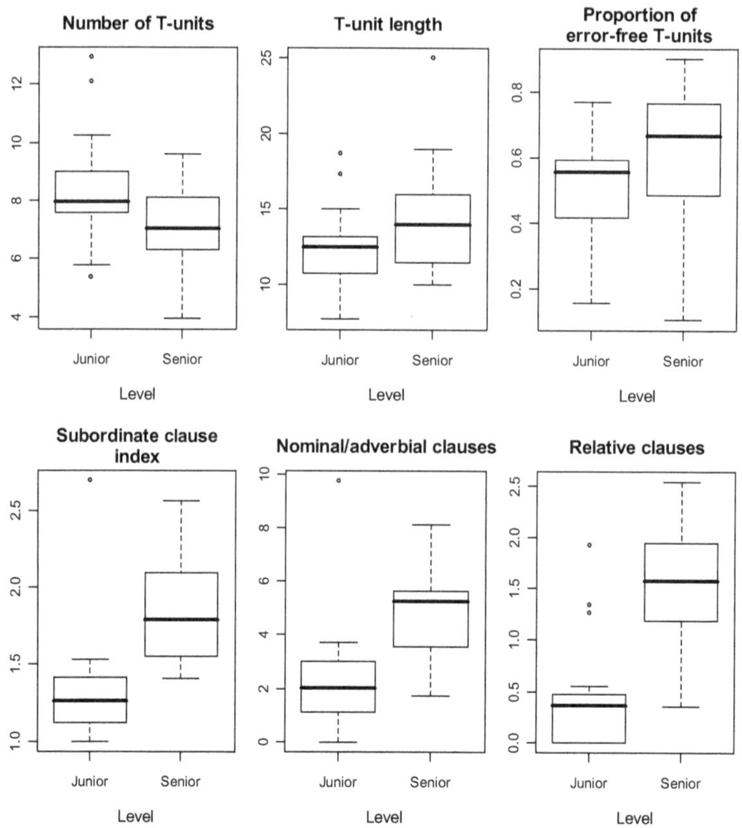

Figure 1: Indicators of syntactic development across Level

(11) *I was in Thailand. About 3 years ago I think. I were there whit my realitives over cristmas and to the 13th of January. [...] Sometimes we take a tuck tuck to the beatch. The sand there were very hot to go on. So I run on it sometimes. Me and my cousin in 7F we get a friend there, his name was kata (i think). He worked on the hotel. He was very nice to us.*
(female student, aged 13, junior high, year 7)

(12) *When i came to Philadelphia i was so happy because i always dreamed about going to USA were everybody talked english, and i am pretty good at english and i use to talk english all the time with some of my friends who are from Africa.*
(female student, aged 15, junior high, year 9)

In example (11) the subordinate clause *So I run on it sometimes* is treated as a main clause. Example (12), on the other hand, shows grammatically correct use of subordination in *when I came to Philadelphia* and *because I always dreamed about*, as well as the relative clause *who are from Africa.*

As regards syntactically error-free T-units, Figure 1 shows an increase in the proportion of error-free T-units between junior high school students' (0.51, or 51%) and senior high school students' writing (0.62, or 62%).

The SCI proved to be an important indicator of syntactic development in our study. According to Hunt (1966: 733), the SCI can be expected to be higher the more advanced the students are. Senior high school students use more subordinate clauses per main clause (1.84) than junior high school students (1.33; see Table 4). More importantly, however, the senior high school students mostly use subordinate clauses in a grammatically correct way, as reflected in the higher proportion of error-free T-units. Compare, for example, (13) with (11) and (12) above.

(13) *I don't belive that people can see into your future, because the things I heard were gonna happen to me, never happened, not once.*
(female student, aged 18, senior high, year 3, English C)

Table 4 shows that the use of nominal and adverbial clauses increases from a normalized frequency of 2.39 in junior high to 4.93 in senior high school. Furthermore, the number of relative clauses increases with student age: senior high school students use 1.53 relative clauses per 100 words, as opposed to junior high school students, who use 0.40 relative clauses per 100 words (see Table 4). Example (14), which is from a senior high school student in the first year (English A), contains both nominal/ adverbial and relative clauses. Example (15), also from an English A student, illustrates the use of relative clauses in senior high school students' writing.

(14) *I think that people who believe in thos things are crazy or just think that they are different from the rest, but their not, in my eyes they are crazy. Little kids dont know what supernaturals phenomena are or what halloween are, so they shouldn't be forced to dress out to ghosts or a pumkin, maybe they dont want to.*
(female student, aged 16, senior high, year 1, English A)

(15) *I don't believe that ghosts exist and people who says they have experienced such things must be crazy, people are not so stupid to believe that???*
(male student, aged 16, senior high, year 1, English A)

Table 2a shows that across the two school levels, junior high and senior high, the strongest indicators of syntactic progression are use of relative clauses, the subordinate clause index, and use of nominal/adverbial clauses. The factors based on the T-unit, by contrast, are statistically weaker indicators.

8. Syntactic development across age

The seven indictors of syntactic development were also tested across the variable School year, which represents an age parameter. Table 5 gives the normalized frequencies of the five statistically significant variables from Table 2b. Figure 2 displays the distribution of the data coded 1, 3, 4, and 6 for school years 7 and 9 in junior high school and year 1 and 3 in senior high school (see the row 'School year coding' in Table 5). As mentioned in Section 5, the variable School year is a slightly stronger predictor than the variable Level: the sizes of the R-square values in Table 2b are generally higher than the corresponding values in Table 2a. Both the number of T-units and T-unit length are statistically more important across School year than across Level. However, Figure 2 shows that there is no difference between year 9 in junior high and year 1 senior high (coded '3' and '4' respectively in Figure 2): the differences in the two variables connected to the T-unit are entirely due to differences between year 7 in junior high and year 3 in senior high. Furthermore, there are no statistically significant differences between year 1 and 3 in senior high school.

Table 5: Distribution of indicators of syntactic development across School year (normalized frequencies per 100 words)

	Junior high		*Senior high*	
	Year 7	*Year 9*	*Year 1*	*Year 3*
number of T-units	9.13	7.54	7.65	6.68
T-unit length	11.16	13.62	13.00	15.90
subordinate clause index (SCI)	1.17	1.49	1.76	1.92
nominal/adverbial clauses	1.50	3.27	5.02	4.85
relative clauses	0.22	0.58	1.48	1.58
school year coding	1	3	4	6

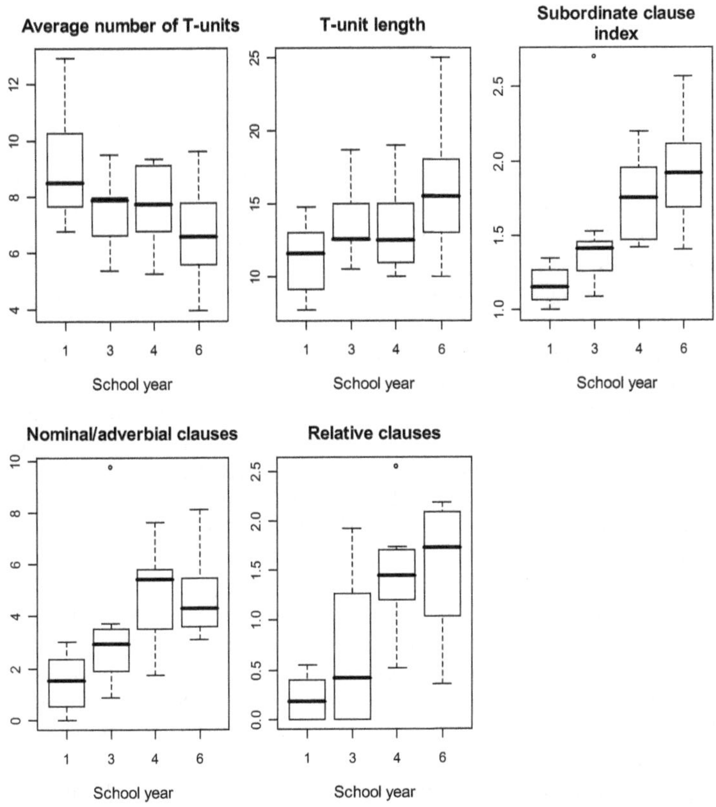

Figure 2: Indicators of syntactic development across School year

9. Getting it right

Four indicators of syntactic development suggest that the character of the student essays changes over this five-year period. As shown in Figure 2 and Table 5, there is clear syntactic progression from year 7 in junior high school to year 3 of senior high school. The students in the third year of senior high school have reached a fairly high level of language proficiency. The strongest indicators of syntactic complexity in our study were the frequency of relative clauses and the frequency of nominal/adverbial clauses. The use of relative clauses with *that* and *Ø* (zero relativizer) in the oldest students' writing is exemplified in (16). In example (17), we see a student making frequent use of *wh*-forms in her writing.

(16) *If I could decide myself, I would believe in supernatural phenomenas but unfortunately I just don't buy the arguments that the "beliving" people*

are using. [...] I believe that the phenomenon Ø we refer to as ghost, relly are the product of our own imagination and paranoia, ...
(male student, aged 18, senior high, year 3, English C)

(17) *... and therefore the spirits search for spiritual people who can help them. Because I think that people who become spirits has something unclarified on the earth that they need to do before they die for real. My friend thinks that she saw a ghost once. She was terrified and she recognized the ghost as a man who followed her in a car once when she was younger, and whom she was very afraid of.*
(female student, aged 18, senior high, year 3, English C)

The relative clauses in the students' writing are generally well-formed; students master both the usage of the different *wh*-forms, *that* and zero as well as the personal/non-personal contrast (see Hawkins 2001: 159-162). Swedish and English are similar with regard to relative clause formation according to the Accessibility Hierarchy (see Keenan & Comrie 1977, Comrie & Keenan 1979, Braidi 1998: 88-94). Furthermore, the English relativizer *that* corresponds to Swedish *som* environments (see Hawkins 2004: 197, 274-275). In any case, both *that* and zero are used frequently in the high school students' writing. The *wh*-forms are used less frequently by the students (but cf. example 17). This could be because the corresponding Swedish *wh*-forms, such as *vilken* and *vars*, are also rare (cf. Hyltenstam 1984: 44-46 and Hawkins 2001: 159-160).

The use of zero and *that* is often looked upon as informal compared with use of the *wh*-forms (see e.g., Biber, Conrad & Leech 2002: 287-289). However, as stated by Hawkins (2004: 151-152), using zero relativizers is not automatically simpler than using *that* or a *wh*-form, since the use of the zero relativizer is more syntactically constrained. Zero is mainly preferred over *that* or a *wh*-form when the antecedent and relativizer are adjacent and when the subject of the relative clause is a pronoun.

The use of nominal and adverbial clauses in syntactically error-free T-units is shown in (18) and (19).

(18) *I belive that we people are so facinated about the unknown because there are no right answers. Everyone can speculate if ghosts exists or not, but no one can prove if they are right and wrong about it. That is I think one of many reasons why we are interrested about the unknown.*
(male student, aged 18, senior high, year 3, English C)

(19) *I've experienced a lot of strange things, at the same time as I've been with my family, so I guess it has to do with the place your'e at. The fact that we don't really know what happens after death is probably the reason why we're so fascinated about it. People who say they've seen ghosts and stuff like that is probably over reacting, or just lying.*
(female student, aged 18, senior high, year 3, English C)

Examples (16) through (19) show that the students in the last year are on their way to getting it right as regards writing in English. Grammatical errors and spelling mistakes may still occur in the essays, but for the most part the students in the third year of senior high school handle sentences and clauses in a satisfactory way.

10. Conclusion

In this study we tested various indicators of syntactic development based on the T-unit, such as the average number and length of T-units per essay, and the proportion of syntactically error-free T-units to the total number of T-units.

The concept of the syntactically error-free T-unit gives rise to additional challenges when measuring syntactic development, particularly in the junior high school students' essays. Students in years 7 and 9 have many syntactically error-free T-units consisting of relatively short main clauses and little use of subordination in their writing (which in itself is a sign of immature writing and a low degree of syntactic development).

The most reliable indicators in our analysis include the subordinate clause index (i.e., how many subordinate clauses per main clause are used) and the normalized frequency of nominal/adverbial clauses and relative clauses. The subordinate clause index increases from junior high school to senior high school and thus indicates syntactic development. Nominal and adverbial clauses are more than twice as frequent in senior high school as in junior high school. In addition, senior high school students use more than three times as many relative clauses.

The indicators of syntactic progression and the pragmatic features examined in this study are statistically significant across age (School year) and school level (Level), but they never reach statistical significance across gender. This absence of statistically significant gender differences should be emphasized, since these results stand in contrast to much of the previous research on the role of gender in second language acquisition.

Acknowledgements

We thank Gregory Garretson and Peter Hughes, Department of English, Uppsala University, for valuable comments on our text.

References

Biber, D. (2006), *University language: a corpus-based study of spoken and written registers*. Amsterdam: Benjamins.

Biber, D., S. Conrad & G. Leech (2002), *Longman student grammar of spoken and written English*. Harlow: Pearson Education.

Braidi, S. (1998), *The acquisition of second language syntax*. Oxford: Oxford University Press.

Casanave-Pearson, C. (1994), 'Language development in students' journals', *Journal of second language writing*, 3: 179-201.

Comrie, B. & E. Keenan (1979), 'Noun phrase accessibility revisited', *Language*, 55: 649-664.

Eckert, P. (2005), 'Language and gender in adolescence', in: J. Holmes & M. Meyerhoff (eds.) *The handbook of language and gender*. Oxford: Blackwell. 381-400.

Ekstrand, L.H. (1980), 'Sex differences in second language learning? Empirical studies and a discussion of related findings', *International review of applied psychology*, 29: 205-259.

Ellis, R. (1994), *The study of second language acquisition*. Oxford: Oxford University Press.

Ellis, R. & G. Barkhuizen (2005), *Analysing learner language*. Oxford: Oxford University Press.

Foster, P., A. Tonkyn & G. Wigglesworth (2000), 'Measuring spoken language: A unit for all reasons', *Applied linguistics*, 21: 354-375.

Gaies, S.J. (1980), 'T-unit analysis in second language research: Applications, problems and limitations', *TESOL quarterly*, 14: 53-59.

Hawkins, J.A. (2004), *Efficiency and complexity in grammars*. Oxford: Oxford University Press.

Hawkins, R. (2001), *Second language syntax: a generative introduction*. Oxford: Blackwell.

Homburg, J.H. (1984), 'Holistic evaluation of ESL compositions: Can it be validated objectively?', *TESOL quarterly*, 18: 87-107.

Hunt, K.W. (1965), *Grammatical structures written at three grade levels. Research report No. 3*. Urbana, IL: National Council of Teachers of English.

Hunt, K.W. (1966), 'Recent measures in syntactic development', *Elementary English*, 43: 732-739.

Hunt, K.W. (1968), *An instrument to measure syntactic maturity*. Tallahassee, (FL): Florida State University.

Hyltenstam, K. (1984), 'The use of typological markedness conditions as predictors in second language acquisition: the case of pronominal copies in relative clauses', in: R.W. Anderson (ed.) *Second languages: a cross-linguistic perspective*. Rowley, Mass.: Newbury House. 39-58.

Johansson, C. (2006), '*Supplemental instruction* och lärarstudenters intresse för grammatik i språkundervisningen och i examensarbeten', in: J. Einarsson,

E. Larsson Ringqvist & M. Lindgren (eds.) *Approaches to teaching and learning in linguistic research: Papers from the ASLA symposium in Växjö, 10-11 November 2005.* Uppsala: Svenska föreningen för tillämpad språkvetenskap. 101-111.

Johansson, C. & C. Geisler (2009), 'The Uppsala Learner English Corpus: A new corpus of Swedish high school students' writing', in: A. Saxena & Å. Viberg (eds.) *Multilingualism: proceedings of the 23rd Scandinavian conference of linguistics*. Uppsala: Acta Universitatis Upsaliensis.181-190.

Keenan, E. & B. Comrie (1977), 'Noun phrase accessibility and universal grammar'. *Linguistic inquiry*, 8: 63-99.

Larsen-Freeman, D. (1978), 'An ESL index of development', *TESOL quarterly*, 12: 439-448.

Larsen-Freeman, D. (2006), 'The emergence of complexity, fluency and accuracy in the oral and written production of five Chinese learners of English', *Applied linguistics*, 27: 590-619.

Larsen-Freeman, D. & V. Strom (1977), 'The construction of a second language acquisition index of development', *Language learning*, 27: 123-134.

Murphy, P. & J. Elwood (1998), 'Gendered learning outside and inside school: Influences on assessment', in: D. Epstein, J. Elwood, V. Hey & J. Maw (eds.) *Failing boys? Issues in gender and achievement*. Buckingham: Open University Press. 162-181.

Saville-Troike, M. (2006), *Introducing second language acquisition.* Cambridge: Cambridge University Press.

Scott, M. & G.R. Tucker (1974), 'Error analysis and English language strategies of Arabic students', *Language learning*, 24: 69-97.

Swann, J. (2005), 'Schooled language: language and gender in educational settings', in: J. Holmes & M. Meyerhoff (eds.) *The handbook of language and gender*. Oxford: Blackwell. 624-644.

Szmrecsányi, B.M. (2004), 'On operationalizing syntactic complexity', in: G. Purnelle, C. Fairon & A. Dister (eds.) *Le poids des mots: proceedings of the 7th international conference on the statistical analysis of textual data. Volume II.* Louvain-la-Neuve, March 10-12, 2004. Louvain-la-Neuve: Presses universitaires de Louvain. 1032–1039.

Age tagging and word frequency for learners' dictionaries

Hanhong Li and Alex C. Fang

City University of Hong Kong

Abstract

In contemporary lexicography, particularly in learners' dictionaries, word frequency information from large corpora has been used for entry selection, sense ranking, and collocation identification as well as selecting defining vocabulary. However, age information in linguistic corpora has not been adequately highlighted or exploited. Early experiments have demonstrated that word retrieval in long-term memory is much more influenced by the age of acquisition than word frequency. For EFL English learners, it is necessary to know what words native speakers tend to use at different ages besides frequent words. Core vocabulary contains not simply those words with high frequency but also those with even distribution in different age groups. Learners' dictionaries with this kind of core vocabulary will be of much help for English learning and teaching as well as research in core vocabulary. Our research makes use of the age group information in the British National Corpus XML Edition (BNC XML 2007). It turns out that higher lexical coverage can be achieved when we select core vocabulary by the combined parameters of a word's dispersion index and distributed frequency in different age groups rather than raw frequency only. Moreover, our study shows that the young age group under 15 rely more on core vocabulary than adults due to its fundamental role in language learning. For the age group over 15 years old, core vocabulary occupies a stable proportion of their vocabulary size despite age increase. Another interesting finding is that each age group tends to acquire more core words selected on a frequency-age basis than those on a raw-frequency basis.

1. Introduction

The use of corpora for word frequency information is unquestioned in contemporary lexicography, particularly in English learners' dictionaries. Word frequency information has been used for entry selection, sense ranking, and collocation identification as well as selecting defining vocabulary or core vocabulary. For example, the *Longman dictionary of Contemporary English* 5th edition (LDCE5 2009) marks out the 3,000 most frequent words in spoken and written English respectively (known as the Longman Communication 3000), based on the computerized analysis of the Longman Corpus Network. It also features a defining vocabulary of around 2,000 common words which are very frequent in their corpora. The *Oxford advanced learner's dictionary* 7th edition (OALD7 2005), as another example, has its own defining vocabulary which is composed of around three thousand of the most frequent, widely distributed and familiar words based on the British National Corpus (BNC).

The frequency in learners' dictionaries mainly falls into two categories: raw frequency in large corpora and distributed frequency in different text types of large corpora. Raw frequency is only based on the counting of a word type's total number of occurrences, or word tokens, in a large corpus, while distributed frequency involves considering word frequency distribution in different sectors or divisions of a large corpus. In word frequency studies, text range refers to the number of text categories or samples in which a word occurs (Juilland & Chang-Rodriguez 1964). Thorndike & Lorge (1944) began to consider the range credit in the vocabulary control movement. Later on, Kučera & Francis (1967) and Hofland & Johansson (1982) introduced range statistics of fifteen text categories in their wordlist based on modern corpora of edited American and British English. However, the text range tells us the number of text categories or corpus samples that a word type occurs in but it fails to make use of the individual word frequency in each text category or corpus sample. In this case, Juilland & Chang-Rodriguez (1964) and Carroll (1970) researched word frequency distribution in different text categories by introducing a "coefficient of usage" called *U*. In effect, the value of *U* is used to evaluate the distributed word frequency in different text categories or corpus samples in large corpora. Subsequently, Carroll's *U* has not only contributed to the making of a school dictionary (Carroll, Davies & Richman 1971) but has also demonstrated its usefulness in the selection of a representative word list with a minimal out-of-vocabulary ratio (Fang & Huckvale 2000). More recently, Carroll's *U* has been used to compute distributed word frequency in a variety of text genres in large corpora (Li 2010).

However, age information in linguistic corpora has not been adequately highlighted or exploited in the above-mentioned frequency studies. Early experiments (Carroll & White 1973) have demonstrated that word retrieval in long-term memory is much more influenced by the age of acquisition than word frequency. For EFL learners, it is necessary and helpful to know what words are used by native speakers at different ages besides those frequent words. Core vocabulary contains not just those common words with high frequency but also the ones with an even distribution in different age groups as recorded in corpora. If learners' dictionaries can incorporate a word profile based on raw frequency and distributed frequency across different age groups, it will be significant and practical for English learning and teaching as well as research into core vocabulary. Moreover, it will open a new area in word frequency studies in lexicography.

We review the frequency marking methods in the latest versions of five English learners' dictionaries (LDCE5, OALD7, CALD3, MED2, and CCD5). Making full use of the age information tagged in the modern corpora, we then compare the core vocabulary provided by learners' dictionaries on raw frequency basis with a core vocabulary based on distributed frequency across different age groups in modern corpora.

2. Word frequency marking in current learners' dictionaries

Despite the development of modern corpora, the review of five of the latest versions of English learners' dictionaries (LDCE5, OALD7, CALD3, MED2, and CCD5) shows that their word frequency information mainly depends on the raw frequency count or range statistics without referring to the age information tagged in modern corpora, not to mention further research in word frequency distribution across different age groups.

2.1 Word frequency in LDCE5

The word frequency information of the *Longman dictionary of Contemporary English* 5th edition (LDCE5 2009) can be traced from its wordlists of the Longman Communication 3000 and the Longman Defining Vocabulary (Bullon & Leech 2007). Based on statistical analysis of the large Longman Corpus Network, words in the Longman Communication 3000 are common English words and "represent the core of English and show students of English which words are the most important for them to learn and study in order to communicate effectively in both speech and writing" (Bullon & Leech 2007: 1). On the other hand, the Longman Defining Vocabulary (LDV) enjoys a long history which "was pioneered over 70 years ago by Michael West in his *New Method English Dictionary*" (Bullon & Leech 2007: 7) and has been regarded as a core vocabulary by other researchers (Quirk 1978, Lee 2001, Li 2010). Nowadays, words in the LDV are constantly being researched and checked to make sure that they are frequent in the Longman Corpus Network.

The word selection criteria for the Longman Communication 3000 are raw frequency and range consideration. Those words in the Longman Communication 3000 are not only frequent but are also well-spread across a full range of language use (Bullon & Leech 2007). However, judging from the screenshot from the Longman corpus analysis system (Bullon & Leech 2007: 5), this kind of frequency distribution is quite simplistic. For instance, Bullon & Leech (2007) do not explain how many text types they have adopted, how many tokens there are in each text type, and how to judge the distribution degree in an accurate computational way. Nor do they mention how to calculate a word's distributed frequency by integrating its individual frequency in each text type. Generally, the final decision of a word being widespread mainly relies on subjective judgment of the spikes appearing in a graph instead of a computational approach. When it comes to the LDV, the major word selection criterion is raw frequency, which ensures that they are frequent in their Longman Corpus Network.

2.2 Word frequency in OALD7

The *Oxford advanced learner's dictionary* 7th edition (OALD7 2005) features a core vocabulary of around 3,000 words titled the Oxford 3000. All these words are indicated in the entries of the dictionary by a preceding key symbol 🔑.

They are also adopted as the defining vocabulary for the *Oxford advanced learner's dictionary* 7th edition. The word selection criteria for the Oxford 3000 are as follows:

(1) most frequent in English corpora
(2) used in a range of different text types
(3) familiar to most English users judged by linguistic and teaching experts

However, they did not mention how many text types had been adopted for selecting their core vocabulary. Neither did they state the minimum number of text types a word had to occur in before it was eligibly selected into the Oxford 3000. Moreover, as to their criterion of being familiar, there is no detail of whether they have carried out a familiarity rating as other researchers did (Gilhooly & Logie 1980, Richards 1976, Wilson 1988)

2.3 Word frequency in CALD3

The *Cambridge advanced learner's dictionary* 3rd edition (CALD3 2008) divides their word frequency into three levels: essential, improver and advanced. Essential words are common, useful and important words to know. The improvers are words to help users move beyond basic English. The advanced words are to make users' English sound more proficient. However, there is no further detailed explanation of the word selection criteria behind these word frequency symbols. What we can be sure of is that they also highlight those basic common words in the sense of core vocabulary.

2.4 Word frequency in MED2

The *Macmillan English dictionary* 2nd edition (MED2 2007) marks 7,500 headwords in red as the English core vocabulary which has been carefully chosen on the basis of frequency and importance. All these core words have a star rating to represent their core degree:

(1) ★★★ the 2,500 most common and basic English words
(2) ★★ very common words
(3) ★ fairly common words

However, the difference between "most common", "very common" and "fairly common" is stated neither explicitly nor statistically. Moreover, MED2 also chose around 2,500 of the most common words in English as its defining vocabulary by examining their word frequency information. The word selection criteria for its defining vocabulary and core vocabulary mainly depend on raw frequency.

2.5 Word frequency in CCD5

Another well-known learner's dictionary, the *Collins COBUILD advanced learner's English dictionary* 5th edition (CCD5 2006) provides word frequency information via three frequency bands. That is, frequent words are marked with a diamond symbol ◆. The most frequent words will have three diamonds in the headword position, the next most frequent two, and those which are less frequent have one diamond. Obviously, raw frequency plays a dominant role in its frequency marking system. It is a pity that the dividing lines of these three frequency bands have not been explained.

In short, this review shows that the word frequency marking in the current major learners' dictionaries is mainly subject to raw frequency, though some of them have touched on the study of range by considering the number of text types in which a word occurs. The selection of defining vocabulary, which has been regarded as a kind of core vocabulary (Lee 2001, Li 2010), is mainly based on raw frequency. Nevertheless, word frequency distribution in different age groups has not yet been considered in their frequency marking and core vocabulary selecting.

3. Frequency vs. age information

Is frequency alone enough for the selection of core vocabulary? Words with high frequency and even distribution in different text genres should be more reliably rated as core words than those only frequent in total frequency (cf. Carter 1998, Li 2010, Stubbs 2001). "A word-type which appears with equal probabilities in a number of different genres of a corpus (e.g., fiction, drama, history, science, etc.) would presumably be more representative of the 'core vocabulary' of a language than a word that appears uniquely in one of these genres, e.g., science" (Carroll 1970: 61). Li (2010) demonstrates that a core vocabulary for EFL learners selected by distributed frequency in different text genres can achieve higher cumulative coverage than those based on raw frequency alone. In this case, distributed frequency should not be excluded when we design core vocabulary.

Another inevitable factor for frequency marking and core vocabulary is age. Early experiments (Carroll & White 1973) demonstrate that word retrieval in long-term memory is much more influenced by the age of acquisition than word frequency. Other research (Li & Fang 2011) shows that word frequency patterns for word classes differ between children and adults and that young children use many more words with concrete and imageable referents. In this case, it is vitally important for EFL learners to know what words are used by native speakers of different ages besides those common words rated by raw frequency.

Therefore, it is necessary to consider both distributed frequency and the age factor when we select core vocabulary and mark frequency in learners' dictionaries. The review above shows that age information in linguistic corpora has not been exploited by learners' dictionaries. Thus, we propose that core vocabulary should comprise not only those high frequency words, but also those with an even distribution in different age groups.

4. Purpose and methodology

The current project explores ways of selecting core vocabulary by two criteria: the frequency of a word and its distribution in different age groups. We compare a core vocabulary list selected by the combined parameters of frequency and age with other core vocabulary lists in learners' dictionaries which are mainly based on raw frequency. The purpose is to test whether the combined factors of frequency and age will achieve a better result.

4.1 Corpora resources

In order to make a new core vocabulary based on distributed frequency in different age groups, we build up a balanced Age-Group Corpus by making full use of the age-group information tagged in the BNC XML (2007), and other age information in the Polytechnic of Wales Corpus (POW), the British English Corpora in the Child Language Data Exchange System (CHILDES), the Lancaster Corpus of Children's Project Writing (LCCPW) and the Child Writing sub-corpus in the LUCY Corpus. We will test the core vocabulary obtained from the Age-Group Corpus in a neutral corpus, the Open American National Corpus (OANC).

4.2 Corpus tagging modification

The age-group information in the spoken part of the BNC XML is indirectly tagged so that words cannot be extracted directly. In order to extract word units according to age group information in the spoken BNC XML, we modify its utterance tagging by replacing <u who="speaker's ID"> with a more detailed uniformed pattern <u ageGroup="X" xml:id="X" role="X" sex="X" soc="X" dialect="X" firstLang="X" educ="X" n="X">. In this case, word units can be collected according to different age group information.

4.3 Construction of the Age-Group Corpus

First, our modification of the age tags in the spoken BNC enables us to extract all the word units from the BNC XML by age group. The tag of Ag0 indicates speakers or writers aged between 0 and 14, Ag1 between 15 and 24, Ag2 between 25 and 34, Ag3 between 35 and 44, while Ag5 represents those aged 60 and over. Table 1 shows all the total tokens of headwords in different age groups of the BNC XML.

Table 1: Word tokens of each age group in the whole BNC XML

age group	*age range*	*spoken tokens*	*written tokens*	*total tokens*
Ag0	0-14	385,234	59,559	444,793
Ag1	15-24	594,400	542,578	1,136,978
Ag2	25-34	1,120,516	2,267,123	3,387,639
Ag3	35-44	1,075,749	6,726,931	7,802,680
Ag4	45-59	1,638,364	7,230,715	8,869,079
Ag5	60+	1,137,433	5,156,077	6,293,510
total		5,951,696	21,982,983	27,934,679

Second, based on these statistics, we try to randomly choose one million word units for each of the age group from both the spoken and written parts of the BNC XML. For each age group, half a million words will be extracted from the spoken part and the other half million from the written part of the BNC XML. In this case, we attempt to build up a balanced Age-Group Corpus which contains both spoken and written language data. The extracted data from the BNC XML is shown in Table 2. It turns out that the first age group (Ag0) cannot reach 1 million words since there are only 385,234 words from the spoken part and 59,559 from the written part of the BNC XML for this age range. In this case, we have to select more words from other corpora with age information.

Table 2: Word tokens sampled from each age group of the BNC XML

age group	*age range*	*sampled spoken tokens*	*sampled written tokens*	*total tokens*	*total type*
Ag0	0-14	302,618	59,559	362,177	16,080
Ag1	15-24	500,397	500,868	1,001,265	24,932
Ag2	25-34	510,863	513,666	1,024,529	25,219
Ag3	35-44	525,850	501,106	1,026,956	26,572
Ag4	45-59	501,575	506,572	1,008,147	26,582
Ag5	60+	505,803	507,623	1,013,426	24,796

Third, on grounds of age range (see Table 3), we supplement the spoken part of Ag0 by all words from the Polytechnic of Wales Corpus (POW, Souter 1989). We also include words from the following three components of the British English Corpora in the Child Language Data Exchange System (CHILDES, MacWhinney 2000): the Howe sub-corpus (Howe 1981), the Manchester sub-corpus (Theakston, Lieven, Pine & Rowland 2001) and the Wells sub-corpus (Wells 1981).

Table 3: Supplementary child corpora for spoken Ag0 in the BNC XML

supplementary spoken corpora	*tokens*	*age range*
Polytechnic of Wales Corpus (POW)	60,717	6-12
The British English Corpora in Child Language Data Exchange System(CHILDES)	530,416	0-7

Similarly, the written part of Ag0 in the BNC XML is supplemented by all words from the Lancaster Corpus of Children's Project Writing (LCCPW, Ivanic & McEnery 1996) and the Child Writing of the LUCY Corpus (Sampson 2005) on grounds of same age range (see Table 4).

Table 4: Supplementary child corpora for written Ag0 in the BNC XML

supplementary written corpora	*tokens*	*age range*
The Child Writing part of the LUCY Corpus	25,995	9-12
Lancaster Corpus of Children's Project Writing (LCCPW)	82,396	8-11

Fourth, with the above data absorbed from other corpus resources, the sub-corpus of Ag0 for our Age-Group Corpus is built up. The general composition of Ag0, the first age group in our Age-Group Corpus is as follows:

Table 5: Composition of the first age group (Ag0) in the Age-Group Corpus

component	*tokens*	*mode*
Ag0 in Spoken BNC	302,618	
The Polytechnic of Wales Corpus (POW)	60,717	Spoken
The Howe, Manchester, and Wells sub-corpora from the Child Language Data Exchange System (CHILDES)	530,416	
Ag0 in Written BNC	59,559	
The Child Writing sub-corpus of the LUCY Corpus	25,995	Written
The Lancaster Corpus of Children's Project Writing (LCCPW)	82,396	
total	1,061,701	

Finally, we accomplished a new balanced Age-Group Corpus with six age groups, with each containing around 1 million words. Moreover, each age group comprises half a million words from the spoken domain and the other half a million from the written domain, except for Ag0. Due to lack of corpus resources for this age group, we had to make a compromise between the spoken and written domains in Ag0. Nevertheless, we succeeded in making the total word tokens in Ag0 reach 1 million. The general composition of this age corpus is in Table 6.

Table 6: Composition of the Age-Group Corpus

age group	*age range*	*spoken tokens*	*written tokens*	*total tokens*
Ag0	0-14	893,751	167,950	1,061,701
Ag1	15-24	500,397	500,868	1,001,265
Ag2	25-34	510,863	513,666	1,024,529
Ag3	35-44	525,850	501,106	1,026,956
Ag4	45-59	501,575	506,572	1,008,147
Ag5	60+	505,803	507,623	1,013,426

4.4 Testing corpus

In order to test the coverage of the core vocabulary based on age group information and that based on raw frequency, we take the Open American National Corpus (OANC) as our neutral corpus for final testing. This corpus contains over 14 million words and a variety of text types (OANC 2005). Table 7 illustrates the OANC's make-up.

Table 7: Composition of the OANC

domain	*text type*	*word number*
Spoken	face to face	198,295
	telephone	3,019,477
Written	government, technical	281,093
	travel guides	1,012,496
	technical	3,349,714
	fiction	61,746
	letters	91,318
	non-fiction	330,524
	journal	4,801,192
	government	1,048,792
total		14,623,927

5. Core vocabulary lists

With the established Age-Group Corpus, we may now design new core vocabulary lists based on word frequency distribution in different age groups. We can then compare them with other core vocabulary lists in the current learners' dictionaries, which are mainly based on raw frequency.

5.1 Computational approach to core vocabulary design

The review of the latest learners' dictionaries shows that distributed word frequency has not been adopted to build core vocabularies such as defining vocabularies. This research adopts a computational linguistic approach to core vocabulary design by calculating distributed word frequency in different age groups in large corpora with age information tags.

The statistical method proposed by Carroll (1970) is applied to calculating distributed frequency across different age groups. By developing Juilland & Chang-Rodriguez's (1964) "coefficient of usage", *U*, Carroll (1970) introduces a better modified "coefficient of usage", U_m, which considers the total frequency of a given word in each sub-category of a corpus, the total word frequency of each sub-category in this corpus, the total word frequency of the whole corpus, and the dispersion index of this word in different categories of this corpus. The formula of calculating the coefficient of usage U_m is illustrated as follows (Carroll 1970: 63):

Let n = the number of categories

f_j = the frequency (number of occurrences) of a given word-type in category j ($j = 1, 2, ..., n$)

F = the total frequency (number of occurrences) of the word in the corpus = $\sum_j f_j$

s_j = the number of tokens in category j

N = the total number of tokens in the corpus = $\sum_j s_j$

p_j = the proportion of tokens in category j that are instances of the given word-type. Thus, $p_j = f_j / s_j$

$P = \sum_j p_j$ (P may take any positive value; it is not in general equal to unity.)

Then:

$H = \log P - (\sum_j p_j \log p_j)/P$; ($p_j \log p_j$=0 for p_j=0)

$D_2 = H/\log n$ = the index of dispersion

$f_{min} = (\sum_j s_j f_j)/N$

$U_m = (1{,}000{,}000/N)\ [FD_2 + (1\text{-}D_2)f_{min}]$

The formula of U_m above was used to choose words for the *American Heritage Dictionary* (Carroll, Davies & Richman 1971). It considers not only the raw frequency (total frequency) of a word but also its dispersion index (*D*) in different categories of a corpus. It has been used to calculate the distributed frequency in different text genres of the BNC XML (Li 2010). Therefore, we can apply it to calculate the distributed frequency in different age groups in a corpus.

With these formulae for dispersion index (*D*) and coefficient usage (U_m), we calculate the *D* and U_m value for each word type in our Age-Group Corpus established in 4.3. Then we filter out those words with a very low dispersion index (*D*<0.5) before we sort the U_m values in descending order. This "coefficient of usage", U_m, integrates frequency and age factor and thus indicates whether a word is frequent as well as widespread across different age groups. In this case, we use it as an index to select words for a core vocabulary list in combination with the dispersion index.

5.2 Comparing core vocabulary lists

In order to compare the different criteria for selecting core vocabulary, we select one representative core vocabulary list from a learner's dictionary. The Longman Defining Vocabulary (LDV) in LDCE5 (2009) has a long history as a product of the vocabulary control movement (Cowie 1999). It has been adopted as the core vocabulary in other research (e.g., Lee 2001, Li 2010). This latest version of the LDV is mainly based on raw frequency counts in large corpora (Bullon & Leech 2007). The LDV is considerably larger than the "around 2000" words it claims, as is noted by other researchers (Herbst 1986). The reason for this is that it also includes 30 prefixes and suffixes which can be combined with the defining vocabulary to form derivatives. After searching all their derivatives in the definitions, we make a full LDV list which contains as many as 2,763 words.

Second, we select the same number of words as in the LDV from the Age-Group Corpus according to their U_m value and dispersion index so as to devise our own core vocabulary list. From the Age-Group Corpus, we first exclude those words with very low dispersion index (*D*<0.5) before selecting 2,763 words with the highest U_m value into our Age-List for comparison with the LDV.

5.3 Results and data analysis

5.3.1 Cumulative coverage

The cumulative text coverage of the Age-List and the LDV will be tested in the neutral corpus, OANC, (see 4.4) in order to find out which kinds of frequency information will produce better core vocabulary: raw frequency or distributed frequency across age groups. It turns out that distributed word frequency across age groups yields a core vocabulary list with higher cumulative coverage by around 4.34% in the testing corpus, OANC (see Table 8).

Table 8: Raw frequency vs. distributed frequency across age groups

core vocabulary	*word type*	*selection criteria*	*cumulative coverage (%)*
LDV	2,763	Raw frequency	70.40
Age-List	2,763	Distributed frequency, Age	74.74

The data show that core vocabulary lists based on distributed frequency across different age groups can achieve higher coverage than those based only on raw frequency when we test their coverage in a neutral corpus.

5.3.2 Contributed coverage

In order to explore the detailed difference between the Age-List and the LDV, we compare the overlapping and different parts of these two core vocabulary lists (see Table 9). The overlapping 1,849 words contribute to the coverage of 69.34%. Those words in the LDV but not in the Age-List account for 1.07% while those in the Age-List but not in the LDV have 5.4% coverage. Therefore, the Age-List based on the distributed frequency across various age groups leads to a higher coverage than the LDV, which is mainly based on raw frequency.

Table 9: Coverage components: Age-List vs. LDV

core vocabulary	*overlap*	*ldv only*	*age-list only*
LDV	1,849 (69.34%)	888 (1.07%)	
Age-List			888(5.40%)

5.3.3 Dispersion index

Coverage and distributed frequency are not the only factors for evaluating the core vocabulary in different age groups. The dispersion index (*D*) also plays an important role in word filtering. For example, the word *doll* ranks 401st in terms of frequency in our Age-Group Corpus. However, the usage of *doll* seems to be mainly associated with the age group AG0 (0-14 years old). It indicates that children tend to use it much more often than any other age group. The dispersion index is as low as 0.18. Therefore, despite its high frequency in the whole corpus, it will not be suitable for our core vocabulary, which needs to be distributed evenly across different age groups. That is to say, a core word must be used by both young and old people frequently at the same time. With the dispersion index, we can also easily spot other examples typical for one age group only such as *feminist* being typical for young people, *bargaining* for middle-aged people, and *trench* for seniors etc. (see Table 10). This sort of imbalance can be filtered out by setting a bottom line of 0.5 for the dispersion index (*D*), the maximum value of which is 1 according to Carroll's theory (1970).

Table 10: Dispersion index vs. intuition

word	*FAG0*	*FAG1*	*FAG2*	*FAG3*	*FAG4*	*FAG5*	*R*	*C (%)*	*D*	*U*	*RF*
doll	1277	13	27	23	11	8	6	0.02	0.18	69.76	401
feminist	0	205	3	5	5	24	5	0.004	0.32	17.33	1854
bargaining	0	0	0	4	328	7	3	0.006	0.09	13.50	1416
trench	1	7	13	1	3	180	6	0.003	0.29	13.76	2105

FAG0=frequency in Age Group (0-14) (see 4.3)
FAG1=frequency in Age Group (15-24)
FAG2=frequency in Age Group (25-34)
FAG3=frequency in Age Group (35-44)
FAG4=frequency in Age Group (45-59)
FAG5=frequency in Age Group (60+)

R=range
C=coverage
D=dispersion index by John Carroll (see 5.1)
U=usage efficient by John Carroll (see 5.1)
RF=the rank of the total frequency in our Age-Group Corpus

5.3.4 Core vocabulary proportion in different age groups

A question at this stage is whether core vocabulary accounts for a stable proportion of each age group's mental lexicon. To answer this question, the core vocabulary is taken as a yardstick to measure its proportion in the word types for different age groups. The total of word types in each age group will be treated as the size of its mental lexicon. The following formula is adopted to calculate the proportion of core vocabulary to mental lexicon for each age group:

Core vocabulary proportion of mental lexicon =

$$\frac{\text{Word type total of a core vocabulary in an age group}}{\text{the relevant age group's word type total}}$$

For example, the Age-List above contains 2,763 word types. Only 2,685 word types from this Age-List show up in Ag0 (aged 0-14) with 15,908 word types in this whole group. Therefore, the core vocabulary proportion of this group's mental lexicon is 2,685/15,908=16.88%. Accordingly, the core vocabulary proportion for each age group is calculated and summarized in Table 11. The results show that the core vocabulary is evenly distributed from Age Group 1 to Age Group 5 (see Figure 1), suggesting that the core vocabulary has a stable and similar ratio in speakers' mental lexicons from age 15 on, regardless of whether the core vocabulary is selected on the criterion of raw frequency or distributed frequency. Core vocabulary plays an important role for speakers of different ages and arguably provides the foundation for language communication. It is thus reasonable that carefully selected core vocabulary can help to formulate an effective pedagogical programme to facilitate teaching and learning English as a foreign language.

Table 11: Core vocabulary proportion in each age group

core vocabulary ratio	*AG0 (%)*	*AG1 (%)*	*AG2 (%)*	*AG3 (%)*	*AG4 (%)*	*AG5 (%)*
LDV	15.29	11.00	10.69	10.21	10.28	11.03
Age-List	16.88	11.50	11.16	10.71	10.68	11.52

It is noticeable that core vocabulary occupies a larger proportion of the mental lexicon in people aged under 15 than those aged above 15, as we see in Figure 1. Obviously, the size of the mental lexicon is not that large for children so core vocabulary will be more frequently turned to and become more accessible. Moreover, the core vocabulary proportion in the Age-List is higher than the LDV in each age group. Hence, we infer that each age group tends to use more core words selected by distributed frequency across age groups than those selected by raw frequency only.

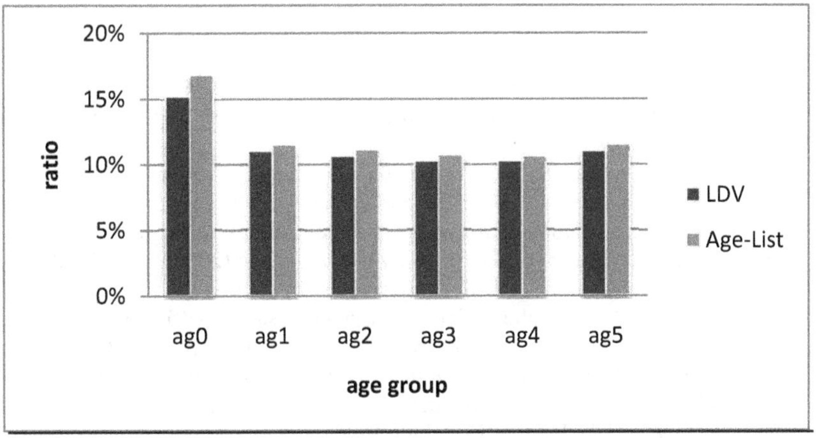

Figure 1: Core vocabulary proportion in each age group

6. Conclusions

When we design core vocabulary for learners' dictionaries, the combined factors of the dispersion index of a word and its distributed frequency in different age groups can achieve higher coverage than raw frequency alone. People aged under 15 rely more on core vocabulary in their daily communication than adults since core vocabulary occupies a larger proportion of their mental lexicon due to its fundamental role in language development. For the age groups above 15, core vocabulary remains a stable and static proportion of their mental lexicon despite increasing age, which signifies the vital role of core vocabulary. Furthermore, it has also been shown that each age group tends to use more core words selected on the basis of distributed frequency across different age groups than those selected on raw frequency alone. Our study is thus significant in bringing into play the importance of balanced vocabulary selection based on distributed frequency with an age dispersion.

Acknowledgement

The work reported in this article was supported in part by research grants to the second author from the City University of Hong Kong (Grant No.s 7008062, 7008002 and 7002387).

References

BNC XML (2007), *The British National Corpus XML Edition DVD*. Oxford: Oxford University Press. Manual available online at: http://www.natcorp.ox.ac.uk/docs/URG/

Bullon, S. & G. Leech (2007), 'Longman Communication 3000 and the Longman Defining Vocabulary', in: S. Bullon and G. Leech (eds.) *Longman Communication 3000*. Harlow: Pearson Education Limited. 1-7.

CALD3 = *Cambridge advanced learner's dictionary* (2008). Third edition. Cambridge: Cambridge University Press.

Carroll, J.B. (1970), 'An alternative to Juilland's usage coefficient for lexical frequencies and a proposal for a standard frequency index (SFI)', *Computer studies in the humanities and verbal behavior*, 3: 61-65.

Carroll, J.B., P. Davies & B. Richman (1971), *The American Heritage word frequency book*. Boston: Houghton Mifflin.

Carroll, J.B. & M.N. White (1973), 'Word frequency and age-of-acquisition as determiners of picture-naming latency', *Quarterly journal of experimental psychology*, 25: 85-95.

Carter, R. (1998), *Vocabulary: applied linguistics perspectives* Second edition. London: Routledge.

CCD5 = *Collins COBUILD advanced learner's English dictionary* (2006). Fifth edition. Glasgow: HarperCollins Publishers.

Cowie, A.P. (1999), *English dictionaries for foreign learners: a history*. Oxford: Oxford University Press.

Fang, A.C. & M. Huckvale (2000), 'Out-of-vocabulary rate reduction through dispersion-based lexical selection', *Oxford literary and linguistic computing*, 15(3): 251-263.

Gilhooly, K.J. & R.H. Logie (1980), 'Age-of-acquisition, imagery, concreteness, familiarity, and ambiguity measures for 1,944 words', *Behavior research methods & instrumentation*, 12(4): 395-427.

Herbst, T. (1986), 'Defining with a controlled defining vocabulary in foreign learners' dictionaries', in: A. Kučera, A. Rey, H.E. Wiegand & L. Zgusta (eds.) *Lexicographica: international annual for lexicography*. Tübingen: Max Niemeyer Verlag. 101-119.

Hofland, K. & S. Johansson (1982), *Word frequencies in British and American English*. Bergen: The Norwegian Computing Centre for the Humanities.

Howe, C. (1981), *Acquiring language in a conversational context*. New York: Academic Press.

Ivanic, R. & T. McEnery (1996), *The Lancaster Corpus of Children's Project Writing (LCCPW)*. Available online at: http://www.lancs.ac.uk/fass/projects/lever/index.htm

Juilland, A. & E. Chang-Rodriguez (1964), *Frequency dictionary of Spanish words*. The Hague: Mouton & Co.

Kučera, H. & W.N. Francis (1967), *Computational analysis of present-day American English*. Providence: Brown University Press.

LDCE5 = *Longman dictionary of Contemporary English* (5th ed. 2009). Edinburgh Gate: Pearson Education Limited.

Lee, D. (2001), 'Defining core vocabulary and tracking its distribution across spoken and written genres: evidence of a gradience of variation from the British National Corpus', *Journal of English linguistics*, 29(3): 250-278.

Li, H. (2010), 'Word frequency distribution for electronic learner's dictionaries', in: S. Granger & M. Paquot (eds.) *eLexicography in the 21st century: New challenges, new applications. Proceedings of ELEX 2009. Cahiers du CENTAL*. Louvain-la-Neuve: Presses universitaires de Louvain. 217-228.

Li, H. & A.C. Fang (2011), 'Word frequency of the CHILDES corpus: Another perspective of child language features', *ICAME Journal*, 35: 95-116.

MacWhinney, B. (2000), *The CHILDES project: tools for analyzing talk*, (3rd ed.). Mahwah, (NJ): Lawrence Erlbaum Associates.

MED2 = *Macmillan English dictionary for advanced learners* (2007) Second edition. Oxford: Macmillan Education.

OALD7 = *Oxford advanced learner's dictionary* (2005). Seventh edition. Oxford: Oxford University Press.

OANC (2005), *The Open American National Corpus (OANC)*. Available online at: http://www.anc.org/OANC/index.html#download

Quirk, R. (1978), Preface to *Longman dictionary of Contemporary English* (1st ed.), in: P. Procter, R.F. Ilson, J. Ayto & G. Walsh (eds.) *Longman dictionary of Contemporary English* (1st ed.). London: Longman Group Limited. vii.

Richards, J.C. (1976), *Word familiarity as an index of vocabulary selection with indices for 4495 Words*, PhD Thesis, Université de Laval.

Sampson, G. (2005), *The LUCY Corpus*. Available online at: http://www .grsampson.net/bufPageLucy.html

Souter, C. (1989), *The Polytechnic of Wales Corpus (POW)*, Manual available online at: http://khnt.hit.uib.no/icame/manuals/pow.htm

Stubbs, M. (2001), *Words and phrases: corpus studies of lexical semantics*. Oxford: Blackwell.

Theakston, A.L., E.V.M. Lieven, J.M. Pine & C.F. Rowland (2001), 'The role of performance limitations in the acquisition of verb-argument structure: an alternative account', *Journal of child language*, 28: 127-152.

Thorndike, E. & I. Lorge (1944), *The teacher's word book of 30,000 words*. New York: Teachers College, Columbia University.

Wells, C.G. (1981), *Learning through interaction: the study of language development*. Cambridge: Cambridge University Press.

Wilson, M. (1988), 'MRC Psycholinguistic Database: machine-usable dictionary, version 2.00', *Behavior research methods, instruments, & computers*, 20(1): 6-10.

Language Documentation

The expanding horizons of corpus analysis

Brian MacWhinney

Carnegie Mellon University

Abstract

By including a focus on multimedia interactions linked to transcripts, corpus linguistics can vastly expand its horizons. This expansion will rely on two continuing developments. First, we need to develop easily used methods for each of the ten analytic methods we have examined, including lexical analyses, QDA (qualitative data analysis), automatic tagging, language profiles, group comparisons, change scores, error analysis, feedback studies, conversation analysis, and modeling. Second, we need to work together to construct a unified database for language studies and related sciences. This database must be grounded on the principles of open access, data-sharing, interoperability, and integrated structure. It must provide powerful tools for searching, multilinguality, and multimedia analysis. If we can build this infrastructure, we will be able to explore more deeply the key questions underlying the structure and functioning of language, as it emerges from the intermeshing of processes operative on eight major timeframes.

1. Introduction

Corpus linguistics has benefitted greatly from continuing advances in computer and Internet hardware and software. These advances have made it possible to develop facilities such as BNCweb (bncweb.lancs.ac.uk), LDC (Linguistic Data Consortium) online, the American National Corpus (americannationalcorpus. org), TalkBank (talkbank.org), and CHILDES (childes.psy.cmu.edu). In earlier periods, these corpora were limited to written and transcribed materials. However, most newer corpora now include transcripts linked to either audio or video recordings. The development of this newer corpus methodology is facilitated by technology which makes it easy to produce high-quality video recordings of face-to-face interactions. Also, we now have common access to software that can link transcripts to the media at the level of the utterance and sometimes the word. These linked transcripts can then be accessed over the web, either through downloading or through browser plug-ins.

Among the various available resources, the collections at TalkBank and CHILDES are unique in providing users with completely open, online access to a large quantity of audio or video that has been linked to transcripts on the level of individual utterances. Using these links, researchers can play back thousands of different conservational interactions and study in detail their interactional and linguistic features. These materials can then be subjected to the analytic methods of corpus-based linguistics. By applying both the traditional methods of corpus analysis and new methods specifically designed for multimedia data, we can achieve a rapid and powerful expansion of the horizons of corpus linguistics.

In this paper, I will argue that this linkage of transcripts to media opens up a unique, new way of understanding human language. My basic thesis is that language emerges through the interaction of forces that operate on several different time scales or timeframes. These timeframes vary in their duration from milliseconds to millennia. However, all of these forces must eventually reveal their functioning within the actual moment of communication. Collections of transcripts linked to video provide us with a methodologically sound way of tracking and evaluating these interactions between timeframes across situations, speakers, and time. In this way, the availability of transcripts linked to video can radically expand the horizons of corpus linguistics. However, to realize these expanded horizons, researchers must commit themselves to the construction of a shared, interoperable database, similar to that currently available in TalkBank. Here, I will explain how this database must be structured to best address the many research challenges we will face within this broadened scope of corpus linguistics.

2. Timeframes meshing in the moment

Let me begin by posing the core question facing linguistic analysis. In his studies of sentence production, Osgood (1971) phrased the question as "Where do sentences come from?" In a similar vein, we can ask, "Where do linguistic forms and functions come from?" A full answer to this question would provide a detailed functionalist account of the shape of human language. In this paper, I will suggest that functions and forms arise from the competing intersection of adaptive processes operating across interlocking timeframes. We can distinguish eight major levels of timeframes; each of these levels includes a variety of individual mechanisms whose timeframes also vary:

1. **Processing**. This timeframe governs the online processing of words and sentences.
2. **Turn-taking**. This timeframe governs how we maintain, complete, extend, and yield conversational turns.
3. **Activity**. This timeframe governs how we structure the overall goals of the current interaction.
4. **Developmental**. This is the timeframe governing language learning by the child and the adult second language learner.
5. **Social**. This is the timeframe within which we track commitments to various social groups and processes across interactions.
6. **Epigenetic**. This is the timeframe across which the genes interact to produce physical and neural structures supporting language.
7. **Diachronic**. This is the timeframe for socially shared changes in language forms and structures.

8. **Phylogenetic**. This is the timeframe that governs the ongoing evolution of the human language capacity.

The shapes of specific linguistic markers are primarily determined by forces on levels 1-3, but are further modulated by the long-scale processes on timeframes 4-7. All of these functions receive inputs from all timeframes. For example, the choice between a noun, pronoun, or zero in subject position is conditioned by forces for the sharing of mental models operating on timeframes 1, 2, and 3. These forces are constrained at the moment of speaking by grammatical and production processes within timeframe 1. Across the timeframe of language development, the growth of control over pronominal marking arises within timeframe 4 and changes in accord with timeframe 5. Finally, the underlying function of deixis and pointing has emerged in the species across timeframe 8 with ongoing support from all the other levels.

A key postulate of functionalism (Bates & MacWhinney 1989) is that functions compete for mapping to forms. In the timeframe model, the outcome of the competition is determined by inputs from clocks running at each time scale. The brain provides support for this type of learning by using circuits with widely divergent time scale properties operating between the basal ganglia, hippocampus, and the cortex. Even in organisms as simple as the bee, we can find discrete neurochemical processes that work to consolidate memories on each of the time scales relevant to the pollen-gathering activities of the bee (Menzel & Giurfa 2001).

For the purposes of illustration, one can compare the timeframes involved in control of language with those used in mechanical calendars. An example from ancient Greece is the Antikythera, a device discovered in 1901 inside a shipwreck in the Aegean. The device uses a set of interlocking gears or wheels to compute times according to the 365-day Sothic year, the 12-month zodiac, the solar year, the lunar phase, the phases between solar eclipses, the 19-year Metonic cycle, and the 76-year Callippic cycle. In addition, it marks the positions of the planets and the times of specific Panhellenic games. Figure 1 provides a glimpse into the shape of this remarkable mechanism. Another example of a clock that meshes across multiple time scales is the Orloj from Prague, which is shown in Figure 2.

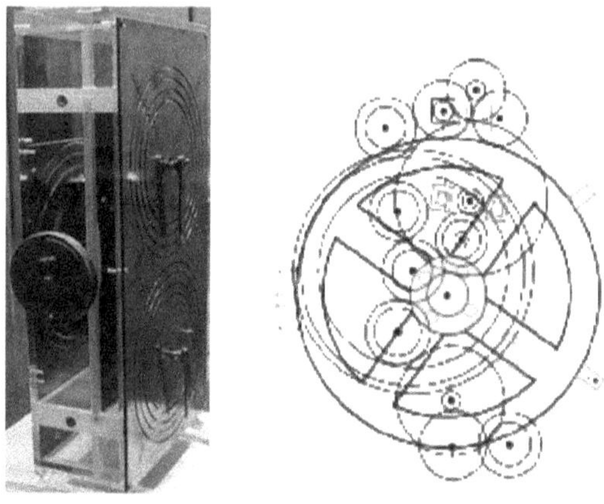

Figure 1: The Antikythera: a reconstruction and a sketch of the gears
Images accessed at Wikipedia Commons:
http://en.wikipedia.org/wiki/Antikythera_Mechanism

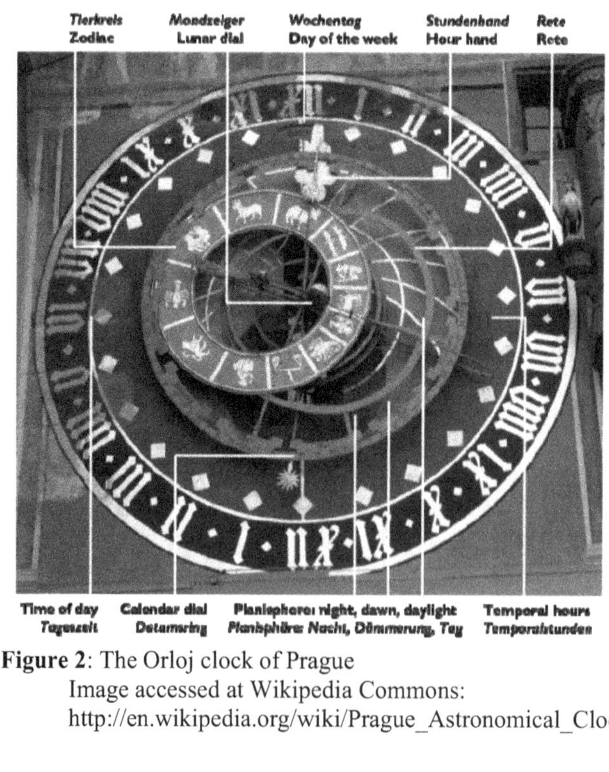

Figure 2: The Orloj clock of Prague
Image accessed at Wikipedia Commons:
http://en.wikipedia.org/wiki/Prague_Astronomical_Clock

The meshing of the wheels of these mechanical calendars provides an analogy to the meshing of the processes operating across the eight time scales determining human communication. The notion of process meshing can also be illustrated through biological systems. For example, metabolic processes in the body link up across a variety of time scales, some tightly linked to the catalytic processes in the Krebs cycle that convert ATP into energy, others involved in the creation of ATP, and still others involved in the overall regulation of the body's heat and energy levels. Even more complex and longer-term regulatory processes govern learning in the brain and its regulation by hormonal systems and exposure to inputs from the environment.

Let us now take a closer look at the shapes of these eight timeframes with attention to how they affect particular linguistic structures or processes. Within each of these timeframes, when we look at specific examples, we will see that there is variation in the actual clocks involved. This is why it is important to use the term "timeframe" to discuss a general class of processes that operate with similar, but not identical, clocks.

2.1 The processing timeframe

The most fast-acting pressures on language form are those that derive from online processing constraints (MacWhinney 2009). These pressures arise from the limitations of memory mechanisms, attention focusing, coordination of sentence planning, code switching between languages, and motor control. These various processing timeframes all rest on top of the basic time required for the firing of a single neuron and transmission of that signal to the next neuron. Although this depends heavily on many factors, a value of 10 milliseconds (ms) is a good approximation for many connections. The brevity of this period allows for the firing of as many as 20 neural connections during the 150 ms period required for production of a single syllable (Massaro 1987). Consider this example: when bilinguals switch from English to Spanish, the initial 250 ms of speaking in Spanish are still under the influence of English phonology until the alternative Spanish patterns become fully active (Grosjean & Miller 1994). Similarly, Goldman-Eisler (1968) found that the majority of retraces and repetitions typically affect nothing more than one or two syllables, extending across perhaps 500 ms. Attentional shifting between perceptual dimensions or languages can also be measured in terms of hundreds of milliseconds (Prior & MacWhinney in press).

The processing timeframe brackets a large number of important processes in language production and perception. In terms of production, this timeframe governs lexical access (including gang effects and competitor effects), phonological activation in the output buffer, morphological combination, and triggering of syntactic combinatorial patterns. This timeframe also governs phonological assimilations occurring in fast speech patterns (Bybee 2003). Using corpus linguistic methods, we can study how these assimilations increase through a discourse and how they vary with the nature of the addressee. In this way we can see interactions between timeframes 1, 2, 3, and 5. When we start to look in detail at fast speech assimilations in the speech mothers provide to their children, we then see further interactions with timeframe 4 (Smith, Durham & Fortune 2007).

On the perceptual side, the processing timeframe brackets all of the basic auditory processes, as well as the input to statistical pattern learning, short-term auditory memory, processes for segmenting by stress patterns, orientation to specially marked signals, and adjustment to speaker variability. Generally, it is easier to apply corpus-based methods to the study of production. However, we can also study perception by using corpora to delineate the shape of the ambient language that serves as input to the learner and the framework for social variation.

2.2 The turn-taking timeframe

When we are engaged in conversational interactions, we are continually taking in data from our conversational partners. We are watching their postures, gestures, and facial expressions. As we are speaking, they may be inserting nods or words indicating their acceptance of what we are saying or at least showing that they are paying attention. However, they may also be indicating impatience or a desire to have the floor. At each point in the conversation, we are involved in the construction and completion of our current turn constructional unit (TCU) (Schegloff 2007). Through syntactic structure, gesture, and prosody we can signal our desire to maintain or yield the floor. When a TCU is completed, we may add a further increment, start a new TCU, or allow an interlocutor to begin speaking. All of these decisions involve the continual ingestion of information by the turn-taking system during real time. The timeframe here is a bit longer than that of basic linguistic processing. The basic system that responds to feedback from listeners operates in a framework of 500 ms, with additional components extending across a few seconds. By studying video data from natural, spontaneous interactions, corpus linguistics can make serious contributions to the understanding of processes in this timeframe. However, achieving this progress requires adherence to a set of coding conventions for conversational features that can be unambiguously processed by computers. This goal has been addressed within the CABank component of TalkBank at http://talkbank.org/CABank.

2.3 The activity timeframe

Beyond our short-term involvement with turn-taking, we also make medium-term commitments to the shape of an interaction as an activity. For each interaction, we set conversational goals that define particular activity types (Leont'ev 1947/1981). For example, we may engage a real estate agent to help us buy a house. Our linguistic interactions with this agent are then shaped by the status of the buying process and our goals in buying a house. After we complete one set of transactions with this agent, we will maintain an ongoing relation that will then shape our further interactions, days or weeks later (Keenan, MacWhinney & Mayhew 1977). Activity types provide a major challenge and opportunity for corpus-based analysis, because the shape of the linguistic resources we use vary widely across activity or situation types. For example, the default reading of the word "bank" will be different if we are discussing economics, as opposed to methods of improving river hydraulics. If we could configure computational corpus analysis to be sensitive to alternative activity types or genres (Biber, Conrad & Reppen 1994), we could markedly improve speech recognition, ambiguity resolution, parsing, and automatic discourse processing.

2.4 The developmental timeframe

Jean Piaget's genetic psychology (Piaget 1954) was the first fully articulated emergentist view of development. Impressively complete in its coverage, it failed to specify details regarding mechanisms of development. To provide this missing mechanistic detail, current emergentist accounts of development rely on connectionism (Quinlan 2003), embodied cognition (Klatzky, MacWhinney & Behrmann 2008), and dynamic systems theory (Thelen & Smith 1994). Emergentist theory has been used to characterize two different, but interrelated, aspects of development. The first is the learning of basic facts, forms, relations, names, and procedures. Connectionist and usage-based models of language learning, such as those that deal with learning of the past tense (MacWhinney & Leinbach 1991), syntactic patterns (Waterfall, Sandbank, Onnis & Edelman 2010), or word segmentation (Monaghan & Christiansen 2010) often focus on this type of development. A second type of development involves the learning of new strategies and frameworks that can alter the overall shape of language and cognition, often through cue focusing and bootstrapping (Regier 2005, Smith & Colunga 2003). The relevance of corpus-based analyses to the study of language development has been demonstrated extensively in recent work based on the CHILDES and BilingBank corpora. There are now over 3,500 published articles based on the use of these corpora. A recent issue of the *Journal of Child Language* (MacWhinney 2010) based on the modeling of corpus data from CHILDES illustrates the high level of analytic precision that this work is now achieving.

The developmental timeframe meshes in complex ways with processing during the ongoing interaction. For example, a child's failure to understand the meaning of the word "dependability" in a classroom discussion of the reliability of batteries (MacWhinney 2005) may be the result of problems in understanding previous classroom and computerized lessons on numerical distributions. Similarly, the failure in lexical retrieval that occurs in aphasia is driven by changes to neural tissue subsequent to a stroke. Thus, online processing emergence can reflect the status of long-term developmental, neuronal, and physiological processes.

2.5 The social timeframe

Many of the pressures that operate during face-to-face conversations derive from long-term social commitments. Our choice of vocabulary, slang, topics, dialect and language is determined by the status of our social relations to the people we meet. We can select particular linguistic options to emphasize solidarity (R. Brown & Gilman 1960), impose our power, or seek favors (P. Brown & Levinson 1987). The time course of these social commitments is often measured in years or decades (Labov 2001). Some basic social commitments, including those forced by gender and race, can never be fundamentally altered. For corpus-based analyses, what is important is being able to link the usage of linguistic forms in the moment to long-term personal characteristics, whether observed directly or measured through questionnaires and surveys. This is the approach taken within the field of sociophonetics (Hay & Drager 2007) which studies the meshing of long-term social indicators with output processing in the moment. To make corpora maximally useful for such studies, we need both good tools for phonetic analysis and systematic coding of the relevant social variables. To achieve this we have been working to configure tools such as Praat (praat.uva.nl), Phon (talkbank.org/phon), and CLAN (talkbank.org/clan) to integrate the phonetic and sociolinguistic aspects of these analyses.

2.6 The epigenetic timeframe

DNA lays out framework that governs the epigenesis (Waddington 1957) of the embryo and the infant. However, this is an emergent framework, rather than a detailed blueprint. Embryologists have shown how biological structures emerge from processes of induction between developing tissue structures in the embryo in cascading waves of catalytic processes (Goodenough & Deacon 2006). The shape of these interactions is not hard-coded in the DNA. Instead, the DNA encodes information that can push the process of differentiation in particular directions at crucial epigenetic choice points. The precursors of autism in the embryo can be traced to particular epigenetic effects, as can the formation of stripes in the tiger. Epigenetic emergence does not cease at birth. To the degree that the brain maintains a level of plasticity, epigenetic processes allow for recovery of function after stroke through rewiring and reorganization. Before birth, epigenetic interactions with the environment are confined to forces that impinge on the uterus and the embryonic fluid. After birth, the environment can trigger a wide variety of variations in gene expression from diabetes to brain reorganization for language in the deaf (Bellugi, Poizner & Klima 1989). As long as the child remains in the womb, few of these processes are relevant to work in linguistics. However, once the infant begins vocalizations and babbling, there is a great deal that can be studied through corpus-based methods, as recently codified in the context of the Phon Project (talkbank.org/phon) organized by Yvan Rose at Memorial University.

2.7 The diachronic timeframe

We can also use emergentist thinking to understand the changes that languages have undergone across the centuries (Bybee & Hopper 2001). Typically, these changes are viewed as resulting from the fast speech processing simplifications or morphological overregularizations. It is the cumulative effect of these myriad short-term effects that drive the long-term changes. However, the distribution of these processes is not necessarily uniform. For example, Labov (2001) notes that teenage males are particularly involved in the generation of new speech patterns. To understand this better, we need to collect corpora that capture the variation in the speech forms produced by these highly active groups.

2.8 The phylogenetic timeframe

The slowest moving emergent structures are those that are encoded in the genes. Changes across this timeframe – which involves millennia rather than minutes – are controlled by natural selection (Darwin 1871). The core engine of emergence is the generation of variation through mutation, followed then by natural selection through both mate choice and differential mortality. Natural selection utilizes the possibilities for reorganization shaped by the DNA and the interactions of polypeptides that it specifies. The unevenness of this underlying landscape makes some mutations more probable and frequent than others, leading to a reliance on the reuse of old forms to serve new functions. Emergentist accounts in this area have emphasized the ways in which language, society, and cognition have undergone coevolution (MacWhinney 2008a) based on the linking of dynamic systems. To trigger this coevolutionary advantage, changes in linguistic abilities must arise in parallel with advances in cognitive or social abilities. Moreover, both effects must interact at the moment of speaking. When this happens in a way that favors reproductive fitness, the mutation will be preserved. To study the linkage of this timeframe to interaction in the moment, researchers must focus on individual and population differences. For instance, one can study clinical patterns such as Specific Language Impairment (SLI), stuttering, autism, or Williams Syndrome in terms of their impact on communication during the moment. As an example, there is evidence that Specific Language Impairment arises from difficulties in integrating diverse types of linguistic information online (Presson & MacWhinney in press). One important line of research seeks to link these patterns to specific genetic patterns in genes such as FOXP2 (Enard et al. 2002). However, we also need to trace the effects of these genetic factors on language both through controlled experimental tasks and corpus analysis. Corpus analysis allows us to track ways in which the language of these populations differs from the standard pattern. By examining these patterns in detail, we can learn which constructions trigger errors, avoidance, or alternative strategies.

2.9 Linking the timeframes in the moment

All of these processes, across all of these timeframes, must have their impact at the moment of speaking. This means that if we can capture the moments of speaking in sufficient quality and quantity, we will be able to study the interplay of all of these processes. To achieve this, the primary TalkBank data structure is an alignment between a digitized transcript (or annotation) and digitized media, much as in the TalkBank database. As Bird & Liberman (2001) have shown, linkages of annotations to media all assume the form of directed acyclic graphs (DAGs) which they call "annotation graphs" (AG). Although this structure is universal, there are dozens of methods for characterizing and displaying these transcript-media linkages. The next page shows two ways in which a transcript can be linked to media. In the first format, from ELAN (www.lat-mpi.eu/tools/elan), we see the transcript displayed in a musical notation format under the QuickTime window (Figure 3). In the second format, from CLAN (childes.psy.cmu.edu/clan), we see the transcript in a standard textual display (Figure 4). In both cases, as the researcher plays through the video, the respective segment of the transcript is highlighted so that the researcher can study the transcript in tight synchrony with the actual experience of the interaction.

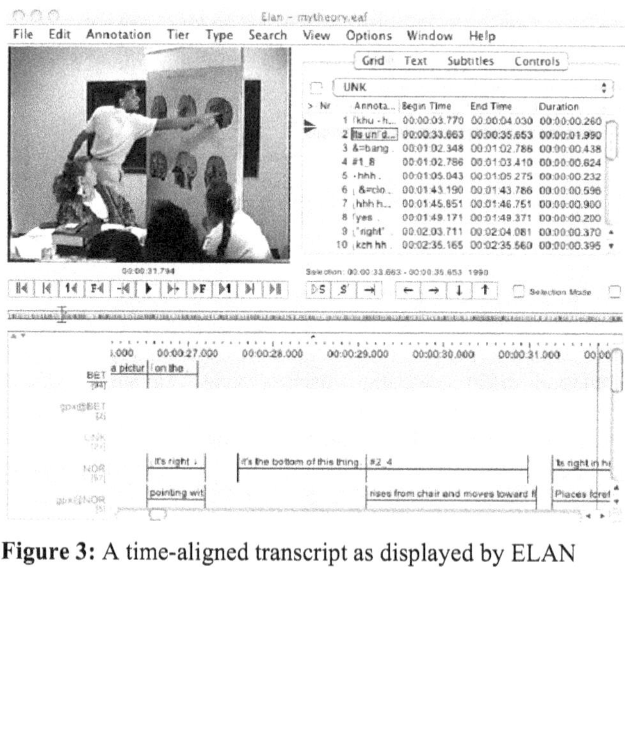

Figure 3: A time-aligned transcript as displayed by ELAN

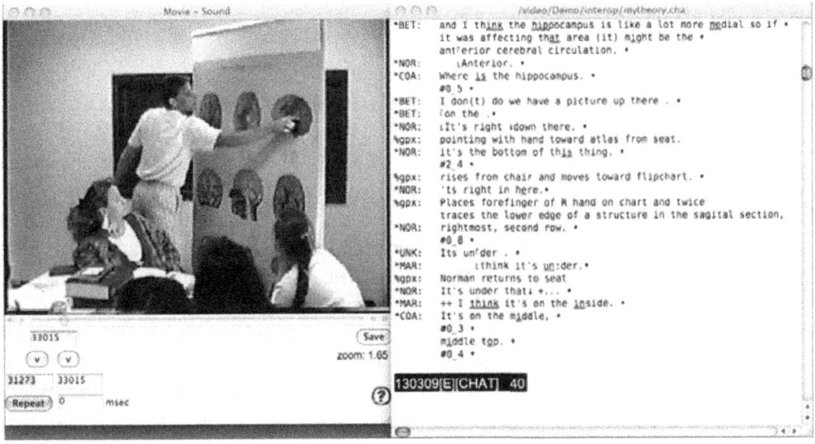

Figure 4: A time-aligned transcript as displayed in CLAN

This particular videotaped interaction was the subject of a special issue of *Discourse Processes* in 1999. In the interaction, medical students in a problem-based learning (PBL) class are trying to link the position of the hippocampus to observed symptoms in a neurological patient. The CD-ROM at the back of the special issue presented the transcripts linked to the media. These transcripts with linked media can be browsed over the web from http://talkbank.org/browser. This particular example is at ClassBank/CogInst/mytheory.cha.

The advantage of the ELAN musical score display format is that it displays clearly the duration of a communicative activity and the synchrony across types of communicative activities (intonation, head nodding, words, etc.). The advantage of the CLAN transcript format is that it is easier to read and presents a better overview of the conversation. Each visualization format has its own advantages and disadvantages. The important point is that, with full data interoperability, researchers can display the same underlying data in whichever viewer or editor they need for the particular project at hand. Toward this goal, we have written programs that can reliably convert data from all of the major transcript-media display programs (AG, Anvil, ELAN, EXMARaLDA, HIAT, SALT, DRT, SyncWriter, MediaTagger, Transcriber, Transana, Praat, WaveSurfer, SoundWalker, and Observer) into the ComNet XML format. Moreover, transcriptions and other annotations can be transformed from XML back into each format and compared with the original to show that no data were lost during the roundtrip conversion.

3. Analysis methods

Corpora composed of multimedia interactions linked to transcripts can be analyzed through a wide variety of methods. Because only some of these methods involve controlled experimentation, there is sometimes a tendency to dismiss corpus analysis as unscientific or pre-scientific. However, many of the most important advances in science have come from non-experimental methods, such as naturalistic observation (Darwin, Linnaeus), model-building (Hawkins), and thought experiments (Einstein). Moreover, corpus analysis can easily be combined with experimental control, when necessary. Therefore, any general attempt to dismiss corpus analysis as unscientific is inappropriate. Instead, methodological critiques should focus on understanding the match between particular methods and their individual scientific goals. In this section, I will review 12 classes of methods that have proven useful in the study of multimedia corpora. To illustrate these methods, I will often refer to specific computational implementations available in the CLAN programs (talkbank.org/CLAN) created by the TalkBank project. In fact, there are dozens of other computational implementations that overlap with features of the CLAN programs and I am using CLAN here only to provide a consistent source of examples.

3.1 Lexical studies

The most widely used methods in corpus analysis involve the study of the distribution of lexical forms. What makes these methods particularly appealing is the ease with which computers can locate specific surface word forms in corpora. Internet search engines such as Google have taken advantage of this fact to construct indices to the vast textual resources of the Internet. These same methods can also be applied to multimedia resources with transcripts linked to video. The various lexical methods fall into several categories or levels, based on the extent to which they rely on additional structures:

1. The simplest lexical methods treat corpora as mere “bags of words”. From this bag of words, we can compute lists of word frequencies, based simply on surface forms. For example, the FREQ program in CLAN provides frequency lists that can be ordered alphabetically or by frequency. As in BNCWeb, the output of FREQ can be used to locate the usages in the original transcripts. Moreover, the output can be shipped over to programs such as Excel for further statistical analysis.
2. Beyond the first level of lexical counting, it is easy to construct a specific search set that targets words from a given semantic domain. For example, FREQ allows the user to track the frequencies of words in specific user-defined lexical groups, such as “morality terms” or “quantifiers”.
3. One can also characterize texts in terms of a variety of lexical profiles. For example, the type/token ratio (TTR), which is also produced by the FREQ program, can be used to indicate the lexical diversity of a text.

However, this index is not constant across sample sizes, because the impact of high frequency words on lowering the TTR is most clearly demonstrated in larger texts. To correct for this, CLAN encourages the user to rely instead on the VOCD measure of vocabulary diversity (Malvern, Richards, Chipere & Purán 2004).

4. On the next higher level, CLAN provides methods of searching lexical combinations through regular expression (Regex) pattern matching (Friedl 2002). Using the KWAL and COMBO programs, users can locate each match to a pattern and double click on the entry to go to relevant line in the original transcript. At that point, they can study the discourse context and play back the audio or video, if needed.
5. In many cases, it is possible to formulate research questions in terms of the surface forms of words. However, in other cases, researchers want to study lexical combinations in relation to part of speech (POS) tags and syntactic tags. To support this, many of the corpora in CHILDES have been tagged for both morphosyntactic composition and syntactic role. These tags are aligned with words on the main orthographic tier in a one-to-one fashion, as verified through the XML validator. The online WebBNC corpus (bncweb.info) provides a good example of how simple Regex searches can be combined directly with POS information. The current versions of COMBO and KWAL in CLAN can perform some of these searches. However, the newer CHATTER program provides fuller support for XML-based Regex queries. Unlike CLAN, which is written in C, CHATTER is written in Java and designed specifically for searching through the XML version of the various TalkBank databases.

These various methods for lexical searching all depend on the use of consistent standards for lexical representation. For spoken language corpora, it is often difficult for transcribers to adhere to a consistent set of standards for lexical representation. MacWhinney (2008b) describes these problems in detail. Many of them can be resolved through simple standardization. However, the most serious problem relates to the desire to represent the actual phonological form of the word directly in the lexical line. Because TalkBank transcripts are typically linked to audio, the need for representing phonology directly through eye-dialect (Ochs 1979) is minimized. In addition, CHAT provides methods for representing phonological form, but then following this with the standard lexical target. Because of these various problems, many of the corpora in the CA segment of TalkBank may never be subjected to POS tagging. Eventually, however, the bulk of the corpora in CHILDES and other segments of TalkBank will be tagged.

3.2 Qualitative Data Analysis = hand coding

Corpora can also be subjected to analysis through coding systems. Areas that rely heavily on the use of hand coding include studies of gesture, speech acts, dialect features, interactional patterns, rhetorical structure, and speech errors. The process of elaborating transcripts with hand-entered codes is known as

Qualitative Data Analysis (QDA). Major programs supporting QDA include NVivo7, ATLAS.ti, Kwalitan, The Observer, HyperResearch, and Transana. Information on these programs is given at http://talkbank.org/software/. Unfortunately, these programs all rely on proprietary transcript formats, and are not linked to any publicly accessible database. As a result, researchers who are interested in coding corpora currently in TalkBank need to rely on the QDA tools provided in CLAN. These tools include the following components:

1. The Coder's Editor program facilitates exhaustive coding of a transcript in accord with a user-specific system. The researcher first specifies a hierarchical coding structure. A good example of this is the INCA speech act coding system (Ninio & Wheeler 1984) given in the CHAT manual. Once a coding system has been specified, the coder then goes through the transcript, line-by-line making a selection of the correct code for each utterance.
2. After using Coder's Editor, the RELY program allows one to compute reliability across two or more coders.
3. GEMs are marks the coder inserts in the transcript to surround interesting blocks of text with code words such as "book reading" or "political discussion". Later on, programs can use these marks to focus analyses on the relevant blocks or "gems".
4. CLAN also allows users to insert codes on any number of additional coding lines such as %coh for cohesion analysis, etc.
5. The TalkBank system also provides a method for work groups to enter blogs or commentary for multimedia-linked transcripts on the web at http://talkbank.org/browser. After registering for this system (MacWhinney et al. 2004), users can see comments from others in their work group and add additional comments of their own. Commentary can also be coded by type, date, and other parameters.
6. Gesture analysis in systems such as ELAN (http://www.lat-mpi.eu/tools/elan/) or Anvil (www.anvil-software.de) provides very accurate alignment of speech to gesture. To interface with these programs, CLAN provides converters between CHAT XML and ELAN or Anvil XML. There are good reasons to consider use of both CLAN and ELAN (or Anvil) for gesture analysis. Within ELAN and Anvil, the screen territory tends to become cluttered with coding tiers. Moreover, it is difficult to get a standard textual overview of the interaction in combination with the gestures. To address this problem, CLAN allows transcribers to nest small files within larger files using hot links. Within the overall transcript for a session, the user clicks a bullet to open up a second embedded transcript, much like zooming in with a microscope. At the second level, a gesture sequence is described and coded in detail and further bullets are available to play back segments of the gesture from thumbnail icons or to open up a third level of gesture analysis. This

Figure 5: Main text window for CLAN gesture analysis sample

Figure 6: Sub-window for CLAN gesture analysis and coding

approach tends to focus on the analysis of gesture sequences, as in Kendon (1982). The screen shots in Figures 5 and 6 show what this coding looks like for an interaction in Danish. The main text window is shown in Figure 5. When the user clicks on the line labeled "torture time sequence", the window in Figure 6 pops up allowing for detailed coding of the gesture sequence for that passage.

3.3 Automatic tagging

As corpora grow in size and as research questions proliferate, it becomes increasingly important to enter codes automatically, rather than tediously by hand. For some domains, automatic coding is still a distant goal, but for others it is possible now. The three areas for which CLAN can now provide automatic coding or tagging include morphosyntax, grammatical relations, and phonology.

1. **MOR and POST**. For morphological tagging and disambiguation, CLAN relies on the MOR and POST programs, as documented in MacWhinney (2008b). MOR provides not only a tagging of the part of speech of the word, but also a full analysis of its morphological composition. We now have open-source MOR taggers with user-modifiable lexicons and rule systems for Afrikaans, Cantonese, Dutch, English, French, German, Italian, Japanese, Mandarin, and Spanish. After tagging by MOR, the user runs the POST disambiguator (Parisse & Le Normand 2000). The accuracy of the disambiguation is well above 95%, as long as the transcription is accurate on the word and utterance level.
2. **GRASP**. After analysis by MOR and POST, it is possible to run the GRASP program (Sagae, Davis, Lavie, MacWhinney & Wintner 2010) to automatically construct a labeled dependency graph, based on a set of user-specified grammatical relations (GRs), such as Adjunct, Subject, or Complement. Although we have GRASP taggers now for English, Japanese, Spanish, and Mandarin, each of these systems is new and further work is needed to improve tagging accuracy.
3. **Phonology**. The CLAN programs have only the most limited abilities to analyze phonological features. To address this problem, we have built a separate Java program called PHON (Rose et al. 2005) that can directly analyze files in the CLAN XML format. Using IPA transcriptions, PHON can perform a variety of automatic analyses, such as segmentation, syllabification, and process analysis. In addition, it provides automatic linkages to Praat for phonetic analysis.

In the future, we hope to extend our automatic analyses to include systems for automatic video analysis (Hauptmann, Yan, Lin, Christel & Wactlar 2007), psychological mood coding (Pennebaker, Francis & Booth 2001), propositional tagging (Palmer, Gildea, & Kingsbury, 2005), and emotional coding (Wiebe, Wilson, & Cardle 2005).

3.4 Language profiles

Using the codes created by MOR, POST, and GRASP, one can automatically compute various language profile indices that were earlier computed tediously by hand. In particular, we have automated the computation of the Developmental Sentence Score (DSS) of Lee (1966) and the Index of Productive Syntax (IPSyn) of Scarborough (1990). These two language profile measures are important for the characterization of the normal course of child language development and the diagnoses of deviations from this normal course. For the study of aphasic language types in the context of the AphasiaBank project, we have constructed the MORTABLE program that automatically extracts a complete tabulation of POS and GR tags for further analysis in Excel. These measures are used to compare individual patients to a wider set of norms found in the one-hour protocols collected from the 150 patients currently in the AphasiaBank database.

3.5 Group and interlocutor comparisons

Many TalkBank data sets were collected in the context of systematic experiments, often involving between-group comparisons. Most of the corpora in the Clinical segment of the CHILDES database include samples from both children with language disorders and normally developing children. For example, the corpora from children with language disorders contributed by Gina Conti-Ramsden (Jones and Conti-Ramsden 1997) involve a comparison between children with Specific Language Impairment (SLI) and their younger language-matched siblings. Also, the AphasiaBank corpus has been structured to highlight the basic comparison between aphasics and age-matched normal controls. In other studies, there is a comparison between children from alternative socioeconomic, racial, or ethnic groups. For example, the Hall corpus (Hall & Tirre 1979) includes children from these four groups of families: Black Professional, Black Working Class, White Professional, and White Working Class. Other corpora compare younger and older mothers, or mothers with various levels of education. For all of these group comparison studies, there is an emphasis on maintaining a consistent method of data collection to maximize comparability between the groups. In the most extreme cases, this involves use of a constant, tightly specified protocol, including specific tasks and questions.

Some of the sociolinguistic studies in TalkBank rely on comparisons between interlocutors, rather than subject groups. For example, the Gleason corpus examines children's language use in three situations: talking with their mother, talking with their father, and interacting with the whole family during dinner conversations. Within the various bilingual corpora, there is often a comparison between interlocutors from different languages or situations that require the use of one language rather than the other (Yip & Matthews 2000). Within this framework, there can also be experimental manipulations that specifically encourage reliance on one language over the other (Nicoladis & Genesee 1998).

3.6 Change scores

The most common use of change scores is to measure the naturalistic course of language development over time. For example, language acquisition researchers use measures such as lexical diversity (VOCD), mean length of utterance (MLU), or developmental sentence score (DSS) to track the course of language development for both first and second languages. These measures can be applied to either longitudinal corpora collected across several years from individual learners or cross-sectional corpora collected at single time points from groups of learners at different ages or levels of first and second language learning. These data can then be modeled to study patterns such as the vocabulary spurt (Bates & Carnevale 1993, Ganger & Brent 2004), learning bursts (Larsen-Freeman 2006), or implicational patterns (Pienemann et al. 2005). The study of change scores over development is the single most important method in the study of both first and second language acquisition.

This basic use of change scores does not involve any clear experimental treatment. However, it is also possible to combine the study of change scores with experimental control. For example, in the context of the AphasiaBank project, researchers apply transcortical magnetic stimulation to improve lexical access in aphasia. To measure the effects of this treatment, participants retell the Cinderella story (MacWhinney et al. 2010) both before and after treatment. The two retellings are then compared using automatic methods such as VOCD and MORTABLE. Differences in the pretest and posttest retellings are also contrasted with those from a control group that did not have transcortical magnetic stimulation.

Change scores can also be used to measure the effects of educational treatments. For example, in their Fluency corpus, de Jong and colleagues examine the effects of production fluency training using the 4-3-2 method (Maurice 1983, Nation 1989). Improvement in fluency after training can be measured in terms of decreasing pause length and reduced errors and omissions.

3.7 Error analysis

Language acquisition studies often focus on ways in which learner corpora diverge from the standards of the target language. In studies of second language learning, Corder (1983) placed an emphasis on the value of Error Analysis. However, other researchers noted that learner grammars are not merely degenerate versions of the target grammar, but have their own systematicity, as expressed in the notion of a learner's interlanguage (Selinker, Swain & Dumas 1975). However, even if one views the learner's productions as structured into an interlanguage, it is helpful to compare divergences between that interlanguage and the target language. To facilitate this type of analysis, the CHAT coding system provides a hierarchical system of error coding. This system has been most extensively and consistently applied to the corpora in AphasiaBank. Aphasic speech involves many types of phonological and grammatical errors only rarely found in speech from normal child and adult learners. However, first and second language learners also demonstrate unique patterns of errors. The goal of the TalkBank error-coding system is to be applicable to coding for each of these groups.

3.8 Feedback studies

The study of learners' errors leads directly to the study of ways in which conversational partners can provide corrective feedback as well as positive exemplars (MacWhinney 2004). The most extreme cases here arise when the learner produces an overt formal error, such as "goed" and the parent or teacher makes an overt formal correction by saying, "No, you can't say 'goed', you have to say 'went'". There is extensive debate in the literature about the extent to which such overt correction occurs and whether it has a positive impact on the learner. Apart from this form of correction, there has also been study of less explicit correction through recasting (Bohannon, MacWhinney & Snow 1990). Researchers also believe that learners can make effective use of clear patterns of language presentation in the form of "variation sets" (Waterfall et al. 2010). In these sets, parents illustrate language patterns through item and replacement schemes. Yet another interactional pattern that is thought to facilitate language learning is the process of fine-tuning that occurs between parents and children. When parents become aware that their children are making use of some new syntactic or lexical pattern, they then increase their own use of this pattern on a level that is appropriate for the child (Sokolov 1993). CLAN programs such as CHIP, CHAINS, and KEYMAP can be used to track these ways of providing fine-tuning, feedback, and examples.

3.9 Conversation Analysis

TalkBank corpora are now also being used for research within the framework of Conversation Analysis (CA) (Schegloff 2007). Beginning in 2002, the CHAT transcription method was adapted to include all of the conventions of standard Jeffersonian CA transcription (Jefferson 1984). Specific Unicode symbols were introduced to mark features such as pitch rise and fall, terminal contours, overlap alignment, and various vocal qualities. These markings, which are summarized in the table at http://talkbank.org/CABank/codes.html, can all be entered through simple pairs of keystrokes. The DK-CLARIN CA Project organized by Johannes Wagner has created "gold standard" CA transcriptions for the Danish SamtaleBank collection and has reformatted Gail Jefferson's Newport Beach and Watergate transcriptions into CA CHAT. The TalkBank CA corpora now also include dozens of other corpora from group conversations, phone calls, and classroom interactions. Like the other corpora in TalkBank, these CA transcripts are linked directly to audio or video media. This linkage allows for greater analytic power in three directions. First, it is now easier to listen repeatedly to specific segments to detect conversationally relevant signals and patterns. This can facilitate analysis by individual researchers, discussion in data sessions, and the sharpening of collaborative commentary over the web. Second, it is now easier to link transcript analysis to phonetic analysis, by directly sending individual segments to Praat for numerical analysis. Third, with the construction of large databases of CA transcripts, it is possible to search for conversational features across interactions. However, to achieve this goal, transcripts must be adapted to display features that can be easily identified by regular expression searches.

3.10 Modeling

Data analyzed using these various methods can be further examined through computational modeling. The goals here are either to account for learning data or to account for conversational patterns. Most current models focus on trying to account for learning of either first or second languages. These models usually assume that learning involves the abstraction of patterns from the input data. This means that the first step involved in building such models is to derive a good picture of the input to the learner. For example, models that seek to account for the learning of the English past tense have first attempted to characterize the frequency of different verb forms in CHILDES corpora. The second step in building these models is to determine the developmental patterns in learners. Once these two profiles have been extracted from the corpora, the model is used to show how the learner's interlanguage can emerge from processing of the input. Neural network models have been used to account for morphological learning (MacWhinney & Leinbach 1991), segmentation (Blanchard, Heinz, & Golinkoff 2010, Monaghan & Christiansen 2010), prosodic patterns (Gupta & Touretzky 1994), lexical organization (Li, Zhao & MacWhinney 2007), and aspects of syntactic development (Elman 1993). Other models have relied on discrimination nets (Ling & Marinov 1993), pattern associators (Gillis, Daelemans & Durieux 2000), hierarchical Bayesian models (Perfors, Tenenbaum & Wonnacott 2010), and basic string comparison methods (Freudenthal, Pine & Gobet 2010). What is common across all of these applications and models is the reliance on data from corpora that include both learners' speech and the speech addressed to them.

4. Building a general database

Recently, researchers associated with the LDC (Linguistic Data Consortium) and the TalkBank Project have developed a proposal for the construction of a general database for the study of human language. This section explains the overall shape of this proposal. Although funding for this project has not yet become available, aspects of this work are progressing as separate projects. The details of the proposed work will undoubtedly change over the course of time, as we learn which ideas are more successful than others. However, in its current form, this proposal can provide us with a vision of what it means to expand the horizons of corpus linguistics.

At the core of this proposal is the observation that, each day, we generate billions of rich communication data streams in the form of conversations, meetings, broadcasts, newspapers, scientific articles, and links to scientific data. These streams of communication can be captured digitally and enriched automatically through systems for linguistic and video annotation. Databases such as TalkBank, CHILDES, Informedia, Let's Go, and LDC have demonstrated how this can be done, amassing the world's largest collections of data on spoken and written communication. However, to properly integrate these materials into a technologically sophisticated network, we must achieve full interoperability, universal access, deep curation, powerful visualization, and wider coverage.

By linking these resources together, we can build an international database for digital data on human communication, including speech (conversations, interviews, radio broadcasts, etc.), text (historical and modern books, journals, newspapers, web pages, blogs, etc.), scientific communication (articles, letters, debates, commentary, reviews, linked to primary scientific data), video, and images. This database, called ComNet, will provide material for students, teachers, businesses, professionals, language communities, government, and the public.

4.1 Basic principles

ComNet will construct a fully interoperable set of tools for data acquisition, curation, analysis, and visualization based on the TalkBank (talkbank.org/talkbank.xsd) XML schema, which will be renamed as the ComNet XML Schema. Using these tools, we will link together an international distributed database on human communication, structured in accord with these basic principles:

1. **Open access.** The core components of ComNet will be freely open to all – students, researchers, government, private industry, and the public. For non-core components, access may be limited by LDC licensing, TEACH Act requirements, or Institutional Review Board (IRB) restrictions.
2. **Integrated structure.** Every item of ComNet data – both core and non-core – will have a unique and specifiable position within a single, comprehensive XML-based data grid. To achieve this tight integration, we will mesh existing formats into the single XML Scheme, thereby overcoming the Format Babel identified by Bird & Liberman (2001).
3. **Interoperability.** To promote interoperability, we will construct roundtrip conversions of ComNet data to other popular analytic programs for display and analysis.
4. **Powerful analysis.** Relying on ComNet XML, the project will build powerful tools for browsing, searching, visualization, statistical analysis, and report generation.
5. **Multilinguality.** ComNet will integrate data from hundreds of

languages, ranging from English and Spanish to minority and endangered languages such as Mapudungún, Ojibwe, and Iñupiaq.

4.2 Links across the sciences

ComNet will be based on the principles of open access and integrated structure. Open access to ComNet data will enable fundamental linkages between research in psychology, education, linguistics, biology, neuroscience, ethology, anthropology, sociology, political science, economics, demographics, computer science, natural language processing, human language technologies, library science, law, area studies, and comparative literature. The system will be capable of linking individual-level transcript data to related neurological, economic, medical, survey, social, and preference data, subject to privacy and IRB constraints. The construction of these additional linkages will be directed and controlled by the participants themselves.

4.3 Example projects

When ComNet resources are in place, it will be possible for users to address hundreds of types of research questions. Here are some illustrations of the types of questions that researchers have been asking, sampled from this much larger space:

1. Analyze the contents of newspapers in six different languages for their reaction to the terrorist attacks of September 11, 2001, using LIWC (Pennebaker et al. 2001).
2. Find out what children in varying social groups have to say about going to the doctor and how parents respond to these expressions (Steward & Steward 2006).
3. Track uses of 鄙人 (bi3ren2) or 在下 (zui4xia4) for "your humble servant" in Chinese texts from the Ming and Ching dynasties in order to understand the time course of changes in class structure (Brown & Gilman 1960).
4. Examine the extent to which high school classes in mathematics in eight different countries engage in the process of "accountable talk" (Michaels, O'Connor & Resnick 2008) and how this discussion plays out in terms of whole class involvement (Pea & Hoffert, 2007).
5. Tabulate and graph the frequency of verb over-regularizations such as *goed* and *runned* in child language samples between ages 1;6 and 3;10 (Marcus et al. 1992). Pass the matches to either Excel or R for further statistical analysis.
6. Compare videotaped story-telling and route descriptions in cultures that construct geocentric spatial terms, such as Tzeltal (P. Brown 2001) or Guugu Yimithirr (Haviland 1993) with those that use allocentric reference. Relate these to ways in which people describe geophysical features of their environment (Mark et al.1999).

7. Extend the analysis of Seyfarth & Cheney (1999) for vervet monkey vocalizations to vocalizations from groups of meerkats (Hollén & Manser 2007), using data currently in TalkBank.
8. Use scene segmentation and gaze alignment to measure how people maintain eye contact (Vertegaal et al. 2001) and postural direction during survey interviews (Groves 2004, Schober & Conrad 2006) when they are producing the disagreement signal *well* or its equivalent in French (*bien*), Hungarian (*hát*), German (*ja, na ja*) or Spanish (*pués*).
9. Link ComNet data to ALFRED (alfred.med.yale.edu) to locate possible genetic markers for indigenous groups whose languages lack recursive syntactic devices (Everett 2007, Hauser, Chomsky & Fitch 2002).
10. Extend the method of Mitchell et al. (2008) that predicts fMRI brain activity from the meaning of nouns to the prediction of brain activity from the reading of types of passages. Extend this method across languages.
11. Create a concordance of terms referring to sustainable energy generation across European and Japanese parliamentary debates and output a set of audio files including the sentences with these references. These materials will support a wider comparison of differences in national energy policies (Jacobsson & Bergek 2004).
12. Study the ways in which Supreme Court justices signal their intentions to vote on a given case to other justices (Johnson 2004) during the years 1957 and 2008. Link these signals to cognitive analyses (Ashley 1991).
13. Study the way bias and perspectives are expressed in social media web artifacts such as blogs or YouTube.

These are sample illustrations taken from a much larger space. Focusing just on the one field of child language, MacWhinney (2008b) lists 50 such research theme types, while the wider literature demonstrates the importance of at least 100 more. When we look at other fields, we find a similar diversity. In each field, however, the barriers to analysis are the same. Absence of published metadata makes it difficult to find, group, select, integrate and analyze appropriate data. Moreover, once located, there are often the barriers of Licensing and Format Babel. By lowering these barriers, ComNet will allow researchers to ask questions in ways that are currently impossible. By allowing researchers to address these new issues, ComNet will enable a transformation in the study of human communication.

4.4 Data curation

The construction of a system as extensive as ComNet requires careful attention to the curation of data through privacy protection, provenance and copyright protection, data validation, organization, metadata generation, and documentation.

Privacy protection: Over the course of 24 years, TalkBank, CHILDES, and LDC have aggregated the world's largest databases of spoken language materials. The fact that this work has never triggered a violation of privacy regulations is indicative of the attention we have paid to this issue. IRB committees across the U.S. are now using our standards in determining their approach to making spoken language materials available. These policies are available at http://talkbank.org/share and have gone through repeated cycles of discussion and refinement from communities as diverse as teachers, parents, aphasiologists, computer scientists, lawyers, and patient advocates. Some of the procedures involved include:

1. Online storage of IRB materials and releases from data contributors.
2. Removal and bleeping of last names and addresses.
3. Password and encryption protection of sensitive materials.
4. Repeated checking with contributors and sometimes participants to make sure that the current level of access is in accord with their wishes and those of the participants.
5. Contacting individual children when they become adults to verify that they wish to allow continued access to their data.
6. Targeted de-accessioning from the database of segments or whole transcripts that seem embarrassing or which could lead to identification of the participant.

Provenance and copyright protection: In addition to issues of confidentiality, ComNet will deal with issues of intellectual property, copyright, provenance, and authenticity. Both LDC and TalkBank publish all of the software we have produced under the GNU Library General Public License (GPL), or equivalent open source license, and we will continue to do so. We choose the GNU Library GPL because it maintains open access, while protecting use for research. By default, we leave the copyright on corpora with the original holders who have agreed to allow us to make their data accessible. In addition, LDC maintains agreements with each of its users that are compatible with agreements previously negotiated with each provider. For books and video, copyright is negotiated in accord with procedures established by the UDL (Universal Design for Learning). The UDL includes a collection of pre-1923 historical texts, which are out of copyright. The UDL has already negotiated copyright permission for every publication from the National Academy of Sciences.

Data validation: Both LDC and TalkBank conduct content validation at the time data are ingested. This process involves checking for transcription accuracy, file correspondence, and metadata entry. Format validation, which is run automatically by current TalkBank programs, applies at the level of the transcript, the corpus, and the metadata. Because the database is structured in XML, it is easy to run tools that validate the adherence of new contributions to the standard Schema. Data must pass through a roundtrip from CHAT to XML and then back to CHAT (the ComNet transcript display format) with no validation errors. For corpora that are linked to media, each media time tag must correspond with a media file correctly stored on the streaming media servers. All ComNet data must fit exactly into this schema.

Organization: To guarantee proper functioning of the database, all data are encoded within a set of five isomorphic trees for:

1. Raw CHAT data,
2. XML CHAT files,
3. Media matching the transcripts,
4. Streaming media matching the transcripts, and
5. Commentary pegged to both transcripts and media.

For example, the transcript for the 10th session of the Yasmin corpus is located at data-orig /romance/es/Yasmin/10.cha. The XML is at data-xml/romance/es/Yasmin/10.xml. The media is at media/romance/es/Yasmin/10.mov. The four alternative compressions of the streaming media are on a streaming server at /CHILDES/romance/es/Yasmin/10/ and the documentation in HTML format is at /CHILDES/romance/es/Yasmin/10.

Metadata generation: The next step of curation involves the creation and maintenance of metadata for ISBN cataloging, DOI (Digital Object Identifier) generation, and OLAC (Open Language Archives Community) indexing. TalkBank files are currently registering automatically to OLAC (www.language-archives.org) and IMDI (www.mpi.nl/IMDI/) metadata systems. Metadata are important for smooth functioning of virtually all aspects of ComNet. This means that, as the project grows, we must continue to improve and extend the metadata set. As an example, let us consider the role that metadata will play in the curation and analysis of speech data. Currently, the /ae/ sound in Canadian English is shifting toward the /ao/ sound (Labov, Ash & Boberg 2006). In 40 years, this transition may be complete and it will then be difficult to correctly process earlier data without having metadata that indicates the time and place of recording and the dialect background of the speaker. This underlines the urgency of placing labels on data as soon as possible. For this sound change, it is also important to record metadata regarding speaker age, gender, geography, and education (Labov 2001). Collection of this sociolinguistic metadata supports a new trend in speech analysis that allows researchers to develop more coherent statistical models. The examination of speech in the context of the oral interviews that accompany major national surveys provides a unique opportunity to link rich metadata to detailed speech analysis.

Documentation: The final step of curation involves the writing of a readable PDF description of each corpus for inclusion in the corpus description manual. This manual is structured both as an independent, readable document and as a set of individual, searchable descriptions with metadata fields. In addition, the manual for the XML coding system is linked to fuller documentation in a manual that describes the format in terms of the CHAT display.

4.5 Interoperability

ComNet will provide interoperability for data, metadata, and programs.

Data interoperability: ComNet is building on 25 years of work on data integration in the TalkBank framework. TalkBank data derive from 158 separate projects, each of which was eventually integrated into the single over-arching XML framework. During this process of integration, it was often necessary to extend the framework to represent new contrasts or distinctions marked in particular corpora. This process will continue within ComNet. Because the schema is a growing framework, TalkBank tools have been constructed to allow for repeated cyclic reformatting and validation of the whole corpus whenever a change is made to the schema. Given the goal of constructing a single, integrated database, a major goal for ComNet will be the integration of LDC materials to the ComNet XML standard. Once this is achieved, users of LDC data will have improved access to LDC materials and can use ComNet tools to process these data. This merger of the two systems will also encourage additional research groups, and even new user communities whose data formats differ, to become LDC members, thereby further strengthening ComNet sustainability.

Metadata interoperability: Computational linguists have devoted a great deal of attention to the development of systems for annotating the ontologies of human communication. Among the efforts in this direction, we should single out OLAC, IMDI, GOLD, and WordNet. ComNet will build on each of these systems. The OLAC metadata set (Simons & Bird 2008) is a subset of the larger IMDI set (www.mpi.nl/IMDI/tools). At a minimum, ComNet data will subscribe to OLAC. However, ComNet will also support IMDI validation, as a further option. The textual segments of ComNet will be curated using the TEI (www.tei-c.org) metadata set. The TEI framework extends beyond metadata to specific language tags. ComNet will also work to integrate these lower level TEI tags into the overall ComNet XML Schema. We will also work to bring the ComNet schema into accord with the developing GOLD (Farrar & Langendoen 2003) ontology (linguistics-ontology.org). This ontology uses the SUMO upper ontology (www.ontologyportal.org) which itself is in accord with the WordNet (wordnet.princeton.edu) framework. GOLD has been most fully elaborated in regards to the features of morphosyntax that encode gender, number, person, case, evidence, evaluation, modality, tense, mood, force, size, aspect, polarity, and voice. This ontology allows us to elaborate the current XML schema to correspond to the decomposition produced automatically by the MOR program for the %mor (morphosyntax) line.

Program interoperability: Our work on program interoperability is fairly advanced. We can now convert between every major display format in this field and the ComNet XML format. However, as ComNet moves into new areas, such as library collections and survey data, we will need to further extend interoperability by extending the ComNet XML schema and the various programming tools that rely upon it to integrate with TEI and other formats.

4.6 Search and visualization

ComNet will also seek to advance methods for search, discovery, and analysis. Users will be able to access ComNet materials through a single entry port interface, using a search engine that can take advantage of the structured, open XML databases we have created. The ComNet searcher will support multilingual, metadata-driven search, composition of regular expression searches, and direct playback of transcripts and media located through the search routines. The search program will implement all standard technologies for concordances, frequency counts, mean length of utterance, tagging, sequence analysis, etc. The searcher will also transmit data to standard statistical analysis in Excel, R, Matlab, and other programs for report generation and data visualization.

For analysis of sociolinguistic data, we will extend the DASLTran tool developed for TalkBank so that it supports search and visualization of hierarchical and tabular data, for example, session and subject-specific metadata. This new tool will also import and export formats used within the quantitative sociolinguistic research community such as NCSLAAP (ncslaap.lib.ncsu.edu), Excel, GoldVarb (http://individual.utoronto.ca/tagliamonte/goldvarb.htm), R (www.r-project.org), and Praat (www.fon.hum.uva.nl/praat).

ComNet will also develop systems for automatic language analysis, such as part of speech tagging, grammatical dependency analysis, and a variety of content analyses, such as Pennebaker's LIWC (Pennebaker, Francis & Booth 2001). In various targeted areas, ComNet will develop tools to build specific information-extraction engines. For example, in the NSF-sponsored "Mining the Bibliome", Mark Liberman and his colleagues created corpora of abstracts of biomedical texts annotated syntactically and for biomedical entities, e.g., *carcinogens*, and the various ways they are named, mentioned, abbreviated, and referenced. These data were then used to build and evaluate systems that automatically identified and classified such entities. The team that built these systems consisted of linguists, computer scientists, programmers, and content experts.

To supplement these tools for data analysis, we will build additional tools for data visualization. Let us mention two as illustrations: BungeeView and Commenter. BungeeView (bungeeview.com) allows the user to discover patterns in metadata across documents and videos. Commenter implements a system for creating collaborative commentary (MacWhinney et al. 2004) much like the DIVER system (http://diver.stanford.edu/contact.html). Commenter provides both a browser front-end and a server database back-end to link comments to the media and to each other. A prototype version of this system is linked to the prototype browser at talkbank.org/browser. The system will allow users to categorize and access comments by type, data, user group, and claim status.

4.7 Multimodal and video analysis

ComNet will provide unique opportunities for the development of new methods for analysis of the multimodal aspects of human communication, including the use of sign language. Many segments of the database will provide high quality transcriptions linked to linguistic, video, and content annotations. Using this rich annotation foundation, researchers will be able to align gestures and postures with changes in scenes, gaps in conversation, and many other structural features of conversational interactions and narratives. The multimodal analysis community currently relies on four major annotation tools: Anvil, ELAN, EXMaRLDA, and The Observer. (Earlier, in Figures 3 and 4, we looked at an example of a TalkBank transcript from a problem-based learning class in medical school displayed in both CLAN and ELAN.)

In order to support efficient multimodal analysis, we must advance the state of the art in the area of video analysis and annotation. Here, we will rely heavily on work conducted in the Informedia Project (www.informedia.cs.cmu.edu). The following sections explain how this work within Informedia can be extended in the ComNet framework.

Video analysis data: The video analysis community has long attempted to bridge the gap from low-level feature extraction to semantic understanding and retrieval of the communicated content. To solve this fundamental problem, we will create a large shared video database as a focused target for further analysis and evaluation. This shared database will include media, transcripts, screen text data, web text metadata, corpus metadata, shot segmentation, image features (Gabor texture, Grid Color Moment, and Edge Direction Histogram), local feature descriptors, motion features (kinetic energy, optical flow, MPEG motion vectors), audio features (FFT, SFFT, and MFCC), and characterizations of the data with the LSCOM concept ontology. Over 60 TRECVID (Text Retrieval Conference Video, trecvid.nist.gov) participants have done this type of sharing of automatically extracted metadata for the non-public TRECVID collections. We will work with this community to create similar metadata for our open-access content.

Video annotation toolkit: To further bootstrap the process of annotation of the video test bank, we will provide a complete video annotation toolkit. This resource will allow researchers throughout the video community to annotate their own data, expand the concept ontology, and explore higher-level search services. We have already fielded several very effective systems, allowing annotators to efficiently label representative key frames in video, as well as longer video clips. We will make a robust version of this tool available to others early on in the project.

Video analysis toolkit: A number of researchers have expressed interest in applying our tools to their own data sets. Responding to this need, we will make key components of the Informedia library system available as open source, including shot detection, speech recognition, alignment, etc. This toolkit will also include modules for finding shots, labeling motions, and classifying content automatically. Using this suite, researchers can quickly customize tools, refine concept ontologies, and re-train classifiers for diverse applications. This allows further shared development of the software for analysis or services such as summarization, without having to expend many additional person-years in development.

Web-based annotation: We will also make use of the cyber-infrastructure opportunity provided by web games, such as the ESP game developed by CMU researcher Luis van Ahn (van Ahn, Kedia & Blum 2006), to allow collaborative annotation of video on the web. For this task we again expect the undergraduate students as well as the high school students participating in the summer programs at CMU to contribute ideas and implement code. This work builds on the notion of "human computation", whereby manual work is efficiently spread out over large numbers of people on the Internet, hereby providing innovative solutions for collaborative annotation of web video. Validation and verification of this annotation effort is done through duplication, which means annotations are only accepted after multiple people independently create the same label. This has been highly effective for image annotation and we will extend this annotation principle to our video collections.

Video annotation evaluation: Finally, to test the efficacy of new annotations against the video test bank, we will provide a benchmark set of tasks for video analysis evaluation.

4.8 Language communities

ComNet will also construct general methods for creating data and methods useful for specific language communities. We will work with four types of communities:

1. non-endangered U.S. minority languages, such as Spanish and Hawaiian.
2. endangered U.S. minority languages, such as Iñupiaq and Ojibwe.
3. non-endangered non-U.S. languages, such as Mapudungan, Welsh, Aymara, and Nahuatl.
4. endangered non-U.S. minority languages, such as Atayal, Cree.

The importance of work in language preservation for endangered languages is widely recognized. Without intervention, more than half of the world's 7,000 spoken languages are not expected to survive this century (Crystal 2000), and many others, even those with millions of speakers, are struggling to maintain a state of stable bilingualism within a surrounding dominant language community.

Many first language communities already have their own websites where group members can access culturally relevant materials. We will work with the developers of these sites to make them interoperable with ComNet tools and formats, while still making sure that communities maintain full control over their sites. Each site will have resources that will allow the target communities to construct social networking systems, cultural documentation, and links to community activities – all in the local language. The social networking software will be developed using open source versions of Facebook, role-playing games, and virtual worlds. These materials will rely on methods for linking transcripts to media, so that speakers can engage in direct dialogs over the web, while still producing written records of their conversations. Our language communities will also use facilities like the ComNet Commenter system to engage in blogging and commentary in the local language with all data being stored on the servers. Apart from these social uses of the web, we will also emphasize tools that assist in language learning and maintenance. These include online dictionaries and methods for grammatical analysis, as well as text-to-speech systems. We will also deploy local versions of the various language learning software methods developed by MacWhinney and colleagues at http://talkbank.org/pslc.

From the materials constructed by these communities, we will develop corpora for each language formatted in ComNet XML. These corpora will then be used for the development of orthographic and linguistic standardization, spelling checkers, online dictionaries, speech recognition and synthesis, information retrieval, telephone dialogue systems, and machine translation.

5. Conclusion

By including a focus on multimedia interactions linked to transcripts, corpus linguistics can vastly expand its horizons. This expansion will rely on several continuing developments. First, we need to develop easily-used methods for each of the ten analytic methods we have examined, including lexical analyses, QDA, automatic tagging, language profiles, group comparisons, change scores, error analysis, feedback studies, conversation analysis, and modeling. Second, we need to work together to construct a unified database for language studies and related sciences. In accord with the proposed ComNet structure, this database must be grounded on the principles of open access, data-sharing, interoperability, and integrated structure. It must provide powerful tools for searching, multilinguality, and multimedia analysis.

If we can build this infrastructure, we will be able to explore more deeply the key questions underlying the structure and functioning of language, as it emerges from the intermeshing of scores of processes operative on eight major timeframes.

References

Abiteboul, S., P. Buneman & D. Suciu (1999), *Data on the web: from relations to semistructured data and XML*: Morgan Kaufmann.

Ashley, K. (1991), *Modeling legal arguments*. Cambridge (MA): MIT Press.

Bates, E. & G. Carnevale (1993), 'New directions in research on language development', *Developmental review,* 13: 436-470.

Bates, E. & B. MacWhinney (1989), 'Functionalism and the Competition Model' in: B. MacWhinney & E. Bates (eds.) *The crosslinguistic study of sentence processing*. New York: Cambridge University Press. 3-73.

Bellugi, U., H. Poizner & E.S. Klima (1989), 'Language, modality and the brain', *Trends in neuroscience,* 12(10): 380-388.

Biber, D., S. Conrad & R. Reppen (1994), 'Corpus-based approaches to issues in applied linguistics', *Applied linguistics,* 15: 169-189.

Bird, S. & M. Liberman (2001), 'A formal framework for linguistic annotation', *Speech communication,* 33: 23-60.

Blanchard, D., J. Heinz & R. Golinkoff (2010), 'Modeling the contribution of phonotactic cues to the problem of word segmentation', *Journal of child language,* 37: 487-511.

Bohannon, N., B. MacWhinney & C. Snow (1990), 'No negative evidence revisited: beyond learnability or who has to prove what to whom', *Developmental psychology,* 26: 221-226.

Brown, P. (2001), 'Learning to talk about motion UP and DOWN in Tzeltal: is there a language-specific bias for verb learning?', in: M. Bowerman & S. Levinson (eds.) *language acquisition and conceptual development*. New York: Cambridge University Press. 512-543.

Brown, P., & S. Levinson (1987), *Politeness: some universals in language usage*. Cambridge: Cambridge University Press.

Brown, R., & A. Gilman (1960), 'The pronouns of power and solidarity', in: T.A. Sebeok (ed.), *Style in language*. Cambridge, MIT Press. 253-276.

Bybee, J. (2003), *Phonology and language use*. New York: Cambridge University Press.

Bybee, J. & P. Hopper (2001), *Frequency and the emergence of linguistic structure*. Amsterdam: Benjamins.

Corder, S.P. (1983), 'A role for the mother tongue', in: S. Gass & L. Selinker (eds.) *Language transfer in language learning*. Rowley (MA): Newbury House.

Crystal, D. (2000), *Language death*. Cambridge: Cambridge University Press.

Darwin, C. (1871), *The descent of man and selection in relation to sex*. London: John Murray.

Elman, J.L. (1993), 'Learning and development in neural networks: the importance of starting small', *Cognition,* 48: 71-99.

Enard, W., M. Przeworski, S. Fisher, C. Lai, V. Wiebe, T. Kitano, A. Monaco & S. Pååbo (2002), 'Molecular evolution of FOXP2, a gene involved in speech and language', *Nature,* 418: 869-872.

Everett, D. (2007), 'Challenging Chomskyan linguistics: thc case of Pirahã', *Human development,* 50: 297-299.

Farrar, S., & T. Langendoen (2003) 'A linguistic ontology for the Semantic Web', *GLOT international, 7,* 97-100.

Freudenthal, D., J. Pine & F. Gobet (2010), 'Explaining quantitative variation in the rate of Optional Infinitive errors across languages: a comparison of MOSAIC and the Variational Learning Model', *Journal of child language,* 37: 643-669.

Friedl, J. (2002), *Mastering regular expressions.* Sebastopol (CA): O'Reilly.

Ganger, J. & M. Brent (2004), Reexamining the vocabulary spurt. *Developmental psychology,* 40: 621-632.

Gillis, S., W. Daelemans & G. Durieux (2000), '"Lazy learning": natural and machine learning of word stress', in: D. Broeder & J. Murre (eds.) *Models of language acquisition.* Oxford: Oxford University Press. 76-102.

Goldman-Eisler, F. (1968), *Psycholinguistics: experiments in spontaneous speech.* New York: Academic Press.

Goodenough, U. & T. Deacon (2006), 'The sacred emergence of nature', in: Clayton, P., & Z. Simpson (eds.) *The Oxford handbook of religion and science.* Oxford: Oxford University Press. 853-872.

Grosjean, F. & J. Miller (1994), 'Going in and out of languages', *Psychological science,* 5: 201-206.

Groves, R. (2004), *Survey errors and survey costs.* New York: Wiley.

Gupta, P. & D. Touretzky (1994), 'Connectionist models and linguistic theory: investigations of stress systems in language', *Cognitive science,* 18: 1-50.

Hall, W.S. & W.C. Tirre (1979), *The communicative environment of young children: social class, ethnic and situational differences.* Champaign, IL: University of Illinois.

Hauptmann, A., R. Yan, W-H. Lin, M. Christel & H. Wactlar (2007), 'Can high level concepts fill the semantic gap in video retrieval? a case study with broadcast news.' *IEEE transactions on multimedia,* 9: 33-39.

Hauser, M., N. Chomsky & T. Fitch (2002), 'The faculty of language: what is it, who has it, and how did it evolve?' *Science,* 298: 1569-1579.

Haviland, J.B. (1993), 'Anchoring, iconicity, and orientation in Guugu Yimithirr pointing gestures', *Journal of linguistic anthropology,* 3: 3-45.

Hay, J. & K. Drager (2007), 'Sociophonetics', *Annual review of anthropology,* 36: 89-103.

Hollén, L. & M. Manser (2007), 'Motivation before meaning: motivational information encoded in meerkat alarm calls develops earlier than referential information', *The American naturalist,* 169: 758-767.

Jacobsson, S. & A. Bergek (2004), 'Transforming the energy sector: the evolution of technological systems in renewable energy technology', *Industrial and corporate change,* 13: 815-849.

Jefferson, G. (1984), 'Transcript notation', in: J. Atkinson & J. Heritage (eds.) *Structures of social interaction: studies in conversation analysis.* Cambridge: Cambridge University Press. 134-162.

Johnson, T. (2004), *Oral arguments and decision making on the United States Supreme Court*. New York: SUNY Press.

Jones, M. & G. Conti-Ramsden (1997), 'A comparison of verb use in children with SLI and their younger siblings', *First language,* 7: 165-193.

Keenan, J., B. MacWhinney & D. Mayhew (1977), 'Pragmatics in memory: a study in natural conversation' *Journal of Verbal Learning and Verbal Behavior*, 16, 549-560.

Kendon, A. (1982), 'The study of gesture: some observations on its history', *Recherches sémiotiques/semiotic inquiry,* 2(1): 45-62.

Klatzky, R., B. MacWhinney & M. Behrmann (eds.), (2008), *Embodiment, ego-space, and action*. New York: Psychology Press.

Labov, W. (2001), *Principles of linguistic change. Volume 2. Social considerations*. London: Blackwells.

Labov, W., S. Ash & C. Boberg (2006), *The atlas of North American English: Phonetics, phonology and sound change*. Berlin: Mouton de Gruyter.

Larsen-Freeman, D. (2006), 'The emergence of complexity, fluency, and accuracy in the oral and written production of five Chinese learners of English', *Applied linguistics* (27): 590-619.

Lee, L. (1966), 'Developmental sentence types: a method for comparing normal and deviant syntactic development', *Journal of speech and hearing disorders,* 31: 331-330.

Leont'ev, A. (1947/1981), *Problems of the development of mind (English translation by M. Kopylova)*. Moscow: Progress Press.

Li, P., X. Zhao & B. MacWhinney (2007), 'Dynamic self-organization and early lexical development in children', *Cognitive science,* 31: 581-612.

Ling, C. & M. Marinov (1993), 'Answering the connectionist challenge', *Cognition,* 49: 267-290.

MacWhinney, B. (2004), 'A multiple process solution to the logical problem of language acquisition', *Journal of child language,* 31: 883-914.

MacWhinney, B. (2005), 'Can our experiments illuminate reality?', in: L. Gershkoff-Stowe & D. Rakison (eds.) *Building object categories in developmental time*. Mahwah (NJ): Lawrence Erlbaum Associates. 301-308.

MacWhinney, B. (2008a), 'Cognitive precursors to language', in: K. Oller & U. Griebel (eds.) *The evolution of communicative flexibility*. Cambridge (MA): MIT Press. 193-214.

MacWhinney, B. (2008b), 'Enriching CHILDES for morphosyntactic analysis',. in: H. Behrens (ed.) *Trends in corpus research: finding structure in data*. Amsterdam: Benjamins. 165-198.

MacWhinney, B. (2009), 'The emergence of linguistic complexity', in: T. Givon (ed.), *linguistic complexity*. New York: Benjamins. 405-432.

MacWhinney, B. (2010), 'Computational models of child language learning', *Journal of child language,* 37: 477-485.

MacWhinney, B., D. Fromm, A. Holland, M. Forbes, & H. Wright (2010), 'Automated analysis of the Cinderella story', *Aphasiology,* 24: 856-868.

MacWhinney, B. & J. Leinbach (1991), 'Implementations are not conceptualizations: revising the verb learning model', *Cognition,* 29: 121-157.

MacWhinney, B., C. Martell, T. Schmidt, J. Wagner, P. Wittenburg, H. Brugman & E. Hoffert (2004), 'Collaborative commentary: opening up spoken language databases', *LREC 2004*. Lisbon: LREC. 11-15.

Malvern, D.D., B.J. Richards, N. Chipere & P. Purán (2004), *Lexical diversity and language development*. New York: Palgrave Macmillan.

Marcus, G., M. Ullman, S. Pinker, M. Hollander, T. Rosen & F. Xu (1992), 'Overregularization in language acquisition', *Monographs of the society for research in child development,* 57(4): 1-182.

Mark, D., C. Freksa, S. Hirtle, R. Lloyd & B. Tversky (1999), Cognitive models of geographical space. *International journal of geographical information science,* 13: 747-774.

Massaro, D. (1987), *Speech perception by ear and eye*. Hillsdale, NJ: Lawrence Erlbaum.

Maurice, K. (1983), 'The fluency workshop', *TESOL Newsletter,* 17: 429-436.

Menzel, R. & M. Giurfa (2001), 'Cognitive architecture of a mini-brain: the honeybee', *Trends in cognitive sciences,* 5: 62-71.

Michaels, S., C. O'Connor & L. Resnick (2008), 'Deliberative discourse idealized and realized: accountable talk in the classroom and in civic life', *Studies in philosophy and education,* 27: 283-297.

Mitchell, T.M., S.V. Shinkareva, A. Carlson, K-M. Chang, V.L. Malave, R.A. Mason & M. Just (2008), 'Predicting human brain activity associated with the meanings of nouns', *Science,* 320: 1191-1195.

Monaghan, P. & M. Christiansen (2010), 'Words in puddles of sound: modelling psycholinguistic effects in speech segmentation', *Journal of child language,* 37: 545-564.

Nation, P. (1989), 'Improving speaking fluency', *System,* 17: 377-384.

Nicoladis, E. & F. Genesee (1998), 'Parental discourse and code-mixing in bilingual children', *International journal of bilingualism,* 2: 85-99.

Ninio, A. & P. Wheeler (1984), 'Functions of speech in mother-interaction', in: C. Garvey, R. Golinkoff & L. Feagans (eds.) *The development of communicative competence*. Norwood (NJ): Ablex. 196-207.

Ochs, E. (1979), 'Transcription as theory', in: E. Ochs & B. Schieffelin (eds.) *Developmental pragmatics*. New York: Academic. 43-72.

Osgood, C.E. (1971), 'Where do sentences come from?', in: D.D. Steinberg & L.A. Jakobovits (eds.) *Semantics: an interdisciplinary reader in philosophy, linguistics, and psychology*. Cambridge: Cambridge University Press. 497-521.

Palmer, M., D. Gildea, & P. Kingsbury (2005), 'The Proposition Bank: an annotated corpus of semantic roles', *Computational linguistics*, 31, 71-105.

Parisse, C. & M.T. Le Normand (2000), 'Automatic disambiguation of the morphosyntax in spoken language corpora', *Behavior research methods, instruments, and computers,* 32: 468-481.

Pea, R. & E. Hoffert (2007), Video workflow in the learning sciences: prospects of emerging technologies for augmenting work practices. In R. Goldman, R. Pea, B. Barron & S. Derry (eds.) Video research in the Learning Sciences. Mahwah (NJ): Lawrence Erlbaum Associates. (427-460).

Pennebaker, J.W., M.E. Francis & R.J. Booth (2001), *Linguistic inquiry and word count (LIWC): a computerized text analysis program.* Mahwah (NJ): Lawrence Erlbaum Associates.

Perfors, A., J.B. Tenenbaum & E. Wonnacott (2010), 'Variability, negative evidence, and the acquisition of verb argument constructions', *Journal of child language,* 37: 607-642.

Piaget, J. (1954), *The construction of reality in the child.* New York: Basic Books.

Pienemann, M., B. Di Biase, S. Kawaguchi & G. Håkansson (2005), 'Processing constraints on L1 transfer', in: J.F. Kroll & A.M.B. DeGroot (eds.) *Handbook of bilingualism: psycholinguistic approaches.* New York: Oxford University Press. 128-153.

Presson, N. & B. MacWhinney (2010), 'The Competition Model and language disorders', in: J. Guendozi (ed.), *Handbook of language disorders.* New York: Routledge. 31-48.

Prior, A., & B. MacWhinney (2010), Beyond inhibition: a bilingual advantage in task switching. *Bilingualism: Language and cognition,* 13, 253-262.

Quinlan, P.T. (2003), *Connectionist models of development: developmental processes in real and artificial neural networks.* Hove, UK: Psychology Press.

Regier, T. (2005), 'The emergence of words: attentional learning in form and meaning', *Cognitive science,* 29: 819-865.

Rose, Y., B. MacWhinney, R. Byrne, G. Hedlund, K. Maddocks, P. O'Brien & T. Wareham (2005), Introducing Phon: a software solution for the study of phonological acquisition. In D. Bamman, T. Magnitskaia & C. Zaller (eds.) 30th Annual Boston University Conference on Language Development (pp. 489-500). Somerville (MA): Cascadilla Press.

Sagae, K., E. Davis, A. Lavie, B. MacWhinney & S. Wintner (2010), 'Morphosyntactic annotation of CHILDES transcripts', *Journal of child language,* 37: 705-729.

Scarborough, H.S. (1990), Index of productive syntax. *Applied psycholinguistics,* 11: 1-22.

Schegloff, E. (2007), *Sequence organization in interaction: a primer in conversation analysis.* New York: Cambridge University Press.

Schober, M. & F. Conrad (2006), 'Does conversational interviewing reduce survey measurement error?', *Public opinion quarterly,* 61: 576-602.

Selinker, L., M. Swain & G. Dumas (1975), 'The interlanguage hypothesis extended to children', *Language learning,* 25: 139-152.

Seyfarth, R. & D. Cheney (1999), 'Production, usage, and response in nonhuman primate vocal development', in: M. Hauser & M. Konishi (eds), *Neural mechanisms of communication*. Cambridge (MA): MIT Press. 57-83.

Simons, G. & S. Bird (2008), 'Toward a global infrastructure for the sustainability of language resources', Proceedings of the 22nd Pacific Asia Conference on Language, Information and Computation, Cebu City, Philippines. 87-100

Smith, J., M. Durham & L. Fortune (2007), '"Mam, my trousers is fa'in doon!": Community, caregiver, and child in the acquisition of variation in a Scottish dialect', *Language variation and change,* 19: 63-99.

Smith, L.B. & E. Colunga (2003), 'Making an ontology: Cross-lingusitic evidence', in: D.H. Rakison & L. Oakes (eds) *Early category and concept development: making sense of the blooming, buzzing confusion.* London: London University Press. 275-302.

Sokolov, J.L. (1993), 'A local contingency analysis of the fine-tuning hypothesis', *Developmental psychology,* 29: 1008-1023.

Steward, M. & D. Steward (2006), 'Children's conceptions of medical procedures', *New directions for child and adolescent development,* 1981: 67-83.

Thelen, E. & L. Smith (1994), *A dynamic systems approach to the development of cognition and action*. Cambridge (MA): MIT Press.

von Ahn, L., M. Kedia & M. Blum (2006), Verbosity: A game for collecting common-sense facts. Paper presented at the CHI 2006, Montréal.

Vertegaal, R., R. Slagter, G. van der Veer & A. Nijholt (2001), 'Eye gaze patterns in conversations: there is more to conversational agents than meets the eyes'. CHI 2001, 3: 301-308.

Waddington, C.H. (1957), *The strategy of the genes*. New York: MacMillan.

Waterfall, H., B. Sandbank, L. Onnis & S. Edelman (2010), 'An empirical generative framework for computational modeling of language acquisition', *Journal of child language,* 37: 671-703.

Wiebe, J., T. Wilson & C. Cardie (2005), Annotating expressions of opinions and emotions in language. *Language resources and evaluation*, 39, 165-210.

Yip, V. & S. Matthews (2000), 'Syntactic transfer in a Cantonese-English bilingual child', *Bilingualism: Language and cognition,* 3: 193-208.

Developing a text-based corpus of the language of Japanese comics (*manga)*

Giancarla Unser-Schutz

Hitotsubashi University

Abstract

*While demands for corpora from media which mix visual and linguistic elements have increased in recent years with developments in corpus-based linguistics research, the actual creation and design of such corpora present many unique problems. Most centrally, there remains much to be considered in terms of how to isolate and meaningfully represent their linguistic data. In line with these trends, in this paper I introduce a 687,654 character (55,415 entries) corpus of the language from Japanese comics (*manga*). Many of the issues encountered in its design are found with other media – newspaper stories, advertisements, political cartoons – which mix the visual with the linguistic. In addition to describing how such unusual text could be of interest to other researchers, the approaches taken here may help others with similar projects.*

1. Introduction: multimodal texts and *manga*

With the development of corpus-based linguistic research, the demand for corpora of non-traditional text sources has seen a sharp increase. Many have called for the expansion into visual mixed media as television scripts and advertisements, pointing to their importance in society and their rich contextual data (overviewed in Allwood 2008). Yet there are many important practical and theoretical problems in designing such corpora, not least how to input the textual elements as meaningful linguistic data. As Bateman, Delin & Henschel (2002: 3) describe, while there have been a wide variety of tools developed for linguistics (i.e., monomodal documents), "(f)or multimodal documents, however, such models and techniques are still largely lacking. A substantial set of problems is raised by the fact that the object of study is not linear, either temporally or in terms of the principles for its consumption; moreover, its multichannel nature makes it difficult to reconcile and peg together the methods of recording, transcription, analysis and annotation that have been developed separately for each mode." The analysis of multimodal texts, then, requires the development of systematic methods of thinking about the text so as to give it the "order'" that it currently lacks.

It is in response to similar issues that I introduce in this paper a 687,654 character (= 55,415 entries) text corpus of the language from Japanese comics (*manga*). With its linguistic data embedded directly into the drawings, *manga* are a true marriage of language with the visual. With text of inherently different natures being presented in a non-linear manner in the same page area, a crucial task in corpus design was to reanalyze the text types found within *manga*, such as lines (text representing conversational dialogue in speech bubbles; see Section 3.3 below) and onomatopoeia. It was also necessary to re-evaluate the relationship between such different types of text in order to give meaning to the abstracted texts, i.e., once they were taken out of their original embedded environments. Ultimately this is a text-oriented corpus, insofar as it is an attempt to deal with how to think about and link together non-linear text which is by nature a part of a larger visual structure. Yet the corpus described here could be said to be a part of the trend to try to link the visual and the linguistic. Furthermore, many of the issues encountered in its design are found with other media—newspaper stories, advertisements, political cartoons—which mix the visual with the linguistic, and the approaches taken here may help others with similar projects.

At the same time, while *manga* may seem an unusual source of linguistic text at first, on closer examination they present themselves as an interesting and widely-read text form that could be of potential interest even to those beyond the field of *manga*-related research. *Manga* by some accounts make up 40% of all items published in Japan (Schodt 1996), and while some (e.g., Nakano 2009) have pointed to recent decreases in readership, they continue to be of great importance because of their overarching reach within Japanese media, with huge licensed industries in animation and live-action television and movies, video games, novels and various non-comic forms of literature, and licensed character products, etc. Translated and published internationally, they are also increasingly the face of Japan abroad, and the number of people studying Japanese as a second language has also sharply increased in recent years, for which *manga* and Japanese popular culture have often been given as one of the important motivating reasons (Kumano & Hirokaga 2008).

There should be no doubt, then, of *manga*'s special role as an important source of text both internationally and domestically, but, as I shall describe below, it is one which is in reality often overlooked. While describing how the corpus was sampled and designed within a larger corpus linguistic framework, as a secondary corollary, this paper serves to outline some of the reasons for being interested in a source of text that has been traditionally undervalued. As I will argue, *manga* form a potentially interesting resource pool not only to those interested in researching Japanese popular culture and how Japanese culture is disseminated and absorbed abroad, but also to those interested in researching topics in Japanese, without any necessary interest in popular culture itself.

With these points in mind, below I will first describe how *manga* are produced and read, paying particular attention to the role of language in those processes and their historical contexts. This will set the stage for talking about how *manga* are currently researched, wherein I will argue that sufficient light has not been given to language. With this background in place, I will then describe how and why the corpus was constructed, particularly in light of sampling and structural issues. After describing the current amount of data in the corpus, I then go over possible ways to use the corpus, discuss some problems that have been encountered thus far, and conclude with some examples of how I have used and plan to use the corpus's data.

1.1 Why manga?

1.1.1 A short history of *manga*

Manga today generally appear first in chapters of approximately 20 to 40 pages in large, phone-book size magazines, which generally include several series and are anywhere between 250 to 600 pages. Magazines themselves are generally viewed as belonging to different genres based upon their target audience, with the traditional division being between titles for young boys (*shounen-manga*) and titles for young girls (*shoujo-manga*). Most such titles are monthly, but some, such as best-selling title *Shounen Jump*, are biweekly. After several chapters have been printed, series are republished as *tankoubon*, pocket-sized books containing approximately 180 pages. Popular series may continue indefinitely, with some continuing to over 100 volumes.

Manga themselves have both a short and a very long history. Depending on one's definition of *manga*, it might include 12th century scrolls depicting people and animals humorously (Ito 2005). The word *manga* itself was first used to describe humorous, one-frame woodblock prints by Hokusai in the 18th century (Shimizu 1991). Along with Westernization after the Meiji Restoration in 1868 came new political comics in magazines like *Japan Punch*. Longer, story-based series began to appear in the early 20th century, but *manga* could be said to have come to their current form in the post-World War II period. Natsume (1997) ascribes this post-war boom to the ease of printing *manga*: they were a cheap, easy-to-produce form of entertainment, with a large audience of entertainment-deprived Japanese readers. The form of *manga* that developed during that period is commonly called *sutoorii-manga* ('story-*manga*') and continues to form the majority of the current market. One of the primary characteristics of *sutoorii-manga* is their strong narratives (I. Takeuchi 2006). They usually feature continuing story arcs which, while extended in length, have eventual endings and whose characters develop over time.

The emphasis on narrative in the modern *sutoorii-manga* might be considered to be directly associated with an emphasis on language: the length and complexity of plot necessitates a way to transmit those stories, and language is clearly one important way of expressing detailed narratives. As Osamu Takeuchi (2005) describes, the use of language found in *sutoorii-manga* is both unique in comparison to previous *manga* types, and essential to creating a sense of time and space in stories. Likewise, while wordless comics do exist, they require more work on the part of both the author and the reader, and "(t)he narrative in wordless comics, therefore, demands more visual competency from readers than in traditional comics" (Beronä 2001: 20). In the case of mass-produced, mass-consumed *sutoorii-manga*, it seems safe to assume that language is a core way of explicating plot to readers.

1.1.2 Language in *manga*

Manga thus constitute an enormous base of linguistic information, and popular reaction to them supports that. A recent 2008 survey by the Agency for Cultural Affairs showed that approximately 45% of respondents gave *manga* as being influential in the speech of young people, coming in only after television, friends and parents (Agency for Cultural Affairs 2010). *Manga* are indeed a wide-read linguistic form amongst young people. In fact, in a survey I conducted in 2007 and 2008 of *manga* reading habits amongst high school students in Tokyo and Okinawa, not only did a majority of students (385 out of 501) say that they had talked to friends about *manga* before, but a majority (288) also said they had a favorite *manga* series. Perhaps because *manga* are widely read amongst young people, they are not uncommonly given as a source of 'unusual' speech patterns. *Manga* are, for example, often given as the reason why some young girls have taken to use the masculine first person pronouns *ore* and *boku*. Endo (2001) found that *manga* was one of the reasons college students' gave for why girls were thought to use these masculine pronouns. As I summarize elsewhere (Unser-Schutz 2010a), this is an explanation common within popular discourse, expressed particularly clearly in posts about girls' usage of *ore* and *boku* on Yahoo Chiebukuro, the Japanese equivalent of Yahoo Q&A.

The question of whether or not *manga* are really influential on young people's speech, and if so, how, is a difficult one and may be better thought of as a complex process. Ueno (2006: 16-17) comments in her analysis of gendered sentence-final particles in *manga* for young girls and older women that *manga* are on the one hand "likely to reflect the characteristics of the desired readership" in order to create a sense of rapport, yet at the same time they may "...influence the readers in framing their gender identities as well as their linguistic behavior." Language in *manga* is subject to the same burdens that other works of fiction are, and there is a clear tension between representing realistic speech that readers can relate to while using speech to create characters and dealing with the interference of the author's own speech patterns. As I found in my own examination of gendered sentence-final particles (Unser-Schutz 2010c), in at least some types of *manga*, sentence-final particles seem distributed somewhat differently from real-life usage. For example, female characters use more realistic forms in series for girls and very conservative ones in series for boys, and factors such as the roles of characters and the sex of authors were all raised as possible reasons for this. Language in *manga* is thus subject to many different factors, offering a rich layer of complexity, and this gap between how *manga* are perceived and their linguistic reality is one worthy of interest from both social and linguistic standpoints.

Whatever the status of their role in society, however, with the clear importance of *manga* in Japan and their role as a source of linguistic information, they would seem an obvious choice of research. Indeed, with the attention given to *manga* as a cultural symbol there has been a rise in interest in *manga* as a serious academic pursuit, symbolized by such events as the formation of the Japan Society for Studies in Cartoon and Comics in 2001. Yet for all that *manga* research is coming to the fore, one notices that there are distinct limiting trends. In particular, there is a tendency to examine them on a visual basis. Such visual-based research tends to examine the role of frames, panels, gutters, etc., in creating a "comics-grammar". An unfortunate result of this focus is that much of the research on *manga*, and comics in general, assumes language to be secondary to their visual aspects. McCloud (1994: 9) is particularly definitive in his dismissal of language, defining comics as "(j)uxtaposed pictorial and other images in deliberate sequence, intended to convey information and/or to produce an aesthetic response in the viewer," and asserting that language text is an 'iconic' element that can be treated as part of comics' visual repertoire. While not as radical, Groensteen (2007) argues that the development of new visual-narrative forms has eclipsed that of the linguistic-narrative in comics. This is something that Ichiro Takeuchi might agree with, arguing that while *sutoorii-manga* are a mixed visual-linguistic media, visual elements are necessary precisely because of language's "incompleteness" and its inability to describe the "essence" of things (2006: 257-258). Others have in fact suggested that linguistic text is essentially ignored by readers in *sutoorii-manga*. Rommens (2000: Section 2) explicitly argues that one of the supposed key methods of reading *manga*, speed-reading, "is made possible through the elimination of textual information."

This of course does not mean that there has been no work on the language of *manga*. Some recent examples of research on language in *manga* include Kinsui's (2003) work on "role language" (*yakuwari-go*), i.e., "speech patterns which are aligned to the images of their speakers" (205; my translation), in comics, stressing the role that stereotypical speech patterns not found in natural speech have character development, in respect to the issue raised above on tension in *manga* as works of fiction. Takahashi's (2009) work touches upon Kinsui's as she examines the role stereotypical female-language has in developing characters in the *shoujo-manga Life*, demonstrating that characters manipulate gendered speech patterns in accordance with the images they are trying to project. Ueno's (2006) research on the usage of gendered sentence-final particles in female-language in comics for girls and women mentioned above also demonstrates that there are distinctly different patterns between characters of different ages as well as between individual series depending on the age of their readership. Inoue (2009), on the other hand, takes on a more specific aspect of language in *manga*, that of onomatopoeia, and how it is used and structured differently in *manga* as opposed to other linguistic environments.

However, while much of the recent research on language in *manga* offers interesting suggestions, the majority of such studies rely upon a smaller number of examples, usually focusing on a few select elements with limited attention to the larger context of such patterns. This makes it difficult to evaluate their arguments. At present, even basic questions such as what kinds of linguistic forms appear, how closely related language in *manga* is to other literary forms or spoken language, and even more concrete questions such as the actual ratio of words to pages or the ratio of words to pictures have yet to be answered. The present situation, then, is not much different from over 20 years ago, when Kai

(1989) posed several key points as being necessary to look at in future *manga* language research. These questions are not only pertinent to assessing how comics themselves function, but also to assessing the linguistic relationship they have with their readers. Without any real concept of what the characteristics of language in *manga* are to begin with, such questions really may only be answered with speculation.

2. Creating a linguistic corpus of *manga*

2.1 Points and problems

The corpus I describe here could be said to be an attempt to deal with the questions raised above. A corpus-based approach might be considered useful for a number of reasons. Not only would it give clear answers to some basic questions such as the ratio of words to the page, it would also undoubtedly shed light on issues such as Kinsui's role-language or, like Ueno's research, the distribution of gendered speech patterns amongst different characters and series. Furthermore, such a corpus would also be usable by those interested in some of the specific kinds of texts found in *manga* – such as thoughts or onomatopoeia – for other, non-comics research. Yet while corpus-based approaches have been suggested before (Maekawa 2008, Ingulsrud & Allen 2009), some major problems have stood in the way of attempts.

First, there is the issue of how to choose an appropriate sample. With thousands of titles published annually, there is an enormous collection of texts to select from. While genre might appear to be one possible option, genre in *manga* has been traditionally defined by market segments based primarily upon readers' gender and, to a lesser degree, their age, rather than the themes or styles of the texts themselves. These segments are rigorously defined by the magazines that *manga* series are serialized in, with individual magazines marketed towards different genders. The legitimacy of such a genre scheme has come into question in recent years, however, with the breakdown of those markets. Young female readers in particular are increasingly reading titles from traditionally male-oriented magazines (Ogino 2001, Allen & Ingulsrud 2005). Such changes in *manga* reading patterns have led some researchers, such as Itou (2005), to press for an expression-oriented definition of *manga* genre which would extend beyond market segments. As an expressive media wherein the author intends to convey some story, or more generally, information in the form of emotions, etc., to its readers, *manga* can be thought of as utilizing many different elements as tools to express that information. Those elements in *manga* include but are not limited to the type of story they tell, the style of drawings utilized and structural elements such as their use of frames and panels. Under an expression-oriented genre scheme, genres would be defined by their use of such elements, focusing on the content one actually sees rather than readership, which may reflect little in terms of common structural or narrative elements and language itself could of course be one such element. Until such attempts are made, however, the extent of the market and the ambiguity of genre lines are such that there is a lack of clear standards for what would be an appropriate general sample.

Second, as Ingulsrud & Allen (2009) point out, language in *manga* is embedded directly in the images, making them inappropriate for text-scanning and thus requiring intensive data entry. A more important corollary, however, is that the non-linear relationship between textual elements demands that any linguistic corpus represent the relationship between different elements dynamically. Maekawa (2008) comments that *manga* should be included as a part of the large-scale written corpus that the National Japanese Language Institute is producing. The incorporation of *manga* in this corpus is attributed to their importance as a symbol of modern Japanese culture and because the genre often motivates non-Japanese speakers to begin studying the language. Nevertheless, there remains the problem of how one should deal with the linguistic data in such a corpus. Some previous attempts at a *manga* corpus, such as Tokuhisa, Murakami & Ikehara (2006), who created a *manga* corpus tagged for facial expressions, have eliminated this concern by selecting only particular elements like lines. But this fails to capture the interdependent relationship that different elements, such as onomatopoeic expressions, notes and narration, have in creating *manga*, and which would theoretically be a major point of interest. Some categorical system for 1) distinguishing between the different types of linguistic text, and for 2) tagging where they appeared in the original *manga*, is essential for properly representing *manga*'s unique linguistic data in any kind of meaningful way.

To summarize the response processes described below, in regards to the first problem, I limited the corpus to series popular with young people, the group said to be influenced by *manga*. This was done in a two-part process, first by creating a list of top-selling series, and then comparing it with the results from surveys of high school students' comic reading habits. Ten series were selected, with an even number of young girl-oriented and young boy-oriented titles. On the other hand, in order to effectively represent the text, two sets of tags—one including contextual information such as the series and page number, and one including categorical information, noting information such as the type of text and the sex of the speaker—were designed and assigned to all elements. For categorical tags, all text was further determined to be in one of eight categories distinguished primarily by their presentation in the text: *Lines*, *Thoughts*, *Narration*, *Onomatopoeia*, *Background text*, *Background lines/thoughts*, *Comments* and *Titles*.

2.2 Sampling issues

As summarized above, in response to the problem of selecting titles from the mass number of possible series, I first restricted the sample to current or recently-ended series popular with young people at the time of the original sampling (summer 2007 to summer 2008). As the previous survey results by the Cultural Agency suggest, young people are the group that *manga* is assumed to have some influence over, and by restricting the sample to titles popular with said group, it may be possible to examine how such readers and *manga* interact. It must be noted that while genre is not a fully reliable marker in *manga*, it is also possible that the language patterns that may be discovered through a corpus could lead to more dynamic ways of thinking about genre, as has been found for literature. With the massive quantity of *manga* published each year, an important starting point for considering genre in *manga* could be said to be examining what, if any, actual common elements may be found in the currently-accepted market-segment genres. Thus, while it may seem somewhat unintuitive given the discussion above, and while holding some reservations and concerns as to their applicability, I selected equal numbers of titles from the most commonly accepted genre groups, *shoujo-manga* and *shounen-manga*, as a starting point to examine whether or not there are any salient characteristics to be found within the two. It should be noted that genre in this case was determined by the market-segment of the magazines running the titles, generally following the Japanese Magazine Publishers Association's groupings.[1] Consequently, the corpus is not a full representation of the market, and does not have that as its aim; rather, it is a sample of male- and female-oriented series popular amongst high school students, and should be interpreted as such.

In order to establish what series were popular amongst young people, I conducted two surveys on high school students' *manga* reading habits. The surveys in question were conducted in July 2007 at a private all-girls school near downtown Tokyo, with 125 female respondents, and at two co-ed public schools in western Tokyo in July 2008 with 148 respondents (73 male, 75 female). The survey itself consisted of seven questions, and was focused on their *manga* reading habits.[2] The number of female respondents was kept artificially high to balance the limited reading patterns of young men: as mentioned earlier, young women tend to read a variety of titles across market genres, whereas boys tend to read exclusively series aimed at boys or older men (Ogino 2001: 141-146, Allen & Ingulsrud 2005: 275-276). The surveys in fact reflect this: few boys mentioned reading any comic magazines for girls, and did not give girls' series as their favorite title, but many female students had read and chose as their favorite series titles for boys.[3] Using students' responses to what their favorite *manga* title was, I created a list of favorite series noted by multiple students. While there were a wide variety of answers, the majority of which were only raised by one or two students, some patterns were seen, and titles selected eight or more times over both surveys were added to the candidate pool. As a point of restriction, I omitted a limited number of older series from the list which, while 'classic', were no longer current at the time of the survey (e.g., *Dragon Ball*, which had ended over ten years previously).

The results of the survey were then compared with a list of top-ten series from the approximately one-year period of July 2007 to July 2008. As Nakano (2009) describes, it can be extremely difficult to get reliable sales figures on *manga*, because detailed sales ranking for *manga* are not fully released by publishers themselves. Data instead comes in from various sources such as distributors and bookstores, and as such, used on their own, sales ranking can be difficult to assess appropriately. They can, however, be thought to be demonstrative of how much a series has permeated popular culture, if not a fully accurate description of which titles are being read by whom. Sales ranking was thus selected as a complementary tool to reassess the results of the surveys above in reflection of the overall market trends. The particular figures used here were those made public by PHP Interface, which announces weekly top ten rankings released by Touhan Shirabe, the research section of the major publication distributer Touhan.[4] Final selection was done by comparing the candidate list from the surveys, and selecting those titles from the top of the list which also appeared on the top-ten list, after first dividing titles into *shoujo-manga* and *shounen-manga*.

Ten series were selected as a result of that process: from *shoujo-manga* Tomoko Ninomiya's *Nodame Kantaabire* ('Nodame's Cantabile', henceforth, *Nodame*), Ai Yazawa's *Nana*, Karuho Shiina's *Kimi ni Todoke* ('Reaching for You', henceforth, *KimiTodo*), Aya Nakahara's *RabuKon* and Yuki Obata's *Bokura ga Ita* ('We Were There'), and from *shounen-manga* Goushou Aoyama's *Meitantei Konan* ('Detective Conan', henceforth, *Konan*), Masashi Kishimoto's *Naruto*, Eiichirou Oda's *One Piece*, Tsugumi Ohba & Takeshi Obata's *Death Note* and Hideaki Sorachi's *GinTama* (Table 1).

Table 1: Current series included in corpus

	title	*author*	*magazine*	*publisher*
Shoujo-manga	*Bokura ga Ita*	Tabata, Yuki	BetsuKomi	Shougakukan
	Kimi ni Todoke	Shiina, Karuho	Bessatsu Margaret	Shuueisha
	Nana	Yazawa, Ai	Cookie	Shuueisha
	Nodame Kantaabire	Ninomiya, Tomoko	Kiss	Kodansha
	RabuKon	Nakahara, Aya	Bessatsu Margaret	Shuueisha
Shounen-manga	*Death Note*	Ohba, Tsugumi; Obata, Takeshi	Shounen Jump	Shuueisha
	GinTama	Sorachi, Hideaki	Shounen Jump	Shuueisha
	Meitantei Konan	Aoyama, Goushou	Shounen Sunday	Shougakukan
	Naruto	Kishimoto, Masashi	Shounen Jump	Shuueisha
	One Piece	Oda, Eiichirou	Shounen Jump	Shuueisha

While most of the series are still continuing, for an equal comparison the first three volumes of each series were chosen. In addition to being highly popular as comics, all of these series have either become animated television series or movies, live action movies, or novels, or have had video games and other related merchandise produced. They can be thus assumed to have been well-absorbed into popular culture.

It should be noted in passing that too many *manga* researchers selecting individual titles as the sample pool rather than magazines may seem unnatural. Many, such as Ogino (2001), claim that serial magazines were the original core of the *manga* market, but, as Nakano (2009) points out, at the start of the 1980s, most of the single-shot titles disappeared from the major magazines, only to be replaced by long-continuing serials. For such serials, republishing as *tankoubon* became a given. In reality, many magazines today are actually losing money, with publishing houses relying upon the *tankoubon* to make up the difference; the number of *tankoubon* published has in fact reportedly doubled in the last ten years—whereas magazine sales have gone down (Nakano 2009). It seems safe to think, then, that reading *manga* series individually is becoming the main reading habit, hence the focus here on series over magazines.

2.3 Structural design

As noted above, linguistic data is presented in comics in a number of different ways. For example, Lines may appear in speech bubbles, or on occasion be written directly on the background, whereas Thoughts may be seen in square bubbles, or on whited-out areas of the background. There is good reason to think that readers process and deal with such information differently. In a telling informal experiment, Ingulsrud & Allen (2009) had readers mark with a felt pen what they looked at on the page as they read *manga*, as a result of which they found that the most common reading pattern was for readers to search out for conversational lines, paying less attention to other types of text and only secondarily at facial expressions, etc., as opposed to the suggestion in Rommens (2000) that the graphic data is more important. Whatever the case may be, clearly any useful corpus would need to distinguish between those differences.

In defining the categories, I took first and foremost their presentational differences into account, such as whether they were in speech bubbles, or on the background. Whether they were written by hand or typed was also taken into consideration, as per Fuse's (2004) findings. In some cases, however, presentational differences were not deemed sufficient to make accurate distinctions. In those limited cases, other information, such as the voice or tense of the utterance were taken into consideration, which I make note of in the discussion of the categories below. With those points in mind I determined a total of eight categories that all the text could be categorized into: *Lines*, *Thoughts*, *Narration*, *Onomatopoeia*, *Background text*, *Background lines/thoughts*, *Comments* and *Titles*. In line with the points above, the definition of each category is as follows, with unclear categories depicted in Figure 1. Note that the order below forms the category number for each type tagged in the corpus (e.g.,

Lines: category 1, Onomatopoeia: category 4, etc.).

1. *Lines* (Figure 1, Frame B, No. 1): Any data found in unbroken speech bubbles representing audible information. Usually in type, Lines include anything from parts of conversation to radio announcements the characters hear. Their common characteristic, however, is that they are presumed to be audible within their *manga* worlds. Not all Lines are human or even voiced. However, Lines spoken by animals and onomatopoeia in speech bubbles are also grouped as Lines. As Groensteen (2007) describes in detail, the different shapes of speech bubbles are often assumed to have meaning, such as jagged edges representing anger, but here such differences will not be assessed given their comparative abstractness.
2. *Thoughts* (Figure 1, Frames A, C, No. 2): Any linguistic data representing characters' inner voices. They generally appear in type, in either speech bubbles with dots going towards the characters, or in squares or whited-out space in the background. As opposed to Lines, they are never said aloud, and represent characters' private thoughts. Put differently, other characters are not privileged to these utterances, and they do not directly address the reader.
3. *Narration* (Figure 1, Frame D, No. 3): Any data which supplies information on plot development, location, etc. directly to the readers. Narration usually appears in type and in square captions, and although they are commonly in the third person, they can be in any person. While its presentational style is similar to that of Thoughts, in contrast Narration's primary role is descriptive, and it often features privileged information that is unknown to the characters. Narration is also directed out towards an audience. Given their presentational similarities to Thoughts, linguistic hints, such as using a past tense and who the utterance is being directed towards, are sometimes used to distinguish between the two types.
4. *Onomatopoeia* (Figure 1, Frames A, C, No. 4): Any words which are written directly on the background to onomatopoeically describe the scene. As a general rule, onomatopoeic words do not form full sentences, and they are assumed to not be spoken by somebody, but rather mimetic of real world sounds or describing the nature or atmosphere of the scene.
5. *Background text* (Figure 1, Frames B, D, No. 5): Any linguistic data that was written as a part of the scene in the comic which is not actually vocalized, such as advertisements written on billboards, building names, etc. Letters and other text that the characters read are also included as Background text.
6. *Background lines/Thoughts* (Figure 1, Frames C, D, No. 6): Lines or Thoughts which are written by hand directly on the background. Because they are not written in speech bubbles, it is impossible to tell whether they actually vocalized or not, and thus they must be differentiated from regular Lines or Thoughts. They are also usually written smaller than utterances in

speech bubbles.

7. *Comments* (Figure 1, Frame B, No. 7): Notes or jokes which are written by hand directly on the background about the characters or the items appearing in the scene. Such Comments may or may not include arrows pointing at the items in question, but they are often full sentences, and supply privileged information about the scenes that has not been made available to the readers through the characters' Lines, Thoughts or Narration.
8. *Titles* (Figure 1, Frame A, No. 8): Data presenting the title, subtitle, author's name, etc., of the series.

Figure 1: Examples of each type of text. Circled numbers next to each block text refer to categories, as noted above. (Original comic "Neko Nikki" by author; frame and category numbers added for illustrative purposes.)

All linguistic data were originally pure text in CSV form for ease of input, but XML tags are now being added so as to possibly be used with Japanese corpus search programs such as Himawari, created by the National Institute for Japanese Language (Yamaguchi 2005). Each individual block of text constitutes one entry in the corpus, and each individual entry is preceded by a set of tags noting where and how it appeared in the text. Respectively, the tags are for the title, volume, frame number, category number, the occurrence number (as multiple entries of the same category may appear in the same frame), and the sex of the speaker (in the case of those categories which have a voice, i.e., Lines, Thoughts, Narration, Background lines/Thoughts and Comments) selected out of five groups: male, female, both/unclear, Onomatopoeia, and animal. By noting the category, page and frame number of each item in this way, it becomes possible to keep track of their occurrences in-context. It also, however, allows one to select just the individual category necessary – such as just Lines or just Thoughts – so as to analyze and compare the different categories as well. Below is an example (1) of how the short comic above (Figure 1) would be represented in the corpus.

(1) Title, Volume, Page, Frame, Category, Occurrence, Sex, Text
NekoNikki,1,1,1,8,1,0, 猫日記＜ｂｙ＞ジャンナ
NekoNikki,1,1,1,4,1,0, タタタ&・・・
NekoNikki,1,1,1,2,1,5, ・・・&今すごく&気持ち&いい&&でも&・・
・お腹&すいた&にゃぁ
NekoNikki,1,1,1,4,2,0, ぺこぺこ〜〜〜
NekoNikki,1,1,2,1,1,1,
あのな&&そろそろ&座りたいん&だから&&どけよ
NekoNikki,1,1,2,7,1,3, 文句&言いつつも・・・
NekoNikki,1,1,2,5,1,0, I❤&猫
NekoNikki,1,1,3,4,1,0, タタタ
NekoNikki,1,1,3,2,1,5, 神様！&ありが&とう！
NekoNikki,1,1,3,6,1,5, お〜！&きたきた！！
NekoNikki,1,1,3,4,1,0, ケケケ・・・
NekoNikki,1,1,4,3,1,3, 沈黙で感謝
NekoNikki,1,1,4,6,1,1, やられた・・・
NekoNikki,1,1,4,5,1,0, ❤&猫
NekoNikki,1,1,4,6,2,5, 何も&してにゃいよ

2.4 Current state of the corpus

Table 2 below organizes data into how many characters, pages and entries are seen in total overall for all series and for each category, as well as by how many entries and characters appear on one page on average and the average length of entries by character. One entry here refers to one entry in the corpus; this is defined as any block of text, such as the text within a speech bubble or a string of onomatopoeic expressions, and does not correspond directly to sentences. Characters, on the other hand, refer to an individual 'letter' of text, including orthographic symbols and blank spaces. Overall, the 30 volumes included in the corpus consisted of 5,289 pages, approximately a little more than 176 pages per volume on average. In total, there were 687,654 characters of text distributed over those pages, or 2,2921.8 characters per individual volume. That text was dispersed over 55,415 entries in the corpus, with an average of 10.48 entries per page. While the number of entries is naturally always less than or equal to the number of characters as characters are what make up entries, the average number of characters per entry also differs from category to category, with Narration (15.88 characters per entry) the longest category on average and Onomatopoeia (3.69 characters per entry) the shortest category on average. Differences such as these point to the characteristics of the categories themselves: where Narration is generally made up of full sentences, Onomatopoeia are individual words or strings of words. As a result, a gap is naturally expected here, and tells us about the different nature of the two categories. Looking next at the amount of text per page, there is an average of 130.02 characters per page, with the majority of those making up lines (94.62, or 72.77%). The average number of Lines per page is 6.49, making the average length of any given Line on a page 14.57 characters. After Lines, Thoughts were the category with the most characters per the page, or 17.37, but Lines clearly make the majority of linguistic information readers flipping through *manga* would find.

Table 2: Basic breakdown of distribution of entries and characters over the page and entries by category

totals	*pages = 5,289*			*entries = 55,415*			*characters = 687,654*		
E per page	All	L	Th	N	O	B-T	B-L/T	C	T
	10.48	6.49	1.23	0.16	1.61	0.41	0.46	0.07	0.05
Ch per page	All	L	Th	N	O	B-T	B-L/T	C	T
	130.02	94.61	17.37	2.56	5.95	4.25	4.28	0.47	0.51
Ch per page	All	L	Th	N	O	B-T	B-L/T	C	T
	12.41	14.57	14.09	15.88	3.69	10.41	9.32	7.17	11.36

Key: L=Lines, Th=Thoughts, N=Narration, O=Onomatopoeia, B-T=Background text, B-L/T=Background lines/thoughts, C=Comments, Ti=Titles; E=Entries, Ch=Characters

Looking at the categories themselves in more detail, as has been hinted at already, Lines made up the majority of all text by far, at 500,393 characters (Table 3). Lines also formed the majority of entries, but the percentage that they comprise is considerably lower (61.97 vs. 72.77%). Given what we know about entries as described above, this suggests that the average length of individual entries for Lines is considerably higher than that of the other categories. Put differently, the other categories tend to be very short in length but are not infrequent per se. This is again undoubtedly at least affected by the nature of categories such as Onomatopoeia and Background Text, since they tend not to be made up of full sentences, but rather, in the case of Onomatopoeia, individual words, and in the case of Background Text, snippets or small sections of greater objects. Thus a gap is found in the second place number of entries and characters: Thoughts (91,889 characters) came to be the second largest collection of characters where Onomatopoeia formed the second highest number of entries (8,519 vs. 6,522).

Naturally, there is also some variation between series. Part of this is due to differences in the number of total pages for each series as the number of pages allocated to *manga* when originally published in chapter form differs both monthly and by magazine. However, the distribution of entries and characters is also dependent upon the structure of the series and stories they express. The number of characters in Lines ranged between 44.12% and 73.36% of characters in all entries. While Lines thus still constitute the largest major category in any series, it is the variation between series that characterizes them. In particular, two categories which seem to have very distinct variation are Background lines /Thoughts and Comments. As can be seen in Table 3, the series that fall under the traditional category of *shoujo-manga* (the lower five entries in the table) seem to have a higher percentage of both types, suggesting that there may be some salient differences between the traditional genres (Unser-Schutz 2010b). Other issues such as story lines may also be worth examining in the future: where the series with the most Lines, *One Piece*, is a fantasy-action story, the series with the least, *KimiTodo*, is a high-school drama. It may be that *One Piece* is more oriented towards conversation and fighting scenes, typified by many Lines and a high percentage of Onomatopoeia (21.22% of entries, 8.23% of characters – the highest percentage of Onomatopoeia in any series) so as to describe the action, whereas *KimiTodo* focuses more on the psychology of the individual characters, characterized by a lower percentage of Lines in favor of a higher percentage of Thoughts (17.70% of entries, 19.90% of characters – the highest percentage of Thoughts in any series).

Table 3: Distribution of entries and characters by category in individual series

pages numbers (series and genre)										
Shounen-manga					*Shoujo-manga*					All
DN	GT	MK	NR	OP	BI	KT	NN	NK	RK	
557	476	547	548	516	540	526	554	519	506	5,289

Series	Data	Text type								
		L	Th	N	O	B-T	B-L/T	C	Ti	Total
DN	E	3,079	620	35	433	463	2	0	30	4,662
	Ch	64,506	15,321	649	1,548	7,988	8	0	285	90,305
GT	E	3,469	112	47	753	311	21	0	41	4,754
	Ch	52,609	1,486	777	2,332	1,416	247	0	621	59,488
MK	E	4,167	717	71	733	171	1	0	31	5,891
	Ch	64,008	10,416	1,308	2,255	1,406	1	0	384	79,778
NR	E	3,036	703	49	1,182	165	96	21	32	5,284
	Ch	39,487	10,272	1,113	3,636	1,042	798	166	354	56,868
OP	E	4,345	90	73	1,252	91	21	0	29	5,901
	Ch	60,145	1,939	883	5,749	588	149	0	378	69,831
BI	E	3,466	1,073	45	510	177	254	43	22	5,590
	Ch	33,674	9,336	523	1,711	1,150	2,139	251	121	48,905
KT	E	2,834	1,137	56	1,235	121	937	89	14	6,423
	Ch	45,348	15,591	876	5,420	953	9,310	692	157	78,347
NN	E	3,300	631	288	449	186	479	23	10	5,366
	Ch	52,825	8,669	4,233	1,547	2,921	4,897	156	149	75,397
NK	E	3,249	733	118	946	252	354	139	18	5,809
	Ch	40,133	9,516	2,015	3,702	3,111	3,058	1,072	156	62,763
RK	E	3,396	706	72	1,026	226	263	34	12	5,736
	Ch	47,658	9,343	1,183	3,577	1,900	2,034	167	110	65,972
All	E	34,341	6,522	854	8,519	2,163	2,428	349	239	55,415
	Ch	500,393	91,889	13,560	31,477	22,475	22,641	2,504	2,715	687,654

Key for Text types: L=Lines, Th=Thoughts, N=Narration, O=Onomatopoeia, B-T=Background text, B-L/T=Background lines/thoughts, C=Comments, Ti=Titles

Key for Series: DN=*Death Note*, GT=*GinTama*, MK=*Meitantei Konan*, NR=*Naruto*, OP=*One Piece*, BI=*Bokura ga Ita*, KT=*Kimi ni Todoke*, NN=*Nana*, NK=*Nodame Kantaabire*, RK=*RabuKon*

Key for Data: E=Entries, Ch=Characters

3. Applications

3.1 Potential uses and interests

Given the underestimation of *manga* as linguistic texts and the general tendency to view them as visual works, the potential uses of this corpus may seem limited. Yet as I have hinted above, there are ample reasons for both *manga* specialists and non-specialists alike to be interested in such data. Of course, one must make certain decisions in order to use the data appropriately. In particular, one must decide what part of the corpus (i.e., which text types) to use and whether or not to look at entries or characters as the unit. In general, entries show how often that type of text appears, whereas characters tell how much data, i.e., the weight of a given category, can be found. Which statistics to utilize will depend on the purpose of the study. In a structural analysis of the types of texts found in *manga,* entries may be telling, whereas when using counts of certain words or grammatical structures, characters may be more appropriate.[5] However, these points add to the corpus's versatility, and can be thought of as one of its points of interest. While many other points might be considered, here I shall demonstrate three others: the possible productivity of unique tags, the mass of specialized data, and the potential for comparing patterns in different linguistic environments.

First, the issue of tags. Given the basic structure described above, it should be comparatively easy to introduce additional notation for different projects. While this is the case for any corpus, the nature of *manga* is such that, given the drawings as references, one can create a wide variety of tags, from basic information such as the gender and name of the speaker/listener to much more complex ones, opening up wide potential fields of analysis. A good example of this would be the emotional tags created by Tokuhisa, Murakami & Ikehara (2006) for their corpus of the lines from a popular *manga* series. Using the expressions on the characters faces, they created a notation system that detailed the emotional status of characters. Not only could this be utilized in this corpus, but it could also be expanded on given the additional categories of text included here.

Secondly, the corpus also offers a large amount of specialized data. Of particular interest is the case of Onomatopoeia. One of the major characteristics of Japanese is its rich vocabulary of onomatopoeia, and *manga* actively use onomatopoeia in order to create a sense of action and atmosphere that would otherwise be static and lacking. Onomatopoeic words are written on the background ("タタタ" '*tatata*', "ぺこぺこ〜〜〜" '*pekopeko~~~*' and "ケケケ・・・" '*kekeke . . .*' in Figure 1) as a kind of special effect, and their abundance has been given varied explanations. Very common in *manga*, Pollman (2001: 12-13) attributes stylized onomatopoeia to a "graphic" element of Japanese writing, whereas Schodt (1983) points towards how *manga* are read by quick scanning, and Peterson (2009) notes that the use of onomatopoeic expressions like this picks up on similar usages in older forms of story-telling. A perhaps more important point is that Japanese simply has more onomatopoeia than many other languages (Lee & Shaw 2006, Peterson 2009).

Where Onomatopoeia are the second most commonly seen text type on any given page, however, they appear less frequently in actual speech, and collecting a variety of examples can be difficult. While such stylized onomatopoeia appear in non-sentence forms in *manga* and thus cannot tell us about their usage in sentences, some researchers have already started to approach them both for the large quantity of data they present. Inoue (2009), for example, has explored how the patterns seen in *manga* fit into the larger phonological and syntactic structure of onomatopoeia. A corpus of *manga* that includes all of the linguistic data found in them would in itself represent a mini-corpus of onomatopoeia that would otherwise be difficult and time-consuming to collect. At 31,477 characters, the onomatopoeia category represents a small portion of the overall data, but a large amount of onomatopoeic data. One promising line of research might be to examine how well onomatopoeia in *manga* conform to the phonological structures described elsewhere, which a corpus would enable researchers to do efficiently through searching for structural patterns. [6]

Onomatopoeia is not the only category to form an interesting mini-corpus, however. Categories such as Lines also offer many opportunities to researchers. While fictional in nature, Lines in *manga* form the majority of the text in the corpus (500,393) and offer large quantities of simulated conversational spoken language. Lines from *manga* have in fact been used by some researchers such as Maynard (2000) on Japanese discourse for precisely those reasons, and a corpus such as this may be of interest to anyone researching Japanese speech. This point, of course, could be extended to the other categories as well, particularly Thoughts and Narration.

Thirdly, the categorical tags make it easy to collect and compare data from different contexts. With all text grouped into one of the above eight categories, an inherent part of the structure of the corpus, and *manga* itself, is such that it is comparatively easy to distinguish between different 'narrative' environments. Whereas in a novel one would have to look for markers such as quotations or sometimes difficult to ascertain linguistic elements (e.g., verbs of thought vs. verbs of narrative) to distinguish between Narratives, spoken Lines and inner voices, for example, in a corpus of *manga* all of these data are clearly divided into easily distinguished categories. This makes it extremely easy and viable to compare the contents of Thoughts versus Lines, or what appears in secondary environments such as Background Text versus more narratively-central conversational Lines. One possible point to consider would be whether characters are consistent in their use of gendered speech patterns in Lines and Thoughts. Because such speech patterns change, based upon the relationship between speaker and listener, one might expect different patterns in Lines, which by nature imply a listener, and Thoughts, which are never directed towards a listener. However, a wide variety of research topics are possible.

3.2 Continuing problems

While the data has many interesting potential uses, the special structure of text in *manga* has meant that there are still some issues which must be properly assessed in order to use the corpus to its full potential. Three particularly critical problematic points are noted here: the use of nonstandard orthography; unusual structures to sentences; and comparing the data within the corpus with other text types. While the former two points primarily have to do with trying to effectively search and parse the text, the latter point is concerned with how to locate the linguistic characteristics found in the corpus within a greater frame of reference.

To begin with, the use of non-standard orthographic conventions in *manga* makes it difficult to break down the text with morpheme parsers. This problem is first characterized by *manga*'s distinct overuse of unusual punctuation. Approximately 21% of all the text is actually orthographic symbols, including but not limited to the question mark ("？"), the exclamation mark ("！") and white space ("　") (Table 4).[7] This is well above the 15.58% average found in newspapers (Nozaki & Shimizu 2000) or the 17.6% found in magazines (Kashino 2007).[8] Likewise, many of the symbols found are in fact *not* commonly used in other texts – in particular white space between words – whereas some common orthographic symbols, in particular the period (*kuten*, "。") and the comma (*touten*, "、") are found very rarely.

Table 4: Number of characters per letter-type (Ch = Characters)

text	*Hiragana*	*Katakana*	*Kanji*	*Roman letters*	*Arabic numbers*	*symbols*	*total*
Ch	354,710	61,462	113,792	10,107	3,656	14,3927	687,654
%	51.58%	8.94%	16.55%	1.47%	0.53%	20.93%	100.00%

The second part of the problem is that authors often use non-standard choices in writing out individual words. Japanese normally utilizes three systems of writing: *kanji* (Chinese characters), *hiragana* (a syllabary used primarily for function words) and *katakana* (a syllabary used primarily for foreign loan words). While most words are written in a more or less accepted way, they are less certain for non-standard spoken language, and it is not uncommon to see great variation and creativity in script choice in *manga*. For example, in male spoken speech, the negative ending marker, *nai* [nai], is sometimes pronounced [ne:] or [nei̯]. Normally *nai* would be written in *hiragana* as "ない", but the masculine form, which is commonly seen in *manga*, is primarily a spoken form and is not as standardized. Thus, one sees versions of [ne:] and [nei̯] written in a variety of combinations of *hiragana* and *katakana*, such as "ねえ," "ねぇ," "ねー," "ねエ," "ネエ," "ネー," and "ネェ" (Example 2).

(2) Three examples of [ne:]/ [nei̯] (my emphasis):
1. Masashi Kishimoto, *Naruto* volume 3: 31:
Naruto, 3,31,3,1,1,1,そーは&いか**ねー**よ
2. Eiichirou Oda, *One Piece* volume 1: 10:

One Piece, 1,10,3,1,2,1,うそつけ！！&バカな事すん&じゃねェ！！
3. Ai Yazawa, *Nana*, volume 2: 93:
Nana,
2,93,3,1,1,1,確かにこれで７万は&激安だよな&&なんか&出るんじゃ&ねえの？

These related points both ultimately affect how easily the text can be effectively searched and parsed. In relation to the former point, Groensteen (2007) notes something similar in some Western comics, suggesting that the overuse of certain kinds of punctuation is meant to give the texts a sense of orality. Whatever the case may be, without a better understanding of how punctuation is being used in *manga*, the overuse of punctuation marks, some of which are not featured in their expected environments, makes it difficult to appropriately parse text into smaller sentences and units. Likewise, the variability in spelling conventions means that not only are none of the more unusual patterns recognizable by morpheme parsers, which are currently oriented towards more conservatively written texts, but that words that are actually derivable to the same base may not be associated with the others. This freedom of script choice is one of great importance to Japanese morpheme parsing in general, but it is one that is especially relevant for a spoken-speech oriented corpus such as this. While still in the elementary stages, I have begun to investigate using n-gram analysis for some of these problems, and am hopeful that it will prove useful in the future.

Secondly, the special structure of linguistic data in *manga* can also affect their usefulness. Utterances are restricted by the size of their environment, whether that be a speech bubble or directly on the background, and their presentation is greatly affected by this. A good example of this would be line breaks. In order to properly represent line breaks within the same utterance, I have utilized the half-width ampersand ("&"), which otherwise does not appear within any of the texts. While I have omitted the ampersand from the character data listed earlier since it is a place marker, if included, it would come to close to 10% of all text (75,428 out of 763,082 characters). Thus, individual sentences, even when in the same bubble (i.e., linguistic environment), are divided into much smaller strings. It is also not uncommon to find sentences broken up into multiple utterances, thereby making each individual entry only fragments without the others. As one limited option, it is possible to remove the ampersand for analysis purposes in the case of line breaks, to create undisturbed text strings. This is less viable for utterances which have been made into separate entries because they were divided into separate blocks in the original *manga*, but it may be possible in the future to connect continuing entries by adding a name-tag to identify the speaker in combination with the occurrence number, to determine the order of utterances.

Finally, an important task will be to determine just how unique the patterns found in the corpus are to *manga*, and, in that respect, how *manga* compare as a linguistic medium to other types of texts. For at least some categories, such as onomatopoeic expressions, it seems that the patterns found in *manga* differ in some key ways from those seen in other types of texts (Inoue 2009). This not only affects one's understanding of how language functions in *manga*, but also changes the viability of using *manga* as a resource for more generalized research. At this point, however, it is also unclear to what degree the patterns in *manga* are unique, and it is difficult to determine what would be appropriate 'parallel' forms to look at, e.g., novels or plays or animation. These are issues which still need to be addressed, but tie-ins with other major industries are some potential resources to look at, e.g., so-called 'light novels' (novellas based upon *manga*) or animated television series and movies of the series used in this corpus.

4. Conclusion: current research trajectories and future plans

Designing and maintaining a corpus is always a work in progress. While, as the discussion above suggests, there are some issues that need to be further examined, there are some immediate tasks which could be of help in such examinations. First, additional basic tags for speakers' names are necessary, so as to be able to identify patterns within the speech of individual speakers. While the current tags for sex allow for generalizations based upon gender, it is currently difficult to track how consistent speakers are and which patterns group together. Secondly, while the current corpus features a not minimal number of overall characters, the number of series included is rather limited. Adding an additional two to four series would allow for better statistical analysis, so as to make greater generalizations about such things as genre and authorial differences.

In terms of future developments, however, a more ambitious plan is that of creating a parallel English corpus. All the titles used herein are available in English, and their translations raise many interesting questions, such as how they deal with the spatial constraints of *manga*. As Baetens (2003) argues, *manga* may be considered to be a form of constrained writing, meaning that the special page conditions of *manga* restrict writers, both in the amount that they write and also in how they write. Unlike in text-only novels, linguistic elements, whatever their form, must appear directly on the drawings, or secondary elements such as speech bubbles must be utilized. Furthermore, while the rich context offered by the drawings in *manga* offer opportunities for plays on words, double entendres and other linguistic complexities, they also limit where utterances may appear and how long they may be because of their linking.

What this means for translation is that the relevant utterances for a scene, whether they be Lines or Onomatopoeia, must appear within the limited space available in any given panel or page, and they may be limited in content or form in order to fit that restriction. Translators may also develop certain artifices to work within that framework. However, because the drawings create a strict order which the relevant linguistic elements must adhere to, the ability of translators to reorder phrases is comparatively limited. This means that one may hypothesize that they are by nature parallel in content and form, which would be highly desirable for comparative Japanese and English research. Furthermore, because each individual linguistic element is clearly tagged for where it appears in the text, adding an additional translation should, in theory, simply require moving them into those identical slots (Example 3).

(3) Example of Japanese and English versions from one page of *One Piece* (volume 1: 179)
A. Japanese version:
One Piece, 1,179,1,1,1,1,・・・・・・・・・
One Piece, 1,179,1,5,1,0, ＭＡＲＩ
One Piece, 1,179,2,1,1,1,何だか&イカつい&おばさん&なんだけど
One Piece, 1,179,2,1,2,1, ２年間も&こいつ&そこで・・・
One Piece,
1,179,3,2,1,1,やめて&下さいよ！！&やめて&下さいよ&・・・・・・！！！
One Piece, 1,179,4,1,1,1,やめて下さいよ！！！！
One Piece, 1,179,4,4,1,0,バキッ
One Piece, 1,179,4,1,2,1,！！？
B. English version:
One Piece, 1,179,1,1,1,1,……...
One Piece, 1,179,1,5,1,0, MARI
One Piece, 1,179,2,1,1,1, SHE WAS&REALLY&MEAN…
One Piece, 1,179,2,1,2,1,AND&FOR&TWO&YEARS, THIS&GUY…
One Piece, 1,179,3,2,1,1, LUFFY!!&DON'T!!
One Piece, 1,179,4,1,1,1, SHUT&UP!!!
One Piece, 1,179,4,4,1,0, THWAK
One Piece, 1,179,4,1,2,1,!!?

Such projects aside, however, no corpus is of any relevance if it is not actually used for linguistic research. In order to demonstrate how such a corpus could be utilized, I am currently involved in two further projects. First, I have taken on the task of examining how gendered language is used within the corpus. Research hitherto on gendered speech in *manga* has shown contradictory results, and in order to reevaluate this, I have begun to examine the use of gendered personal pronouns in *manga*. While still in the beginning stages, a first attempt at looking at their distribution in *manga* has been summarized in Unser-Schutz (2010a). Secondly, the use of different linguistic patterns in *manga* may be useful in determining more expression-oriented genre lines. In order to examine this, I have also begun analyzing what the distribution of different text categories between series tells us about their genres and structure (Unser-Schutz 2010b).

Although there are clearly problems that need to be dealt with in order to better utilize the data, these plans point to the potential that a *manga* corpus may have. While *manga* may seem obscure at first, when reevaluated in light of their special linguistic characteristics, they clearly form a unique and relevant resource, but one which is perhaps not easily accessible structurally. Introducing the corpus here has been an attempt to think about those issues, and how they may be dealt with. These are things that, naturally, can also be said for similar media, from other cartoon forms to things like advertisements, which use text in unusual ways. In that sense, the lessons learnt from this attempt may be of use to other individuals interested in non-traditional sources of text.

Notes

1 The only exception was *Nodame Kantaabire*, whose publishing magazine, *Kiss*, is listed as being for women by the Japanese Magazine Publisher Association, but which has generally been received as a *shoujo-manga* series, winning awards such as the Koudansha *shoujo-manga* award in 2004.

2 Seven questions were asked in both surveys: what comic magazines they had ever read; how often do they read comic magazines; do they buy comic books (non-magazines); had they ever talked to their friends about comics; had they bought any non-comic/non-academic books recently; their favorite series; and spending money. The survey had multiple-choice selections available, with space to write additional comments. However, the structure of the survey varied slightly between the earlier and the later surveys. In the first survey, there were three additional questions, asking their favorite celebrity, television show and class; the question on spending money asked them how much allowance they received per month. In the later surveys, those three questions were removed, and the question on spending money asked how much money they used and on what.

3 Specifically, at the two co-ed schools in eastern Tokyo, out of the 44 boys who said they had a favorite series, only one boy gave a *shoujo-manga* series. In comparison, of the 55 girls who said they had a favorite title, 10 of them gave a *shounen-manga*, and 16 a *shoujo-manga*. This trend of girls reading titles for both boys and girls but for boys to only read titles for boys is even more obvious when asking what magazines they had ever read: of the 64 boys who had read comic magazines before, seven had read ones aimed for girls, whereas of the 72 comic magazine reading girls, 44 had read series for boys.

4 Such data, including current and previous rankings, can be found on PHP's website (http://www.php.co.jp/fun/ranking/books.php?genre=f).

5 Some of these are points which are actually typical issues for corpus-

based studies in Japanese because of the nature of Japanese text: as Japanese does not utilize spaces, defining the number of words in a text can be difficult, and corpora are often described by the number of characters in them instead. See Gotou (2007) for more details on working with Japanese corpora.

6 Onomatopoeia in Japanese typically follows a limited number of well-described phonological structural patterns, such as the repetition of a basic morpheme. See Inoue (2009) for a review of these structures with particular light on how they appear in *manga*.

7 All symbols intermixed in Japanese text were input as full-width characters, hence the use of full-width symbols over the more orthodox half-width symbols found in English language texts.

8 Note that Kashino (2007) includes numbers with symbols, so the number of orthographic symbols only should actually be considerably lower, making the percentage difference between them and *manga* higher.

References

Agency for Cultural Affairs (2010), 'Heisei 19 nendo "Kokugo ni kansuru yoron chousa" no kekka nitsuite'. Available online at: http://www.bunka.go.jp/kokugo_nihongo/yoronchousa/h19/kekka.html.

Allen, K. & J. Ingulsrud (2005), 'Reading *manga*: patterns of personal literacies among adolescents', *Language and education*, 19(4): 265-280.

Allwood, J. (2008), 'Multimodal corpora', in: A. Lüdling & M. Kytö (eds.) *Corpus linguistics: an international handbook*. Berlin: Mouton de Gruyter. 207-225.

Baetens, J. (2003), 'Comic strips and constrained writing', *Image & narrative*, 7 (October 2003). Available online at: http://www.imageandnarrative.be/inarchive/graphicnovel/janbaetens_constrained.htm

Bateman, J., J. Delin & R. Henschel (2002), 'Multimodality and empiricism: methodological issues in the study of multimodal meaning-making,' *GeM report* 2002/1: 1-35.

Beronä, D. (2001), 'Pictures speak in comics without words: pictorial principles in the work of Milt Gross, Hendrik Dorgathen, Eric Drooker, & Peter Kuper', in: R. Varnum & C.T. Gibbons (eds.) *The language of comics: word and image*. Mississippi: University Press of Mississippi. 19-39.

Endo, O. (2001), 'Onna no ko no "boku/ore" wa okasikunai', in: O. Endo (ed.) *Onna to kotoba: onna wa kawatta ka, nihongo wa kawatta ka*. Tokyo: Meiji-shoten. 30-39.

Fuse, H. (2004), *Manga wo kaibou suru*. Tokyo: Chikuma Shobou.
Gotou, H (2007), 'Koopasu-gengogaku to nihongo kenkyuu', *Nihongokagaku* 22: 45-58.
Groensteen, T. (2007), *The system of comics*. B. Beaty & N. Nguyen (trans.). Jackson: University of Mississippi Press.
Ingulsrud, J. & K. Allen (2009), *Reading Japan cool: patterns of manga literacy and discourse*. Plymouth: Lexington Books.
Inoue, K. (2009), 'Onomatopoeic neologisms in Japanese comics', *Journal of language and culture*, 18: 69-85.
Ito, K. (2005), 'A history of *manga* in the context of Japanese culture and society', *Journal of popular culture*, 38(3): 456–475.
Itou, G. (2005), *Tezuka izu deddo: hirakareta manga hyōgenron e*. Tokyo: NTT Shuppan.
Kai, M. (1989), '*Manga* no kotoba: mondai teiki', *Nihongo-gaku*, 8(9): 33-38.
Kashino, W. (2007), 'Kanji no shiyou wa, izen to hikaku shite hetteiru no deshou ka', *Moji to shakai* 20: 69-71.
Kinsui, S. (2003), *Vaacharu nihongo: yakuwari-go no nazo*. Tokyo: Iwanami-shoten.
Kumano, N. & M. Hirokaga (2008), 'An examination of "anime and *manga*": regional information overseas and Japanese-language materials,' *Kokusai kouryuu kikin nihongo kyouiku kiyou*, 4: 55-69.
Lee, W. & Y. Shaw (2006), 'A textual comparison of Japanese and Chinese editions of *manga*: translation as cultural hybridization', *International journal of comic art,* 8(2): 34-55.
Maekawa, K. (2008), 'Kotonoha "gendai nihongo kaki-kotoba kinkou koupasu" no kaihatsu', *Nihongo no kenkyuu*, 4(1): 82-95.
Maynard, S.K. (2000), 'Speaking for the unspeakable: expressive functions of *nan(i)* in Japanese discourse', *Journal of pragmatics*, 32(8): 1209-1239.
McCloud, S. (1994), *Understanding comics: the invisible art*. New York: Harper Paperbacks.
Nakano, H. (2009), *Manga shinka-ron: kontentsu bijinesu wa manga kara umareru!* Tokyo: Blues Interactions.
Natsume, F. (1997), *Manga wa naze omoshiroi no ka*. Tokyo: Nihon housou shuppan kyoukai.
Nozaki, H.& Y. Shimizu (2000), 'An analysis of kanji frequency in newspaper articles, and the development of a kanji list for teaching newspaper Japanese', *Nihon kyouiku kougaku zasshi*, 24(2): 121-132.
Ogino, M. (2001), 'Manga wo shakaigaku suru', in: K. Miyahara & M. Ogino (eds.) *Manga no shakaigaku*. Kyoto: Sekai Shisousha. 134-156.
Peterson, R.S. (2009), 'The acoustics of *manga*', in: J. Heer & K. Worcester (eds.) *A comic studies reader*. Jackson: University of Mississippi Press. 163-172.
Pollman, J. (2001), 'Shaping sounds in comics', *International journal of comic art*, 3(1): 9-21.
Rommens, A. (2000), '*Manga* story-telling/showing', *Image & narrative*.

Available online at: http://www.imageandnarrative.be/inarchive/narratology/aarnoudrommens.htm
Schodt, F.L. (1983), *Manga! Manga!: the world of Japanese comics*. Tokyo: Kodansha International.
Schodt, F.L. (1996), *Dreamland Japan: writings on modern manga*. Berkeley, CA: Stone Bridge.
Shimizu, I. (1991), *Manga no rekishi*. Tokyo: Iwanami-shoten.
Takahashi, S. (2009), 'Akujo no 'yakuwari':shoujo *manga* 'raifu' ni miru shoujo no 'onna-kotoba', *Gender and sexuality*, 4: 17-38.
Takeuchi, I. (2006), *Tezuka Osamu = sutorii-manga no kigen*. Tokyo: Kondasha.
Takeuchi, O. (2005), *Manga hyougengaku nyuumon*. Tokyo: Chikuma Shoten.
Tokuhisa, M., J. Murakami & S. Ikehara (2006), 'Construction and evaluation of text-dialog corpus with emotion tags focusing on facial expression in comics', in: B. Gabrys, R.J. Howlett, & L.C. Jain (eds.) *Knowledge-based intelligent information and engineering systems*. Berlin: Springer-Verlag. 715-724.
Ueno, J. (2006), '*Shojo* and adult women: a linguistic analysis of gender identity in *manga* (Japanese comics)', *Women and language*, 29(1): 16-25.
Unser-Schutz, G. (2010a), 'Personal pronouns and gendered speech in popular *manga* (Japanese comics)', in: *LSA Annual Meeting Extended Abstracts*. Available on line at : http://www.elanguage.net/journals/index.php/lsameeting/article/viewFile/639/596
Unser-Schutz, G. (2010b), 'Exploring the role of language in *manga*: text types, their usages and their distributions', paper presented at the Popular Culture Association Annual Meeting, St. Louis, MO, March 31-April 3.
Unser-Schutz, G. (2010c), 'Girls, boys and *manga*: sentence final particles in Japanese comics for girls and boys'. Paper presented at the 2010 International Gender and Language Association Conference, Tokyo, September 18-20.
Yamaguchi, M. (2005), 'Kaisetsu: zenbun kensaku shisutemu "Himawari"', *Kokugoken no mado*, 24: 4.

Appendix. Series used within the corpus

Aoyama, G. (1994-present), *Meitantei Konan*. Tokyo: Shougakukan.
Kishimoto, M. (1999-present), *Naruto*. Tokyo: Shuueisha.
Nakahara, A. (2001-2007), *RabuKon*. Tokyo: Shuueisha.
Ninomiya, T. (2001-2009), *Nodame Kantaabire*. Tokyo: Koudansha.
Obata, Y. (2002), *Bokura ga Ita*. Tokyo: Shougakukan
Oda, E. (1997-present), *One Piece*. Tokyo: Shuueisha.
Ohba, T. & T. Obata (2003-2006), *Death Note*. Tokyo: Shuueisha.
Shiina, K. (2005-present), *Kimi ni todoke*. Tokyo: Shuueisha.
Sorachi, H. (2004-present), *GinTama*. Tokyo: Shuueisha
Yazawa, A. (1999-present), *Nana*. Tokyo: Shuueisha.

Corpus linguistics and language documentation: challenges for collaboration

Christopher Cox

University of Alberta

Abstract

Recent literature in corpus linguistics (e.g., McEnery & Ostler 2000) and language documentation (e.g., Johnson 2004) suggests both disciplines may share natural points of interaction, having in common an interest in the construction and use of permanent collections of diverse linguistic data. Although considerable benefit might be anticipated from close collaboration between these two areas, divergences in their respective purposes, practices, and products may render such an interaction more difficult to foster than might initially be expected.

This paper considers points of commonality and difference between corpus linguistics and language documentation in four specific areas of practice, drawing upon examples from ongoing corpus construction and language documentation efforts centered on Mennonite Plautdietsch in Canada. Given the results of this comparison, this study proposes viewing corpora as descriptive applications of language documentation, to be built directly upon the permanent documentary record. By founding corpora upon documentary materials, such an approach opens language documentation more readily to the analytical and methodological contributions of corpus linguistics, while providing a solid empirical basis for future corpus construction.

1. Introduction

In a recent commentary on responses within linguistics to issues of language endangerment, Himmelmann (2008) remarks on the concentration of one such initiative, language documentation, upon the construction of reusable, permanent collections of primary linguistic data. Paralleling other definitional statements in the current literature on documentary linguistics (e.g., Himmelmann 1998, 2006, Woodbury 2003, Austin 2010), Himmelmann observes that

> [l]anguage documentations [...] focus on observable linguistic behavior and knowledge. The goal is a lasting, multifunctional record of the linguistic practices attested at a given time in a given speech community and the knowledge speakers have about these practices. (Himmelmann 2008: 346)

Programmatic definitions such as these aimed at the goals and practices of language documentation bear notable similarity to sentiments often expressed in corpus linguistics, where a similar emphasis is placed upon multifunctional records of attested linguistic acts (cf. Leech 1992: 112, Stubbs 2001: 221). Commenting on the benefits of reusable corpus-linguistic materials in the context of language endangerment, McEnery & Ostler (2000) note that

> [...] in collecting corpus data for endangered and minority languages, researchers are not only paving the way towards better descriptions of those languages, they may also be allowing work to begin on [a] range of language technology applications [...]. Corpora are multifunctional resources, and their potential for reusability is high. Consequently, although the trend towards minority and endangered languages to be studied largely in the context of ethnolinguistics is understandable, this work, as it becomes corpus based, also opens up the prospect of reuse and retargeting of corpus data gathered by such work to language-processing applications. (McEnery & Ostler 2000: 417)

A closer review of the recent literature in both disciplines suggests such similarities between present-day corpus linguistics and language documentation to be more than skin deep. In addition to this shared interest in producing and analyzing reusable collections of linguistic data, studies in both disciplines have (i) laid claim to a common intellectual heritage, (ii) acknowledged language endangerment as a significant motivation for certain aspects of their development, and (iii) often involved critical reflection upon the empirical foundations of linguistic research. Each of these commonalities is discussed in greater detail below.

1.1 Reusable collections of linguistic data

As the introductory quotation by Himmelmann suggests, the theoretization of practices surrounding the production of permanent, multifunctional stores of primary linguistic data has represented a central issue for language documentation. This concern reflects in part a broader effort to ensure that documentary records are suitable for use in as wide a range of linguistic and socio-cultural applications as possible. Corpus linguistics intersects with language documentation in this regard inasmuch as it deals with the construction and analysis of consistent, reusable collections of linguistic data. At their core, both disciplines are rooted in a common concern for what in corpus linguistics has occasionally been termed "first-order data" (Stubbs 2001: 66), or, in language documentation, "primary data" (Himmelmann 2006: 7).

1.2 Common intellectual heritage

This concentration upon primary data compilation and analysis in both disciplines has sometimes been cited as reflecting a common intellectual heritage, as well. In particular, studies in both corpus linguistics and language documentation have laid claim to the anthropological linguistic tradition established by Franz Boas and his students. McEnery & Ostler (2000: 404) identify the "recording [of] dying languages for posterity in the form of paper-based corpora" as a component of Boasian fieldwork, establishing a clear connection between the construction of linguistic corpora and Boasian text collection. Likewise, although they are careful to distinguish between the characteristics of current language documentation and other preceding traditions, both Woodbury (2003: 35) and Himmelmann (2006: 14) similarly acknowledge the formative influence of "[l]inguistic and anthropological fieldwork in the Boasian tradition" (Himmelmann 2006: 16) in the development of documentary linguistics, particularly in its emphasis upon the recording of texts.

1.3 Language endangerment

As in the Boasian Americanist linguistic tradition, issues of language endangerment have also contributed substantially to the development of language documentation (Himmelmann 2008, Austin 2010: 14). While less central to its historical development, contemporary corpus linguistics has similarly viewed corpus development as a possible response to language endangerment. McEnery & Ostler (2000: 414) present a particularly clear statement to this effect, perceiving a critical role for the development of spoken corpora in the study and support of endangered languages, while underscoring the importance of the data-gathering required for such corpora as a component useful to both linguistic analyses and language revitalization efforts.

1.4 Empirical foundations of linguistic research

This consideration of potential applications of reusable language resources has also brought attention in both disciplines to the empirical underpinnings of linguistic research. Practitioners in both areas have repeatedly advocated replicable studies which draw upon such resources, whether in the form of corpora from the corpus-linguistic tradition, or the collections produced in language documentation.[1] Himmelmann (2006: 1) remarks on bolstering the "empirical foundations" of linguistics through greater reliance upon the primary data available in documentary collections, thus supporting greater accountability in published analyses through replication and falsification (2006: 6). These comments are essentially mirrored in Leech (1992: 112), who similarly proposes falsification as a desirable trait of linguistic models based upon open corpora.

1.5 Mutual interests of corpus linguistics and language documentation

These commonalities are not limited to a parallel history or shared positions on what constitutes desirable research practices in linguistics, but also encompass a mutual interest on the part of each discipline in the practices of the other. For corpus linguistics, the results of documentary linguistic research offer strikingly diverse, well-catalogued samples of natural language, materials which might serve as the basis for the construction of linguistic corpora. These same language materials often represent comparatively understudied languages whose integration into digital corpora and tools for corpus-based analysis presents a long-standing challenge for corpus linguistics (cf. McEnery & Ostler 2000). In both respects, the prospects for corpus-linguistic involvement in the development of documentary linguistic materials appears promising, presenting an opportunity to extend the scope of corpus-linguistic methods, tools, and standards to include languages whose typological features may not have been addressed in corpus construction to date.

Similarly, language documentation might seek to benefit from closer engagement with developments in corpus and computational linguistics. From the perspective of documentary linguistics, corpus linguistics might be seen as potentially offering another methodological perspective upon the documentary record, as well as another set of tools for this record's analysis. Several decades of research in corpus linguistics on collocation and corpus-based lexicography, for instance, present no shortage of elaborated methods which might be harnessed in the production of documentation-based dictionaries, one of the more common descriptive applications of language documentation (Teubert 2001, Heid 2008). Corpus-linguistic procedures may present new methods of opening the documentary record to analysis, and thus encourage further reuse of the documentary record in a wider range of descriptive applications.

More generally, corpus-linguistic methods present another means of rendering the documentary record accessible to *both* academic and non-academic communities. Providing even a simple, concordance-based search facility for a documentary collection – a search interface comparable to that of an internet search engine, and thus perhaps less daunting to less technically-inclined users – may be of use to many individuals interested in exploring the contents of a documentary collection. This kind of interface clearly does not prevent other methods of access, or obviate the need for discussion among those parties engaged in documentation to determine the appropriateness of such a view of the documentary materials involved. Nevertheless, corpus search interfaces offer another way of sharing documentary collections with a general audience, an issue which remains a standing challenge for documentary linguistics (cf. Nathan 2006).

1.6 Convergence and divergence

A gradual convergence of both disciplines in matters of corpus construction thus presents an opportunity to encourage greater interdisciplinary collaboration from which both disciplines may benefit. Yet, such an interaction may not be as simple to foster at it would seem at first glance. The anticipated strengths of such a collaboration lie in the distinctive contributions of each discipline – in the degree to which the contributions of the one might both meet the needs of and present instructive challenges to the other. Such distinctiveness might also be expected to extend to the respective practices and purposes of each discipline, however, and thus not guarantee immediate compatibility of interests in either respect.

The following sections examine such commonalities and differences between corpus linguistics and language documentation through the lens of ongoing corpus-based documentation of Canadian Mennonite Plautdietsch. Mennonite Plautdietsch (ISO 639-3: pdt) is the traditional, West Germanic language of the Dutch-Russian Mennonites, an Anabaptist Christian denomination. The repeated persecution, emigration, and exile of Mennonite Plautdietsch speakers over the course of several centuries has contributed to the exceptional character of the language, having been separated from the larger continental West Germanic dialect continuum during this time, as well as to the unusually broad distribution of present Mennonite Plautdietsch speech communities over four continents and more than a dozen countries (Epp 1993). Although estimates of the total population of Mennonite Plautdietsch speakers are difficult due to this geographical dispersion, Epp (1993) and Gordon (2005) place the worldwide speaker population at approximately 300,000, with the Canadian population contributing substantially to that number. The endangerment of most Canadian varieties of Mennonite Plautdietsch and their unique status as 'parent' dialects to several currently thriving speech communities in Latin America partly motivates efforts to develop permanent linguistic records useful to Plautdietsch speech communities and to researchers. An element of this ongoing work involves not only the preservation of existing language records and the creation of new language resources, but also corpus construction as a parallel component of documentation.

The aim of this paper is thus twofold, seeking to offer a general comparison of current practices in language documentation and corpus construction and their apparent compatibility in several areas, while grounding its conclusions in the specific experiences of language documentation and corpus construction in the case of Canadian Mennonite Plautdietsch. As such, this study does not claim to present an exhaustive or authoritative comparison of both disciplines. Differing perspectives may well exist on the relative compatibility of both areas, and other recommendations might justifiably be made on the basis of differing experiences in resolving potential points of difference between the practices of the two fields. The conclusions of this study are based upon consideration of issues which appear relevant with Mennonite Plautdietsch, and invite further consideration in the light of other corpus construction and language documentation efforts.

2. Corpus linguistics and language documentation

The concentration upon corpus linguistics and language documentation in the following sections calls for more thorough consideration of what is understood by both terms. Following Himmelmann (1998, 2006, 2008) and Woodbury (2003), this study takes language documentation to be an independent discipline within linguistics, concentrating upon the theoretization and practice of developing and analyzing permanent, multipurpose collections of linguistic data. As such, it is distinct from, though not entirely independent of, linguistic description in the form of lexicography, grammatography, and other aspects of linguistic inquiry which make use of the contents of the permanent documentary record. By comparison, the focus of most of the discussion which takes place here under the label of 'corpus linguistics' is upon corpus building and the development of facilities for the analysis of corpus resources – that is, upon the process and products of corpus construction and the accompanying technical infrastructure, rather than upon any particular methodological standpoint on the 'proper' interpretation of the resulting corpora. This paper thus attempts to remain essentially neutral in the debate over the status of corpus linguistics as a distinct area of research within linguistics, or as a methodology of potential service to other linguistic subdisciplines.

The discussion that follows concentrates upon four specific areas of comparison, focusing on the practices of language documentation and corpus construction as they relate to the relationships between project stakeholders, methods of linguistic sampling, conventional technologies, and the treatment of data and metadata in both disciplines. Each of these areas is considered in turn, beginning in each case with a comparison of perspectives from both disciplines and concluding with comments on how the issues thus raised are reflected in the documentation of Canadian Mennonite Plautdietsch.

2.1 Stakeholder relationships

Common to both corpus construction and language documentation is the involvement of multiple parties in the development process. Even where the teams responsible for development are relatively small, efforts are commonly still made to develop a final resource amenable to the audiences and end-uses envisioned by the developers. This study refers to these audiences, both those directly involved in development and those providing guidance and evaluation to the development process, as *stakeholders* – individuals or groups having an interest in the development or results of development of the language resources under consideration.

Within the context of corpus construction, decisions concerning the overall composition of a corpus and the eventual selection of its contents are often the result of careful corpus planning. This process serves to determine the distribution of corpus documents over demographic, geographical, social, and textual categories of interest, and thus informs the later choice of language materials which might fill these categories (Sinclair 2005). More often than not, these corpus planning decisions are made in accordance with the linguistic interests of the developers and the intended final uses of the corpus, rather than beginning with an assessment of the language materials on hand and proceeding from there to determine categorical boundaries. Where corpus planning suggests that access may be required to materials which are not available to or cannot be easily produced by the corpus development team, terms of use are typically negotiated with the copyright holders of such materials when and where the need arises.[2]

The relationship which exists between corpus developers, copyright holders, and the intended end-users of the corpus is and was typically one of business, being characterized by relatively short-term interactions centered around the formal negotiation of terms of access and redistribution acceptable to each stakeholder. In such circumstances, it is rare that a publisher holding the rights to materials sought after in building a new corpus will express any immediate interest in the interface which will be applied to the final corpus, for instance, or raise concerns over the application of part-of-speech tagging or orthographic normalization to the texts provided, as long as the agreed-upon terms of use, redistribution, and access are strictly maintained. It is rarer still for individual authors represented by that publisher to have much say in the ultimate representation of their works in the corpus. As corpus elements, these authors' texts are treated first and foremost as linguistic data, rather than as works intended for the aesthetic or artistic appreciation of a general audience. In the end, the decisions which define the composition and contents of a corpus are typically made by linguists for linguists, with negotiation of access to the relevant texts being negotiated essentially 'on demand' with the relevant stakeholders. These stakeholders' interest in the resulting compilation of linguistic data only infrequently extends beyond the protection of their asserted intellectual property rights.

This situation stands in contrast to the relationships which commonly exist between stakeholders in language documentation. Here, planning often emerges as a product of active partnership between linguists and community members (where these are not already one and the same), with both groups determining the composition and contents of the collection, either directly or indirectly through their interactions. In such cases, stakeholders representing the language community and the academic community participate in shaping the ultimate form of the documentary record through long-term participation and negotiation (Leonard & Haynes 2010). This interactive process of definition seeks to develop common goals and outcomes which meet the needs of all stakeholders involved, and is thus not entirely under the direction of any linguists involved, as is often the case in corpus construction.

Interactions between stakeholders in language documentation may resemble those found in corpus construction, involving short-term, business-like negotiation of access and distribution rights with the holders of intellectual property rights. In many cases, however, language documentation proceeds on a more familiar and longer-term basis, depending critically upon relationships of trust built between individuals in communities over the course of years and even decades of interaction. Such relationships are often essential in situations where language documentation is perceived to be a politicized activity (cf. Ostler 2009), whether this politicization stems from previous interactions between the stakeholder communities or from attitudes towards the language(s) and/or language materials involved. Interactions between stakeholders under such conditions, particularly in determining appropriate access and reuse conditions, are arguably of a different quality than the comparatively less politicized negotiations between corpus linguists and copyright holders. The relative disinterest on the part of the latter copyright holders in the ultimate representation of the provided language 'data' would be unexpected in the kinds of language documentation situations described above. Where individual language materials bear considerable cultural, historical, or personal significance, their intermediate treatment and final presentation in language documentation may require more extensive collective deliberation between stakeholders.

Language documentation involving Canadian Mennonite Plautdietsch faces many of the issues noted above in both corpus linguistic and language documentation stakeholder relationships. As in corpus linguistics, some existing language materials have been made available for language documentation and corpus construction without an extended period of consultation. Bible translation agencies, first-language literacy initiatives, and radio programs in particular have often been willing to share their language materials with a wider audience, in accordance with their respective mandates. Even in these cases, however, there is often the concomitant expectation that the contributed resources will be used in a respectful manner and with due acknowledgement, which in turn requires a mutual understanding of what proper reuse entails. In one instance, a series of discussions concerning historical Plautdietsch language materials appearing in a prominent Mennonite periodical concluded with the blessing of the editor for the documentation project to "do whatever you like" with the sources – as long as everyone was clear on what was meant by 'whatever you like'!

More often, language documentation has followed from long-term relationships with community members and institutions who have an expressed interest in Mennonite Plautdietsch, and whose contributions and guidance codetermine the final products of documentation. Several prominent Mennonite Plautdietsch authors, including the lexicographer Herman Rempel and scholar Reuben Epp, have made portions of their respective Mennonite Plautdietsch literary estates generally available under Creative Commons agreements, having been encouraged to consider doing so in consultation with close colleagues and friends. In contrast to many other minority language communities in Canada, where language documentation and description efforts have typically involved the presence of interested 'outsiders' to the speech community, the vast majority of academic linguistic description and language documentation concerned with Canadian Mennonite Plautdietsch has been undertaken by members of Mennonite Plautdietsch-speaking communities themselves. All dictionaries of Mennonite Plautdietsch published to date have been compiled by native speakers of the language, for instance. This situation has perhaps contributed to a less politicized view of language documentation within Canadian Mennonite communities, where it has generally been seen as bringing welcome, if somewhat unexpected attention to the language. As in the case of the periodical discussions mentioned above, however, the familiar, community-internal nature of most linguistic scholarship serves to underscore the expectation of a thorough understanding of what constitutes 'appropriate' materials and practices for language documentation.

2.2 Methods of sampling

A concern shared by both corpus linguistics and language documentation centers on determining adequate coverage of linguistic contexts in the collection under development. This includes deciding what should be part of the final collection and in what proportion; when collection activity itself should cease for the sake of processing, release, and archival; and the degree of first-hand involvement of the collators of linguistic materials in the linguistic acts being recorded. Each of these aspects is considered below before returning to review the situation with Canadian Mennonite Plautdietsch.

2.2.1 Representativeness and balance

As noted in the introduction, corpus linguistics has long discussed what materials should comprise a corpus and in what proportion, such that the resulting resource might be taken to be a reasonable sample of the group of speakers and speech practices under consideration. Typically, corpus construction seeks to achieve *balance* (representation of variation across the types of corpus sources sampled that is proportional in some way to their occurrence in the larger, unsampled population) and *representativeness* (coverage of all those types of corpus sources deemed relevant to the reproduction of the linguistic practices or knowledge to be modeled by the corpus). Both balance and representativeness are often taken in corpus development as "target notions", in the terms of Sinclair (2005: 9), who acknowledges that "(w)hile these are not precisely definable and attainable goals, they must be used to guide the design of a corpus and the selection of its components."

The lack of representativeness or balance may limit the research questions which may be asked of a corpus, as well as the degree to which generalizations derived from such a corpus can be applied to other situations (cf. Biber, Conrad, & Reppen 1998: 246). A study of the language used in English prose fiction, for example, would find it challenging to argue convincingly that its conclusions about that genre are in fact of broader scope if it used a corpus of science fiction novels alone. Likewise, psycholinguistic research drawing upon corpus samples for general frequency measures of words as possible response predictors might justifiably express concern if the contents of a given corpus are skewed in the direction of a particular demographic, geographical, social, or textual category. These 'distortions' might further exacerbate problems caused by sample non-randomness when deriving reliable frequency estimates from corpora (cf. Evert 2006). Such concerns commonly manifest themselves in corpus linguistics through an emphasis upon careful design, planning, and selection in corpus construction to ensure that balance and representativeness are maintained throughout.

Discussions of documentary linguistic practice are generally sympathetic to issues of balance and representativeness in sampling, given an overarching concern for broad and balanced coverage of linguistic practices and metalinguistic knowledge in permanent documentary collections. Only rarely, however, are practitioners of language documentation able to exercise control over the planned coverage of sampled contexts to the extent commonly expected by corpus linguists to ensure representativeness and balance. There are several reasons why this may be the case:

Naturalness and opportunistic recording. When language documentation aims to represent naturally-occurring (i.e., unstaged, non-elicited) language events within a speech community, the recording of a wide range of communicative events in natural contexts is, by necessity, partially opportunistic (cf. Woodbury 2003: 39). Woodbury (2003: 47) identifies the opportunistic nature of this aspect of documentary linguistics as a hallmark of "good corpus production." Individuals involved in language documentation can decide what to record and what to leave unrecorded, or aim to be present at particular events or in particular situations in order to shape the balance of the documentary collection. Even then, however, it is still largely impossible for these individuals to know in advance what precisely will come out of different, unscripted contexts, let alone attempt to control *a priori* for coverage of discourse categories to the same extent as in corpus linguistics.

Issues of subsampling. Another way of achieving corpus-like balance of materials within a documentary collection involves *subsampling*, or selecting a subset of the available records to produce more 'balanced' or 'representative' collection. While potentially effective, such efforts may not be met with equal acceptance by all stakeholders in documentation. Materials may have cultural or personal significance to individual stakeholders which extend beyond these materials' membership to particular corpus categories. It may be difficult to justify leaving out one speaker or author's contributions to documentation while including another's, simply because one particular corpus design category has already been saturated. Likewise, the decision to keep only a snippet of two thousand words from a sacred text may prove highly controversial, even though it follows a corpus design practice established in the influential Brown family of corpora (cf. Francis & Kučera (1964), though note the more recent recommendation of Sinclair (2005: 7) to have corpus documents represent whole sources).

Collaborative determination of documentary coverage. Language documentation is commonly undertaken with a commitment to share and develop documentary records with all stakeholders wherever ethically possible within the framework of a given project. Broad and balanced coverage may be among the goals of participating stakeholders, but are almost certainly not the only guiding principles. No less determinant are the goals of language community members themselves, who may define appropriate balance of coverage differently from possible stakeholders in the academic linguistic community. As Himmelmann (2006: 4) observes, the degree to which broad documentary coverage might be achieved is, to a significant extent, determined by relationships with and within the language community, as well as by the larger social setting in which documentation takes place. What comes to be part of the documentary record is, in many cases, not only the result of *a priori* planning to address concerns over balance and representation, but also of ongoing discussion of the priorities of all parties – each of whom may favor increased representation of certain contexts or genres deemed to be of greater interest or intrinsic importance.

Language endangerment. Where documentation takes place within the context of language endangerment, in which a language of wider communication or higher overt prestige has begun to occupy domains of traditional language use, it may be difficult to find instances of all genres of interest still being practiced in their original settings, if that is goal of balanced sampling. Section 2.2.3 revisits this point in greater detail.

2.2.2 Project completion

As noted above, it is not uncommon in corpus linguistics to set explicit goals for corpus size and composition as part of an initial corpus design, and, thus, to have some notion of when the corpus is ready for release. In his recommendations concerning corpus development, redistribution, and preservation, Wynne (2005b: 72) explicitly reminds corpus builders to know when to stop developing their corpora, both to avoid the "danger of excessive perfectionism" and to permit corpus use and reuse by a wider audience. Wynne is careful to make an exception for monitor corpora, where changes over time enter into the corpus in a principled way, although still stressing the importance of predictable and well-documented management of such a resource for it to be of practical use.

By contrast, language documentation may not be 'predictable' in the same sense, with predetermined goals for corpus size and coverage being established before any public release is possible. Although clearly dependent upon the details of individual documentation projects, in cases where data gathering is in part opportunistic, development often follows a more gradual and cumulative process. Documentary materials often become available to more project stakeholders as their annotation progresses. Major language documentation projects funded by multi-year grants may have end-dates and definite goals for the production of particular language materials associated with them, but this certainly does not imply that the development of the documentary record is completed when the grant funding comes to an end, or that additional materials or annotations might not be added in the future. The ongoing nature of language documentation can make a single release event difficult to accommodate, although milestones may certainly be set in the data-gathering or annotation processes (cf. Woodbury 2003: 47).

2.2.3 Involvement in language production

Linguistic sampling in both corpus linguistics and language documentation may also differ in the degree to which individuals are presumed to be involved in both the planning of the collection and in the recorded linguistic events themselves. It has been common practice in much of corpus linguistics to rely upon existing, naturally-occurring examples of language as the basis for corpus construction. This practice of adopting existing materials for secondary uses in corpora is reflected in Stubbs's (2001: 221) insistence that "corpus data [be] part of natural language use and not produced for the purposes of linguistic analysis." Even if sampling procedures may be influenced by the interests of the researchers involved in corpus compilation, the corpus compilers are themselves not represented in the corpus *per se*, thus effecting a division between observation and analysis.

This ideal of a clean separation between data gathering and interpretation is not always met in corpora containing spoken language intended to be broadly representative of a given speech community. Certain important genres (e.g., private conversations) are often poorly represented in generally-available sources of language data, and therefore require more active data-gathering paradigms to represent adequately in corpora. The influence of the researchers involved may be mitigated somewhat by providing recording equipment to friends-of-friends or to hired 'recruits,' who then perform the required recording. A similar process is described as part of the construction of the spoken component of the British National Corpus, as outlined in Crowdy (1993) and Aston & Burnard (1998: 32-33). Even still, one might recognize potential issues posed by the direct involvement of such delegates in producing language intended for inclusion in a corpus. This solution does not wholly address the possibility of recordings being influenced by speakers' knowledge of the recordings' intended purposes (if this information is communicated in advance as part of informed consent), or by speakers' awareness of the presence of recording equipment. Although some corpus construction projects have attempted to circumvent these issues by initially concealing recording equipment and later seeking informed consent (e.g., Torreira & Ernestus 2010), in many cases, spoken corpus construction must still contend with manifestations of the Observer's Paradox.

Issues such as these are of no lesser relevance in language documentation, where observation and recording may inadvertently introduce bias into the collection. Most definitions of language documentation are careful to cast a wide net, making room for existing materials not produced explicitly for documentation to serve as welcome parts of the documentary record. This may potentially lower the risk of pervasive bias going undetected. Nevertheless, language documentation efforts appear on the whole hesitant to rule out more active investigations of language, which may include documenting interactions involving members of the documentation team. This may be partially for reasons of practicality acknowledged in the corpus-linguistic literature: since language materials are often not available in such abundance that corpus construction can proceed through secondary sampling alone, additional recording are sometimes required (cf. McEnery & Ostler 2000: 414).

Such procedures may well run afoul of Stubbs' (2001: 221) stated concentration of corpus linguistics upon "attested texts – real acts of communication used in a discourse community." However, focusing on only those communicative acts taking place currently in the language of interest may inadvertently underestimate the degree of linguistic knowledge still present but rarely enacted within the speech community, particularly in cases of recent language shift. Moreover, documentary linguists have repeatedly insisted that elicitation not be ruled out as a component of language documentation alongside naturally-occurring language (cf. Woodbury 2003: 42). Rather, elicitation presents another tool for investigating aspects of linguistic and metalinguistic knowledge not easily approached by observing naturally-occurring language alone – albeit with the understanding that "the whole elicitation procedure is to be considered a special, somewhat artificial communicative event and is to be documented as such" (Himmelmann 1998: 13).

2.2.4 Mennonite Plautdietsch

Each of the aforementioned issues bears upon documentation and corpus construction in the case of Canadian Mennonite Plautdietsch, as well. General concerns over balance and representativeness in the resources under development must be weighed in the context of both specific Mennonite community interests in language documentation, and in the light of an ongoing shift to English in most Canadian Mennonite communities. Collaborative documentation of a broad range of linguistic practices is certainly of general interest, perhaps particularly given a growing awareness within Canadian Mennonite communities of the gradual decline of Mennonite Plautdietsch from domains of language usage outside of the home (cf. Reimer, Reimer & Thiessen 1983: 1).

In the Saskatchewan Mennonite communities with which the present documentation has been most closely involved, recent public events centered around Mennonite Plautdietsch have drawn audiences of hundreds of speakers, who often offer comments on the importance of the language as a vital element of Russian Mennonite history and culture. Interest in language documentation in these communities has commonly reflected this pervasive association between Mennonite Plautdietsch language use and local historical-cultural knowledge, as well as the perceived importance of the preservation of such knowledge. As might be anticipated from this framing of the consequences of language loss, community recommendations for areas of documentation have often prominently favored Mennonite oral history, to be conducted among the eldest generation of speakers. This interest is certainly not an impediment to documentation, and presents in itself many chances for a richer documentary collection to be developed. It also presents an opportunity, however, to discuss the priorities of documentation more generally and to balance historically-oriented research with other kinds of recordings (e.g., involving the younger generations of speakers in non-interview contexts) to produce a collection which is both diverse and of cultural interest.

Given the progress of language shift in many Mennonite communities, it is not immediately clear what 'representativeness' in the corpus-linguistic sense should entail for practical purposes. Devoting primary attention to Mennonite Plautdietsch among those languages maintained within traditionally multilingual Russian Mennonite communities in the first place implies a demographic skew towards the older cohort of speakers who have maintained the greatest degree of Plautdietsch fluency, and the concomitant underrepresentation of child-directed speech, the language of younger individuals who have maintained only a passive knowledge of the language, and of semi-speakers more generally. Strictly speaking, achieving demographic 'balance' between age-based cohorts in language materials collected may not be impossible, but is almost certainly not realistic in reflecting the current state of language vitality in the community – and, thus, not representative of Plautdietsch language use in the contexts where it remains practiced in these Canadian Mennonite communities.

In a similar way, language shift results in a higher representation within documentation of those domains where Plautdietsch language use remains comparatively robust (namely in private conversations between family members and friends), and lesser representation of other, traditional domains still familiar to those generations of speakers who have experienced this language shift first-hand. Documentary representation of recent Plautdietsch-language church services, for instance, a domain in which a stage-wise transition from Mennonite Standard German to Mennonite Plautdietsch to English had already run its course in many Canadian Mennonite communities several decades ago (cf. Doell 1987: 60, Regehr 1996: 312-315), is necessarily sparse as a consequence of this shift, rather than of documentary inattention. Plautdietsch-language church services may thus be conspicuously absent from the present-day record – but it is also not realistic to leave unrepresented individuals' knowledge of language use in these domains, which are still well within the abilities of many speakers. It would arguably be remiss to neglect these culturally important contexts of language use for reasons of corpus balance alone. While historical recordings of language use in these and other contexts might assist in providing diachronic examples of Plautdietsch in domains which have since shifted to English, setting 'balance' and 'representativeness' as general guidelines does not provide a simple solution to the pervasive problem of wishing to record now-uncommon linguistic practices. Likewise, the separation between involvement in corpus construction and documentary recording advocated by Stubbs (2001) does not afford the opportunity to pursue investigation of these domains through more active means of inquiry. In practice, documentation has involved 'corpus planners' participating in language recording events, with this involvement forming part of the metadata later associated with such sessions.

2.3 Conventional technologies

The range of technologies conventionally employed in corpus linguistics and language documentation represents the area of greatest similarity between these two disciplines, sharing commonalities in name, at least, if not always in practice. Both disciplines make heavy use of digital technologies, although both still commonly deal with 'legacy' materials (and often in quite different fashions). Table 1 summarizes these comparisons, which are taken up individually in more detail in the sections that follow.

Table 1: Technologies in corpus linguistics and language documentation

	corpus linguistics	*language documentation*
Representation of data and metadata	XML-based data and metadata (e.g., XCES, TEI) typical, although SGML and plain-text still common	XML-based data and metadata (e.g., OLAC, IMDI) typical, although plain-text records still common (e.g., Toolbox databases)
Treatment of audiovisual materials	Time-aligned transcription of audiovisual materials (e.g., with CLAN, Praat)	Time-aligned transcription of audiovisual materials (e.g., with Transcriber, ELAN, EXMaRALDA)
Distribution of language materials	Distribution via the Linguistic Data Consortium, TalkBank, individual websites	Distribution via language archives (e.g., DoBeS, ELAR, AILLA), individual websites, although paper copies still common
Annotation tools	Semi-automated annotation tools for tagging, lemmatization, etc.	Annotation rarely automated; tools seldom amenable to changing, provisional analyses

2.3.1 Representations of data and metadata

In both disciplines, XML-based standards for representing textual data and accompanying metadata are essentially ubiquitous. In the case of corpus linguistics, it is common to deal with SGML and plain-text sources for earlier corpora (e.g., the British National Corpus). Similarly, plain-text, semi-structured records are still exceedingly common in language documentation, particularly in the form of Shoebox or Toolbox lexical databases. Somewhat less commonality is noted in the choice of particular XML-based standards by each discipline, however. Whereas corpus linguistics has concentrated upon XCES (Ide, Bonhomme & Romary 2000), TEI (TEI Consortium 2010), LAF/GRaF (Ide, Romary, & de la Clergerie 2004, Ide & Suderman 2007), and related formats for data and metadata (where not inventing custom schemas for individual projects), documentary linguistics has largely focused on other families of standards, such as OLAC (Bird & Simons 2001) and IMDI (Broeder et al. 2001) (where any formal standard is in use, rather than free-form prose text).

2.3.2 Time-aligned transcription of audiovisual materials

Time-aligned transcription has become common practice in both disciplines, not just in areas concerned with multimodality in corpus and computational linguistics, or gesture and sign language in language documentation. As with standards for representing data and metadata, similar general practices might be identified, but less agreement on transcription tools or associated standards for storing the resulting data. Corpora with significant audiovisual components, such as the Santa Barbara Corpus of Spoken American English (Chafe, Du Bois, & Thompson 1991) or SCOTS (Douglas 2003), have commonly relied upon tools such as CLAN or Praat for producing time-aligned annotations, while language documentation projects have seen a greater adoption of Transcriber, ELAN, and EXMaRALDA for similar purposes (e.g., Johnston 2010).

2.3.3 Distribution of language materials

Both corpus linguistics and language documentation have made substantial use in recent years of computational infrastructures developed to support the preservation and distribution of digital language materials. In this respect, the lines between the two disciplines are blurred: language documentation materials are sometimes hosted with distribution services more typically used for corpora (e.g., the Linguistic Data Consortium (www.ldc.upenn.edu), TalkBank (talkbank.org)), and corpora are being deposited in archives largely centered around language documentation (e.g., DoBeS (www.mpi.nl/DOBES), AILLA (www.ailla.utexas.org), ELAR (elar.soas.ac.uk)). While rarer in corpus linguistics, it is not unusual in language documentation for materials to be made available in a variety of 'popular' presentation formats to interested parties, be they consumer video DVDs or audio CDs, or even on paper.

2.4 Annotation tools

Perhaps the single largest gap between the current technical practices of corpus linguistics and language documentation lies in their approaches to annotation. Corpus linguistics is often able to avail itself of computational tools for automated or semi-automated annotation tasks, such as the assignment of part-of-speech tags, lemmata, or syntactic parses. This is seldom the case for language documentation, where even the most basic annotation tasks are rarely automated to a comparable extent. This presents a significant challenge not only for language documentation efforts, where annotation levels comparable to those found in existing corpora may involve considerably more time and expense to attain, but also for corpus and computational linguistics, which face non-trivial problems in adapting existing tools and techniques to the analysis of lesser-studied languages and to changing, provisional analyses (cf. Bird 2009).

2.4.1 Mennonite Plautdietsch

Mennonite Plautdietsch documentation and corpus construction finds itself between two worlds with regards to conventional technology. Its commitment to the long-term preservation of and access to collected language materials presents motivation to participate in digital archiving and the creation of multiple interfaces to the documentary record. These 'interfaces' also assist in producing printed versions of these materials for situations where digital access does not meet the needs of stakeholders. Considering the emphasis placed by community stakeholders upon oral history with older speakers in documentation (cf. Section 2.2.4), and the general importance of documentary materials being reviewed by and returned permanently to their contributors, it would not be reasonable to expect that all Mennonite elders would feel comfortable reviewing their contributions in digital form alone, even if help were offered in doing so. As well, some contributors to documentation may have decided not to make use of digital technologies in their daily lives, either as a matter of personal preference or religious conviction. Although this issue has not arisen so far in documentation, it is certainly possible within the Mennonite communities involved. Being able to provide printed copies of digital materials to such contributors (and, where appropriate, to locally-accessible, community-run archives and libraries) may help address this possible problem. Documentary linguistic presentation tools such as CuPED (Cox & Berez 2009) provide assistance in this regard.

Although favoring documentary linguistic annotation tools and standards generally, Mennonite Plautdietsch documentation has still sought to make use of some semi-automatic annotation techniques from corpus and computational linguistics. Cox (2010) details how part-of-speech tags were assigned to materials from the documentary collection, adapting a tag set proposed for a related language and an existing probabilistic tagger for use with Mennonite Plautdietsch. While ultimately successful, this process required several custom scripts to be written to convert between documentary and corpus linguistic data formats, a need which no 'off-the-shelf' software tool in either area was able to meet.

2.5 Treatment of data and metadata

Corpus linguistics and language documentation might be contrasted not only in the technical standards and tools prevalent in each discipline, but also in the amount and treatment of data commonly available to them. In many corpus construction projects, data are relatively plentiful, presenting ample sources out of which multi-million word corpora might be produced. Given the volume of data available, corpus construction typically achieves much of its tractability through normalization, distilling the complexity and heterogeneity of the available sources to more easily compared corpus samples. This may involve 'correcting' or standardizing spelling and punctuation, removing visual formatting from written sources, applying consistent tokenization schemes, and so on. Such processes seek to render texts more consistent, and thus more readily searched and automatically annotated by tools which make use of this uniformity.

By comparison, data resulting from language documentation are often relatively scarce. It is rare for individual documentation projects to have access to the millions of words of running text that are often available in mainstream corpus construction. More commonly, documentary records must be treated as being essentially irreplaceable, whether due to language endangerment or the degree of effort and expense which entered into their production. Unlike corpus sources, documentary materials are commonly preserved in their full diversity, producing collections of featurally-rich primary data which have not been subject to an initial stage of permanent normalization. While certainly feasible, this solution nevertheless incurs a potential loss in overall searchability for the entire documentary collection, given the diversity of its component records.

Normalization is problematic for Mennonite Plautdietsch materials, especially where orthographic conventions are concerned. Multiple distinct orthographic systems exist for representing written Mennonite Plautdietsch (cf. Nieuweboer 1998). Although several proposals have gained support across Mennonite communities, no single standard is prevalent, and the choice of orthographies remains controversial. In light of the potential benefits of consistent orthographic representation for effective search and retrieval across language records, some form of normalization to a single spelling system would seem desirable for Mennonite Plautdietsch materials. Yet, as noted above, this is not merely a technical issue. While multiple orthographies may be problematic for processing materials, it is not possible to replace one system with another without the risk of alienating the original contributors. One might instead choose to lemmatize orthographically-diverse sources, but this merely displaces the problem of orthographic choice to the representation of lemmata, and still prevents reliable non-lemmatized searches (cf. Cox 2010). No less problematic is the potential loss of association between those original sources contributed by writers and publishers to language documentation efforts and the simplified forms of these materials that would typically enter into corpus construction. Converting a series of page scans into plain text, associated with one another only in name, might risk the offence of authors who wish to see their works preserved in their full original presentation.

Social and technical issues such as these are pervasive in the present documentation, and require attention if the materials involved are to be both computationally tractable and culturally acceptable. Several methods of addressing these challenges are therefore discussed in the following section.

3. Bridging the gap

The preceding sections have attempted to offer a comparison of current practices in corpus linguistics and language documentation, concentrating upon issues pertaining to stakeholder relationships, methods of sampling, conventional technologies, and the treatment of data in both fields. This comparison finds several reasons to expect compatibilities between these two disciplines. The similar paths followed in their use of conventional technologies is encouraging, for one, and suggests a relatively close alignment of both disciplines in technical practices. Potentially more challenging are those differences between language documentation and corpus linguistics which bear upon issues of corpus planning, and in particular expectations made of corpora with respect to representativeness, balance, and the sampling of language materials. Here, the opportunistic nature of key aspects of language documentation, the specific interests of stakeholder parties in particular aspects of documentation, and the direct involvement of stakeholders in the production of documentary materials need to be taken into consideration when language documentation is revisited from a corpus linguistic perspective.

Both corpus linguistics and language documentation share at their core an interest in the compilation of collections of linguistic information. Yet, as the preceding section has noted, even this fundamental concern itself is not without significant divisions. A tension might be perceived between the reductionist pressures of corpus construction and the preservationist tendencies of language documentation, a difference stemming in part from the relative abundance and 'replaceableness' of the linguistic records commonly available to each discipline, as well as from the perceived acceptability of a reduction in these sources' complexity as a precondition to their inclusion in a collection or corpus. When added to the differences in perspective noted above, this tension may risk producing a gulf between the two disciplines. In cases where the link between corpus documents and documentary sources is not made explicit, the creation of a corpus arguably does little to augment the documentary record; it presents at best a temporary exploitation, rather than a lasting enrichment of those sources from which it draws its data. Moreover, the stages of normalization commonly required of materials for their use in corpus construction render the corpus itself less than ideal as the primary documentary record. The permanent normalization of language data runs afoul of the basic commitment of language documentation to preserve language materials for future reuse – reuse which may not require, or even find acceptable, the initial simplifications undertaken as part of the normal course of corpus development.

Observations such as these motivate an alternative proposal for the general relationship between corpus construction and language documentation. At the centre of this proposal is the notion that corpora might be viewed productively as *applications* of language documentation, built upon permanent records within the documentary collection which are referenced wherever possible throughout the corpus. From the perspective of documentary linguistics, this proposal establishes the corpus as another component of the larger descriptive apparatus, i.e., as one perspective among many others possible upon the contents of the documentary collection (cf. Woodbury 2003: 42, Himmelmann 2006: 11).

In practical terms, this proposal implies that corpus development is to be largely contingent upon the contents and development of the documentary collection to which it makes reference. The corpus thus essentially grows out of permanent documentation, rather than that documentation being made to fit the Procrustean bed of a single, corpus-linguistic representation. Indeed, on this view, it is entirely possible for multiple corpora to be built out of the materials provided by a single documentary collection, with no one of them being necessarily authoritative.

Critically, explicit and detailed citation of documentary materials in their corpus counterparts might be seen as contributing a 'corpus' interpretation to those materials. If such references between documentary sources and corresponding corpus interpretations are carefully constructed, the possibility exists not only to proceed from a corpus text to its documentary source, but also from a given documentary source to its interpretation within the corpus. The bidirectionality of this relationship, permitting back-and-forth navigation between corpus texts and their documentary sources, enriches both the documentation and the corpus. The accuracy and completeness of the corpus texts, which are often themselves produced through automatic or semi-automatic means like optical character recognition, are more easily confirmed against the documentary sources from which they were derived when such navigation is facilitated. Where elements of a particular transcript within a spoken corpus appear suspect, given the predictions of a particular linguistic model or personal intuition, it is possible to check the transcript against the original recording when the spoken corpus documents make reference to the corresponding sections of the original documentary recording. Similarly, if some part of a written text in the corpus appears to be missing (not an altogether uncommon error for optical character recognition procedures), the corpus text can be held up for immediate comparison against the corresponding page image in the documentary collection.

The benefits of such a deeply interwoven dependency between the derived corpus and the permanent documentation upon which it is based extend to practices of normalization, as well. Recall that normalization of spelling is controversial in Mennonite Plautdietsch, given the presence of multiple competing orthographies. Much less controversial is the preservation of materials in their original orthographies, a function well handled by the documentary collection, which is typically able to curate unedited page scans of printed materials or other digital facsimiles. Where corpus texts make persistent reference to these original documentary sources, the opportunity exists for corpus normalization to be non-replacive, not supplanting the existing representations found in the documentary materials, but rather supplementing those sources with a secondary representation in another orthography. In this way, then, there is the potential to respect the orthographic choices reflected in the original documents while nevertheless permitting corpus normalization, the latter processes being rendered less controversial through the persistent availability of unaltered documentary sources.

This proposal may further allow for a more dialectic relationship to develop between corpus development and language documentation. Much as with the development of documentation-based dictionaries and grammars, the construction of a corpus on the basis of a documentary collection presents opportunities to identify potential weaknesses in coverage which might otherwise escape notice, were this corpus-centered perspective not present. Corpus linguistic concerns of balance and representativeness in the documentary materials feeding into the corpus might help inform the priorities of ongoing documentation, presenting some notion of areas in which documentation might particularly benefit from expansion. Likewise, as has already been suggested in preceding sections, the diversity of materials entering the documentary collection might present healthy challenges to corpus construction, in both the variety of sources and the typological features represented in such data.

Viewing corpora as applications of language documentation does not itself present a solution to persistent issues of representativeness and balance. These 'target notions' may remain difficult to achieve using opportunistically gathered documentary materials, although progress here is certainly not impossible. As stakeholders in the development of an important part of the documentary apparatus, corpus linguists working from documentary sources might enter more fully into discussions concerning the development of the documentary collection itself, and continue to advocate for broad and balanced coverage for much the same reasons expounded in the corpus linguistic literature. Furthermore, as in the case of normalization even where only a small portion of a culturally or personally-significant documentary source is included in a corpus for reasons of balance, references from that corpus to the corresponding documentation still permit users to return to the original source in its full and unedited form. These references then provide one possible means of addressing concerns over the editorial treatment of sensitive documentary materials in linguistic corpora (cf. Section 2.2.1). A corpus which draws selectively upon the documentary record does not present the same danger of permanently limiting reuse of the original documentary sources themselves; the whole records remain accessible in the documentary collection, however they are ultimately represented in the corpus.

For such a proposal to succeed technically, corpus construction must be able to make use of documentary sources as the basis of corpora. Documentary sources must therefore be open to reference within corpus documents, and corpus formats and tools must be able to represent and process such references. Encouragingly, as Section 2.3 notes, strong commonalities exist between the technologies currently in use for corpus linguistics and language documentation, placing a definite emphasis on consistent data and metadata, and on the use of open, often XML-based digital standards for greater interoperability. Standards for the representation of data and metadata in both disciplines differ, but might be hoped to be rendered compatible where serving a comparable function. Computational and corpus linguistic software tools may prove more difficult to adapt to typological features not resembling those found in languages for which corpora already exist, although this remains to be seen.

Lastly, as participants in language documentation, it is likely that corpus builders involved in the construction of documentation-based corpora would eventually be required to come to terms with the 'politicization' of their work, and with the requirements of equal stakeholders from outside the academic and publishing communities. This situation is somewhat atypical in corpus construction based upon other publicly-accessible documents (e.g., those harvested from the web), but arguably of potential benefit for corpus compilation in the long term. A closer, more productive relationship with other stakeholders in documentation may help avoid potential missteps, either political or technical, which would otherwise hinder such corpus construction.

4. Conclusion

The commonality observed between corpus linguistics and language documentation runs deep, proceeding from a fundamental shared interest in the construction and reuse of lasting collections of linguistic data, produced to support both empirically-grounded linguistic research and efforts to address issues of language endangerment. Notable similarities exist between both disciplines in their selection of digital technologies to address common challenges faced in developing permanent language resources. Such similarities, along with other shared traits, give reason to believe that a productive interaction may be possible between both disciplines in meeting their respective needs for increased access to documentary linguistic materials on the one hand, and increased corpus linguistic attention to a wider range of languages on the other.

It bears stressing, however, that this is commonality, and not uniformity, either in purpose, process or product; it would seem premature to take both disciplines to be immediately compatible as such. Although technically feasible, it is no trivial undertaking to address the distance which presently exists between corpus linguistic tools and typologically diverse documentary linguistic data, between corpus documents and their corresponding documentary sources, and between corpus normalization techniques and the aim for the permanent preservation of rich documentary materials. Yet, as was noted in the introduction, it is precisely in the challenge of this divergence between disciplines that one might expect to arrive at a more significant reward – that the contributions of each might ultimately be greater than the sum of their parts.

Acknowledgements

This paper has benefited substantially from discussions with John Newman and Sally Rice, as well as from the comments of two anonymous reviewers and participants in the American Association for Corpus Linguistics 2009 conference. This research has been supported financially by the Social Sciences and

Humanities Research Council of Canada (SSHRC), the Killam Trusts, and the Pierre Elliott Trudeau Foundation.

Notes

1 A terminological distinction is made throughout this paper between "corpora," which are taken here to be the products of corpus-linguistic treatments of language data, and "collections," the stores of primary data and associated metadata which arise out of documentary linguistic research. References to 'corpora' and 'collections' are shared across both disciplines, albeit not always with the same connotations. Corpus linguists have frequently distinguished between "collections" and "corpora," the latter demonstrating efforts at a balanced representation of some linguistic phenomenon of interest across a range of contexts, efforts which may or may not have been present in the compilation of a 'raw' collection (cf. Leech 1991: 10, Biber, Conrad & Reppen 1998: 246, Wynne 2005a: vii). A comparable distinction would appear to be less commonly made in documentary linguistics. Johnson (2004: 3), for instance, takes both terms to be essentially synonymous, stating that a "collection, or corpus, is the body of documentary materials created by linguists and native speakers in the course of their research." Woodbury (2003: 42) similarly refers to the "documentary corpus" when discussing primary materials assembled in the course of a documentation project, an entity which Himmelmann (2006: 10) simply terms a "corpus of primary data."

2 Indeed, for desired materials not to be freely available is far from unusual in the history of European corpus linguistics. Before the advent of the world-wide web, it was exceedingly difficult to assemble sufficient amounts of text in the desired proportions for the construction of balanced, multi-million word corpora without relying on materials "almost all in commercial hands," as Leech (1992: 10) observes.

References

Aston, G. & L. Burnard (1998), *The BNC handbook: exploring the British National Corpus with SARA*. Edinburgh: Edinburgh University Press.

Austin, P.K. (2010), 'Current issues in language documentation', in: P.K. Austin (ed.) *Language documentation and description. Volume 7.* London: School of Oriental and African Studies. 12-33.

Biber, D., S. Conrad & R. Reppen (1998), *Corpus linguistics: investigating language structure and use*. Cambridge: Cambridge University Press.

Bird, S. (2009), 'Natural language processing and linguistic fieldwork', *Computational linguistics,* 35(3): 469-474.

Bird, S. & G. Simons (2001), 'The OLAC metadata set and controlled vocabularies,' in: T. Declerck, S. Krauwer & M. Rosner (eds.) *Proceedings of ACL/EACL Workshop on Sharing Tools and Resources for Research and Education*. Toulouse: unpublished.

Broeder, D., F. Offenga, D. Willems, & P. Wittenburg (2001), 'The IMDI metadata set, its tools and accessible linguistic databases', in: S. Bird, P. Buneman & M. Liberman (eds.) *Proceedings of the IRCS Workshop on Linguistic Databases*. Philadelphia: Linguistic Data Consortium. 48-55.

Chafe, W.L., J.W. Du Bois & S.A. Thompson (1991), 'Towards a new corpus of spoken American English', in: K. Aijmer & B. Altenberg (eds.) *English corpus linguistics: studies in honour of Jan Svartvik*. London / New York: Longman. 64-82.

Crowdy, S. (1993), 'Spoken corpus design', *Linguistic and literary computing*, 8(4): 259-265.

Cox, C. (2010), 'Probabilistic tagging of minority language data: a case study using Qtag', in: S.Th. Gries, S. Wulff, & M. Davies (eds.) *Corpus linguistic applications: current studies, new directions*. Amsterdam: Rodopi. 213-231.

Cox, C. & A. Berez (2009), 'Software demonstration: CuPED (Customizable Presentation of ELAN Documents'. Paper presented at First International Conference on Language Documentation and Conservation (ICLDC09), University of Hawai'i, March 12-14, 2010. Available online at: http://hdl.handle.net/10125/4969.

Doell, L. (1987), *The Bergthaler Mennonite Church of Saskatchewan: 1892-1975*. Winnipeg: CMBC Publications.

Douglas, F.M. (2003), 'The Scottish Corpus of Texts andSpeech: problems of corpus design', *Linguistic and literary computing*, 18: 23-37.

Epp, R. (1993), *The story of Low German & Plautdietsch: tracing a language across the globe*. Hillsboro, Kansas: Reader's Press.

Evert, S. (2006), 'How random is a corpus? The library metaphor', *Zeitschrift für Anglistik und Amerikanistik*, 54(2): 177-190.

Francis, W.N. & Kučera, H. (1964), *Brown corpus manual*. Providence, Rhode Island: Brown University.

Gordon, R.G. Jr. (ed.) (2005), 'Plautdietsch', in: R.G. Gordon Jr. (ed.) *Ethnologue: languages of the world.* Fifteenth edition. Dallas, Texas: SIL International.

Heid, U. (2008), 'Corpus linguistics and lexicography', in: A. Lüdeling & M. Kytö (eds.) *Corpus linguistics: an international handbook*. Berlin / New York: Walter de Gruyter. 131-153.

Himmelmann, N.P. (1998), 'Documentary and descriptive linguistics', *Linguistics*, 36: 161-195.

Himmelmann, N.P. (2006), 'Language documentation: what is it and what is it good for?', in: J. Gippert, N.P. Himmelmann & U. Mosel (eds.) *Essentials of language documentation*. Berlin / New York: Mouton de Gruyter. 1-30.

Himmelmann, N.P. (2008), 'Reproduction and preservation of linguistic knowledge: linguistics' response to language endangerment', *Annual review of anthropology*, 37: 337-50.

Ide, N., P. Bonhomme & L. Romary (2000), 'XCES: an XML-based encoding standard for linguistic corpora', in: M. Gavrilidou, G. Carayannis, S. Markantonatou, S. Piperidis & G. Stainhaouer (eds.) *Proceedings of the Second International Conference on Language Resources and Evaluation (LREC 2000)*. Paris: European Language Resources Association.

Ide, N., L. Romary & E. de la Clergerie (2004), 'International standard for a Linguistic Annotation Framework', *Natural language engineering,* 10: 211-225.

Ide, N. & K. Suderman (2007), 'GrAF: a graph-based format for linguistic annotations', in: B. Boguraev, N. Ide, A. Meyers, S. Nariyama, M. Stede, J. Wiebe & G. Wilcock (eds.) *Proceedings of the Linguistic Annotation Workshop, Prague, June 28-29, 2007*. Stroudsburg (PA): Association for Computational Linguistics. 1-8.

Johnson, H. (2004), 'Language documentation and archiving, or how to build a better corpus', in: P. Austin (ed.) *Language documentation and description. Volume 2*. London: School of Oriental and African Studies. 140-153.

Johnston, T. (2010), 'From archive to corpus: transcription and annotation in the creation of signed language corpora', *International journal of corpus linguistics*, 15(1): 106-131.

Leech, G. (1991), 'The state of the art in corpus linguistics', in: K. Aijmer & B. Altenberg (eds.) *English corpus linguistics: studies in honour of Jan Svartvik.* London / New York: Longman. 8-29.

Leech, G. (1992), 'Corpora and theories of linguistic performance', in: J. Svartvik (ed.) *Directions in corpus linguistics: proceedings of Nobel Symposium 82, Stockholm, 4-8 August 1991*. Berlin: Mouton de Gruyter. 105-125.

Leonard, W.Y. & E. Haynes (2010), 'Making "collaboration" collaborative: an examination of perspectives that frame linguistic field research', *Language documentation and conservation*, 4: 268-293. Available online at: http://hdl.handle.net/10125/4482.

McEnery, T. & N. Ostler (2000), 'A new agenda for corpus linguistics – working with all of the world's languages', *Literary and linguistic computing*, 15: 403-418.

Nathan, D. (2006), 'Thick interfaces: mobilizing language documentation with multimedia', in: J. Gippert, N.P. Himmelmann & U. Mosel (eds.) *Essentials of language documentation*. Berlin / New York: Mouton de Gruyter. 363-380.

Nieuweboer, R. (1998), *The Altai dialect of Plautdiitsch (West-Siberian Mennonite Low German)*. Doctoral thesis, Rijksuniversiteit Groningen.

Ostler, N. (2009), 'Corpora of less studied languages', in: A. Lüdeling & M. Kytö (eds.) *Corpus linguistics: an international handbook*. Berlin / New York: Walter de Gruyter. 457-483.

Regehr, T.D. (1996), *Mennonites in Canada, 1939-1970: a people transformed.* Toronto: University of Toronto Press.

Reimer, A., A. Reimer & J. Thiessen (eds.) (1983), *A sackful of Plautdietsch: a collection of Mennonite Low German stories and poems.* Winnipeg: Hyperion Press.

Sinclair, J. (2005), 'Corpus and text – basic principles', in: M. Wynne (ed.) *Developing linguistic corpora: a guide to good practice.* Oxford: Oxbow Books. 1-16.

Stubbs, M. (2001), *Words and phrases: corpus studies of lexical semantics.* Oxford: Blackwell.

TEI Consortium (eds.) (2010), *TEI P5: Guidelines for electronic text encoding and interchange.* Version 1.8.0. November 5, 2010. Available online at: http://www.tei-c.org/Guidelines/P5/

Teubert, W. (2001), 'Corpus linguistics and lexicography', *International journal of corpus linguistics*, 6: 125-153.

Torreira, F. & M. Ernestus (2010), 'The Nijmegen Corpus of Casual Spanish', in: N. Calzolari, B. Maegaard, J. Mariani, J. Odjik, K. Choukri, S. Piperidis, M. Rosner & D. Tapias (eds.) *Proceedings of the Seventh International Conference on Language Resources and Evaluation (LREC 2010).* Paris: European Language Resources Association. 2981-2985.

Woodbury, A. (2003), 'Defining documentary linguistics', in: P. Austin (ed.) *Language documentation and description. Volume 1.* London: School of Oriental and African Studies. 35-51.

Wynne, M. (2005a), 'Preface', in: M. Wynne (ed.) *Developing linguistic corpora: a guide to good practice.* Oxford: Oxbow Books. vi-vii.

Wynne, M. (2005b), 'Archiving, distribution, and preservation', in: M. Wynne (ed.) *Developing linguistic corpora: a guide to good practice.* Oxford: Oxbow Books. 71-78.

The Speech Accent Archive: towards a typology of English accents

Steven H. Weinberger[1] and Stephen A. Kunath[2]

[1]George Mason University
[2]Georgetown University

Abstract

The theoretical and practical value of studying human accented speech is of interest to linguists, language teachers, speech recognition researchers, and computational linguists. It is also part of the research program behind the Speech Accent Archive. The Archive is a growing annotated corpus of English speech varieties. All samples include a complete digital audio version and a narrow phonetic transcription. Each speaker is located geographically and crucial demographic parameters are supplied. This paper will discuss the architecture of the Speech Accent Archive and a computational mechanism we developed to assist in analyzing the archive, the Speech Transcription Analysis Tool (STAT). We show how such a tool generates a "typological corpus" of English accents that can benefit researchers in the fields of theoretical and applied linguistics.

1. Introduction

It is well known that human listeners immediately and automatically notice that different speakers of a second language have discernable accents (Scovel 1995). For example, for native English listeners, Russian speakers of English sound different from Arabic speakers of English. But what exactly constitutes these differences? Just what specific information alerts a human listener that a speaker from one native language background sounds different from a speaker from another? Questions like these seem obvious, but for linguists, there is no exact comprehensive definition of a foreign accent that can be used to answer this question (Gut 2007). Certainly humans are able to rate the degree of accent in non-native speech (Magen 1998, Major 2007, Munro, Derwing & Morton 2006, Zechner, Higgins, Xi & Williamson 2009), but there is far less research on listeners' abilities to categorize the type of accent -- the ability to distinguish one accent from another (E.M. Brennan & J.S. Brennan 1981, Cunningham-Andersson & Engstrand 1989, Scheuer 2002). As linguists, we seek to define a set of phonological characteristics that determine these accents, and we require an adequate database with a large variety of accented speech from which to determine these characteristics.

In this paper, we describe a project that has been underway at George Mason University that collects and presents varieties of English accented speech. The Speech Accent Archive (http://accent.gmu.edu) is a growing corpus of accented varieties of spoken English. As a collaborative enterprise, it shares the characteristics of most well-designed corpora: It is annotated and machine-readable, it is systematic and representative, it catalogs a wide distribution of speakers, and it is freely accessible to researchers. The nature of the archive allows us to do principled work in accent detection and classification. Because the various speech samples have a uniform consistency, we are able to compare any two samples, segment by segment.

We have developed a web component for the Archive that computationally compares any two phonetic transcriptions from our corpus. The Speech Transcription Analysis Tool (STAT) (Kunath & Weinberger 2009) will soon be incorporated into the archive. It takes samples and automatically aligns them with a two-level process. We discuss STAT and its contribution to the formulation of a linguistic classification of speech accents.

The paper is organized as follows: Section 2 describes the Speech Accent Archive in terms of its construction and architecture. Section 3 proposes a set of discrete speech accent characteristics, or what we term phonological speech patterns. Section 4 discusses the incorporation of STAT and its use in deriving a finite set of phonological speech patterns. We conclude with further research potentials and some lessons learned in Section 5.

2. The Speech Accent Archive architecture

The Speech Accent Archive was started at George Mason University in 1999. It originally began as a teaching project for a graduate phonetics class. Students were to gather, record, and analyze the speech of non-native speakers of English. It started as a relatively small collection of speech samples that illustrated the various phonological difficulties that second language learners had when producing English speech sounds. The archive quickly surpassed the local pedagogical needs of our phonetics class and has acquired a life of its own on the internet. The project has evolved through many web-based iterations, and is now a relatively large and comprehensive source of English speech accents and affiliated resources. An audio sample, a phonetic transcription, and demographic information about each speaker are included. The Archive is stored as a MySQL database and accessed via a PHP web interface. It now includes both native and non-native varieties of spoken English from over 165 countries. The Archive continues to grow with new samples added weekly. As of March 2011, there were 1422 speech samples represented.

2.1 Speaker demographics

Prior to eliciting and recording the uniform speech sample, each speaker must agree to a standard George Mason University Human Subjects Review Board (HSRB) statement. The speaker-participant is then interviewed and asked a series of demographic questions. The answers to the interview questions are posted in the Archive database. Research on inter-language phonology has historically converged upon most of these demographic variables (Purcell & Suter 1980).

Each of the eight variables is discussed below. The SEARCH facility attached to the Archive allows users to sift through these data. For example, any of these demographic variables can be independently selected and searched in combination with any other variables.

2.1.1 Native language

During the interview, each speaker is asked a series of questions to ascertain his or her native language. Participants who report that they are balanced bilinguals are removed from the study. We generally report the language name given by the speaker and we authenticate it with Ethnologue.com (Lewis 2009), and the ISO 639-3 Standard 3-letter code for each language is listed in the database. Alternate names are included where necessary. The archive currently contains speakers from approximately 310 different language backgrounds.

We also include uniform phonetic inventories for more than 150 of these native languages. Each inventory includes a vowel chart and a consonant chart. Figure 1 shows an example set of these inventories for the Dari language. The structure of these charts allows for straightforward contrastive analyses between languages. In fact, if these charts were made into transparencies, simply holding one language's inventory over another's would yield an immediate and rudimentary hypothesis about the specific sound differences between languages.

CONSONANTS (PULMONIC)

	Bilabial	Labiodental	Dental	Alveolar	Postalveolar	Retroflex	Palatal	Velar	Uvular	Pharyngeal	Glottal
Plosive	p b			t d				k g	q		ʔ
Nasal	m			n				ŋ			
Trill				r							
Tap or Flap											
Fricative		f		s z	ʃ ʒ			x ɣ			h
Affricate					tʃ dʒ						
Lateral fricative											
Approximant							j				
Lateral approximant				l							

Where symbols appear in pairs, the one to the right represents a voiced consonant. Shaded areas denote articulations judged impossible.

VOWELS

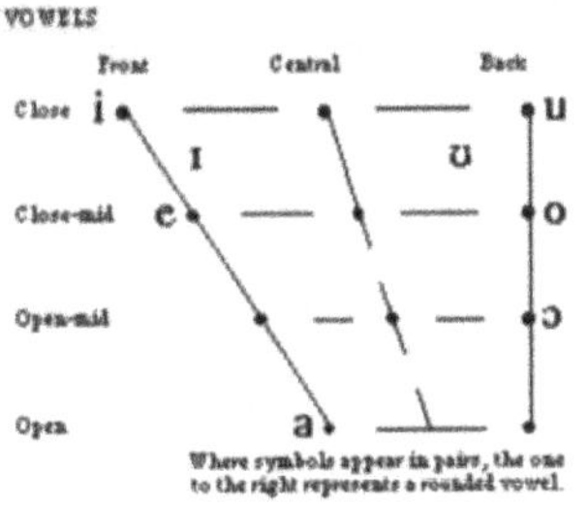

Figure 1: Phonetic inventory of Dari

2.1.2 Other languages

Many of our speaker-participants have some knowledge of one or more languages besides their native language and English. The Archive records this information. Up to five other known languages are listed for each speaker in order of dominance.

2.1.3 Place of birth

The Archive contains the city and country of birth as reported by the speaker. If the speaker indicates that he or she spent only a brief time at that location, the other geographical areas where the speaker reported living are also listed in the database. We locate each speaker's birthplace on individual maps provided by The World Factbook (Central Intelligence Agency 2010).

2.1.4 Age

The mean age of speakers in the Archive is 32.8 and the median age is 29. Although the general policy of the Archive is to only accept speech samples from individuals who are 18 years and older, there are a few cases where the speakers are a bit younger. There are just a handful of these younger speakers, and the youngest was age six at the time of the recording. By contrast, the oldest speaker represented in the Archive is 97 years old.

2.1.5 Gender

The Archive includes both male and female speakers. Of the total, 55 percent are male and 45 percent are female.

2.1.6 Age of onset

Age of onset refers to the age at which the speaker was first exposed to sustained English language input. This is perhaps one of the most significant variables in second language acquisition studies (Long 2007). Most linguists agree that there is an age-sensitive time period for completely acquiring a language. After this time period, it remains unlikely that a human can become a native speaker.

All of our native English speakers have an English onset age of 0. This means that they all have been exposed to English since birth. Our non-native English speakers have English onset ages that range from 1 to 53 years.

2.1.7 English residency

Language input matters, and an important pair of variables reflect the degree to which speakers are exposed to the English language. Speakers must report which English-speaking countries they have lived in and their length of stay in those countries. While many of the non-native speakers in the sample have never lived in an English-speaking country, quite a few speakers have lived for years in the

United States, New Zealand, Nigeria, or other English-speaking countries.

2.1.8 Learning style

While certainly a language learner can gain knowledge of a grammar through multiple avenues, we essentially group these into two major methods of learning: naturalistic and academic. A naturalistic method of learning assumes no formal classroom instruction in English. The learner is typically immersed in a target language environment and simply "picks up the grammar". Alternatively, a speaker who reports that he or she learned English formally in a classroom is categorized as academic. Needless to say, all of the Archive native English speakers are classified as naturalistic learners. Of the non-native speakers, 88 percent are categorized as academic learners, and 12 percent are classified as naturalistic learners.

2.2 The elicitation paragraph

Each speaker reads the same elicitation paragraph (shown in example (1)). It consists of a string of 69 common English words that most beginning-level non-native speakers can recognize. The limited size of the elicitation paragraph reflects the historically narrow bandwidth of data transmission available in 1999 when the Archive began. Nevertheless, because a multitude of speakers are engaged in reading this paragraph, the Archive contains 98,118 words recorded in comparable environments.

(1) *Please call Stella. Ask her to bring these things with her from the store: six spoons of fresh snow peas, five thick slabs of blue cheese, and maybe a snack for her brother Bob. We also need a small plastic snake and a big toy frog for the kids. She can scoop these things into three red bags, and we will go meet her Wednesday at the train station.*

The paragraph contains almost all of the consonants and vowels of English. Because it was originally designed for non-native learners of English, it also includes numerous initial and final consonant clusters, a known difficulty for many learners of English. Table 1 depicts the distribution of consonants, vowels, and clusters in the elicitation paragraph.

Table 1: The sounds in the elicitation paragraph (numbers indicate occurrences)

single consonants		vowels	clusters	
initial	final		initial	final
k (3)	z (5)	i (12)	pl (2)	sk (1)
t (3)	l (4)	ɑ (4)	st (4)	ŋz (2)
ð (6)	ŋ (1)	ɛ (4)	bɹ (2)	ks (1)
θ (3)	θ (1)	æ (10)	fɹ (3)	nz (2)
w (5)	m (1)	ɪ (11)	sp (1)	bz (1)
s (2)	ɹ (5)	ʌ (2)	sn (3)	nd (3)
f (3)	v (3)	ə (10)	sl (1)	dz (1)
tʃ (1)	ʃ (1)	u (5)	bl (1)	gz (1)
n (1)	k (4)	oʊ (3)	sm(1)	
b (3)	b (1)	aɪ (1)	sk (1)	
l (1)	d (2)	eɪ (5)	θɹ (1)	
ʃ (2)	g (2)	ɔ (3)	tɹ (1)	
d (1)	n (4)	ɔɪ (1)		
ɹ (1)	p (1)			
g (1)	t (2)			
m (2)				
h (4)				

We also compared the relative frequency of individual sounds represented in the elicitation paragraph with the relative frequency of these sounds in natural speech (Edwards 1992). Figures 2 and 3 show these comparisons for consonants and vowels, respectively. As demonstrated in the figures, there appears to be reasonable agreement in sound frequency between the two sources of speech. Of course, there are a few incongruities. For consonants in the paragraph, there seems to be a lower frequency of /t/, and a higher frequency of /θ/, /z/, and /s/. For vowels, there was a lower frequency of /aɪ/ and a higher frequency of /i/ and /u/.

There may also be arguments that paragraph reading is quite unlike naturally occurring spontaneous speech, i.e., that the speech style would influence the resulting types of phonological processes produced by the speaker. But work by Munro & Derwing (1994) found that non-native speech from text reading and naturally occurring non-native speech are both judged in a remarkably similar fashion in accent ratings made by native listeners. Scheuer (2002) also reports that for her subjects, there was no significant difference in the accent evaluations of speech from reading tasks and free speech tasks. This suggests that accented speech retains its unique linguistic characteristics regardless of the elicitation method.

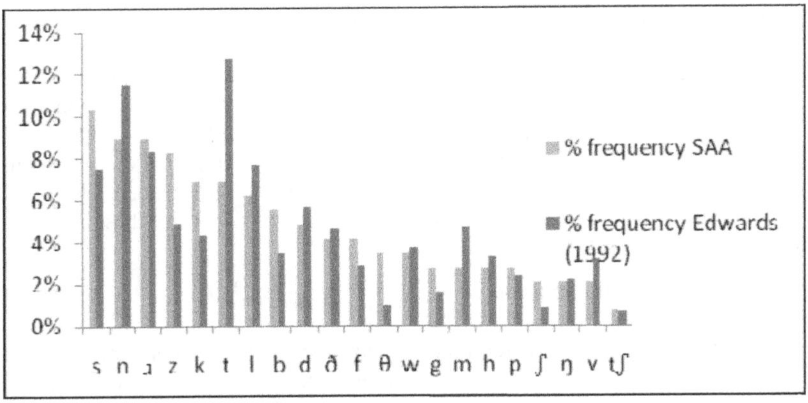

Figure 2: Consonant frequency of elicitation paragraph versus natural speech (SAA=Speech Accent Archive)

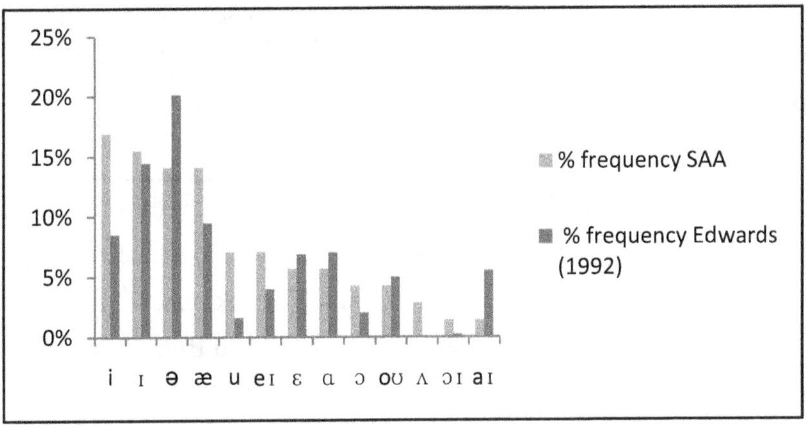

Figure 3: Vowel frequency of elicitation paragraph (SAA=Speech Accent Archive)

As part of the elicitation protocol, speakers each have the opportunity to look over the elicitation paragraph for one minute and ask any questions about the meanings of the words. After that, speakers are recorded as they read the paragraph once through.

2.3 Audio samples

All speakers are recorded according to a strict interview protocol at CD quality: 44.1 kHz., 16-bit mono. For web delivery, we compress the samples eight times. Samples are reduced with IMA 4:1 at 22.05 kHz., 16-bit, and are presented as

Quicktime movie soundtracks. We keep all raw audio files for future processing.

We have used various recording equipment over the history of the Archive. Many of the earlier recordings were made with a Sony TC-D5M cassette recorder using a Radio Shack 33-3001 unidirectional dynamic microphone. We later switched to Sony minidisk recorders, MDR-70, with Sony ECM-MS907 stereo microphones. We then moved on to Olympus DM-10 digital recorders with external mini microphones. We are currently recording with Samson Zoom H2 digital recorders. Our graduate linguistics students typically carry these recorders with them when conducting interviews.

2.4 Phonetic transcriptions

Each of the audio samples is represented with a segmental phonetic transcription. We do not indicate any prosodic information in the transcription. Transcriptions are carried out by three transcribers: two phonetically-trained graduate students plus the first author of this paper. Initial agreement is generally high, and where it is not, all transcribers are required to meet consensus after some detailed discussion. We use the International Phonetic Alphabet symbols and diacritics (International Phonetic Association 1999). The transcriptions are done with the Unicode Doulos SIL font (SIL International, 2010), and spaces are inserted between the transcribed words to enhance readability. An example transcription of a Vietnamese speaker of English (Vietnamese7) is shown in (2).

(2)

[pəliz kʰɑ ṣ stɪlə æs hə tə pɹĩn̪ d̪ɪs t̪ĩŋgs wɪt hɚ fɹʌ̃m d̪ə stɔɹ sɪks spũns ɻ̩ ʌf fɹɛs sno pʰis faɪ θɪk slɑɸs əf blu tʃis æ̃n meɪbi ɛ snæx fɔɹ hə bɹʌðə bɑ wi ɑlˠso nid ə smɑ plæstɪk̚ sːneɪkʰ æ̃n ə bɪg̚ tʰɔɪ fɹɑx̆ fɔː ðə kʰɪs ʃi kæ̃ skup̚ ðɪs θ̃ɪŋz ĩntu θɹi ɹɛd̚ bæxs æ̃n wi wɪlˠ goʊ mit hɚ wɛ̃nsdeɪ æt̪̚ ðə tʃɹẽn steʃə̃n]

The phonetic transcriptions are presented on the web as gif images to ensure proper rendering, but since all of the data is stored as Unicode text files, we are moving to display the text file directly and to simply rely on users to procure the proper font. All transcriptions remain open to new analysis, and we often receive notes from users who may notice an error or suggest a change. We maintain that this is the proper strategy in any collaborative enterprise.

3. Phonological speech patterns

We are now ready to return to the issue of differences in individual speech accents mentioned in Section 1. Native English listeners have the ability to distinguish between varieties of spoken English. Not only can they immediately tell if a speaker is from outside their own native speech community, listeners can typically determine that the English speech from one native language background is different from that of another native language background. So, for example, native English listeners can discriminate between the English speech of a Vietnamese speaker and the English speech of a Tigrigna speaker. Of course, we do not mean to imply that English listeners can correctly *identify and label* the accent as Vietnamese or Tigrigna, because we believe this requires a different type of independent experiential knowledge of accent types and geography. Instead, we are concerned with the more mysterious and instantaneous knowledge that allows humans to simply discriminate between accents. It is this ability we take to be automatic. Listeners seem to be able to do it subconsciously, and this is precisely the kind of tacit knowledge that linguists strive to understand and represent.

We assume that humans, when listening to speech, perform some sort of comparison between their own internalized native phonology and the perceived phonology from a non-native speaker. These differences form the basis for the judgments a listener makes about the speaker. These phonological differences can take many forms, but here we will be dealing only with segmental ones.

Now, if we were able to somehow compare speech varieties, we may be able to tease out some of these crucial characteristics that get noticed by native listeners. The phonetic transcriptions in the Archive provide us with an ideal collection of the items to compare. Conceptually, if we were able to superimpose one transcription over another, we should be able to notice differing elements. For example, if we arbitrarily pick one native English transcription as the so-called "standard", and we superimpose a transcription from a speaker from say, a Vietnamese background, we may notice that there are numerous places where the Vietnamese speaker uses /t/ and /d/ where the native English speaker uses /θ/ and /ð/ (*these things* [d̪ɪs t̪ɪŋgs]). There may also be cases where the Vietnamese speaker deletes final obstruent consonants or devoices them – things that our native English model does not do (*Bob* → [bɑ], *kids* → [kɪs]). And in various places where we find the native English speaker producing stop consonants, we find the Vietnamese speaker producing these as fricatives (*snack* → [snæx]). These observed differences between transcriptions (interdental fricative → /t/, /d/, obstruent deletion, final devoicing, and stop → fricative) we will call phonological speech patterns (PSPs). A subset of some of these PSPs for all speakers represented in the Archive is given in Table 2.

Table 2: Phonological speech patterns (PSPs)

consonants	*vowels*	*syllables*
final devoicing	vowel shortening	consonant deletion
non-aspiration	vowel lengthening	vowel insertion
consonant voicing	vowel raising	consonant insertion
interdental fricative --> t/d	vowel fronting	
interdental fricative --> s/z	vowel backing	
interdental fricative --> f/v	vowel lowering	
w --> v		
ɹ --> trill		
ɹ --> uvular		
ɹ <----> l		
liquid --> flap		
stop --> fricative		
dentalization		
palatalization		
nasal fronting		

Our question is whether or not a set of PSPs derived from systematic comparisons is sufficient to define a specific class of non-native speakers of English. Certainly some of these phonological speech patterns will be idiosyncratic to individual speakers and some may be conditioned by the English proficiency of the speaker. And yet others may be shared across accent types. Our preliminary work suggests that these PSPs are not infinite, and we find that there remains a finite set of patterns that uniquely define categories of accented speakers of English. Returning to our Vietnamese example, the specific PSPs associated with a typical Vietnamese speaker of English are given in Table 3. A comparison to a speaker of Tigrigna is given in Table 4.

Table 3: Phonological speech patterns for Vietnamese7

consonants	*vowels*	*syllables*
final devoicing	vowel shortening	consonant deletion
non-aspiration		
consonant voicing		
interdental fricative → t/d		
stop → fricative		

Table 4: Phonological speech patterns for Tigrigna3

consonants	*vowels*	*syllables*
final devoicing	vowel raising	vowel insertion
non-aspiration	vowel lowering	
consonant voicing		
interdental fricative → s/z		
ɹ → trill		

4. STAT: speech transcription analysis tool

Comparing the phonetic transcriptions of hundreds of speech samples is time-consuming and arduous for humans. We have built a computational device to handle this task. This device is functional and will be integrated into the archive architecture soon. Our "machine", the speech transcription analysis tool (STAT), essentially compares speech samples (Kunath & Weinberger 2009). Conceptually, the machine superimposes, or aligns, one narrow phonetic transcription over another, and the differences are tabulated. In this case, the one transcription is of a native speaker of English, and the other is from a non-native speaker. The alignment is performed using a set of phonetic features that distinguish the differences and relationships between sounds. A key aspect of this process is determining a distance measure between two speakers' pronunciations of the same target utterance. The features used to calculate the distance include the different articulatory descriptions of utterances. Once two utterances have been aligned, a closer comparison begins that identifies patterns of L2 phonology throughout the utterance. For example, a comparison could be based on a speaker aspirating a stop consonant, which would then trigger the system to look for other instances of aspirated stops. Finally, differences between the transcriptions are returned as PSPs like those listed in Section 3.

In addition to the time and accuracy advantages, STAT incorporates some very useful features. First and foremost, it can easily perform comparison alignments with any native sample. So not only can we compare a non-native speaker with an arbitrary "standard" English1 sample as we did above, we can easily also choose any of our 431+ native English samples as the "standard". Moreover, STAT can easily compare the complete set of samples from one language background and distill a composite accent profile. For example, we can run all 89 or so of our Spanish samples and find out just what typifies an archetypal Spanish accent.

Results can also be tailored to suit specific research questions. For example, STAT can be programmed via an easy-to-use web-based interface to only attend to the various substitutions for inter-dental fricatives within single or multiple comparisons. That is, we could find out how various speakers of English deal with /θ/ and /ð/. Is /t/ the most common substitute for these interdental fricatives, or is /s/? And how do the variables of native language background or syllable position interact? STAT allows for such focused queries. And, of course, since STAT has the ability to count and rank PSPs, there is an obvious potential for automatic speaker assessment.

An example of STAT output for native Vietnamese speaker, 'Vietnamese7', is given in Figure 4. As you can see, STAT discovers native/non-native differences that are not yet listed in our set of PSPs in Table 2.

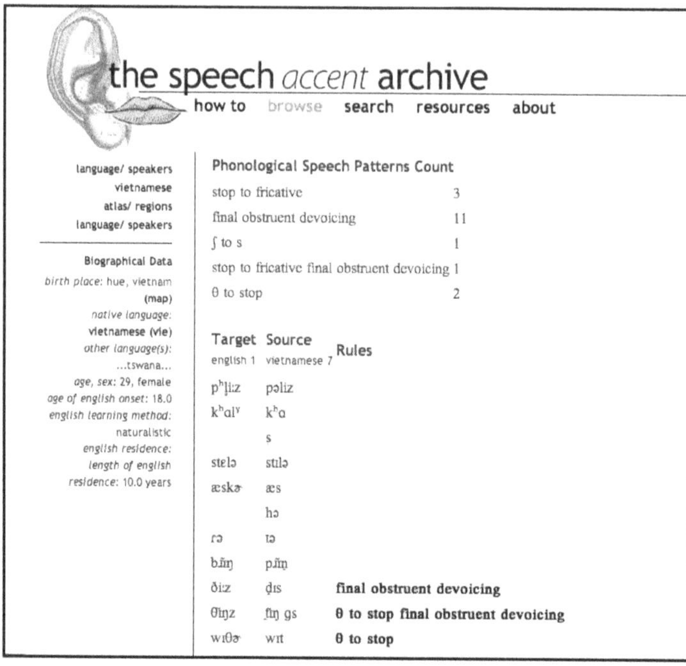

Figure 4: Example alignment results for Vietnamese7

4.1 STAT architecture

The STAT system incorporates several distinct components. These include a front-end interface used by linguists and other researchers, a phonetic analysis and alignment processor, and a resource database. Users interact with the system primarily via a web interface that manages communication with the Accent's transcription database and STAT's own processing mechanisms. All user web interfaces are implemented with Ruby on Rails and various JavaScript libraries. Back-end processes and algorithms are implemented in Java and are made accessible to the web interface via REST services. We believe that the transcription alignment and speech pattern analysis components of STAT make it a unique tool for linguists studying speech processes. An open source web application bundle including the front-end web interfaces and back-end libraries suitable for use in other applications will be made available in the future.

4.2 Phonetic feature database

To make phonetic and word-level alignments possible, we built a database describing various phonetic features. This database includes a list of phonemes with a description of all relevant articulatory features. These features indicate phoneme qualities such as voicing, place and manner of articulation. Other features can be incorporated as needed for particular research projects. Items in the database can be accessed either by providing the IPA character for the phoneme or by searching a list of features. Additionally, the database contains information about diacritics and how they would combine with other IPA characters to select the correct feature set to return. For example, if one were searching for /d̥/, the returned features would specify a voiceless consonant.

4.3 Alignment process

When the STAT mechanism receives an alignment request, a number of steps are involved in generating the final analysis. The first step involves effectively tokenizing the input phonetic transcriptions. Once the transcriptions have been verified to contain well-formed input and are tokenized, the phoneme-level alignment is performed. After this, a word- or utterance-level alignment is performed. The final step STAT performs is an examination of all alignments for differences that identify possible phonological speech patterns. All these differences are then compared to other previously identified phonological speech patterns and any new patterns are flagged and made available for further analysis. We will now describe each step in detail.

4.3.1. Input validation and phonetic tokenization

An essential step before STAT can align transcriptions is to ensure proper input. Due to the structure of Unicode and the varieties of ways phonetic information may be transcribed in it, STAT enforces compliance of transcriptions with a certain set of Unicode characters. The characters permitted include all phoneme and diacritical marks used in IPA. Transcriptions processed by STAT are all verified to comply with this set of Unicode characters.

After the transcription has been verified, the second step of pre-processing is undertaken. This consists of tokenizing the transcription input into distinct phonetic blocks. Since IPA allows for multiple diacritics to be used with one underlying phonetic character, our tokenizer aggregates the initial phonetic character together with all the associated diacritics. STAT then searches the phonetic feature database for each individual phonetic unit identified in the tokenization process. Once this process is completed, the initial IPA transcriptions have been correctly tokenized and now have all their phonetic features integrated.

4.3.2 Phoneme-level alignment

After STAT has verified and tokenized the input transcriptions, the first alignment process can be started. This first alignment process aligns the individual phonemic units of each transcription together. Individual phonemic alignments are made possible by performing feature vector comparisons for each unit of the transcription within a context window. The features used in this analysis are the set of linguistically-motivated phonetic features like voicing, vowel height, continuance, etc. It is important to note here that the items aligned need not match exactly, they must simply be the most likely candidates for alignment given the particular context and the relevant features of each alignment item.

4.3.3 Word-level alignment

Following the phoneme-level alignment, the individual words of the transcript, segmented by the use of a white space character, are aligned. This step is necessary to allow for contextual analysis of phonetic changes including final devoicing. Additionally, some speakers will repeat a word multiple times and this step of the process allows for the optimal pairing of words between transcripts, which typically involves selecting the final attempt at the utterance.

4.3.4 Phonological speech pattern identification

Following validation, tokenization, and alignment, the analysis of phonological speech patterns can begin. This step involves looking at the discrepancies that occur in the two transcripts and determining which differences constitute a systematic pattern. Differences in the two transcriptions can involve any of the processes described in Section 3 above. Previously, linguists carried out this step by using a rule to identify such patterns by finding at least two occurrences of the same pattern in each transcription. STAT and the phonological feature database together allow for the system to look across the entire corpus of accents to identify potential pattern candidates. Any new pattern identified is stored and flagged so that linguists can verify both presence and relevance of the pattern to ensure that only relevant patterns are incorporated into the database. Once both new and old patterns have been identified, their occurrences are stored in the phonetic feature database.

4.3.5 Manual intervention capabilities

A problem that can arise with any attempt to automatically process human language data is the propagation of errors due to the lack of human oversight. In order to prevent this, STAT has incorporated a number of manual verification and intervention methods. Linguists can look at the results of any part of the STAT process and make changes as they see fit that will be propagated throughout any remaining steps and will also be used to improve the accuracy of the underlying computational procedures.

5. Conclusion: lessons learned and further work

The research program that we are engaged in is a linguistic one. In our investigations into speech accents and their categorizations, we begin with a standard phonological position: that all human grammars are systematic and describable. The PSPs identified (by STAT) from the speech samples in the Speech Accent Archive appear to support this. Moreover, we are observing good results from a purely segmental focus. We assume that these phonological speech patterns are entities that human listeners notice. Unlike most of the computational studies done with the acoustic information from non-native speakers (e.g., Bartkova & Jouvet 2007, Deshpande, Chikkerur, & Govindaraju 2005), we ensure that the analysis has a linguistic foundation by employing a hybrid procedure that includes the contributions of both machines and humans. Humans create the phonetic transcription and the machine processes it. Ultimately, as machine algorithms begin to advance and result in better performance (which would rival what humans do instantaneously and subconsciously), the human contributions will wither away. But in the meantime, we believe that our linguistic approach can best inform purely computational studies.

There are certainly things we have learned that, with hindsight, we would have done differently. One of these has to do with the notion of completeness. Were we to start over, we would construct a much more comprehensive elicitation paragraph, ask our speakers more detailed demographic questions, and confirm every phonetic transcription with spectrographic analysis. We are acting on some of these lessons. For example, all of the audio speech samples are being formatted into time-coded files for instrumental analysis. Each uncompressed sound file is being tagged by word and segment so that more precise acoustic research can be done with the data. This will not only result in more accurate phonetic transcriptions, but it will be of great value to speech recognition researchers. More detailed speaker notes about residency are being incorporated into the searchable database. Finally, our background language materials (the phonetic inventories and syllable structure inventories) are being revised and expanded.

The Speech Accent Archive is a unique resource. To our knowledge, it is the only uniform web-accessible corpus of native and non-native English speech accents. The systematic demographic and phonetic annotations make the archive a valuable research tool, and the incorporation of STAT adds considerable potential to the database.

References

Bartkova, K. & D. Jouvet (2007), 'On using units trained on foreign data for improved multiple accent speech recognition', *Speech communication*, 49: 836-846.

Brennan, E.M. & J.S. Brennan (1981), 'Measurements of accent and attitude toward Mexican-American speech', *Journal of psycholinguistic research*, 10(5): 487-501.

Central Intelligence Agency (2010), The world factbook 2010. Washington, DC: Central Intelligence Agency. Available online at: https://www.cia.gov/library/publications/the-world-factbook/

Cunningham-Andersson, U. & O. Engstrand (1989), 'Perceived strength and identity of foreign accent in English', *Phonetica*, 46: 138-154.

Deshpande, S., V. Chikkerur & V. Govindaraju (2005), 'Accent classification in speech', in: *Proceedings of the Fourth IEEE Workshop on Automatic Identification Advanced Technologies*. Buffalo (NY): IEEE Computer Society. 139-143.

Edwards, H.T. (1992), *Applied phonetics: the sounds of American English*. San Diego: Singular Pub. Group.

Gut, U. (2007), 'Foreign accent', in: C. Muller (ed.) *Speaker classification*. Berlin: Springer Verlag. 75-87.

International Phonetic Association (1999), *Handbook of the International Phonetic Association: a guide to the use of the International Phonetic Alphabet*. Cambridge: Cambridge University Press.

Kunath, S. & S. Weinberger (2009), 'STAT: Speech Transcription Analysis Tool', in: F. Poppowich & M. Johnston (eds.) *Proceedings of NAACL HLT 2009: Demonstrations*. Boulder: Association for Computational Linguistics. 9-12.

Lewis, M. P. (2009), *Ethnologue: languages of the world* (16th ed.). Dallas: SIL International.

Long, M. H. (2007), *Problems in SLA*. Mahwah (NJ): Lawrence Erlbaum.

Magen, H. (1998), 'The perception of foreign-accented speech', *Journal of phonetics*, 26: 381-400.

Major, R.C. (2007), 'Identifying a foreign accent in an unfamiliar language', *Studies in second language acquisition*, 29(4): 539-556.

Munro, M. & T. Derwing (1994), 'Evaluations of foreign accent in extemporaneous and read material', *Language testing*, 11: 253-266.

Munro, M., T. Derwing, & S. Morton (2006), 'The mutual intelligibility of L2 speech', *Studies in second language acquisition*, 28: 111-131.

Purcell, E. & R. Suter (1980), 'Predictors of pronunciation accuracy: a re-examination', *Language learning*, 30: 271-287.

Scheuer, S. (2002), 'What makes foreign accent sound foreign?', in: A. James & J. Leather (eds.) *Proceedings of New Sounds 2000*. Klagenfurt, Austria: University of Klagenfurt. 306-314.

Scovel, T. (1995), 'Differentiation, recognition, and identification in the discrimination of foreign accents', in: J. Archibald (ed.) *Phonological acquisition and phonological theory*. Hillsdale (NJ): Lawrence Erlbaum. 169-181.

SIL International (2010), Doulos SIL. Avalilable online at: http://scripts.sil.org /cms/scripts/page.php?item_id=DoulosSIL_download.

Zechner, K., D. Higgins, X. Xi & D.M. Williamson (2009), 'Automatic scoring of non-native spontaneous speech in tests of spoken English', *Speech communication*, 51(10): 883-895.

Creating and using *A frequency dictionary of Contemporary American English: word sketches, collocates, and thematic lists*

Mark Davies and Dee Gardner

Brigham Young University

Abstract

We have recently published A frequency dictionary of Contemporary American English: word sketches, collocates, and thematic lists *(Davies & Gardner 2010). The dictionary is based on the 400 million word Corpus of Contemporary American English (COCA), 1990-2009. It contains the top 5,000 lemmas of American English, along with the top 20-30 collocates for each word, which help to paint a useful "word sketch" for each word. In addition, there are more than thirty frequency-ranked thematic lists – family terms, clothing, new words in American English, American / British contrasts, top phrasal verbs, and so on. In this paper, we discuss the creation of the dictionary and how it can be used to facilitate the teaching and learning of English vocabulary.*

1. The value of a frequency dictionary of English

"I don't know that word." "What does that word mean?" "How is that word used?" These are some of the most common pleas for help by language learners—and justifiably so.

Not knowing enough words, or the right words, is often the root cause of miscommunication, the inability to read and write well, and a host of related problems. This fundamental need is compounded by the fact that there are simply so many words to know in any language, but especially in English, which may contain well over two million distinct words (Crystal 1995)—and growing fast. Thirty years ago, who would have thought that we would be "surfing" in our own homes, or that "chips" would be good things to have inside our equipment, or that we would be excited to "*google* this" or that we would "get *freaked out* by that". Without belaboring the obvious, it is little wonder that learners, teachers, researchers, materials developers, and many others are interested in establishing some sense of priority and direction to what could easily become vocabulary chaos.

To address this issue, we have recently published *A frequency dictionary of Contemporary American English: word sketches, collocates, and thematic lists* (Davies & Gardner 2010). We wanted to know which of the vast number of English words to start with, and we also wanted to know which other words these words "hang out with" — their neighbors (or collocates) — which provides crucial information about the meaning and use of these words. Perhaps even more importantly, we wanted to know this for our current day, not for some English of the past, when punch cards were used to program computers, and when surfing was only done at the beach. In short, our goal in creating the dictionary was to create a tool that would benefit those who are trying to learn English, as well as for those who desire to assist them.

2. Overview of the dictionary content

The frequency dictionary is designed to meet the needs of a wide range of language students and teachers, as well as those who are interested in the computational processing of English. The main index contains the five thousand most common words in American English, starting with such basic words as *the* and *of*, and quickly progressing through to more intermediate and advanced words. Because the dictionary is based on the actual frequency of words in a large 400 million word corpus (collection of texts) of many different types of English texts (spoken, fiction, magazines, newspaper, and academic), the user can feel comfortable that these are words that one is very likely to subsequently encounter in the "real world."

In addition to providing a listing of the most frequent five thousand words, the entries provide other information that should be of great use to the language learner. Each entry also shows the main collocates for each word, grouped by part of speech and in order of frequency. These collocates provide important and useful insight into the meaning and usage of the word, following the idea that "you shall know a word by the company it keeps" (Firth 1957: 11). The entries also show where each of the collocates occur with regards to the head word (before, after, or both), which indicate whether they are subject, object, and so on. Finally, the entries indicate whether the words are more common in one genre of English (e.g., spoken or academic) than in the others.

Aside from the main frequency listing, there are also indexes that sort the entries by alphabetical order and part of speech. The alphabetical index can be of great value to students who, for example, want to look up a word from a short story or newspaper article, and see how common the word is in general. The part of speech indexes could be of benefit to students who want to focus selectively on verbs, nouns, or some other part of speech. Finally, there are a number of thematically-related lists (clothing, foods, emotions, etc.) as well as comparisons of vocabulary across genres and over time, all of which should enhance the learning experience. The expectation, then, is that the frequency dictionary will significantly maximize the efforts of a wide range of students and teachers who are involved in the acquisition and teaching of English vocabulary.

3. Comparison to other frequency dictionaries of English

Historically, most frequency dictionaries (also referred to as "word books" and "word lists") have been created to meet educational needs, with many designed specifically to meet the needs of foreign- and second-language learners of

English. Prominent among these are *The teachers word book of 30,000 words* (Thorndike & Lorge 1944)—based on 4.5 million words from general English texts, magazines, and juvenile books, *The general service list of English words* (West 1953)—a list of the 2,000 highest frequency words (with semantic distinctions and counts) based on visual inspections by semanticists of five million words from various sources (encyclopedias, magazines, textbooks, novels, etc.), the Brown Corpus list (Francis & Kučera 1982)—based on one million words of written American English, and its British English counterpart—the LOB Corpuslist (Johansson & Hofland 1989).

For many purposes, these latter two replaced the older lists of Thorndike & Lorge. Additionally, there are several more specialized school lists, such as the *American Heritage word frequency book* (Carroll, Davies & Richman 1971) based on five million running words of written school English (grades 3 through 9), the *Academic word list* (Coxhead 2000) with 570 academic word families based on 3.5 million running words of academic texts, and the very early *A basic vocabulary of elementary school children* (Rinsland 1945), based on six million running words of children's writing samples.

A great debt is owed to the pioneering scholars who generated these and other frequency lists to facilitate English vocabulary learning, research, and description. Building on these earlier efforts, the *Frequency dictionary of American English* addresses several vocabulary needs in the field of English language education. First, and perhaps most obvious, it is based on contemporary American English, thus making it more ecologically valid in educational and research settings where American English is the target, and where many are still relying on the nearly 50-year-old Brown Corpus (Francis & Kučera 1982) for frequency information about American English vocabulary. (Note: the actual texts for the Brown Corpus were from 1961.) Second, unlike the Brown Corpus (one million words of written English only), the frequency counts in the dictionary are based on a very large and balanced corpus of both written and spoken materials (400 million words from five major genres).This increases one's confidence that the highest frequency words have indeed been determined and properly ranked, and that these words have a high degree of utility across major genres of importance to English language learners (spoken, fiction, newspapers, magazines, and academic).

Third, the inclusion of collocates (by part of speech) for each of the 5,000 high-frequency node words adds a semantic richness to the dictionary that is often lacking when only the forms of words are tallied without consideration of their potential meanings (Gardner 2007). The tightness of some of these node-collocate relationships (*big deal, bad habit, make sense, trash talk*, etc.) also highlights the phrasal nature of many English vocabulary items (Cowie 1998). Such collocational knowledge is a crucial component of what it means to know a word (Nation 2001) and has also been recognized as a characteristic difference between native and non-native language abilities (Nesselhauf 2005). Therefore, language learners and their teachers should benefit from the rich semantic and pragmatic information the collocates provide, thus taking us one step closer to Read's

(2000) call for new high-frequency word lists that are based on large electronic corpora, but which also account for the many meanings that language learners need to negotiate. Although semantic frequency is not fully realized in the dictionary, the collocates do provide some support for semantic interpretations, and will certainly aid in determining which meanings of a word form to teach and learn.

Finally, the 30 call-out boxes in the dictionary are packed with useful vocabulary information for language learners and their teachers, including words that make up many of the basic semantic sets of the language (*animals, body, clothing, colors, emotions, family, food*, etc.), words that characterize a specific genre of the language (spoken, fiction, academic, etc.), words that are new to American English, words that tend to be characteristically American or British, productive suffixes and the actual content words they are found in (nouns and adjectives), and the highest frequency phrasal verbs of American English. (Compare with Gardner & Davies 2007, which lists the highest frequency phrasal verbs of British English.) These and other call-out boxes in the dictionary can be used for self-study, teaching, assessment, materials development, and research purposes.

To our knowledge, there is only one other publicly-accessible frequency dictionary of English that is based on a large mega-corpus – *Word frequencies in written and spoken English* (Leech, Rayson & Wilson 2001). However, our dictionary is quite different in at least three major respects. First, the Longman frequency dictionary represents British, not American, English, and it bases its word-frequency information on the British National Corpus (BNC). Second, most of the texts in the BNC are at least twenty years old, while texts in the Corpus of Contemporary American English (COCA) are current through late 2008. Third, while both corpora are balanced for genre (e.g., spoken, fiction, newspaper, and academic), COCA (400 million words) is nearly four times as large as the BNC (100 million words), allowing us to have more confidence in determining the words that should "make the list" and in finding their meaningful neighbors.

In addition to the differences in focus, age, and sampling size between the two dictionaries, there are also differences in the presentation formats. The Longman dictionary is mainly composed of straight frequency lists of words and lemmas, while the dictionary is oriented specifically to language learners, supplementing the frequency listings with the unique features previously mentioned: (a) frequency-ranked collocates (co-occurring words) for each headword in the frequency dictionary—which can help learners and their teachers better understand the *meanings* and *uses* of the high frequency words; and (b) the more than 30 thematically-oriented vocabulary lists (call-out boxes) for particular semantic, grammatical, or lexical categories that would be helpful for language training purposes.

4. The corpus

A frequency dictionary is only as good as the corpus on which it is based. The Corpus of Contemporary American English (COCA, see Davies 2009) is the largest balanced corpus of American English, and the largest balanced corpus of any language that is publicly available (http://www.americancorpus.org). In addition to being very large (400 million words; 20 million words each year 1990-2007), the corpus is also balanced evenly between spoken (unscripted conversation from 150+ radio and TV shows), fiction (e.g., books, short stories, movie scripts), 100+ popular magazines, ten newspapers, and 100+ academic journals – for a total of 150,000+ texts.

The more than 150,000 texts come from a variety of sources:

Spoken: (79 million words) Transcripts of unscripted conversation from more than 150 different TV and radio programs (examples: *All Things Considered* (NPR), *Newshour* (PBS), *Good Morning America* (ABC), *Today Show* (NBC), *60 Minutes* (CBS), *Hannity and Colmes* (Fox), *Jerry Springer*, etc).

Fiction: (76 million words) Short stories and plays from literary magazines, children's magazines, popular magazines, first chapters of first edition books 1990-present, and movie scripts.

Popular Magazines: (81 million words) Nearly 100 different magazines, with a good mix (overall, and by year) between specific domains (news, health, home and gardening, women, financial, religion, sports, etc). A few examples are *Time, Men's Health, Good Housekeeping, Cosmopolitan, Fortune, Christian Century, Sports Illustrated*, etc.

Newspapers: (76 million words) Ten newspapers from across the US, including: *USA Today, New York Times, Atlanta Journal Constitution, San Francisco Chronicle*, etc. In most cases, there is a good mix between different sections of the newspaper, such as local news, opinion, sports, financial, etc.

Academic Journals: (76 million words) Nearly 100 different peer-reviewed journals. These were selected to cover the entire range of the Library of Congress classification system (e.g., a certain percentage from B (philosophy, psychology, religion), D (world history), K (education), T (technology), etc.), both overall and by number of words per year.

In summary, the corpus is very well balanced at both the "macro" level (e.g., spoken, fiction, newspapers) and the "micro" level (i.e., the types of texts and the distribution of the sources) within each of these macro genres.

5. Annotating and organizing the data from the corpus

In order to create a frequency dictionary, the words in the corpus must be tagged (for part of speech) and lemmatized. Tagging of course means that a part of speech is assigned to each word — noun, verb, and so on. Lemmatization — which is crucial for the frequency dictionary – means that each word form is assigned to a particular "head word" or "lemma", such as *go, goes, going, went*, and *gone* being marked as forms of the lemma GO.

The tagging and lemmatization was done with the CLAWS tagger (Version 7), which is the same tagger that was used for the British National Corpus (http://www.natcorp.ox.ac.uk/) and for other important corpora of English as well. One of the most difficult parts of tagging, of course, is to correctly assign the part of speech for words that are potentially ambiguous. In cases like *computer, disturb, lazy*, or *fitfully*, these are unambiguously tagged as noun, verb, adjective, and adverb, respectively. But in a case like *light*, the word can be a noun (*he turned on the light*), verb (*should we light the fire?*), or adjective (*there was a light breeze*). In these cases, the tagger looks at the context in which the word occurs in each instance to determine the correct part of speech. While the CLAWS tagger is very good, it does produce errors. We have tried to correct for most of these, but there are undoubtedly still some that remain.

It of course makes sense to provide separate entries in the dictionary for words with different parts of speech, such as noun and verb. For example, the word *beat* as a noun has collocates like *hear, miss, steady, drum*, and *rhythm*. As a verb, however, it takes collocates like *heart, egg, bowl, severely*, or *Yankees*. Even in cases where the word appears as a noun and an adjective (*magic, potential, dark, veteran*), the collocates for the two parts of speech are very different, and it would probably be too confusing to conflate them into one entry. Perhaps the most problematic are function words like *since*, which appear up to three times in the dictionary. In the case of *since*, for example, it appears as preposition (*he's been here since 1942*), adverb (*several other schools have since been constructed*), and conjunction (*since they won't be here until 5pm, we'll just leave for a minute*). In these cases, we have simply followed the output of the tagger. If it says that there are multiple different parts of speech, then the word appears under each of those parts of speech in the dictionary.

6. Frequency and dispersion

After the tagging and lemmatization of the 400 million words in the corpus, our final step was to determine exactly which of these words would be included in the final list of the 5,000 most frequent words (or lemmas). One approach would be to simply use frequency counts. For example, all lemmas that occur 5,000 times or more in the corpus might be included in the dictionary. Imagine, however, a case where a particular scientific term was used repeatedly in engineering articles or in sports reporting in newspapers, but it did not appear in any works of fiction or in any of the spoken texts. Alternatively, suppose that a given word is spread throughout an entire register (spoken, fiction, newspaper, or academic), but that it is still limited almost exclusively to that register. Should the word still be included in the frequency dictionary? The argument could be made that we should look at more than just raw frequency counts in cases like this, and that we ought to look at dispersion as well, or how well the word is "spread across" all of the registers in the entire corpus.

In our dictionary, we have used Juilland's "D dispersion index" (see Juilland & Chang-Rodriguez 1964). A score of 1.00 means that the word is perfectly spread across the corpus, so that if we divided the corpus into one hundred equally-sized sections (each with four million words, in the case of our 400 million word corpus), the word would have exactly the same frequency in each section. A dispersion score of .10, on the other hand, would mean that it occurs a lot in a handful of sections, and perhaps not at all or very little in the other sections.

As a clear example of the contrast between "frequency" and "dispersion", consider the Table 1. All of the words in Table 1 have essentially the same frequency – an average of about 3,000 occurrences in the corpus. The words to the left, however, have a dispersion score of at least 0.95, which means that the word has roughly the same frequency in all of the 100 sections of the corpus that we used for the calculation. The words to the right, on the other hand, have a much lower dispersion score. Most would easily agree that the words shown at the left would be more useful in a frequency dictionary, because they represent a wide range of texts and text types in the corpus. Therefore, as we can see, frequency alone is probably not sufficient to determine whether a word should be in the dictionary.

Table 1: Differences in dispersion (PoS = Part of speech, D = Juilland's D dispersion index)

good dispersion				*poor dispersion*			
freq	*lemma*	*PoS*	*D*	*freq*	*lemma*	*PoS*	*D*
3134	CONVINCING	j	0.96	4653	HEALTHCARE	n	0.56
3107	SENSIBLE	j	0.95	4282	ELECTRON	n	0.58
3041	HONESTY	n	0.96	4181	SKIER	n	0.43
3033	UNUSUALLY	r	0.95	4113	COMPOST	n	0.31
3020	CONFUSING	j	0.97	3685	WATERCOLOR	n	0.41
3014	EXAGGERATE	v	0.96	3769	SKI	v	0.47
2950	DISTRACTION	n	0.95	2028	NEBULA	n	0.46
2922	RESENT	v	0.96	2547	PALETTE	n	0.57
2891	WRESTLE	v	0.95	2536	ANGLE	v	0.55
2876	URGENCY	n	0.96	2479	ALGORITHM	n	0.52
2873	HINT	v	0.96	2437	PASTEL	n	0.25
2842	OBSESSED	j	0.95	2388	SOCKET	n	0.60
2833	GENUINELY	r	0.96	2350	NASAL	j	0.44
2813	RESPECTED	j	0.95	2281	CACHE	n	0.43

7. The final calculation

The calculation to determine which words are included in the frequency dictionary was a fairly straightforward one. The formula was simply:

score = frequency * dispersion

For example, consider the words near 3210 in the frequency dictionary, as shown in Table 2. The word *furthermore* has a higher frequency (9,594 tokens) than the other two words, but it has lower dispersion (.86). *Orange*, on the other hand, has a lower frequency (8,881 tokens) but it has better dispersion across the corpus. *Taxpayer* (frequency of 9,140 and dispersion of .90) is in the middle of both of these. But with the formula that takes into account both frequency and dispersion, these three words end up having more or less the same score.

Table 2: Effect of frequency and dispersion on rank order

ID	*lemma*	*PoS*	*frequency*	*dispersion*	*score*
3199	ORANGE	j	8881	0.93	8270
3201	TAXPAYER	n	9140	0.90	8256
3205	FURTHERMORE	r	9594	0.86	8235

The 5,000 lemmas with the top score (frequency * dispersion) are those that appear in the frequency dictionary.

8. Collocates

A unique feature of the frequency dictionary are the listing of the top collocates (nearby words) for each of the 5,000 words in the frequency listing. These collocates provide important and useful insight into the meaning and use of the keyword. To find the collocates, we did the following. First, we decided which parts of speech to group together in order to rank the collocates and show the most frequent ones. In the case of verbs, we grouped noun collocates (subject: *the evidence supports what she said*, and object: *this supports the claim*), and all other collocates were grouped as miscellaneous (e.g., *with, directly, difficult*, and *prepare* for the verb *deal*). For nouns, we looked for adjectives (*green grass*), other nouns (*fire station*), and verbs (e.g., *desire to succeed*). For adjectives, we looked for nouns (*fast car*) and all other collocates were grouped as miscellaneous (*completely exhausted, willing to stay, black and white*). Finally, for adverbs and other parts of speech, we see collocates from all parts of speech listed together (*sharply reduce, fewer than, except for*).

To find the collocates for a given word, a computer program searched the entire 400 million word corpus and looked at each context in which that word occurred. In all cases, the context (or span) of words was four words to the left and four words to the right of the node word. The overall frequency of the collocates in each of those contexts was then calculated, and the collocates were examined and rated by at least four native speakers.

Obviously, common words like *the, of, to*, etc. were usually the most frequent collocates. To filter out these words, we set a Mutual Information (MI) threshold of about 2.5. The MI calculation took into account the overall frequency of each collocate, so that common words were usually eliminated from the list.

Using MI is sometimes more an art than a science. If the MI is set too low, then high frequency "noise words" show up as collocates, whereas if it is set too high, then only highly idiomatic collocates are found. As an example, the most frequent collocates of *break* as a verb – when the MI score is set high at 5.5 – are: *deadlock, logjam, monotony, and stranglehold.* These are quite idiomatic and don't really show well the core meaning of *break.* On the other hand, the most frequent collocates when the MI threshold is set very low at 1.0 are *down, into, up*, and *off*, which again do not provide a good sense of its meaning. Finally, however, when we set the MI threshold to 2.5, we find the most frequent collocates are: *heart, silence, rules, loose, leg, and barriers*, which (for native speakers, at least), probably do relate more to the core meaning and usage of *break*. But getting the MI threshold set just right for each of the 5,000 headwords was a bit daunting, to say the least.

9. The main frequency index

Chapter 2 of the dictionary contains the main index in the dictionary – a rank-ordered listing of the top five thousand words (lemma) in English, starting with the most frequent word (the definite article *the*) and progressing through to *warehouse, paradise*, and *nominate*, which are the last three words in the list. The following information is given for each entry, as in (1):

(1)

rank frequency (1, 2, 3, …), lemma, part of speech
collocates, grouped by part of speech and ordered by frequency
raw frequency, dispersion (0.00 – 1.00), (indication of register variation)

As a concrete example, let us look at the entry (2) for the verb *break*:

(2)

494 break *v*

n. law, heart, news, .rule, silence, story, .ground, .barrier, leg, bone, .piece, .neck, arm, .cycle, voice. *misc*.into, .away, .free, .apart, .loose up marriage, .fight, boyfriend, meeting., girlfriend, union, band, pass, .demonstration, .monotony down.into, .barrier, car., .cry, .door, .tear, talk., enzyme., completely, negotiation.out war., fight., fire., sweat, fighting., riot., violence., .laugh, .hive off piece, talk, .engagement, negotiation, branch, abruptly, .relation

72917 0.97

This entry shows that word number 494 in our rank order list is the verb *break*. The last line of the entry shows the raw frequency for the lemma (72,917 tokens) and the dispersion (.97 in this case). The collocates are given in the intervening lines. As can be seen, they are partially grouped by part of speech. In the case of verbs, we see the noun collocates and then other parts of speech (miscellaneous).

Note also that for some collocates, there is an indication of the placement of the collocate. When the "." is before the collocate, this means that the node word (headword) is typically found before that collocate (*break the law, break into pieces*). When the "." is after the collocate, this means that the node word is typically found after the collocate (*her voice broke, all hell broke loose*). This symbol can provide useful information, for example, on whether the collocates are subjects or objects of a given verb, or whether the node word noun acts as a subject or object of the verbal collocate. (Note, however, that with passives and relative clauses, the noun that is object of a verb will occur before the verb, which does confuse things a bit.) In order to display the "." symbol, 80% or more of the tokens of a given collocate had to occur either before or after the node word. In the case of ADJ / NOUN and NOUN / ADJ, word order is typically so consistent (*blue house*, never **house blue*) that the "." is not used to show placement.

Finally, as is seen above, in the case of some verbs that can act as phrasal verbs (*break up, turn down, cut off*, etc.), these are listed in bold (with their own collocates) at the end of the regular collocates list for verbs. Phrasal verbs are only listed when they have a frequency of at least 1,000 in the corpus, and when there are at least three collocates with a frequency of at least five occurrences each.

Let us consider one other example:

(3)

3396 hypothesis *n* j null, following, consistent, alternative, working, general, initial, original, theoretical, competing n study, support., result, test, research, testing, evidence, analysis, method, set v.predict, suggest, reject, examine, confirm, base, develop, formulate, .state, .explain 9282 0.82 A

This entry is for *hypothesis* (word number 3396 in our list). As before, the collocates are listed in frequency order and grouped by part of speech. In this case, however, note that there is an "A" at the end of the entry. This indicates that the lemma *hypothesis* occurs at least twice as frequently in the Academic genre as it does overall in the corpus (Spoken, Fiction, Magazines, Newspapers).

10. Thematic vocabulary (call-out boxes)

Placed throughout the main frequency-based index are approximately thirty call-out boxes, which serve to display in one list a number of thematically-related words. These include thematic lists of words related to the body, food, family, weather, professions, nationalities, colors, emotions, and several other semantic domains. There are also lists of words that are much more common in each of the five main genres (spoken, fiction, popular magazines, newspapers, and academic) than overall, as well as comparisons of frequent American and British vocabulary, as well as new words in the language. Finally, there are lists related to word formation issues, such as irregular past tense and irregular plurals, and common suffixes to create nouns, adjectives, and verbs. In each case, the entries are of course ordered by frequency.

Partial lists for seven of the more than thirty thematic lists are given in the Appendix.

11. Electronic version

In addition to the basic 5,000 word list with 20-30 collocates each, expanded word frequency and collocates lists that are based on the same corpus can also be found at http://www.wordfrequency.info. This site contains lists of the top 10,000 and 20,000 words with 20-30 collocates each. In addition, it also includes the top 200-300 collocates for either the top 10,000 or top 20,000 words. For the largest list, then, there are about 4,300,000 node word / collocate pairs, along with their frequency and Mutual Information score. Finally, this site also contains the full set of trigrams from the corpus along with their frequency, a total of more than 155 million unique three-word sequences.

12. Delimitations

The following are the major delimitations of the frequency dictionary:

1. Frequency is form-based (lemma), not semantically-based (homographs -- *bank, run*, heterophones – *lead* 'metal' vs. *lead* 'be in front', *contract* vs. *contract,* etc.). But our approach is an improvement over many similar frequency listings because the collocates give some indication of potential variant meanings. For example, the entry for *lead* (n) [entry 1598] and *bow* (n) [entry 4139] show that for *lead*, there are collocates for the two meanings 'metal' and 'in front' and for *bow* there are collocates for *bow* in the context of 'ship', 'arrow', 'hair', and 'violin'.
2. Except in the case of high-frequency phrasal verbs, only single-word nodes were included. When a lemma occurs almost exclusively in a given multi-word expression (*as far as, in charge of, lots of*), that multi-word expression is listed as part of the entry.
3. All collocates are single word collocates. In cases like *in terms of, by means of*, etc., each of the collocates are listed separately.
4. The most frequent form of a given collocate lemma may be an inflected form, not the head word form as listed (e.g., *long* as a collocate of *no* almost always appears as *longer* in the corpus).
5. In general, proper nouns were not included in the dictionary, either as node words or collocates. However, a few highly salient proper noun collocates were included for certain node words (e.g., *Iraq* as a collocate of *invade*; *China* as a collocate of *export*).

13. Summary

A frequency dictionary of Contemporary American English: word sketches, collocates, and thematic lists (Davies & Gardner 2010) is the first frequency list of its type for English. It is based on the 400+ million word Corpus of Contemporary American English (COCA), which is the largest, freely-available corpus of English. Because it is balanced between spoken, fiction, popular magazines, newspaper, and academic, and because it contains texts from 1990 to the present time, users can be sure that the words in the dictionary are those that they will actually encounter in the "real world".

Rather than just containing a list of the most frequent words or lemmas (as do some other frequency lists and dictionaries), this dictionary provides much more. Each entry contains the top 20-30 collocates for the head word (sorted by part of speech and ordered by frequency), which provides extremely valuable insight into meaning and usage. Entries also indicate whether the word is more common in one genre than another. Finally, there are more than thirty thematically-organized call-out boxes, which contain information not just on thematic vocabulary such as clothing and family terms, but also lists on American

/British differences, "new words" in American English, genre-based differences, and also several grammatical topics, such as word formation and phrasal verbs – all organized by frequency, of course. In summary, we believe that the dictionary offers a range of features that make it highly useful for learners and teachers of English.

References

Carroll, J.B., P. Davies & B. Richman (1971), *The American Heritage word frequency book*. New York: American Heritage Publishing Co., Inc.

Cowie, A.P. (ed.) (1998), *Phraseology: theory, analysis, and applications*. Oxford: Clarendon Press.

Coxhead, A. (2000), 'A new academic word list', *TESOL quarterly*, 34(2): 213-238.

Crystal, D. (1995), *The Cambridge encyclopedia of the English language*. New York: Cambridge University Press.

Davies, M. (2009), 'The 385+ Million Word Corpus of Contemporary American English (1990-2008+): design, architecture, and linguistic insights', *International journal of corpus linguistics*, 14: 159-90.

Davies, M. & D. Gardner (2010), *A frequency dictionary of Contemporary American English: word sketches, collocates, and thematic lists*. London: Routledge.

Firth, J.R. (1957), *Papers in linguistics 1934-1951*. London: Oxford University Press.

Francis, W.N. & H. Kučera (1982), *Frequency analysis of English usage: lexicon and grammar*. Boston: Houghton Mifflin.

Gardner, D. (2007), 'Validating the construct of "word" in applied corpus-based vocabulary research: a critical survey', *Applied linguistics*, 28(2): 241-265.

Gardner, D. & M. Davies (2007), 'Pointing out frequent phrasal verbs: a corpus-based analysis', *TESOL quarterly*, 41(2): 339-359.

Juilland, A. & E. Chang-Rodriguez (1964), *Frequency dictionary of Spanish words*. The Hague: Mouton de Gruyter.

Johansson, S. & K. Hofland (1989), *Frequency analysis of English vocabulary and grammar: based on the LOB Corpus, Volume 1: tag frequencies and word frequencies*. Oxford: Clarendon Press.

Leech, G., P. Rayson & A. Wilson (2001), *Word frequencies in written and spoken English: based on the British National Corpus*. London: Longman.

Nation, I.S.P. (2001), *Learning vocabulary in another language*. Cambridge: Cambridge University Press.

Nesselhauf, N. (2005), *Collocations in a learner corpus*. Amsterdam: John Benjamins.

Read, J. (2000), *Assessing vocabulary*. Cambridge: Cambridge University Press.

Rinsland, H.D. (1945), *A basic vocabulary of elementary school children*. New York: The Macmillan Company.

Thorndike, E.L. & I. Lorge (1944), *The teacher's word book of 30,000 words*. New York: Columbia University, Teacher's College.
West, M. (1953), *A general service list of English words*. London: Longman.

Appendix

Examples of (partial) thematic lists:

Clothing: (suit) *n* $_{35280}$, shoe $_{26007}$, (ring) *n* $_{21069}$, shirt $_{20470}$, dress *n* $_{20389}$, hat $_{17462}$, (tie) *n* $_{17060}$, coat *n* $_{15297}$, jacket $_{14938}$, boot *n* $_{14436}$, belt *n* $_{13966}$, pants $_{11412}$, glove $_{9852}$, uniform *n* $_{9809}$, skirt *n* $_{8858}$, jeans $_{8037}$, sock *n* $_{6486}$, sweater $_{5179}$, robe $_{4751}$, shorts $_{4626}$, gown $_{4387}$, scarf *n* $_{3551}$, (slip) *n* $_{3545}$, vest $_{3313}$, blouse $_{3110}$, underwear $_{3037}$, necklace $_{2914}$, diaper $_{2738}$, earring $_{2720}$, cloak $_{2624}$, bracelet $_{2394}$, bra $_{2378}$, apron $_{2205}$, sneakers $_{2181}$, stocking $_{2027}$, slipper $_{1943}$, blazer $_{1932}$, pajamas $_{1491}$, bikini $_{1418}$, sweatshirt $_{1342}$,

Family: child $_{323005}$, mother $_{163282}$, father $_{140176}$, (kid) $_{126054}$, parent $_{115339}$, wife $_{80380}$, son $_{77848}$, (baby) $_{65615}$, brother $_{60753}$, husband $_{57625}$, daughter $_{57551}$, sister $_{45904}$, mom $_{39021}$, dad $_{34364}$, uncle $_{18091}$, twin $_{15073}$, aunt $_{13184}$, grandmother $_{13045}$, daddy $_{12748}$, cousin $_{11640}$, mama $_{10838}$, grandfather $_{10663}$, ancestor $_{6336}$, sibling $_{5864}$, bride $_{5677}$, (widow) $_{5265}$, grandparent $_{5147}$, grandchildren $_{4846}$, grandma $_{4529}$, papa $_{4007}$,

Transportation: car $_{128671}$, train *n* $_{43971}$, ship $_{38312}$, plane $_{32339}$, truck $_{31140}$, boat $_{31036}$, bus $_{25488}$, van $_{22988}$, bike $_{17795}$, jet $_{13873}$, helicopter $_{9660}$, airplane $_{8339}$, automobile $_{6652}$, bicycle $_{6354}$, cab $_{6320}$, (metro) $_{5776}$, taxi $_{4635}$, subway $_{4485}$, ferry $_{4455}$, ambulance $_{4020}$, motorcycle $_{3480}$, jeep $_{3364}$, tractor $_{3100}$, carriage $_{3049}$, SUV $_{2813}$, convertible $_{2048}$, limo $_{1810}$, pickup truck $_{1716}$, space shuttle $_{1634}$, limousine $_{1583}$, minivan $_{1512}$,

Academic (more than twice as frequent in academic than in other genres):
[noun] student $_{163046}$, study $_{108068}$, teacher $_{73873}$, education $_{67286}$, level $_{61510}$, research $_{61043}$, community $_{56722}$, result $_{55682}$, process $_{53533}$, development $_{51798}$, use $_{51365}$
[verb] provide $_{73643}$, suggest $_{40118}$, develop $_{39775}$, require $_{37581}$, base $_{33053}$, indicate $_{31471}$, describe $_{30752}$, identify $_{29310}$, represent $_{26974}$, increase $_{26032}$, present $_{24867}$
[adjective] social $_{80721}$, political $_{63690}$, economic $_{43584}$, significant $_{37691}$, cultural $_{30243}$, environmental $_{29711}$, physical $_{27783}$, specific $_{23780}$, similar $_{23717}$, individual $_{23127}$
[adverb] however $_{70754}$, thus $_{39524}$, (for) example $_{36060}$, therefore $_{21538}$, e.g. $_{18417}$, significantly $_{15657}$, generally $_{14601}$, highly $_{12450}$, (in) addition $_{12087}$, relatively $_{12025}$

Word increasing most in frequency, 1990s to 2000s:
[noun] e-mail $_{14326}$, terrorism $_{10360}$, terrorist $_{8889}$, affiliation $_{8713}$, adolescent $_{7212}$, homeland $_{4157}$, website $_{3909}$, wireless $_{3492}$, insurgent $_{2433}$, globalization $_{2354}$,
[verb] host $_{5535}$, click $_{4094}$, e-mail $_{2139}$, download $_{1851}$, preheat $_{1364}$, bully $_{916}$, makeover $_{853}$, freak $_{649}$, partner $_{638}$, mentor $_{587}$, morph $_{349}$, vaccinate $_{286}$, restart $_{258}$
[adjective] online $_{9219}$, terrorist $_{7908}$, Afghan $_{2776}$, Taliban $_{2095}$, Shiite $_{2052}$, Pakistani $_{1967}$, same-sex $_{1397}$, sectarian $_{1138}$, upscale $_{1057}$, embryonic $_{1036}$, Islamist $_{929}$

[adverb] online $_{6034}$, famously $_{1173}$, postoperatively $_{226}$, offline $_{158}$, wirelessly $_{141}$, healthfully $_{72}$, preemptively $_{66}$, intraoperatively$_{58}$, triply $_{33}$, day-ahead $_{30}$

American vs. British vocabulary: (Amer. V): call, report, focus, guess, sign, step, figure, roll, fire, hire, file, oppose, wrap, interview, accomplish, testify, bake, track, evolve, violate, target (Brit. V): ensure, suppose, regard, voice, bind, retain, undertake, phone, allocate, knit, book, abolish, envisage, incur, fancy, commence, enclose, enquire (Amer. N): student, president, percent, kid, guy, nation, photo, arm, American, Republican, phone, movie, store, lawyer, Democrat, professor, expert, senator (Brit. N): council, minister, union, pound, scheme, shop, principle, village, provision, sector, appeal, parliament, mum, tea, lord, cabinet, pension, flat (Amer. ADJ): American, federal, tough, native, Iraqi, crazy, smart, Israeli, Mexican, congressional, elementary, online, gifted, athletic, ongoing (Brit. ADJ) British, European, English, royal, French, industrial, Scottish, lovely, working, bloody, parliamentary, alright, statutory, keen, Welsh, Tory, socialist

Phrasal verbs: go on $_{56638}$, come back $_{40285}$, come up $_{37168}$, go back $_{35719}$, pick up $_{33613}$, find out $_{28067}$, come out $_{26705}$, go out $_{26094}$, grow up $_{25268}$, point out $_{23949}$, come in $_{23563}$, turn out $_{23284}$, set up $_{21711}$, end up $_{19900}$, give up $_{18558}$, make up $_{18207}$, be about $_{17658}$, sit down $_{17375}$, look up $_{17356}$, come on $_{16116}$, get up $_{15388}$, take on $_{14697}$, go down $_{14609}$, figure out $_{14505}$, show up $_{14368}$, get back $_{13668}$, come down $_{12733}$, go up $_{12618}$, get out $_{12600}$, stand up $_{12559}$, work out $_{11512}$, be back $_{11233}$, wake up $_{10733}$, look back $_{10698}$

www.ingramcontent.com/pod-product-compliance
Lightning Source LLC
LaVergne TN
LVHW020634300926
849161LV00004B/696